# LAND USE POLICY
## IN THE
# UNITED STATES

# LAND USE POLICY
## IN THE
# UNITED STATES

*Edited by Howard W. Ottoson*

## BeardBooks

Washington, D.C.

ISBN 1-58798-099-1

Reprinted by arrangement with the University of Nebraska Press.

Reprinted 2001 by Beard Books, Washington, D.C.

Printed in the United States of America.

# *Foreword*

MAY 20, 1962, was the one hundredth anniversary of the signing of the Homestead Act by President Lincoln, marking the end of an era of land policy in the United States, and the beginning of another. This occasion provides a convenient point in time at which to review the course U.S. land policy has taken during the past 180 years, to appraise some of the land use problems which concern us today, and to speculate on future trends in land use and the unresolved issues we will face.

The thoughts of twenty nationally known students of land policy have been brought together in this book. They include economists, historians, a political scientist, and a geographer, selected so as to make possible an interdisciplinary product. It might be feared that so many topics and authors would make for disorganization and repetition. However, the material falls logically into five major sections; these can be read independently by persons interested in specialized phases of land policy. Yet they logically flow together, providing the reader with a broad sweep over the whole range of land policy issues.

Land policy history includes some mythology, and much attention to the legislative acts; inadequate attention has been paid to how the policies actually operated. One finds that early policies were conditioned on the one hand by the urge to raise public funds from the sale of land, and on the other, to get the land into private hands. The emphasis of Congress was largely on disposal rather than resource management, and there is evidence that in the process economic development was impeded rather than aided.

With all of the repeated criticisms of the Homestead Act, its importance is not to be minimized. In the words of Gates, "The Homestead Act of 1862 is one of the most important laws which have been enacted in the history of this country, but its significance has been distorted and grossly misrepresented." The success of the act occurred early in its history, while the most glaring abuses occurred later, after 1880.

The other side of homestead history is the story of the homesteaders themselves. Poor or rich, young or old, Hoosier or European, they came to take up free land. Theirs is a story of adventure and monotony, of joy and pathos, of achievement and suffering. Some succeeded, many failed. Representing at the beginning a largely exploitative movement, and necessarily self-sufficient, the people created a new culture, new communities, and new capital in what had been called "The Great American Desert."

The forces which created and have influenced U.S. land policy are complex, and the resulting policies have been anything but neat, precise instruments for public action. Providing some of the philosophical underpinnings for the "free land" idea was the Jeffersonian ideal, which suggested a "casual relationship between [family] farming and the political system of democracy." The family farm still dominates the U.S. rural scene, but the old definitions are outmoded. It is not appropriate today to attribute the present high level of efficiency and development of agriculture to the family farm by itself. Many economic forces have been at work. Labor-saving technologies have enabled farm workers to farm increasing acreages of land. The creation of nonfarm job opportunities occurred rapidly enough to employ the farm workers released by this technology. Specialized farm credit, agricultural research and education, and conservation activities have enhanced technological progress in farming.

On the political side, one is impressed by the number of agencies which have been involved in land policy. For instance, at the federal level alone we find six congressional committees, totalling 177 members, with a legislative interest in this topic. Three executive departments, and eight agencies within them, have administrative responsibility relating to land use. Talbot suggests the need for more coordination in land policy administration, less of a "pork barrel" type of approach in Congress, and more emphasis on the public interest.

At present, agriculture is the most important claimant upon land. It is perennially suggested that soon our supply of land will be insufficient to provide food for a growing population. However, it appears that U.S. agriculture will be able to meet the demands for its products in 1980 with 11 per cent (51 million acres) less land in crops than in 1959. The expected population increase will be more than offset by the increase in crop yields, illustrating the power of technological advance. Contrary to the hopes (or fears) of some, nonagricultural uses for land will not cut into farm acres in magnitudes great enough to either solve the surplus problem or create food shortages. However, these nonfarm uses will increase significantly—perhaps by 33 per cent (49 million acres) by 1980. An acre of land is used for every four to six persons added to the urban population; transportation and outdoor recreation will require additional land acres. Urbanization will also affect water supplies and river systems. In the face of the increasing complexity of problems arising from the competition for land at particular strategic locations we are as yet without a formal national policy governing the use of urban land. For instance, decisions about plant locations are made by private firms, without regard to the effect on public costs. It is likely, however, that the role of the federal government in urban land policy will expand in the future, with the social costs—and national efficiency—becoming more important criteria in decision making about urban land use. However, all levels of government will have to become more adept in resolving steadily increasing numbers of land use conflicts.

The control of land resources presents another complex but intriguing field of study. In addition to ownership in fee simple, an inheritance from our Anglo-Saxon forebears, we have worked out intricate arrangements for the division of control between landlord and tenant for the private use of land. Government also brings its power to bear to make private property serve the public interest, with devices like police power, taxation, eminent domain, and spending power. Governments also own land. It is not likely that the area of land owned by the federal government will change much in the future. However, the extent of city, county, and state lands will almost certainly increase, for such uses as recreation, roads, streets, and other facilities.

Americans have been singularly uninformed about land policies in Europe. However, we may well turn our attention to the European experience, since some of our future problems may be mirrored in the confrontation between an intensive agriculture and a highly industrialized society which we find in some of these countries. Examples of the more interesting land policies of Europe have been the "rural renewal" of Sweden and the "Real Estate Transaction Law" of Germany. On the other hand, we must be cautious in our recommendations on land policies to underdeveloped countries of Asia and other areas; our system may be an inappropriate ideal for them because of differences in social structures and systems of ideas. Despite the emphasis placed on land reform in many of these areas it is unlikely that such programs can initiate economic growth; we must recognize them as secondary measures supporting development.

The material in this book was presented at a Homestead Centennial Symposium at the Nebraska Center for Continuing Education, University of Nebraska, on June 11-14, 1962. This symposium was made possible because of the efforts and thoughts of many persons, and the cooperation of several agencies.

Financial support in the form of a grant was provided by Resources for the Future, Inc., Washington, D.C. The members of the general planning committee, and their agencies, include the following:

Marion Clawson, Resources for the Future, Inc.
Joseph Ackerman, Farm Foundation
Gilbert C. Fite, Agricultural History Society
Marshall Harris, Agricultural Law Center, State University of Iowa
C. Edward Hoyt, U.S. Department of Interior
Warren D. Hotchkiss, National Park Service
John Muehlbeier, Great Plains Agricultural Council
Wilfred Pine, Kansas State University
John Timmons, Iowa State University, Ames
Philip Raup, University of Minnesota
Harry Steele, U.S. Department of Agriculture

They met several times to plan the topics covered in the symposium and contributed in many ways to its success.

Also contributing their time and ideas on the local arrangements committee were staff members of the University of Nebraska, including Loyd K. Fischer, Leslie Hewes, L. W. Hurlbut, Bruce Nicoll, James C. Olson, Carl Schneider, Harry M. Trebbing, and Arthur B. Ward, and William D. Aeschbacher of the Nebraska State Historical Society.

The continuing support of the Interregional Land Tenure Research Committee from the inception to the completion of this project is recognized. Also helpful at all times were the members of the administration of the University of Nebraska and of the office of Governor Morrison.

HOWARD W. OTTOSON
University of Nebraska

# Contents

# THE HISTORICAL BACKGROUND

# THOMAS LE DUC

# History and Appraisal of
# U. S. Land Policy to 1862

IN ALL HISTORY, no other new republic was so richly endowed at its birth as the United States. By conveyance from a number of the states that formed the federal union, the new nation acquired title to much of the land between the Allegheny Mountains and the Mississippi River. To this enormous initial birthright was added, within little more than half a century, sovereignty over the remainder of the continental territory. Progressively, the possessory rights of Indian tribes were acquired so that the public became the owner in fee of a high proportion of all the land.

Here, obviously, was a magnificent opportunity for the American people to make a fresh start. Here they could apply their intelligence, their cumulative knowledge, and their capital to the task of realizing the ideal of the commonwealth to which they had so recently dedicated themselves.

Seventy-five years later, when the passage of the Homestead Act supposedly planted a milestone in the history of the nation, how would a perceptive contemporary have assessed the performance of the American people in managing their vast estate? How well had they used the national resources to promote the public interest? How far did the record support the proposition that men were competent to organize their intelligence so as to govern themselves wisely?

To these Olympian questions we may not find universally acceptable answers. I believe, however, that they are the questions we should be asking. As an historian, I have to confess that the written history of the federal public lands for the period before 1862 is unsatisfactory. As in our study of many other areas of government, we have tended to concentrate on studying the legislative history of policy rather than on investigating how the policy really operated. We have failed also to understand

3

fully the meaning for American development of the existence
of a vast public domain of natural resources and the meaning
of public policies as they were administered. The survival of an
embarrassingly large volume of detailed land records has made
it difficult to manage the data reflecting the operation of the
laws and so we have been largely content to tackle the relatively
compact subject of legislative history.

An even greater barrier to historical perception has been
the failure of many historians to attain the measure of detach-
ment necessary for perspective and objectivity. To put it candidly, a significantly large part of the written history of the
public lands is so saturated with class bias that it cannot be
classed as scholarship. Captive to folk tradition, we have accepted
uncritically a number of interpretations formulated and perpet-
uated by politicians.

From the distance of a century and more, it should be possible
for the scholar to attain some perspective in understanding and
measuring the performance of democratic government in managing the national resources before 1862. To do this we must strip
off the mythology fabricated by demagogues and try to determine what really happened.

In tackling this assignment, let me say I am well aware that
our factual knowledge is still so imperfect in many respects that
some of our conclusions must be highly tentative. It is possible,
nevertheless, to recognize certain clear lines of policy development and to attach to them a fairly certain meaning.

We can see now that the most fateful and basic decision was
the one made at the outset and allowed to stand until the end
of the nineteenth century: that the lands should be disposed of
rather than retained in public ownership. The corollary of this
principle was that nothing should be done to protect or develop
the land, or even to determine and describe adequately the nature
and location of its natural wealth, so long as it remained in
social ownership.

Just why it was initially taken for granted that the federal
government should not retain ownership of its western lands is
not clear to me, and I have supposed that men's reasons for
accepting the policy differed. Some whose memories reached

back into Colonial days entertained phobias of quitrents, crown lands, and royal forests. Others looked upon the public domain as a capital asset pledged to sink the national debt created by the American Revolution. Others may have indulged themselves in the optimistic view that proceeds from the sale of the public lands would support current expenditures of a modest and prudent federal government. One of the many myths about federal policy in the first forty or fifty years is the assertion that its object was to maximize cash proceeds, rather than to promote migration or economic development. The fact is, however, that almost at once the new government began to give away significant quantities of land and thus undercut its own sales. Tallying the disposals through the year 1828, one finds that almost half the conveyances represented donations.

I suspect that the asserted reasons for putting the land in private hands are not the real reasons and that the real reasons were never explicitly set forth. In the background, always, was the assumption that profit was to be made from land speculation. More significant, perhaps, were the prevailing conceptions about the role of government. Starting from the premise that farming was the use to which the lands in the interior would be put, and recognizing that the raw land would have to be converted by the input of capital, it was taken for granted that investment and development, as well as farm operation, should be left to the private sector of the economy. Corollary to these assumptions was the principle that private ownership was the condition of private development. Akin to this complex of ideas was the physiocratic view that the yeoman farmer, the owner-operator, was not merely the salt of the earth but the flesh of the body politic. While it was the Jeffersonian defenders of plantation slavery who most systematically assimilated French economic theory, it is clear that the idealization of the family farm was widely accepted among Yankees and Yorkers.

As we shall see later, the decision to desocialize ownership of the land carried with it the delegation to private interests of a large measure of authority. This authority was ultimately to formulate a host of other decisions that seriously affected the nature and pace of migration, patterns of land use, and trends in the geographic flow of capital.

That basic decision meant also that the design of federal administration would be oriented to the disposal rather than to the conservation and management of public resources. Of the meaning of this orientation I shall say more later; but at this point I am compelled to notice one decision made at the outset. It was of such fundamental import that its effects continue even today to testify to its wisdom. That decision was that all grants of land by the federal government should embody a description of the land not merely in quantity, but *in place as defined by relation to an actual survey.* Implicit in this policy was the establishment of a uniform system of surveying in objective units of measurement run along compass lines from established meridians and base lines.

Scholars familiar with other land systems tell me that Americans fail to appreciate the amount of grief our system has obviated. This I have no reason to doubt, but I suspect that those who introduced the system well knew the kind of confusion and litigation they were eliminating. Everyone was familiar with the mischief wrought by surveys based on ephemeral landmarks; many were familiar with the even greater mischief wrought by the practice of eighteenth-century sovereigns of making grants in quantity but undefined by metes and bounds. Determined to avoid these twin evils, the founders created a system of title related to a survey design so durable and objective that titles founded on it could be concisely expressed and easily verified.

The system was not everywhere well adapted to the lay of the land and it was not everywhere honestly and accurately applied. With the technology now available we could and might well employ a radically different system. But as a way of meeting contemporary problems it represented a victory of order over anarchy. The necessity in later years of determining the location and extent of titles derived from grants made by French, Spanish, and Mexican governments continuously reminded Americans of the wisdom of our system; only when that chaos was finally ordered did we begin to pick flaws in the American plan.

With a plan of survey established, it was possible to begin

selling the land. Although for practical purposes the disposal of the public lands begins only with sales under the Act of 1800, that law reflected earlier experience. Even before 1789 the old Confederation Congress had made some effort to determine the optimum mode of sale and had fixed on a policy of negotiating contracts with large-scale buyers as a way of avoiding the problems of direct sale in farm-size units. The experience was not a happy one, partly because the supply of unimproved lands in nonfederal hands was still so large and so attractive in site and quality.

When the new federal union was established, the tireless Alexander Hamilton, in 1790, presented Congress with a set of proposals embodying a realistic appraisal of the market possibilities. He envisaged a dual system under which genuine settlers could take not more than a hundred acres at a cash price of thirty cents an acre and others could buy large tracts on credit. Congress ignored Hamilton's suggestions but failed until 1796 to adopt any policy. Then, fearing that a low price would encourage speculative purchase to the disadvantage of the genuine settler, it established terms equally uninviting to settler and speculator. By the Act of 1796 it was provided that the land should be offered at auction in units of 640 acres at a minimum price of two dollars an acre, payable one-half down and the other half in twelve months.

While sales were negligible under this act, it did institute the practice of public auctions that remained, nominally at least, the cornerstone of the sales system until the 1860's. The theory of the auction was first, that it would protect the public interest against the evils of negotiated contracts such as those obtained by many politicians during Confederation; and second, that competitive bidding would serve to classify the land by quality or market value and thus save the Treasury the work of classification and differential pricing. The best lands would sell instantly at prices above the minimum and the land unsold at the auction would thereafter be open to purchase at the minimum. Obviously, this pricing system would function only if the government limited the quantity of land put up at the auction. In fact, however, the government steadily offered more land than the

market could absorb at the minimum price and the auction
system soon became a joke. So much first-class land was offered
that bids never rose much above the minimum, speculative buying was encouraged, a lot of land remained unsold, and so far
as any settlement followed sale, it was scattered among tracts of
idle land in public or in speculative hands. Thus administrative policy subverted legislative intent, but Congress made no
move to restrict the quantity of land offered.

One may divide the span of years from 1800 to 1860 into
three periods, each almost equal in length and each brought to
a close by the onset of a major depression that reduced sharply
the volume of speculative purchase of public land. Now the
interesting thing to note is that every time speculative purchase
collapsed there arose a loud demand, in the name of justice to
the genuine settler, for modifications in the land laws that would
supposedly give the true pioneer more favorable terms for acquiring land ownership.

The first period runs from the enactment of the land law to
the year 1820. The Act of 1800 set a minimum price of two dollars
an acre on units of 320 acres, required a down payment of 25
per cent, and gave the buyer four years in which to meet later
installments. The act did not function well, and little land was
sold until after the War of 1812. Then a flood of migration to the
Gulf states and the lower Lake states triggered a fever of speculative purchase.

This is not to say that the migrants and the buyers were necessarily the same persons. Some of the settlers were buyers but many
were squatters; some of the buyers were settlers, but many were
absentees out to make a speculative killing by resale of raw land
to the expected throng of migrants.

This is to say that now we meet, for the first time on a large
scale, one of the significant realities to which folk myth has
blinded us: the independence of the three variables: transfer of
land from federal title, actual settlement, and economic development of the land. Lots of land stayed unsettled and undeveloped
long after it moved out of federal ownership; other land was
settled by squatters who neither bought nor developed it; other
land was exploited by graziers or timber trespassers who neither

settled nor bought it. Somewhere in the picture were those who bought land, settled it and developed it, but the pioneer stereotype was less common and, in aggregate, less significant than the others.

On the one hand, we must recognize that after 1815, squatting became universal. Congress had forbidden occupancy of the public lands in 1807 and had authorized the President to use the Army to eject intruders. Behind the statute, of course, stood the doctrine that the public lands were not a public commons open to private appropriation but rather a proprietorship that rested on the same basis as federal ownership of a customs house or post office. That concept sounded fine in 1807, but with the tide of migration after 1815, enforcement became politically inexpedient and collapsed.

The economic reality that laid the basis for squatting was simply that most of the migrants lacked sufficient money to buy the public land. Their capital consisted mainly of some elementary tools and more or less livestock. If they had no liquid capital with which to buy land, neither did they have it to hire labor to develop unimproved land. Given the primitive technology of the time, the tasks of clearing forest land or sodbusting on the prairie or otherwise making farms required immense inputs of labor. From our perspective, with a well-developed awareness of the conditions of economic development, we can recognize that the interior of the United States between 1815 and the Civil War furnished a prime instance of the underdeveloped area. Incredibly varied and intense in its resources of soil, climate, vegetation, energy, and metals, its greatest need was a tremendous dose of capital.

Not much of the available capital flowed into farm making. A lot of it flowed as land-sales proceeds through the district land offices into the federal treasury. So much money came in that it was possible in 1818 to repeal all federal taxes. Little of the raw land purchased with these funds, however, went into production; most of it was held idle for speculation. The low price and the low down payment embodied in the Act of 1800 fostered the hope that the lands could be resold at advanced prices to the expected swarm of genuine farm makers. Not all the speculators were absentees with large means. Even before 1819 the petty resident speculator was a familiar figure, complaining that he had to pay high rates of interest to make his down payment and trying to find a customer for his claim before he had to make the next installment. Big and little, these speculators were all doomed to disappointment.

A combination of circumstances wrecked their hopes. The failure of the government to enforce its sanctions against trespass on the public lands tended to divert migrants from purchase to rent-free squatting at a time when the supply of land far exceeded the demand. Not only did the federal government offer excessive quantities for sale, but simultaneously created further competition by making to states and military veterans large grants, most of which soon came on the market. We can see now that the land market was overbought and there was little prospect of a rise in land prices.

The bubble was burst by the onset of the financial panic and the commercial depression of 1819. The flow of eastern capital dwindled; speculators could not find private funds with which to refinance their debts to the federal government and settlers could not find mortgage money. Quite predictably, the Treasury was confronted with widespread delinquency among its debtors. The Act of 1800 had done a better job of promoting disposal than of promoting development.

Faced with a clamorous horde of unhappy speculators, Congress moved to their rescue with relief laws allowing them to salvage their equities. So corrosive was the situation that Congress resolved to scrap the credit system altogether, and put sales on a cash basis, with an auction minimum reduced to $1.25 an acre. That price had no known relation to the economic value of the land; it represented a purely political adjustment, assertedly in the interests of the settler but actually, as was then recognized, designed to encourage speculation.

Had the politicians genuinely desired to promote farm making and to discourage speculation, they would have moved in precisely the opposite direction by raising the price of land, lengthening the term of credit, and even advancing development credit. There was nothing wrong in principle with credit sales.

The trouble was that the credit term was too short and the price too low. It enticed speculators without really aiding authentic farm-making settlers. On their land purchase most settlers needed more than four years' credit, for they could not hope in that time to bring raw land to a point of development where it would yield sufficient net savings to permit payment. Even so, land costs were a relatively small fraction of the total investment necessary in making a farm and moving a family to it. If Congress had been interested in promoting migration and real development, a program of development credit should have been introduced. Early and late, it is clear that the lack of credit retarded genuine development and that low prices on government land tended to channel credit into speculative purchase of land.

The policies followed for twenty years under the Act of 1820 represented little improvement. The government continued to offer for sale more land than the market could absorb at the minimum price, and the inventory of offered, but unsold, land steadily accumulated. It was this situation that set the stage for the famous Webster-Hayne debates of 1830 on Senator Foote's resolution to withhold marketing of more land until the inventory should be absorbed. If the intent of that resolution was merely to reduce offerings so that the sales price would rise, it was soundly conceived. If, however, it was intended as a device to discourage westward migration and thus enlarge the supply of wage labor in the cities, it was delusive. The simple historical fact is that settlers were under no obligation to buy land. After 1820, there was a steady growth of squatting. Migrants settled on government land, offered and unoffered; they settled on private land; they settled on land that had passed as grants to the states. In the entire period from 1820 to 1860 there probably occurred a steady widening of the gap between ownership and occupancy. In considerable measure, the buyers were not settlers and the settlers were not buyers. We know, for example, that in Illinois in the 1820's, thousands of rural male voters owned no land while, at the same time, hundreds of thousands of acres had passed from public ownership and were being held idle.

Out of the conflict between squatters and speculators came the demand, eventually satisfied, for legal recognition of the prin-

ciple that the act of squatting on public lands created an inchoate
title that could be perfected by payment of the statutory minimum price. Squatters tended to arrive early and pick out the
choice sites which at auction would have commanded immediate
sale and high prices. Squatters wanted exemption from competitive bidding on the tracts they occupied; that is, a preemptive
right to buy the land at $1.25 an acre. The theoretical defense of
preemption was that the squatters were public beneficiaries
engaged in actual development of the West. Exposing to public
auction the tracts they had improved would permit others to
confiscate the fixed improvements by purchasing the fee in the
land. The defect in this theory is that the alleged improvements
were generally negligible in value if not altogether invisible.
Since not all squatters were farm makers, it was necessary, therefore, to put the defense of the squatters on other grounds. The
chief architect of the defense, not surprisingly, was one who spent
thirty years in the United States Senate busily running errands
for those predatory interests that were trying in every possible
way to get something for nothing out of the public resources. In
our own age we are familiar with demagogues whose assertions of
devotion to the people ring false to those who happen to know
what they are really up to. In the age of Jackson the woods were
full of such persons and while they were not all Jacksonians,
that durable Missouri politician Thomas Hart Benton will illustrate the type. The genius of Benton was that he recognized the
political mileage that could be found in promoting private
exploitation of the public resources. With his many services to
St. Louis business interests we are not here concerned. About
them he said little, but he never stopped singing the praises of
the petty predator on the nation's property. It was Benton who
perfected, if he did not conceive, the doctrine that since the
national resources belonged to the people, any one of those people
had a moral right to appropriate permanently timber, minerals,
or land surface. Congress never acquiesced in this specious reasoning, but in his lifetime, Benton saw public policy accept more
and more the principle of preferential treatment of squatters.

The squatters' clamor for preemption rights had been heard
even before the establishment of the federal union in 1789;

beginning in 1813 Congress began to satisfy it piecemeal with favors to limited groups. In the 1830's, the laws became more general in scope but retained the limitation that they benefited only those who had already settled. In fact, however, successive laws afforded the squatters almost continuous protection and, as President Van Buren pointed out, tended to encourage squatting and the expectation that Congress would continue to favor it. At last, out of the depression that followed the boom and bust of the middle 1830's, came the permanent, prospective, preemption Act of 1841.

By the provisions of that law, the squatter was authorized to purchase at the minimum price up to 160 acres, providing that prior to the public auction of the area in which his claim was embraced he paid up and proved his asserted occupancy and improvement.

The laws and regulations governing proof of settlement and cultivation afford an interesting insight into the contemporary state of administrative procedures, and the behavior of squatters illuminates our understanding of frontier ethics. The government made no effort to protect the public interest by an independent determination of the validity of the claims asserted by the squatter. It was content to rely on ex parte testimony in the form of affidavits. The extent of perjury cannot of course be determined, but just as in the twentieth century we are aware of widespread evasion of taxes on income and intangible personal property, so the mid-nineteenth century was familiar with evasion of the letter as well as the spirit of the laws requiring settlement and improvement as conditions for claiming the benefits of the preemption laws. Yet in all the documents and literature I have never found a single report of prosecution for perjury. One might say that the sovereign people delegated to a sovereign Deity all responsibility for punishing false swearing.

Even the benefits of the preemption law and lax enforcement of its requirements did not satisfy the squatters. Preemption, in fact, was a protean thing that not only survived the adoption of the Homestead Law in 1862, but continued to grow in legal content until it was finally outlawed in 1891. Until 1853, Congress had pretty well adhered to the principle that it would create no titles or equities on unsurveyed land. Then, by a series of measures, it began to open unsurveyed lands to preemption vestings. When the courts construed these statutes to mean that the act of settlement, apart from any formal filing of claim, operated to vest an enforceable right, the door was opened to the mischievous chaos that the original founders had tried to avoid. The logical extension of preemption is perhaps well illustrated by a holding of the Illinois Supreme Court that permitted a squatter to eject the United States Army from Fort Dearborn. Even then, the southeast corner of Michigan Boulevard and Wacker Drive was too valuable a property to be left in public hands.

At the point where legal rights ended, the squatters constructed extra-legal agencies, sometimes using illegal methods, to enlarge their gains. The preemption law limited the squatter's taking to 160 acres and required him to pay up before the public auction started. It was generally recognized that in existing farm technology even a quarter-section was more than a family could develop and operate. To get control of more land than the law allowed, squatters formed "claims clubs" or "squatters' associations." We shall never know how widespread these vigilante organizations really were. In many cases, the fabric was so informal that it amounted to nothing more than a petition to the President to postpone the public auctions until the squatters could raise money to buy their claims. In cases where the organization was designed to introduce violence to intimidate outside bidding at the auction, the activity was obviously secret. Exclusion of outside bidders was designed to achieve either or both of two ends. The claims club might attend the auction in a body and prevent *any* bidding. At the close of the auction the squatters would return to their claims and continue to enjoy rent-free use. Or they might designate one of their number as a clerk to bid off the tracts for the squatters. Now the interesting aspect is that almost universally the claims club attempted to protect the members in buying—not the 160 acres which, if they had had the money, they could have bought the preceding day—but some multiple of the quarter section to which they were legally entitled. The commonest arrangements enabled the squatters to bid in at the minimum price 320 or 480 acres, although I have

seen records showing them buying 640 acres. It is obvious, therefore, that the claims club was not an innocent neighborhood
organization to protect hard-working settlers against rapacious
speculators, but a conspiracy to defeat the law.

From all this, one infers that squatters and others thought
that the land was worth more than $1.25 an acre, and would soon
bring much higher prices at resale. That inference is sustained by
another kind of evidence. One is not surprised to find that
interest rates tended to rise directly with the distance from money
centers. Nor is one surprised to find that loans secured only by
unimproved land commanded high rates of interest. If, however,
the facts were not so thoroughly established, one would be skep-
tical of reports that speculators big and little frequently borrowed
money at 25 per cent to 50 per cent per annum in order to buy
land. These stories have about them the authentic flavor of
agrarian complaint myth. They happen, however, to be true and
the only rational explanation of this behavior is that the borrowers believed that even after paying interest sufficient to double
their investment they were making a wise buy.

We cannot now determine the extent of this borrowing since
it is not reflected in public records, but we know that it was
widespread. Its existence sustains also, I think, the interpretation
that many of those buying land had no capital with which to
develop their purchases. This interpretation is supported by such
evidence as we have of agricultural production on lands that had
gone into private ownership. Undoubtedly, there was a lag in
the peopling of land after it passed from public ownership; there
was an even more pronounced lag in putting the land into production. If these facts have escaped full recognition it is partly
because of the incredible acceptance for almost half a century
of an erroneous reading of the evidence by Frederick Jackson
Turner. Turner was a romantic young historian who in 1893
announced that the frontier, defined as a supply of free land, had
just vanished. There is no reason to believe that Turner ever
made any attempt to determine when the supply of free land was
exhausted. The only basis he offered for his declaration was census data relating to population density. His assumption, in other
words, was that population density and free land were reciprocals.

By his standards, Cherry County, Nebraska, with a population density of 1.4 in 1960, would still be free land.

Now if Turner had bothered to tally the records of land disposal, he would have discovered that the supply of free, arable, humid land was pretty well exhausted by 1870, twenty years earlier than the date he assigned. In the two decades before 1870 the pace of disposal had accelerated markedly. Much of this land was still idle in 1870, but it was not free.

To this increased rate of desocialization a substantial contribution was made by sales under the Graduation Act of 1854. In an effort to head off the demand for free homesteads, Congress finally adopted the principle of differential pricing of the land. Had this measure been enacted thirty years earlier and administered in conjunction with a program of limiting the amount of land offered on the market, the country would certainly have been better off. Apart from the gains to the Treasury, the policy would have insured compact settlement, with correspondingly lower social costs for roads and schools. Rejecting such a program, Congress had so saturated the market that a backlog of unsold land, amounting perhaps to 100 million acres, had accumulated. Some of it had been on the market for thirty years or more; almost 80 million acres had been on the market for at least ten years. By pricing it on a sliding scale, Congress managed to put into private hands almost 40 million acres before the act was repealed in 1862. The original provision of the Act of 1854 (that the buyer must occupy and develop his purchase) was soon modified and, while we are not certain, it is believed that much of the land went into the hands of those who wanted the timber or the minerals, or who planned to hold it speculatively.

Even more significant than graduation as a factor in speeding up disposal was the stepping up of the rate of donations after 1847. Despite the enormous volume of cash sales in the 1850's, accumulated donations continued to exceed accumulated sales. Seemingly, it was more expedient for federal politicians to give away land than to give away Treasury cash, for there were few to point out that grants of land not only reduced the capital assets of the commonwealth but also competed with lands offered for sale and so reduced the cash proceeds. One may be permitted to view many of the land grants, as well as the spending of land-sales proceeds, as kinds of deficit spending in which the government spent off its capital to support current policies, instead of levying taxes and appropriating the revenue.

By and large, donating land seems to have proven a poor way to support the public policies for which the grants were assertedly made. In many categories, small cash grants would have done a better job. The weaknesses of the donation policy were evident so early that one is compelled to question the sincerity of legislative recitals and to ask whether the intended beneficiaries were the nominal grantees or another group altogether.

Take, for example, the donations to military veterans. During the War of 1812, Congress provided for grants to the soldiers and officers. After the war, three large tracts were reserved for the satisfaction of the veterans' claims. As a matter of historical fact, most of the veterans never even visited the lands granted to them, but sold out to itinerant solicitors who offered them modest cash settlements. The net effect was that the soldiers realized little. The government had conveyed a lot of choice land through the hands of the veterans to a second group of intermediaries who hoped to unload it profitably on genuine settlers. It is interesting to note that Congress, notwithstanding the history of this transaction, embarked in the years from 1847 to 1855 upon an even bigger program of land bonuses to veterans. The legislation is highly diverse and need not be summarized here. No attempt was made to assign specific tracts to veterans; they received instead warrants entitling them to a specified number of acres. All told, warrants for 61 million acres were issued. After 1852, the warrants were fully negotiable and they came to be traded in the open market like other government obligations. Most of the veterans sold their warrants for less than $1.25 an acre, and most of the land paid for with warrants fell into the hands of intermediaries rather than farm makers. The issue of the warrants undermined the cash marketing of land; it undermined any intent to restrict to genuine farm makers the initial entry on the public lands; and it speeded up exhaustion of the supply of public, humid, tillable land. Almost 40 per cent of the state of Iowa was taken with warrants, so also were choice areas in Illinois, Minnesota, and the eastern parts of Kansas and Nebraska. The whole experience so explicitly fitted into the experience with the 1812 bounty and so completely fulfilled the expectations of those contemporaries who asserted that later bounty acts were designed to promote speculation, one is forced to conclude that in issuing the warrants Congress was far less interested in either soldiers or settlers than in speculators.

Somewhat akin to soldiers' bounties were a series of grants to settlers in specified areas. As early as 1842, Congress tried to promote settlement in northern Florida by offering free homesteads to those who would settle, cultivate five acres, and remain five years. The act was an almost complete failure and even the lifting of the cultivation requirement did not attract settlers.

Diagonally across the country, a larger and more instructive program was tried under the so-called Oregon Donation Act of 1850. For years Missouri politicians had talked of rewarding migrants to Oregon with free land. The act, as finally passed, provided that a man could take 320 acres and his wife could take an additional half-section, while latecomers arriving between 1850 and 1853 could qualify for half these quantities. The sole condition of the grant was occupancy for four years. What happened under this act is highly revealing. Most of the beneficiaries had no use for as much as 320 acres, much less 640. They lacked the capital to develop that amount and the man power to farm it. What they wanted was a negotiable title that could be sold. Congress came to their rescue with a law permitting them to buy their land at $1.25 an acre after two years' residence. Bona fide settlers could sit out their four-year term and get the land free, but 72 per cent of the claimants elected to buy their land. The full meaning of this experience needs further study, but this much we can say: the main effect of the Oregon Donation Act was to create another large group of petty intermediaries whose interest in the land was purely speculative.

These several programs of donations to individuals were dwarfed by the donations made to the public-land states. In view of their magnitude, it is surprising that their operation has been so little studied. Here, as with the land bonuses to individuals, one observes the tendency of Congress to accelerate the flow of donations after 1840. John C. Calhoun had never been able to persuade Congress to surrender all the public lands to the new states in which they were situated, but at the close of his life he could celebrate a partial victory. Eventually the magnitude of the surrender would approach 200 million acres, far more than the aggregate sales from the beginning.

The performance of the states in conscientiously applying earlier grants to the public purpose for which they had been made was so lax that one is puzzled by the action of Congress in giving them ever greater quantities to mishandle. The best explanation, perhaps, is that Congress interpreted the Constitution as authorizing land subsidies to the states to encourage the performance of functions not within the powers of the federal government.

At an early date, the federal government had entrusted to the states small grants in support of elementary education. A restriction against sale of these lands was met by more or less perpetual leases to political favorites. Eventually, the early states were released from the trust and they, like the newer states, were allowed to sell the lands. So far as it has been studied, the administration of these grants can hardly be called an example of dedicated service to the cause of education. By a variety of devices, the interests of buyers were put ahead of fiduciary responsibility. Congress made no effort to introduce controls that would assure fulfillment of the terms of the trust and indeed proceeded, in the 1840's, to double the rate of grant.

Even more grotesque is the story of the donation of the wet or swampy lands to the states in which they were situated, on condition that they reclaim them by drainage. Why this policy was adopted we may never know; it is so fanciful that one may speculate whether the voting of the grant has some undiscerned relationship to the voting of the Oregon Donation Act, the Illinois Central Railroad grant, and the various measures we call the Compromise of 1850. Is it only a coincidence that all were passed in the same week of September, 1850?

The entire idea of reclaiming swampland was so preposterous that the sober mind is astonished it should have been suggested at that stage in American development. Arable land was still so plentiful, and labor costs were so high in relation to commodity prices, that it was evident few swamps could be economically drained. It is not surprising, therefore, to find that while few of the 64 million acres donated to the states under this act were ever reclaimed by them, much land valuable for timber or hay or minerals passed through their hands with little regard for the public interest.

Finally, we must notice the Congressional policy of appropriating to the states enormous quantities of land as subsidies intended to encourage investment in roads, canals, river improvements, and eventually, railroads. During the first forty years of the federal union, Congress appropriated only cash. To foster road building, a small fraction of the proceeds of land sales was distributed to the states in which the sales fell. Although the aggregate funds thus distributed were not inconsiderable, no one has found much trace of the construction supposedly supported. The federal government itself financed construction of the National Road and invested modest sums in improvements to rivers and harbors.

In the 1820's, several unrelated developments converged to support the idea that investment in transportation facilities should be undertaken by the states and supported by a program of federal land grants. The completion and instant success of the Erie Canal demonstrated that cheap transportation would permit a cash-crop specialization that could liberate the interior from the penury of subsistence farming. New York's achievement seemed also to justify confidence that other states could build and operate facilities of comparable character and magnitude. It was recognized, of course, that the western states and territories possessed neither the tax base nor the credit standing that would enable them to finance any sizable program of public works. This difficulty would be overcome by a federal land grant sufficient to serve as collateral security for borrowing the construction outlays.

If one asks why the job was not turned over to private capital, the answer is to be found, I think, in the nature of the projects. At the time the policy crystallized, men were thinking of canals and roads as public highways and were reluctant to put them into the hands of private monopolists.

Another set of reasons was offered to exclude the federal government from construction and management. Sincerely or otherwise, constitutional objections were raised to such an expansive definition of federal power. Furthermore, if the federal government appropriated cash to pay for construction it would have to increase the yield from tariffs, lay internal taxes, or borrow the money. Any of these possibilities terrified vote-conscious politicians who early recognized that few cared if they gave away public lands.

So powerful were these diverse attitudes that it was politically necessary to delegate to the states the job of improving transportation. To justify the federal land grants it was argued that they would speed the sale and enhance the market price of the federally owned lands. Altogether, almost 56 million acres passed to the states under the guise of aids to transportation.

We can see now that the western states were not the optimum agencies to carry out federal policy. The record is not all bad, but it is filled with mismanagement and corruption. One must recognize, however, that the ability of the states to raise money on the security of the land grants was steadily impaired by the cheap-land policy of the federal government. Financing in many instances was so retarded that by the time the roads or canals were built they had already been rendered partly obsolete by the technical superiority of the steam railroad.

Although it was clearly understood that the railroad could not serve as a public highway but must function as a common carrier, there was little opposition to a policy of allowing private interests to develop it and much support for land grants that would entice private capital into tapping undeveloped areas. I say "entice," because I am satisfied that without some kind of public guarantee, eastern and European capital could not have been induced to embark upon construction through undeveloped areas. In the light of the earlier federal programs for roads and canals, it was natural to conceive of government help in terms of land grants. This is not to say that the railroads had to be built when they were, or that the grants had to be scaled as they were, or that the federal government could not have managed them in a more systematic way. With the advantage of hindsight, the imaginative mind can conceive of a variety of choices.

It is now almost a century since Congress made the last land grant to a railroad venture, but historians are still debating the wisdom of the policy. The debate, unfortunately, has never risen much above the level of the old feud between the grangers and the railroads. I am doubtful that the policy can be evaluated in such parochial terms. It must stand or fall on its contribution to national economic growth. In that sense, the issue is much bigger than an aspect of land policy and we would warp the perspective if we viewed it only in the more limited sector.

If this paper has so far dealt largely with policies for the disposal of the public lands and if it has seemed to assume that most of the lands were suitable for tillage agriculture, it is because those are the central themes of historical reality before 1862. I should, however, like to say a little about what might be called "nonpolicy." The heart of this nonpolicy is the failure of Congress to formulate and support a program for the protection of the public interest in timber, coal, and metals found on the public property. These resources were neither managed affirmatively nor opened to private development on a basis that would guard the people's equity. Congress chose, instead, to tolerate depredation and depletion of such resources as did not pass by sale or donation under laws contemplating the transfer of lands suited primarily for agriculture.

If one is inclined to think the whole idea of conservation and public ownership is a recent concept, it may be worth noting that the Land Ordinance of 1785 reserved to the public an interest in minerals and that early in national history one finds a number of measures surprisingly modern in their recognition of the public interest. The year 1807, which saw Congress authorize the President to use the army to expel intruders from the public lands, saw also passage of a law authorizing the leasing of the Missouri lead lands in consideration of payment of royalties on the ore extracted. The system was later extended to the lead lands in Illinois and Wisconsin, but it must everywhere be written off as a failure. Although a challenge to the constitutionality of leasing was successfully met, the system was systematically and successfully sabotaged by private interests. Much of the lead land was never segregated and reserved for leasing; even where the process moved that far, administration was halfhearted and ineffectual. Eventually the system was scrapped and the lands sold at nominal prices.

Despite occasional indications of Congressional interest in differentiating mineral lands from other types, intelligence could not be sufficiently mobilized to protect the public interest and, as a result, such substantial resources as the iron and copper lands of the upper Great Lakes were either given away or sold at token prices.

Coal lands, not considered mineral lands until 1864, were not differentiated from agricultural lands even where the deposits appeared at the surface. Except for a few tracts of Indian tribal trust land that never came into the public domain, the whole mid-continent coal field, extending from Indiana to Kansas passed into private ownership under laws intended for the conveyance of farm land. Only then did Congress lock the stable door.

The most spectacular display of the incompetence of democratic government is seen in the way the precious metals were mishandled. Until 1866, Congress not only did nothing to regulate the removal of 1 billion dollar's worth of gold and silver from public property, but actually bought and paid for ores taken from federal lands. When one state attempted to lay a tax on the ores, the taxpayer asserted the ores could not be taxed because they were federal property. The Supreme Court did not acquiesce in this reasoning; on the contrary, it became an accessory to the crime by holding that the metal, although unlawfully removed from federal land, had become private property. In the light of such a relaxed attitude on the part of federal authorities, and in view of the negligible amount of capital needed in the enterprise of carrying gold from the public lands to the public mint, it is not surprising that California and Colorado magnetized labor that might better have been left in productive work.

Finally, Congress achieved an almost perfect record of ignoring the public interest in timber resources. Except for the designation of minor tracts with stands of timber especially needed for construction of naval vessels, valuable timberlands were not reserved or segregated from the mass of public land subject to disposal under the regular laws. Even where the timber was extremely valuable and the land surface was unsuited to tillage, the government made no effort to introduce a system of administered stumpage. As a result, most of the pine land of the three northern Lake states and the timberlands of Arkansas and the Gulf states passed either by donations or by sales at token prices. Before this happened, however, a great deal of the best timber had been removed by depredators. Although timber trespass had been made a criminal offense in 1831, Congress failed to provide adequately for enforcement and the law was generally ignored.

The matter of federal nonenforcement must be put in its proper context. While it is my assignment here to deal with public resources, I do not want to leave the impression that Congress was singularly blind in this one field. We should recognize that, by and large, federal criminal laws were not effectively enforced in the period here dealt with. It is true that for many crimes grand juries would not indict and trial juries would not convict. But probably more significant was the failure of Congress to create a general agency for the detection and apprehension of criminals. The federal marshals were political hacks whose main occupation was collecting fees for serving writs in civil suits. The Post Office and the Customs Service had their own specialized agencies and in those fields enforcement was probably more realistic. One may note, however, that Andrew Jackson's Collector of the Port of New York went unpunished in the embezzlement of over a million dollars. Even in respect to behavior generally condemned by public opinion, enforcement was lax. The prohibition of the importation of slaves, for example, was never conscientiously enforced and our best estimates indicate that the illicit flow continued undiminished and unpunished.

It is unnecessary to cite other examples, for its is clear that in the gap between the definition and the suppression of crime, the historian is confronted with an aspect of group behavior that was general in American culture. Americans seem to have felt a greater need for ritualistic declaration of a moral code than for achieving even minimal adherence to it. Why this was so I must leave to the cultural anthropologists.

To the economist and the historian a more urgent question is put by asking how the public land policies affected the processes of economic growth. To this question some responses have been suggested earlier in this paper. They should perhaps be made more explicit.

It is my contention that, by and large, the land program before 1862 tended to retard economic development. Low prices, together with free grants, tended to put land in the hands of intermediaries between the federal government and the ultimate farm makers. One need not argue the question of the profitability of this ownership. Certainly, the endless flooding of the market with public land and grant land disappointed the expectations of many a speculator, big and little. But the dream of easy profits never died and it tended to channel into mere ownership capital that might have flowed into development. Because they thought land was cheap, settlers beggared themselves trying to control more land than they could develop or operate. To buy land they borrowed heavily and so raised interest rates on development capital. And, so far as they engaged in agriculture, their enterprise was skewed towards the crops that required minimum capital and minimum labor.

These tendencies were, I believe, most marked in the Corn Belt. In using that term I am consciously emphasizing the idea that the optimum land use in the northern Middle West was in livestock production. I am persuaded that it was even "more optimum" a century ago, and that those who put their capital into livestock were well rewarded. On the great prairie stretching from here to western Ohio the native grasses afforded excellent pasturage, and the environment was well adapted to raising corn for finishing the steers. Above all, this was a crop that need not wait for commercial transportation, for it could be profitably driven to hungry markets on the east coast. It was the most economic crop and only the want of capital kept more men from raising it. So far as settlers farmed at all, they tended to glut the market with corn and wheat. But anyone who analyzes the volume of agricultural production in the 1840's and 1850's will be struck with the small output in relation to the quantity of land that had passed from public ownership.

If the record was somewhat better in the Gulf states, it is because the South had found in chattel slavery an institution that would circumvent the evils of cheap land. Slave labor was not cheap, but it was certain. On it was built an economic structure into which enormous quantities of development capital flowed. The dynamic strength of the southern economy stands in striking contrast to the structural weaknesses visible in the Middle West in the later 1850's.

It was the land disposal boom of the mid-1850's that set the stage for the eventual enactment of the Homestead Law. With the tremendous increase in the flow of public land into the hands of a variety of donees, it was only natural that politicians should find it expedient to argue for donations to all settlers. With the transfer of much of the donation land into the hands of speculative intermediaries, the political clamor was given a moral justification. Finally, the economic collapse of 1857 made it clear that the land market was flooded and that settlers would have difficulty either in selling their claims or in borrowing money to pay for them. Just as the depression after 1837 generated the demand for permanent, prospective preemption, so the depression at the end of the 1850's contributed to the movement for free homesteads.

We can see now that the price of land was not the critical determinant in the success of the authentic farm maker. An eighty-acre farm at $1.25 an acre would cost him $100. This was only a small fraction of his total farm-making costs. If he lacked the skills and the capital necessary to develop a farm, free land wouldn't help him. The high rate of abandonment under the Homestead Act, like the high rate of failure under a system of low cash prices, demonstrated that cheap land magnetized a class of settlers who had nothing to lose and few qualifications for farm entrepreneurship. One cannot escape noticing the striking reality that stability of tenure and success in farm making is in direct proportion to the price paid for land. So far as the land-grant railroads were genuinely concerned in fostering farm making as the source of recurrent traffic, they found that the optimum arrangement was to put a high price on land and extend long-term credit to the buyers. Selling at low prices tended to put the land in the hands of speculative buyers.

By 1860, the country had built up a mass of experience with land disposal. That body of experience clearly demonstrated that disposal and development were independent elements, and that development required vast inputs of capital. Experience showed also that running through American life was a persistent dream of speculative profits that was reflected in endless political response. Since we are talking about democratic government, perhaps we should say that there were more people interested in unearned increment than in economic development. In this setting, the Homestead Act can be seen as another stage in the evolution of a set of policies better suited to desocializing capital gains than to harnessing the nation's resources. The interesting thing is that while the real thrust of the land laws was never affirmed as public policy, the declared national objective was steadily undermined by politicians trading the public property for votes.

PAUL W. GATES

# The Homestead Act: Free Land
# Policy in Operation, 1862–1935

Two GENERATIONS of agitation by land reformers, including workingmen's advocates, Jeffersonian arcadians, and western agrarians, finally produced the Homestead Law of 1862 which offered free a quarter section of public land in the West to citizens or intended citizens who settled upon and improved it. These free-land advocates anticipated Henry George in maintaining that wild, undeveloped land on the frontier had no value until it was improved by the toil of farm makers; the taxes of residents that provided roads and schools; town and county government; subventions that assisted in opening up canals and railroads; and high transportation rates that helped to pay for the railroads. Since it was the investment of the farmer's labor and the public's money that made land valuable, it seemed to the western citizen double taxation to make him pay for government land.[1] The Homestead Act was intended to reward him for his courageous move to the frontier by giving him land, the value of which he and the community would create.

If classical economists found little but sophistry in this reasoning, the western pioneer and the eastern land reformers cared not.[2] Free land, they hoped, would make the life of the pioneer easier, enable him to use his meager capital to purchase farm machinery and livestock, relieve him of debt to the government or to loan sharks (who frequented the land offices to lend their funds at frontier interest rates of 20 to 40 per cent), remove the specter of crushing mortgages, and thereby assure a larger proportion of success among farm makers.

The Homestead Law was the culmination of a series of moves intended to end the policy of using the public lands as a source of revenue for the government. Prior to 1862, the revenue policy had been frequently modified but prices had been reduced only moderately. Now, in one simple act, it seemingly had been replaced by what conservatives regarded as a radical policy of giving land freely to anyone willing to undertake the obligations of farm making.

Not all westerners subscribed to the view that land on the outer fringe of settlement had no value. Some could see that as the western population movement expanded, it shortened the period in which, on successive frontiers land values rose swiftly from little or nothing to a number of dollars an acre. Like speculators from the East, they were prepared to gamble that the land would acquire value with the expected immigration and the improvements the people made. Consequently, they looked for every opportunity to accumulate ownership, whether by one or two quarter sections beyond their needs or acres numbered by the hundreds or thousands. The ambivalence of western attitudes is clear, for with free land established, the West interposed every kind of objection to plans to curb the alienation of homesteads or to provide effective administration of land laws that would prevent accumulation.

The Homestead Law was not without opponents in 1862. Some held it was partial and discriminatory in that the donation would go only to persons who went West. Others held it would drain off population from high-priced land and thereby lower land values in eastern communities; that it would deprive older states of their share in the lands and reduce the value of soldiers' land bounties and railroad grants. But these were the cries of conservatives who feared the elevating effect that free land would have on the propertyless poor, the day laborer, the immigrant.

If conservatives viewed with alarm the social results they foresaw from homesteading, the land reformers were disappointed that the thoroughgoing reconstruction of American land policies they had sought was not achieved. Homesteads were to be alienable, and weak and inadequate safeguards were included to prevent abuse of the law and accumulation of homesteads by capitalists. The privilege of buying public land in unlimited quantities to anticipate settlers' needs was not ended. Huge grants of land were made after the adoption of the Homestead Law to railroads, wagon roads, and states and territories which could make their

selections before settlers appeared and thereby acquire the better
and more desirable tracts. Indian land, when opened to settlement, was commonly to be sold, not given to settlers, and individual Indian allotments were likewise to be sold. Altogether,
between 400 and 500 million acres were selected by states and
territories, railroads, and investors and were held for future sales.
These were not, therefore, subject to homestead.[3] In fact, the
area not open to homestead, though undeveloped, was much
greater than the total acreage that homesteaders finally won as
free grants. Congress even required in 1889 and 1890 that the
23 million acres it granted the six new states that entered the
Union during these years should be sold at a minimum of ten
dollars an acre.[4]

Free-land policy as embodied in the Homestead Law was then
grafted upon a land system to which it was ill-fitted and incongruous. The two systems existed side by side for the next twenty-
eight years, indeed longer, during which time the choicer selections of the railroads, states, and speculators were being sold.
Hence the amount of homesteading was smaller than otherwise
it surely would have been.[5]

That revenue was not abandoned as a basic feature of government land policy is shown by the fact that homesteaders,
desiring to expand their holdings beyond the 160 acres they
could acquire by right of development, had the choice of buying
additional tracts from railroads, states, or territories—or from the
federal government if in areas where land had been proclaimed
for sale in unlimited amounts. If the land was in unoffered areas,
they might secure a preemption, or take a desert-land entry which
would cost them $1.25 an acre, or enter a tree claim with its
obligation of setting out trees on forty of the 160 acres. Actually,
more government land was sold between 1862 and 1891 than
was successfully homesteaded and patented between 1862 and
1899. Or, to put it differently, the government derived from the
sale of public land in the sixty years following the adoption of
the Homestead Act a far greater sum ($223,000,000) than it did
in the first sixty years of its land administration ($186,000,000).

The land reformers had not succeeded, when writing the
Homestead Act, in providing that all public lands henceforth

should be reserved for actual settlers. Nor had they succeeded in restricting the quantity of land that might be purchased in offered areas. But they did prevail on the government not to offer newly surveyed land at unlimited sale except for timbered land in Michigan, Wisconsin, Minnesota, Colorado, Oregon, and Washington.[6] Henceforth, there were two classes of land in official terminology: offered land which was subject to private entry in unlimited amounts and unoffered lands which could only be acquired through settlement laws: homestead, preemption, timber culture, timber and stone, and their variations. Approximately two-thirds of Kansas, a larger fraction of Nebraska, all of Oklahoma and the Dakotas, and all of the public land farther west except for California and small areas in Colorado, New Mexico, and Washington were not offered. In these states, speculators could not use their cheaply acquired military bounty-land warrants, or their agricultural college scrip that cost them as little as fifty or sixty cents an acre, to build up huge holdings such as the 263,000 acres that the Brown-Ives-Goddard group of Providence, Rhode Island, established mostly in Illinois, Iowa, and Nebraska; the half million acres of pine lands in Wisconsin to which Ezra Cornell acquired the patent; or the huge 650,000 acres of land that William S. Chapman came to own in California.

Yet it is true that in the unoffered areas large estates were created, such as the bonanza farms of the Dakotas, and the equally large cattle ranches of Wyoming and elsewhere. Some of these holdings, like the bonanza farms, were bought partly from the railroads which placed few limitations on the size of tracts they would sell, and partly from the states. And partly they were acquired through the use of dummy entrymen who took advantage of the loopholes in the settler laws.[7] Others, including some of the large cattle ranches, were not ownerships but enclosures, illegally erected on the public lands which, when the order went out for the removal of the fences, became thereafter open to settlement. These large holdings, together with even larger acquisitions of the timber companies (elaborately documented in the report on forest ownership of the Bureau of Corporations of 1913),[8] and the discovery that millions of acres of land have passed into private hands by the fraudulent use of the settlement laws, have led historians to misunderstand and underestimate the role of the Homestead Law and related settlement measures. Recent textbook writers have declared that the Homestead Law was "not a satisfactory piece of legislation"; it was "a distressing disappointment"; "farmers only benefited slightly" from it; it ended "in failure and disillusionment"; two-thirds of all "homestead claimants before 1890 failed."[9]

A reason for the frequency of these misconceptions of homestead is the continued reiteration in the annual reports of the Commissioners of the General Land Office, of the widespread and indeed common violation of the spirit and even the letter of the law by land-hungry settlers, land lookers, petty and large speculators and their agents, and cattle and mining companies. Defective legislation, insufficient staff, poorly paid personnel in the Washington office, the low level of people filling the local land offices, and the practical impossibility of scrutinizing critically the entries made under the various land laws, all combined to make the Commissioners' task of administering the laws most frustrating.[10] Their comments on the amount of perjury, subornation, and misuse of the law became increasingly sharp until finally, the Commissioner under Cleveland, harassed by the degree of maladministration and the widespread dishonesty of people trying to take advantage of the government, took the drastic step of suspending many thousands of land entries moving toward patent to allow time for examination and the cancellation of fraudulent entries. This action led to swift political pressures by western politicians, forcing Cleveland to reverse his subordinate, no matter how just his action. So absorbed were the Commissioners in their efforts to make homestead function as it was intended to, that they devoted the space allowed them for recommendations for future action very largely to the frauds and malfunctionings of the system. Historians have reflected this jaundiced view, relying upon these continued reiterations, and not finding much in the reports about the hundreds of thousands of people successfully making farms for themselves.

I must confess that I may have contributed to this misunderstanding some twenty-six years ago when I wrote a paper, "The

Homestead Law in an Incongruous Land System." As the title suggests, the paper was intended to show that the principle of free lands to settlers clashed with the revenue principle on which the federal land system was based. My opening sentence might well do for introduction here, and I quote:

> The Homestead Act of 1862 is one of the most important laws which have been enacted in the history of this country, but its significance has been distorted and grossly misrepresented.[11]

The article was intended as a corrective for some of the ideas then prevalent concerning the measure, as, for example, the notion that most of Iowa passed into private hands through the Homestead Act; that homestead replaced other methods of land disposal; that cash sales in unlimited amounts ended in 1862; or that the revenue basis of the land system was abandoned.[12] Correction was necessary but, as is often the case, the revision was carried too far, until some writers seem ready to discount the Homestead Law as of little more than minor significance. Such judgment is unsound.

In any attempt to appraise the significance of the Homestead Law it should be borne in mind that settlers on unoffered land had more protection for their selections and improvements than they did on offered land. Since speculators could not enter or offer to buy their selections or improvements by falsely swearing at the land office that there were no claims against the land, the settler had less fear, once he had filed his original entry, of being dispossessed.

Having filed his original entry (even though he lacked the means with which to develop his claim), the homesteader had an equity that became increasingly valuable and negotiable as population increased the pressure upon the land supply. In the vanguard of settlement on every frontier were land speculators great and small who spied out choice tracts they wished to hold for the expected rise in value that incoming immigration would bring. The extensive speculator might assemble tracts running to tens of thousands of acres. But of equal importance, possibly, was the small man with no capital for the arduous task of farm

making who nevertheless took up a piece of land to which he
expected to acquire a preemption right. Frontier custom assured
that his claim of one hundred to two hundred acres was his to
do with as he wished. With patience and little labor he might
improve slightly, sell, and then move to another tract and do
the same thing. Government conceded only one preemption right,
but that right was almost sacrosanct on the frontier and the same
person might make a number of fortunate selections in succession and dispose of them profitably. Some contemporaries were
not certain whether the first occupation of pioneers was farm
making or land speculation. A settler on his homestead claim in
central Kansas in 1878, noting how so many of his neighbors
were attempting to engross and acquire title to far more land
than they could utilize observed:

> The curse of this country is land-grabbing. Few men are
> satisfied with one claim; they must have a pre-emption, home-
> stead and timber filing, and between the three they have so
> much work they don't know which end they stand on.[13]

In addition to the three usual claims it was not unknown for
different members of a family to file on adjacent tracts, even
though they were violating the spirit if not the letter of the law.

Having established a number of claims which they might be
doing little or nothing to develop, settlers had the choice of
selling relinquishments to others, borrowing to commute and
then skipping the country, attempting to make their improvements with loans until they could get the benefit of rising land
values, or holding for long range development. The location, sale,
and relinquishment of claims became a major business on the
frontier as it proceeded into western Kansas, Nebraska and
Dakota.[14] Relinquishments in the middle Eighties sold for $25
to $50 in Kansas, for $50 to $400 in South Dakota and for as little
as $5 and a shotgun to $700 in North Dakota.[15] Variations in
price partly depended upon the nature of improvements. Undoubtedly, the business of selling relinquishments was carried
beyond all justification but it should be emphasized that it
permitted persons who lacked the means with which to begin
farming to acquire some cash, farm machinery, and stock and

after two or three false starts and sale of relinquishments to succeed finally in establishing ownership of a going farm. The process of claim making with the intention of selling was greatly
abused, particularly in the Eighties, but despite that abuse it
provided opportunities for many settlers to reach their goal of
farm ownership.

Land office reports, accounts of the cattle and lumber industry, and other government documents are replete with stories of
the use of dummy entrymen by individuals and companies eager
to get control of large areas of the public lands. The process was
fairly simple. Employees of the cattle, mining, or lumber companies would be induced to file claims under one of the settlement laws, possibly make some slight improvements on their
claims, take title by commuting their claims and swear before
the land officials that their claims were intended for their own
use and that they had entered into no agreement to transfer ownership. Funds for their commutation and a fee for their services
that ranged from $50 to $200 were provided by the company.[16]
As competition for land intensified, compensation to dummy
entrymen reached as high as $1,000 for a quarter section.[17]

A third source of income that the weakly administered public
land system made possible to westerners was the practice of mortgaging newly entered land with insurance companies at well
beyond its going value and then skipping out with the proceeds
of the loan and unloading the property on the credit agency. The
West had not always been blessed with abundance of capital but
in the Eighties, attracted by high interest rates, money flowed
into the Great Plains in such quantities that agents of eastern
insurance companies and petty capitalists vied with each other
in pushing their loans on settlers, offering some well beyond the
cash value of the land at the time. So marked was this rivalry
that agents, eager for their fees, paid little attention to the quality
of improvements on the land and only insisted on a mortgageable
title. It was reported from northwestern Nebraska in 1886 that it
was easy to get an $800 loan on any quarter section of wild land
on which a settlement right had been established.[18] In central
North Dakota, in 1903, loans to permit commutation of homesteads were being made as high as $1,500.[19] Settlers who had put

little effort into their claims could commute their timber claim (before 1891) or homestead, at a cost of $200 for 160 acres, pay all fees and still have left from $600 to $1,300 for a second try under one of the other settlement laws, the privilege of which they had not yet used.

Many western settlers had larceny in their hearts when it came to dealing with the government, and it did not stretch their consciences unduly to take advantage of the insurance companies or other absentee sources of capital. As one insurance adjuster later said, "it became really too easy for settlers to cash in on their western venture and 'go back to their wives' folks.' They borrowed more than the land was worth and fled."[20] An agent for a Kansas bank said of the borrowers in western Kansas: "As soon as their loans are completed they abandon the land, if they can sell it to someone for a nominal sum above the mortgage they do so."[21]

Whether the early settler was defrauding the government, cheating the insurance company, or making the later immigrant buy a relinquishment from him, he was accumulating the means with which he could finally establish himself as a stable farm maker. This is not to say that all persons establishing claims on the public lands were ultimately to become farmers; many had no such intention. They were out for a speculation. But a very considerable portion of the misuse of the public land laws resulted, it appears, from the credit needs of actual settlers.

A common error in appraising the Homestead Law has been the assumption that homesteading was only important in the Great Plains and Interior Basin where the unit of farming characteristic of the more humid regions was not suitable. The fact is that 23 per cent (689,000) of all original homestead entries were filed in the states east of the Mississippi and in the first tier west of that river. Twenty-four per cent of the homestead entries that went to final patent were located in this region. During the first ten years of the operation of the Homestead Law, Minnesota outranked all states in number of final entries of homesteads and was exceeded only by Kansas in the number of original entries. Altogether, 82,845 free homesteads were patented in Minnesota.[22] This constitutes 66 per cent of the farms of Minnesota of 100

acres or more as listed in the census of 1920. It probably would
not be far from the truth to say that the abstracts of two-thirds
of Minnesota farms trace back to the patent of the homesteader.
East of the Mississippi, 143,360 homestead entries for 15,990,533
acres were carried to patent, mostly in Alabama, Florida, Wisconsin, Mississippi, and Michigan.

In all the states around the Great Lakes, in the South, and in
the first tier west of the Mississippi, a considerably higher proportion of the original filings were carried to final entry than
elsewhere and there were fewer commutations.

In substantial portions of the second tier of states beyond
the Mississippi (extending from Dakota to Oklahoma), the 160-
acre unit of farming was not altogether unsuited for farm practices in the late Nineteenth Century. The line of 20-inch rainfall
begins roughly just west of the Red River of the North and
extends in a gentle southwestward direction. East of that line is
perhaps a fifth of North Dakota, a third of South Dakota, more
than half of Nebraska, and two-thirds of Kansas. The line of
24-inch rainfall leaves, to the east, a small corner of South
Dakota, a fifth of Nebraska, and half of Kansas. To and somewhat
beyond the 24-inch rainfall line, corn flourished and the 160-acre
unit of agriculture seemed reasonably well adapted to farming.
I have conservatively estimated that 150,000 homestead applications were filed in the more humid portions of the Great Plains.
This means that, together with the 689,000 entries previously
mentioned, 839,000 homesteads or 28 per cent of the total number of homesteads were commenced in areas generally suitable
in the Nineteenth Century for 160-acre farm units.

Furthermore, it is important to note that of these early
homesteads established from Kansas north to Dakota territory
before 1881, 58 per cent of those in Kansas were successfully
carried to final entry, 61 per cent in Nebraska and 52 per cent
in Dakota. Sixty-seven per cent of the entries in Dakota made
before 1876 were patented by 1880. This is perhaps the best test
of the applicability of homestead to these areas. For the country
as a whole, slightly less than 50 per cent of the original homesteads were carried to patent.[23]

Doubtless there are other and perhaps smaller areas in the

West where the 160-acre homestead unit seemed to work well at the time. One example is in California where 63 per cent of the original entries made in the years from 1863 to 1875 were carried to completion.

A second error frequently observed in appraisals of the Homestead Act is forgetting that it took five years, later reduced to three (veterans' military service could be counted), for the original entries to mature.[24] Actually, even more than five years was required for many homesteaders who were driven out by drought, grasshoppers, or other misfortunes, and who had to be allowed extensions of time in which to prove up.

In the land selection process many choices were made by settlers and speculators who were misled by the descriptions on the surveyors' plats; by the land lookers who for fees guided settlers to what soon proved to be questionable locations; and by settlers themselves who may have had little knowledge of the quality of land in the vicinity of the 100th meridian. Some settlers, like those who participated in the great rushes into Oklahoma or who desperately tried to get a claim on the Rosebud Reservation in South Dakota, had no time to pick and choose but had perforce to take the first vacant land they could find. Inevitably, mistakes were made. Study of the correspondence of the General Land Office and of western congressmen illustrates the frequency with which errors of location were made from the very outset of the public land system, and the disappointments and frustrations of the land locators who sought the privilege of making exchanges. In the absence of land classification, settlers made many errors that resulted in a high rate of failure on homesteads.

Nebraska well illustrates this tendency to err in the selection of land. When homestead was adopted, or shortly thereafter, the grants to the state for educational purposes, and to railroads for aid to construction had reduced the public domain to less than 37 million acres. Of this amount speculators quickly grabbed up an additional million acres. Yet the records show that settlers filed on nearly 51 million acres either for homesteads or timber-culture claims. Some of these filings led to contests between homesteaders and the railroads or between different homesteaders; other filings proved to be unattractive and were abandoned or relinquished, and perhaps the rights transferred to others. For Nebraska, 51 per cent of the homestead entries and 46 per cent of the combined homestead and timber-culture entries were carried to patent as free land. If commuted entries are included, the percentages reaching patent becomes 58 and 53. Those that did not reach patent were either relinquished for a fee to others or simply abandoned for better selections elsewhere. What is important is that ownership of 74 per cent of the land available for homesteading in Nebraska was actually achieved either through the Homestead Act or the Timber Culture Act, with their privilege of commutation. Or, we may go one step farther and say that at least 80 per cent of the land area of Nebraska available for settler location became owned by homesteaders through settler-oriented laws, though some of this ownership was quite unstable and was not acquired by the first owner for farming.

In Kansas, where little more than 24 million acres were available for homesteading when the act was passed, settlers filed for homesteads and timber-culture claims for more than 35 million acres. The business in relinquishments was large in Kansas as in Nebraska: an estimated 93,000 homestead claims were either relinquished or abandoned. Of the land available for homesteading 50 per cent was carried to patent as free land, 14 per cent was patented as commuted homesteads and 8 per cent was patented to timber-culture claimants.

Since 1607, settlers had been moving westward adapting themselves to different ecological conditions from those to which they were accustomed. The oak openings of Michigan and the rich bluegrass region of Kentucky were as strange to settlers from New York and Virginia as were the prairies of Illinois and Iowa and the Great Plains of Kansas and Nebraska. Adaptation to environment wrought swift changes in methods of farming; those who could not adapt failed. American settlers on whatever frontier were prepared to make these changes and soon did. They did not realize, so general was this process of adaptation, how different their methods—and indeed their whole way of life—had become from those they had followed previously.

Not long after the hungry land seekers crossed the Missouri they came into contact with a region where rainfall was less than they had been accustomed to and the variations greater from year to year; where drought, winter blizzards, and grasshopper plagues were met, and where more extensive farm practices were essential. These conditions made larger farm units necessary. It is interesting to note how the average size of farms in Kansas increased with a certain regularity from east to west as is shown by the census of 1920: 153 acres was the average in Miami County on the eastern Kansas front, 167 in Osage County, 192 in Lyons County, 244 in Morris County, 354 in Ellsworth County, 590 in Ness County, and 900 acres on the western border in Greeley County.[25]

Historians have been troubled that the homestead unit was fixed at 160 acres just when, as they say, settlers were preparing to break into the less humid region of the Great Plains where larger farm units were desirable. Paradoxically, they have also been troubled that the Preemption Law which, with homestead, made possible larger farm units, was kept on the statute books.[26] Following the judgment of the Commissioners of the General Land Office who harped on the amount of fraud involved in preemption, they have given undue emphasis to this aspect and insufficient attention to the fact that preemption was consciously retained by Congress surely because of the greater flexibility it allowed settlers in adapting themselves to farming in the dryer portions of America where land was not offered.[27] There is no mention of repeal of preemption in the discussion leading to the adoption of homestead in 1862 and the Law itself carefully provided for saving all preemption rights that may have been established prior to its adoption. Furthermore, just a few days after the adoption of the Homestead Law, Congress, without a word of opposition in either house, enacted a bill that said all lands to which Indian title had been or should thereafter be extinguished should be subject to preemption. We must conclude that Congress had no intention of establishing an inflexible 160-acre unit for settlers in the unoffered areas.[28]

In 1872 and 1873 the two houses of Congress finally came to agreement on a bill to encourage the planting of trees on the

Great Plains. An additional quarter section was thereby offered
to settlers who would plant and care for forty acres of trees (later
reduced to ten acres) for a period of ten years. An effort to limit
its benefits to settlers who had not taken up a preemption or
homestead, failed. Timber culture was designed further to adapt
the post-1862 land system to farming in sub-humid America. The
law was not carefully drafted and as with all other land legislation it quickly became subject to abuse and was repealed in 1891.
But it had in the meantime, notwithstanding its abuse, served its
purpose. With preemption and homestead it provided a flexibility that after its repeal was to be assured by the more direct
method of enlarging the homestead unit to 320 and then
640 acres.

How significant was the Homestead Law in enabling settlers
to acquire land and to establish themselves on going farms? It
is clear that it was most successful in the period from 1863 to
1880 when the greater proportion of homesteads were being
established in the states bordering on the Mississippi River.
It was successful also in parts of Kansas and Nebraska well east
of the 98th meridian where there was abundance of rain, and
where commutations, relinquishments, and abandonments were
fewer than they were to be in other areas later. In these eighteen
years, homesteaders filed on 469,000 tracts and by 1885 had made
their final entries and were in process of getting title on 55 per
cent. Doubtless some would complete their residence requirements in later years.

The misuse of the Homestead Law was becoming common
between 1880 and 1900. As shown, misuse was by persons not
primarily interested in farm making but concerned to sell relinquishments to immigrants or to transfer rights to cattle, timber,
and mining companies. But the most glaring abuses occurred
later. Between 1880 and 1900, approximately half of the homestead entries were filed in the six states and territories extending
from Oklahoma to North Dakota and including Minnesota.
These all were major farm states and the Homestead Law was
contributing largely to the development of farm ownership,
notwithstanding its abuses.

In these states and territories, free government land, adver-

tised by the America letters which earlier immigrants had sent
back to their families in the Old World, by the government immigration bureaus, by even the colonization departments of the
railroads and land companies, provided the lodestone, the direct-
ing force, that set in motion continued waves of settlers in search
of free land. It was the prospect of disposing of their lands to
these settlers and transporting their goods that made possible
the financing and construction of the railroads through the
Plains, into the Interior Basin and to the Pacific Coast. Homestead, above all other factors, made possible the fast growth of
the West and all the problems this rapid growth brought with it.

Altogether, 1,413,513 original homestead entries were filed
between 1863 and 1900, but even more were to be filed in the
twentieth century for a substantially larger acreage. The great
day of farm making with the material aid of Uncle Sam was
over, however. True, some twentieth century entries were made
with the enlarged units for small stock raising farms or ranches
or even wheat farms but the evidence seems strong that the great
bulk of the entries filed after 1900 were for large ranching,
mining, and lumbering companies. The numbers of original and
final homestead entries, when compared with the number of
farms in the Rocky Mountain States, provides startling evidence
that the homesteads were being assimilated into larger aggrega-
tions of land. Using round figures, we find that Idaho had 92,000
original homestead entries, 60,000 final entries and in 1910–1930
its highest number of farms was 42,000. Colorado had 205,000
original, 107,000 final entries, and at its most 59,000 farms.
Arizona had 38,000 original, 20,000 final entries, and 9,000 farms.
Wyoming had 115,000 original, 67,000 final entries, and 15,000
farms. In six mountain states the original entries came to 848,000,
final entries 492,000, and the maximum number of farms 217,000.
Thus it seemed to take about four original entries and two final
homestead entries to produce a farm, and most of these homesteads were of the enlarged variety.

Major John W. Powell's recommendation of 1879 that the
public lands be classified for use and that a 2,560-acre pasturage
homestead be established for lands fit only for grazing was
somewhat premature, but certainly by 1900, land classification

and larger homestead units were essential.[29] Yet the evidence is strong that the enlarged units of 1904, 1909, and 1916 were not altogether wise or successful. The old evils of careless drafting of land legislation, weak and inefficient administrations (inadequately staffed), and the anxiety of interests to take advantage of loopholes in the laws, all brought the Homestead Acts into contempt and censure. But their noble purpose and the great part they played in enabling nearly a million and a half people to acquire farm land, much of which developed into farm homes, far outweigh the misuse to which they were put.

## NOTES

1. The western point of view concerning the public lands and homestead was perhaps best expressed over and over again in the 1850's by Horace Greeley in the *New York Tribune* when he was vigorously campaigning for the adoption of a homestead law and for drastic curbs on speculative purchasing of public lands. Theodore Roosevelt, no radical as almost everyone would agree, accepted, with his keen understanding of western problems, the traditional western view concerning land values in his *Winning of the West* (4 volumes, New York, 1889–1896), III, 252–253.

2. Reference should be made to the standard works on public land policy for the period to 1860: George M. Stephenson, *Political History of the Public Lands from 1840–1862* (Boston, 1917); Benjamin F. Hibbard, *History of the Public Land Policies* (New York, 1924); Roy M. Robbins, *Our Landed Heritage. The Public Domain, 1776–1936* (Princeton, 1924); Paul W. Gates, *The Farmers' Age* (New York, 1961).

3. The following statistics of acreage of land and numbers of entries are compiled from the *Annual Reports* of the Commissioner of the General Land Office. Compilations that sometimes differ from data continued in these reports are Thomas Donaldson, *The Public Domain. House Miscellaneous Documents*, 47 Cong., 2 Sess., No. 45, Part 4, 1884, and *Report of the Public Land Commission, Senate Documents*, 58 Cong., 3 Sess., No. 189, 1905.

4. Herbert S. Schell, *History of South Dakota* (Lincoln, 1961), p. 222.

5. Paul W. Gates, *Fifty Million Acres: Conflicts Over Kansas Land Policy, 1854–1890* (Ithaca, N.Y., 1954), pp. 237ff. Also the same author's "The Homestead Law in an Incongruous Land System," *American Historical Review*, XLI (July, 1936), 652 ff.

6. Between 1866 and 1876 the public lands of Alabama, Arkansas, Florida, Louisiana, and Mississippi were open only to homesteaders but in the latter year they were restored to unlimited entry and the best of them were quickly

bought up by lumbermen from the North. Paul W. Gates, "Federal Land Policy in the South, 1866–1888," *Journal of Southern History, VI* (Aug., 1940), 303 ff. Elsewhere, lands that had once been offered for unrestricted sale and later withdrawn to permit railroads to select their alternate sections as granted by the United States were restored to the offered and unrestricted status when the selections had been made.

7. Harold E. Briggs, "Early Bonanza Farming in the Red River Valley of the North," *Agricultural History, VI* (Jan., 1932), 20 ff.

8. Bureau of Corporations, Department of Commerce and Labor, *The Lumber Industry,* 3 Parts, 1913–1914 (Washington, 1913–1914), especially Part 1, Chap. VI, "Public-Land Policy a Primary Cause of the Concentration of Timber Ownership," pp. 218 ff.

9. T. Harry Williams, Richard N. Current and Frank Freidel, *History of the United States* (2 Vols., New York, 1959), II, 142; Thomas D. Clark, *Frontier America* (New York, 1959), p. 727; Ray A. Billington, *Westward Expansion. A History of the American Frontier* (New York, 1949), pp. 696 ff.; Dumas Malone and Basil Rauch, *Empire for Liberty, The Genesis and Growth of the United States of America* (2 Vols., New York, 1960), II, 43. Actually 58 per cent of those who homesteaded through 1890 succeeded in gaining title to their land either through final entry or through commutation. James C. Olson, *History of Nebraska,* (Lincoln, 1955), p. 166, contemplating the slow alienation of public lands in Nebraska by the homestead route before 1900, asks why did the Homestead Act "fall so short of expectations." Much of western Nebraska was still in public ownership and largely unused save for grazing in 1900 but this was nature's fault, not the fault of the act. In 1900 there were 121,525 farms in Nebraska. It may not be unfair to say that 68,862 of these had been partly or wholly acquired through homesteading for that is the number of homesteads that had gone to patent at that time. In addition, 5,004 homesteaders were to reach the final entry stage in the next five years and should be included in the number of homesteads which were probably a part of the farms of the time.

10. Harold H. Dunham discusses the inadequacies and weaknesses of the personnel of the General Land Office in *Government Handout: A Study in the Administration of the Public Lands, 1875–1891* (New York, 1941), pp. 124 ff.

11. *American Historical Review,* XLI (July, 1936), 652.

12. Edgar Harlan, director of the Iowa Historical, Memorial, and Art Department assured the writer in 1936 that most of the land of his state was homesteaded and was greatly surprised when he was shown that only 4 per cent went to patent. Congressman Harvey B. Ferguson stated in 1914: "It was great statesmanship that created the homestead laws under which such a State as Iowa developed." *Grazing Homesteads and the Regulation of Grazing on the Public Lands,* Hearings before the Committee on the Public Lands, House of Representatives, 63 Cong., 2 Sess., 1914, Part 1, p. 358. See also Leifur Magnuson, *Disposition of the Public Lands of the United States With Particular Reference to Wage-Earning Labor* (Washington, 1919), p. 29; Theodore L. Nydahl, *Social and Economic Aspects of Pioneers in Goodhue*

*County, Minnesota,* Norwegian-American Historical Association, *Studies and Records,* V (Northfield, Minn., 1930), 53.

13. John Ise, ed., *Sod-House Days. Letters from a Kansas Homesteader, 1877–1878* (New York, 1937), p. 212; Francis J. Rowbotham, *A Trip to Prairie-Land* (London, 1885), p. 240.

14. On the basis of careful research in newspapers and in correspondence of the land offices in Kansas, George W. Anderson emphasizes the institutional character of the location of claims by land lookers and the purchase and sale of relinquishments in "The Administration of Federal Land Laws in Western Kansas: A Factor in Adjustment to a New Environment," *Kansas Historical Quarterly,* XX (Nov., 1952), 233 ff. Newspaper proprietors, he found, were deeply involved in this business.

15. Anderson, *ibid,* p. 240; Herbert S. Schell, *History of South Dakota,* p. 173; *North Dakota Historical Collections,* II (1908), 169, 202, 237; and III (1910), 167; *North Dakota History,* XVIII (October, 1951), 242.

16. For the prevalence of the $200 fee see General Land Office, *Report,* 1886, p. 83. Charles Lowell Green has summarized some of the evidence of frauds in the administration of the public land laws in South Dakota in "The Administration of the Public Domain in South Dakota," *South Dakota Historical Collections,* XX (1940), 199 ff.

17. *Report of the Public Lands Commission, Senate Documents,* 58 Cong., 3 Sess., 1904, p. 121. This sum was paid for the services of eight dummy entrymen and women in southern Pierce County, by the Prowly & Church Cattle Co.

18. The Aetna Life Insurance Company, which had an average of $8,677,000 invested in western farm mortgages from Ohio to Texas between 1867 and 1890, was forced to take over 812 properties having a book value of $1,877,000. The number of foreclosures was doubtless greater in Kansas, Nebraska, and Dakota than in the region farther east. The figures were kindly provided by Robert H. Pierce, formerly of the Aetna Company. Allan G. Bogue in his *Money at Interest: The Farm Mortgage on the Middle Border* (Ithaca, N.Y., 1955), p. 193, shows that J. B. Watkins of Lawrence, Kansas, and his mortgage company took over 2,500 farms between 1873 and 1893, or between 10 and 20 per cent of the total number of farms on which they made loans.

19. Beatrice *Gage County Democrat,* June 25, 1886; *Report of the Public Lands Commission, Senate Documents,* 58 Cong., 3 Sess., 1904, No. 189, p. 122.

20. Seth K. Humphrey, *Following the Prairie Frontier,* p. 95; General Land Office, *Report,* 1885, p. 54. Humphrey was a claim agent who tried to chase down some of the defaulting mortgagors. His disillusionment with absconding debtors led him to write: "By far the greater number of landseekers took up government land with the intention of unloading it on somebody else...." *op. cit.,* p. 132.

21. Quoted in Allan G. Bogue, *op. cit.,* p. 146.

22. Since much of Minnesota land had been offered and was therefore subject to purchase in unlimited amounts there was less resort to the use

of dummy entrymen in this state than in areas farther west. The Mesabi Range, partly, and much of the timber land, was open to cash purchase and well over a million acres of potentially valuable land were acquired through outright purchase in large blocks by capitalists.

23. I have omitted Oklahoma from consideration because its lands came into settlement so much later.

24. Cf. Roy M. Robbins, *Our Landed Heritage, The Public Domain, 1776–1936,* p. 240; Fred A. Shannon, *The Farmers' Last Frontier* (New York, 1945), p. 54.

25. *Fourteenth Census of the United States, 1920,* Vol. VI, *Agriculture,* 732–41.

26. Cf. Hibbard, *History of the Public Land Policies,* p. 409; Robbins, *Our National Heritage,* pp. 238, 285–86.

27. In 1870, Joseph Wilson, Commissioner of the General Land Office, recommended that persons be allowed to enter only one tract of 160 acres under either the preemption or the homestead laws. His successor, Willis Drummond, urged the repeal of the preemption law in 1871–1873. In 1877, Commissioner J. A. Williamson, and in 1882, Commissioner N. C. McFarland, resumed the attack upon the preemption law with recommendations that it be repealed. Thereafter, until 1891 when the act was repealed, the successive commissioners laid down an increasing barrage against its continuation on the ground that it enabled persons having no intention of developing the land to acquire ownership.

28. *Congressional Globe,* 37 Cong., 2 Sess., April 17, 1862, p. 1711; May 29, 1862, pp. 2432, 2439.

29. The recommendation for the 2,560-acre homestead on "pasturage" lands is made in the Preliminary Report of the Public Lands Commission, *House Ex. Doc.,* 46 Cong., 2 Sess., 1880, Vol. 22, p. lxxvi.

MARI SANDOZ

# *The Homestead in Perspective*

THE HOMESTEAD ACT was the hope of the poor man. Many who
had wanted a piece of government land felt that preempting,
which required an eventual cash payment of $1.25 or more an
acre, was too risky for the penniless. If the preemptor failed to
raise the money at the proper time, in addition to building a
home in the wilderness and making a living for a family, he
lost the land and with it all his improvements, his work, and
his home. The Homestead Act offered any bona fide land seeker
160 acres from the public domain with no cash outlay beyond
the $14 filing fee and the improvements he would have to make
to live on the place the required five years. His house, barn, sheds
and corrals, his well, the tilled acreage and the fencing, all
counted toward the final patent to the land, and most of these
improvements could be made by the homesteader's own hands,
his and the family's.

It was this offer of free land that drew my father, Old Jules
Sandoz, west to a homestead in the unorganized region that was
to become Sheridan County, Nebraska, and he stressed "free
land" in all the letters he wrote to the European and American
newspapers for the working man, letters that drew the hundreds of settlers he located.

The home seeker, as late as the end of the Kinkaid Homestead days of my childhood, came by every possible means, even
afoot. I was born too late to see the Czechoslovakian couple who
crossed much of Nebraska pushing a wheelbarrow loaded with
all their belongings, including, it was said, the wedding feather
tick. But we saw many land seekers walk in, some coming much
farther than the seventeen miles from the railroad. There were
dusty men, worn and discouraged until they got a good wash-up
at the Niobrara River near our house or at our well, followed
by one of mother's hearty suppers and a big dose of Old Jules'
enthusiasm and faith in the country. Some came by livery rig
or the mail wagon, or were picked up by a settler returning

home from town. Many of the more serious land seekers left
their families back east until they were located. Often these drove
in by wagon in the old way although the wire fences of settlers,
and, in the free-land regions, the cattlemen, prevented the accustomed movement up along the streams, as Old Jules himself had
come, following the Niobrara to Mirage Flats.

We children had the usual curiosity about outsiders but we
were even more thoroughly disciplined than most homesteader
children, who were taught to keep out of the way and never
push into grown-up affairs. But we tried to hear the answer to
Old Jules usual western query: "What name you traveling
under?"

This question from a rough, bearded man with a strong
foreign accent and a gun on his arm was not reassuring to
strangers. But perhaps a potential settler should realize from the
start that homesteading was not for the timid, and as soon as a
man could say "I'm looking for me a piece of government
land——" he was among friends. He and any family he had
were welcome to eat at our table and sleep in our beds even
if we children were moved to the floor. This was naturally all
free beyond the twenty-five dollar locating and surveying fee
Old Jules charged whenever the settler managed to get the
money. Often the family stayed with us until their house was
up, the wife perhaps criticizing father's profane and bawdy
tongue and complaining contemptuously about mother's bread
from unbleached macaroni wheat that we grew and hauled to
the water mill on Pine Creek.

For us children the important home seekers were the boomers, the covered wagon families. Evenings we watched them come
down into the Niobrara valley, rumble over the plank bridge,
and climb the steep sandy pitch to the bench on which our
house stood. There, on a flat camping-ground, the panting
horses were allowed to stop, and barefoot children spilled out of
the wagon, front and back, to run, galloping and bucking like
calves let out of a pen. We stared from among the cherry trees,
or in the summer, from the asparagus patch where the greenery
stood over our heads. We saw the tugs dropped, the harness

stripped off and piled against the wagon tongue, while the woman ordered the children to this and that task as the fire began to smoke in the little pile of stones always there for campers.

Finally the man might come to draw a bucket of the clear water from our well, water so cold it hurt the teeth on hot days.

By the time we were old enough to notice, father had no trouble waiting until after supper to talk land to such men.

"Boomers!" he would say, in contempt. "Probably been to Oregon and back, living off the country, picking up anything that's loose. Hey, Mari, go hide all the hammers and bring in my rifle——" meaning the 30-30 that usually hung on the antlers outside the door.

"And shut up the chickens——" mother would add.

Old Jules was usually right about the boomers of the 1906–12 period. The man would come in to talk land but even if he showed any enthusiasm for homesteading, the family might be pulling out at dawn, seldom with anything of consequence that belonged to us. That stack of guns in a corner of our kitchen–living room, and father's evident facility with firearms, discouraged more than petty thefts of, say, a pair of pliers or a slab of bacon from the smokehouse.

"Sneaky thieves!" mother would snort. "If they were so hungry I would have given them more than that, so long as we could spare it."

A few stayed to follow father's buckskin team into the sandhills, to live in the covered wagon until a dugout or a soddy could be prepared on the new homestead. Some of these left when the drouth and hot winds of August struck, along with others who had walked in or came by hired rig. The winters seemed particularly hard to the latter-day boomers, and often the first fall blizzard sent them rolling toward Texas or Arkansas. Some stuck it out. Several of these Kinkaid-day boomers are growing fine blooded stock in Nebraska, the older members spending the winters in Florida or California and damning the government.

We tend to forget that the homesteaders were not a type, not as alike as biscuits cut out with a baking-powder can. They varied as much as their origins and their reasons for coming west. There were Daughters and Sons of the Revolution located next to the communal communities of the Mennonites, say, or the Hutterians. An illiterate from some other frontier might be neighboring with a Greek and Hebrew scholar from a colony of Russian Jews in the Dakotas. A nervous-fingered murderer who fled west under a new name might join fences with a nonviolent River Baptist or a vegetarian who wouldn't kill a rabbit eating up his first sprouts of lettuce, no matter how hungry the settler might be.

Yet there was apparently a certain repetition of characters in the homestead communities. Those who thought that Old Jules Sandoz was incredible or at least unique should go through the many thousands of letters I received from homesteaders and descendants of homesteaders. Apparently, men with some Old Julesian traits lived in every pioneer community—even as far away as Australia and New Zealand—men with the vision of the community builder, the stubbornness to stick against every defeat, the grim ruthlessness required to hold both themselves and their neighbors to the unwelcoming virgin land.

There was considerable difference between the homesteaders who came into western Nebraska in the 1884–90 period and the Kinkaiders of 1906–12, that is, after the cattleman fences were removed from the government land. The homesteaders of the earlier period were generally young, many under the required twenty-one years, but with a family or a flexible conscience. In the height of the Kinkaid Homestead days many were in their forties and some much older—usually office workers or teachers and so on—retired people or those who had lost their jobs in the retrenchment of 1906–08. There were many women among these, not only among the fraudulent entries by the cattlemen (often only names of old-soldier widows) but among the bona fide homesteaders. These women were classified roughly into two groups by the other settlers. Those with genteel ways, graying hair, downy faces and perhaps good books to loan to a settler's reading-hungry daughter, were called Boston school teachers, no matter who or where from. The others, called Chicago widows, weren't young either, or pretty, but their talk, their dress, and their ways were gayer, more colorful, more careless; their books, if any, were paperback novels, with such titles as *Wife in Name Only,* or *Up from the Depths.* Several had a volume of nonfiction called *From Ballroom to Hell,* with every step of the way well illustrated and described. Among the tips offered was a solution for a recurring problem: To fill out your corset cover, roll up two stockings and pin into place, but be sure the stockings are clean, to avoid an offending odor.

It is true that in the largely male population of our homestead regions more of the Chicago widows got married than the Boston school ma'am type.

There was a saying among the settlers that the first spring of a new homesteader told whether the man or the woman was the boss. If the house was put up first, plainly the woman ran things; if a corn patch was broken out before any building, the cowboys told each other that this homesteader would be hard to drive off. But there were other factors to be considered. An April settler was wise to throw up a claim shack of some kind and leave the sod breaking for May, after the grass was started well enough so it would be killed by the plowing. Nor were the women, bossy or not, always easy to drive out. Some clung to the homestead even after their husbands were shot down by ranch hirelings. Nebraska's State Senator Cole grew up in the sandhills because his mother stayed with her two young sons after their father was shot off his mower.

Old Jules' first claim dwelling was half dugout, half sod, but the home of his family was a frame house in which the water froze in the teakettle in January. We envied our neighbors with good sod houses, the deep window seats full of Christmas cactus, century plants, and geraniums blooming all winter, the fine shadowiness of the interior cool and grateful in the summer, while our house was hot as an iron bucket in the sun. Old Jules permitted no cooling blinds or curtains at the windows. He wanted to see anyone coming up. Evenings he always sat back out of line of the lighted windows.

Although I never lived in a sod house I went to school in one and taught school in two others, both pretty decrepit at the time, with mouse holes in the walls; one with a friendly bullsnake living there. Sometimes the snake was fooled by the glowing stove on a chilly fall day and came wandering out and down the aisle during school hours. A snickering among the boys always warned me, and the snake too. Licking out his black forked tongue speculatively, the autumn-logy snake turned slowly around and moved back to his hole in the wall.

The three immediate needs of the new settler were shelter, food, and water. Of the three, only the food that he must grow had a tyrannical season. As locater Old Jules never showed a home seeker a place without a piece of corn land. At a potential site he would push his hat back, estimate the arable acreage, and sink his spade into an average spot. Turning up a long sod, he examined the depth and the darkness of the top soil and shook out the rooting of the grass. If he was satisfied, he looked around at the weeds, not just on spots enriched by some animal carcass long ago, but in general. Where sunflowers grew strong and tall, corn would do well.

But even the best of sod had to be turned and planted at the proper time. With two fairly good draft horses, preferably three or four against the tough rooting, and a sod plow, the settler could break the prairie himself. Or he could hire it done, usually by exchange of work with some of his neighbors. I like to remember the look on the faces of some of these new home-steaders as they tilled the first bit of earth they ever owned. Like any toddler, when I was two, three years old I couldn't be kept from following in the furrow of any plowing done near the house. Later it seemed to me there was something like a spiritual excitement about a man guiding a breaker bottom through virgin earth, with the snap and crackle of the tough roots as they were cut, the sod rolling smooth and flat from the plow, a gull or two following for the worms, and blackbirds chattering around.

Sometimes corn, beans, or potatoes were dropped in the fur-row behind the sod plow and covered by the next round but more often the corn was planted later by a man, a woman, or an energetic boy or girl. With an apron or a bag tied on for the seed, and a spade in the hand, the planter started. At every full man's step or two steps for the shorter-legged, the spade was thrust down into the sod, worked sideways to widen the slit, two kernels of corn dropped in, the spade swung out and the foot brought down on the cut to seal it. All day, up and down the sod ribbons, the rhythmic swing of step and thrust was maintained. To be sure, the spade arm was mighty work-sore the next morning, but every homesteader's child learned that the remedy for that was more work.

Millions of acres were planted this way, sometimes with beans and pumpkin seeds mixed with the corn for a stretch. Good breaking grew few weeds except a scattering of big sunflowers, so the sod field was little care. With the luck of an early August rain, turnip and rutabaga seed could be broadcast between a stretch of rows for the winter root pit. Up in South Dakota, some homesteaders tried flax instead of corn, the seed harrowed into the sod just before a rain, and were rewarded by an expanse as blue as fallen sky in blooming time.

The second spring the sod was backset, and ready for small grain, perhaps oats or rye but more often the newer varieties of wheat broadcast on the fresh plowing from a bag slung under one arm, much like the figure of the Sower on the Nebraska capitol. The seed was covered by a harrow or drag. If there was no harrow, a heavily branched tree, a hackberry, perhaps, would be dragged over the ground by the old mares or patient oxen. Mechanical seeders drawn by fast-paced horses or mules helped spread bonanza wheat farming from the Red River down to Oklahoma and deep into Montana and Alberta. But the new homesteader still broadcast his small grain by hand.

The settler too late for the land along the streams was in urgent need of water from the day of his arrival. True, there might be buffalo wallows and other ponds filled by the spring rains for the stock a while, but many settlers hauled at least the household water ten, twelve miles, and farther, until a well could be put down, or had to be, to quiet the womenfolks. Where the water table was not too deep the first well was usually dug— cheap but dangerous for the novice. Every community had its accidents and tragedies. Uncurbed wells caved in on the digger.

People, adults and children, fell into the uncovered holes and were perhaps rescued by a desperate effort of everyone within fifty miles around, or were left buried there, with a flower or a tree planted to mark the grave.

The well in our home yard was the usual dug one, curbed to the bottom, with a windlass and a bucket that had been a black powder can, larger than the usual pail, the fifty-pound powder size, I think, and came painted a water-proof blue outside. All of us were very careful around wells, perhaps because we had a constant example before us. Old Jules was crippled his first summer on his claim on Mirage Flats. He had finished his new well and was being drawn up by his helpers. As he neared the top the two practical jokers yanked the rope to scare him. The rope, frayed by all the strain of lifting the soil from the sixty-five foot hole, broke. The digger was dropped to the bottom and crippled for the rest of his life. Only the extraordinary luck of getting to Dr. Walter Reed, of later yellow-fever fame, at the frontier post, Fort Robinson, kept him alive at all.

Our well on the river had a solid ladder inside the casing, the kind of ladder that could have saved Old Jules all those crippled years if he had nailed one into the curbing of his first well and climbed out instead of standing in the dirt bucket to be drawn up. Whenever a foolish hen jumped up on the water bench of our well and let the wind blow her in, it was Old Jules who clambered ponderously down the deep hole after her. Practically any other emergency, except something like sewing up a badly cut leg, he let his wife or his children handle— ordered them to handle—but he was determined there would not be another well accident in his household.

In the deep-soiled sand hills, most homesteaders put down their wells with a sand bucket—a valve-tipped short piece of pipe on a rope to be jerked up and down inside the larger well piping that had an open sand point at the bottom. Water was poured into the pipe, to turn the soil into mud under the plunging sand bucket and be picked up by the valve in the end. Full, it was drawn out, emptied and the process repeated. Occasionally, the larger pipe was given a twist with a wrench until its own weight forced it down as fast as the earth below was soaked and lifted out in the sand bucket. When a good water table was reached the end of the sand point was plugged, a cylinder and pumprod put in, and attached to a pump, home-made or bought from a mail order catalogue, and the home-steader had water.

"Nothing's prettier'n a girl pumpin' water in the wind," the cowboys used to say, obviously of homesteader daughters, for no others were out pumping.

As long as there were buffaloes, settlers could go out to the herd ranges for meat and even a few hides to sell for that scarcest of pioneer commodities, cash in the palm. The early settlers learned to preserve a summer buffalo or two in the Indian way, cutting the meat into flakes thin as the edge of a woman's hand to dry quickly in the hot winds, with all the juices preserved. Well-dried, the meat kept for months and was good boiled with a touch of prairie onion or garlic. With vegetables, the dried buffalo or deer or elk made good boiled dinners or meat pies, and was chopped into cornmeal mush by the Pennsylvanians for scrapple until there was pork.

Much could be gleaned for the table before the garden even started. Old Jules brought water cress seed west and scattered it wherever there was a swift current and in the lake regions where the earth-warmed water seeped out all winter, and kept an open spot for cress and mallard ducks. Dandelions start early and as soon as they came up brownish red, we cut them out with a knife for salad, very good with hard boiled eggs, the dressing made with vinegar from wild currants, plums, or grapes and the vinegar-mother we borrowed from a neighbor who had brought it in a bottle by wagon from Kentucky. Later there was lambs-quarter, boiled and creamed and perhaps on baking days spread into a *dunna,* which looked like a green-topped pizza. Meat the homesteaders could provide—antelope and deer, and after these were gone, grouse, quail, and cottontails, with ducks and geese spring and fall. Old Jules was an excellent trapper and hunter as well as gardener and horticulturist, with his wife and the children for the weeding and the harvest. Consequently we seldom lacked anything in food except the two items that cost money—sugar and coffee. Roasted rye made a cheap and poor coffee substitute. Other homesteaders grew cane and cooked the sap into hard and soft sorghum but our sweetening was often nothing but dried fruits eaten from the palm or baked into buns and rolls. Once a whole winter was sweetened by a barrel of extra dark blackstrap molasses father got somehow as a bargain. It made fine pungent cookies.

Mother was a good pig raiser and we usually had wonderful sausage looped over broomsticks in the smoke house with the hams and bacon, the good sweet lard in the cellar in crocks. In our younger days butchering was a trial. It meant father had to be disturbed from his plans, his thinking, to shoot the fat hog. The washboiler was put on the stove, with buckets and the tea-kettle filled for extra scalding water. A barrel had to be set tilted into the ground with an old door laid on low blocks up against the open barrelhead. When everything was ready, the hog up close and everybody out to keep it there, Old Jules had to be called, mother shouting to him, "That one there! Shoot quick!"

But by then the hog might be gone, to be fetched back after a chase through the trees. When father got a shot he put the bullet cleanly between the eyes but he was often experimenting with the amount of powder that would kill without penetrating into the good meat. Sometimes the hog was not even stunned but ran squealing for the brush, and had to be shot again. Sometimes it fell soundlessly and mother thrust the sticking knife into father's hand. With disgust all over his face, he drove the knife in the general direction of the jugular vein and when the dark blood welled out, stepped back while mother ran in to roll the animal to make the blood flow faster. When grandmother was still alive she usually hurried out with a pan for the makings of her blood pudding but none of the rest of the family would even taste it.

Now the hog was dragged up on the old door, ready for the scalding. Everybody ran for the boiling water, the washboiler, the buckets.

"Look out! Look out!" father kept shouting most of the time as he limped around. When the barrel was steaming with the hot water, he and mother shoved the dead pig down into it head first, because that was the hardest to scald well, and worked the carcass back and forth by the hind feet, to get every spot wet, while mother yanked off handsful of the loosening bristles, shaking the heat from her fingers. Then the hog was drawn out upon the door, turned and the hind half thrust into the stinking hot water, and pulled out upon the door again. Now everybody fell to scraping, clutching butcher knives by the back or working with ragged-edge tin cans, the bristles rolling off in wet clumps and windrows.

No butchered animal looks finer than a well-scalded and scraped hog—pink and plump and appetizing. That evening there was fresh liver for supper, and the frothing brain cooked in a frying pan. I liked pork tenderloin with the animal heat and sweetness still in it. I fried this for myself, and never tasted a finer dish. Meat still animal-warm was credited with helping to cure many sufferers from bleeding stomachs sent west to a government claim by their doctors. Whole communities of stomach patients settled on the Plains, and usually died of other complaints, including old age.

Butchering for most homesteaders, particularly the lone ones, was a matter for neighborly help, as were many larger undertakings, particularly threshing. Most of the threshing outfits that finally reached the homesteader were small horse-powered machines with the owner probably feeding the separator himself to keep greenhorns from choking it, tearing it up. Usually three, four hands, including the horse-power driver, came with the outfit. The rest of the sixteen, eighteen man crew was drawn from the settlers, exchanging work. Often neighber women came to help with the cooking. Reputations were made or broken by the meals put out for the threshers, and many a plain daughter owed a good marriage match to the wild plum pie or the chicken and dumplings of her mother at threshing time.

The homesteader got most of his outside items through mail-order catalogues, including, sometimes, his wife, if one could call the matrimonial papers, the heart-and-hand publications, catalogues. They did describe the offerings rather fully but with, perhaps, a little less honesty than Montgomery Ward or Sears

Roebuck. Unmarried women were always scarce in new regions. Many bachelor settlers had a sweetheart back east or in the Old Country, or someone who began to look a little like a sweetheart from the distance of a government claim that got more and more lonesome as the holes in the socks got bigger. Some of these girls never came. Others found themselves in an unexpectedly good bargaining position and began to make all kinds of demands in that period of feminine uprising. They wanted the husband to promise abstinence from profanity, liquor, and tobacco and perhaps even commanded allegiance to the rising cause of woman suffrage. Giving up the cud of tobacco in the cheek was often very difficult. A desperate neighbor of ours chewed grass, bitter willow and cottonwood leaves, coffee grounds, and finally sent away for a tobacco cure. It made him sick, so sick, at least in appearance, that his new wife begged him to take up chewing again. Others backslid on the sly, sneaking a chew of Battle Axe or Horseshoe in the face of certain anger and tears.

But many bachelors had no sweetheart to come out, and some of these started to carry the heart-and-hand papers around until the pictures of the possible brides were worn off the page. In those days the usual purpose really was marriage, not luring the lonely out of their pitiful little savings or even their lives. "We married everything that got off the railroad," old homesteaders, including my father, used to say.

Usually the settler was expected to send the prospective wife a stagecoach or railroad ticket. Perhaps, even though he had mortgaged his team to get the ticket, the woman sold it and never came and there was nothing to be done unless the U.S. mails were involved. Most of the women did arrive and many of these unions, bound by mutual need and dependence, founded excellent families. Of course, there was no way to compel a mail-order wife to stay when she saw the husband's place. Usually she had grown up in a settled region, perhaps with Victorian sheltering, and was shocked by her new home, isolated, at the best a frame or log shack with cracks for the blizzard winds, or only a soddy or dugout into some bank, with a dirt floor and the possibility of wandering stock falling through the roof.

The long distance to the stagecoach or the railroad, with

walking not good, kept many a woman to her bargain. There are, however, stories of desperate measures used to hold the wife—ropes or chains or locked leg hobbles, but the more common and efficacious expedient was early pregnancy. That brought the customary gift for the first child—a sewing machine, and many a man, including my own father, scratched mightily for the money.

The women, particularly the young ones, brought some gaiety to the homestead regions, with visitings, berryings, pie socials, square dances, play parties, literaries at the schools, and shivarees for the newlyweds. The women organized Sunday Schools, and sewing bees. When calamity or sickness struck, the women went to help, and if there was death they bathed and dressed the corpse, coming with dishes of this and that so the bereaved need not trouble to cook and were spared the easing routine. Doctors were usually far away and scarce and expensive. Old Jules, with his partial training in medicine, had a shelf of the usual remedies and for years he was called out to care for the difficult deliveries. Several times middle-aged people have come to me to say that Old Jules brought them into the world, perhaps back in the 1880's or 1890's.

There were problems besides sickness and death, besides the lack of cash and credit that dogs every new community, besides the isolation and drouth and dust storms. Fires swept over the prairies any time during practically ten months a year, although the worst were usually in the fall, with the grass standing high and rich in oily seed. The prairie fires could be set by fall lightning, by the carelessness of greenhorns in the country, by sparks from the railroads and by deliberate malice.

"Burning a man out" could mean destroying his grass, crops, hay, even his house and himself. Once started, the heat of the fire created a high wind that could sweep it over a hundred miles of prairie in an incredibly short time. Settlers soon learned to watch the horizon for the pearling rise of smoke from prairie grass. At the first sign of this, everyone hurried to fight the flames with water barrels, gunny sacks, hoes, and particularly plows to turn furrows for the backfiring. Even more important was the awareness of the danger ahead of time, early enough so fireguards were plowed around the homestead, at least around the buildings. In addition everyone was told the old Indian advice: "Come fire, go for bare ground, sand or gravel or to big water. Make a backfire against small creek or bare spot, to burn only into wind, and stay where ashes are. Best is to go on a place with no grass, and do not run."

Old Jules' Kinkaid in the sandhills bordered on the Osborne valley, which had a prairie-fire story. An earlier settler and his wife and two small boys had lived in the Osborne—a wet hay flat with miles of rushes and dense canebrakes, and a small open lake in the center that dried up in the summers. Early one fall a prairie fire came sweeping in toward the place. The settler and his wife hurried out to help fight the flames, commanding the two boys to stay in the house. It was sod, with a sod roof, and surrounded by a wide fireguard. Here they were safe. But when the smoke thickened and the fire came roaring over the hill toward the house the boys ran in terror to the swamp, clambering through the great piles of dead rushes and canes for the lake bed. The fire caught them.

After that the settler and his wife moved away but the story of the boys remained as a warning to all of us. When my brother James and I were sent down to hold the Kinkaid for a few months alone, we often went to the Osborne swamp to hunt ducks but never without searching the horizon for prairie-fire smoke. There were mushrooms growing where the sod house of the early settler had been, good mushrooms, fine fried with young ducks or prairie chicken.

The most dreaded storm of the upper homestead region was and still is the blizzard. The first one to kill many people was the Buffalo Hunter's Storm of the 1870's, although the School Children's Blizzard of 1888 is sadly remembered, and even the one of 1949. Most of the people who died in blizzards died through some foolishness, some stupidity, and a few years later would have known better. There are always signs before the worst storms: unseasonal warmth, calm, and stillness, as on January 12, 1888, and old timers were ready with warnings of what to do if caught in a blizzard. "If lost in the sand hills, any blowout will give the directions. The wind cuts the hollows from the northwest and moves the sand out southeastward. If so confused that directions are useless or you are too far from shelter, dig in anywhere to keep dry, with a fire if possible, but dry, even if it's only under a bank somewhere, into the dry sand of a blowout. Don't get yourself wet and *don't* wear yourself out. Practically anyone with a little sense and a little luck can outlast a blizzard."

Not all the danger is in the storm itself. The homestead region had few trees and fewer rocks and a May blizzard left an unbelievable glare of unbroken whiteness in the high spring sun, enough to make cows snowblind, and people, if the eyes were not protected. Of all the dangers of homestead life, our family escaped all but two, Old Jules' well accident and my snowblindness in a May blizzard that cost me all useful sight in one eye.

Much of what I have been saying comes out of my childhood but could have come out of the childhood of practically anyone brought up on a homestead. Those first years on a government claim were a trial, a hardship for the parents, particularly the women, but the men too. Usually only one in four entrymen remained to patent the claim; in the more difficult regions and times only one in ten, or even fifteen. A large percentage of those into any new region had been misfits in their home community, economic, social, or emotional misfits, both the men and the women. Some of these, unsettled by the hardships and the isolation, ended in institutions or suicide if they did not drift on or flee back to relatives or in-laws. Those who stayed might be faced by drouth, grasshoppers, and ten-cent corn, sometimes followed by the banker's top buggy come to attach the mortgaged team or the children's milk cow. The men gathered at the sales and at political meetings, with many women, too, speaking for reforms, for a better shake for the sparsely settled, sparsely represented regions.

None of these things could be kept from the children. They saw the gambles of life and the size of the stakes. They shared in the privation and the hard work. All of us knew children who put in twelve-, fourteen-hour days from March to November. We knew seven-, eight-year-old boys who drove four-horse teams to the harrow, who shocked grain behind the binder all day in heat and dust and rattlesnakes, who cultivated, hoed and weeded corn, and finally husked it out before they could go to school in November. And even then there were the chores morning and evening, the stock to feed, the cows to milk by lantern light. If there had been tests for muscular fitness as compared to European children then, we would have held our own.

Often there was no difference in the work done by the boys and the girls, except that the eldest daughter of a sizable family was often a serious little mother by the time she was six, perhaps baking up a 49 pound sack of flour every week by the time she was ten. Such children learned about life before they had built up any illusions and romanticisms to be clung to later, at the expense of maturity. Almost from their first steps, the homesteader's children had to meet new situations, make decisions, develop a self-discipline if they were to survive. They learned dependence upon one's neighbors, and discovered the interrelationships of earth and sky and animal and man. They could see, in their simpler society, how national and international events conditioned every day of their existence. They learned to rescue themselves in adulthood as they had once scrabbled under the fence when the heel flies drove the milk cows crazy. What they didn't have they tried to make for themselves, earned money to buy, or did without. Perhaps somewhere there are individuals from homestead childhoods who grab for fellowships and grants, for scholarships and awards, for special influence and privilege but I don't know of any. The self-reliance, often the fierce independence, of a homestead upbringing seems to stay with them. They may wander far from their roots, for they are children of the uprooted, but somehow their hearts are still back there with the old government claim.

# SOCIAL FACTORS INFLUENCING
## U. S. LAND POLICY

CARL O. SAUER

# Homestead and Community
# on the Middle Border

A PUBLIC ANNIVERSARY in the present American mood is likely to consider the date as a determinate point between the past and the future. The past thus is of interest chiefly because it shows what change has taken place and what its direction has been. The present is the base from which we project the future. Perhaps more than any other people, or at any other time, we are committed to living in a mundane future, confident we shall control it by anticipation, that is, by planning the march of the material progress desired.

The immediate instrument of change is provided by the spiraling advance of technics that appear to put limitless material possibilities in our hands, and it is of these that we think primarily. What we have gained, at least for the present, is the ability to produce many more goods of more kinds for more people. We not only think to hold the horn of plenty but we believe we can and should pass it on to the rest of the world. Capacity to produce and capacity to consume form a reciprocating system that we desire to expand without end. Growth in material wants and in the ability to satisfy them and so to stimulate new wants is what we are agreed is progress. We measure progress by such things as gross national product, income per capita, standard of living (a term we have introduced to the world; perhaps it is the most widely known of all American phrases), level of employment, new construction, and other quantitative indices of an expanding economy. The system, insofar as we have seen it work, depends on continued acceleration and perhaps on being kept jogged by the stimuli of debt and taxes as well as of consumption and obsolescence. The American image is becoming that of the compulsive spender of neo-Keynesian doctrine. Thorstein Veblen formed his thesis of conspicuous waste too soon by a generation.

Output grows with input and so on, requiring more and more engagement of expert technicians. The objective of growth necessitates making and carrying out more and more decision about public policy, which becomes an increasingly limited and coveted prerogative. For the individual and the community the choice as to how one would live becomes more restricted in the interest of the will and authority of what is proposed as the commonweal. Reducing the risks of livelihood we also diminish the diversity of purposes and ends of individual living, once richly present in rural America.

On this occasion we call to remembrance an event of a hundred years ago when American life differed greatly from the present in mode, mood, and meaning. We may take a look back over a formative span of our history which lasted for several generations, a long time as our history goes. In its first part we were a rural nation, the first major shift to city living coming as the result of the Civil War and its industrial mobilization. Thereafter, population flowed more and more from country to city but the ways and values of rural living continued for two more generations to have much the accustomed meaning and content. We are here in fact taking part in an Old Settlers Reunion, as descendants of those who left their previous places and conditions of life to take part in making a new West, the Promised Land which a chosen people came to possess. There was an Old Testament sense of fulfillment in the western migration which should not be forgotten.

The Homestead National Monument, situated where wooded valley met upland prairie, is a model geographic expression of the manner in which the West was settled. This first homestead as taken under the act lies well out into the farther and later part of the Midwest. Its specific location records still the original pioneer requirement of a living site with wood and water, requisites that the building of railroads soon made unnecessary. When this tract was taken up, only three young and raw towns were in the Territory of Nebraska, all of them on the Missouri River. Through them emigrant trails led to Oregon and California, bearing westward over prairie and wooded stream, in a land still ranged over by Indian, buffalo, antelope, and deer. In very short order the wild land was brought into cultivation and fully settled. By mid-century, the westward course of homesteading had begun to cross the Missouri line at the west, to be halted later by dryness farther on. In simple outline, I should like to direct attention to the peopling of that part of the interior we know as the Corn Belt. The Wheat Belt is another, though derivative, story. What sort of rural living was established on the Middle Border; what were its attainments and satisfactions, its lacks and failures?

The date of the Homestead Act marks conveniently for our recall a moment of significance in the mainstream of American history, the great westward movement of families seeking land to cultivate and own. This movement began from states of the eastern seaboard, swelled to surges across the wide basin of the Mississippi-Missouri and ebbed away in the High Plains. To the south and north there were other westward movements sufficiently different in kind and route as to be left out of present consideration. The Middle Border, as it has been named appropriately, was the wide, advancing wave of settlement that spread over the plains south of the Great Lakes and north of the Ohio River, making use of both waterways as approaches. Its advances made Cleveland, Toledo, and Chicago northern gateways. At the south it gave rise to border cities on rivers, such as Cincinnati on the Ohio, St. Louis at the crossing of the Mississippi, and Kansas City on the great bend of the Missouri. The Mississippi was crossed in force in the 1830's, the Missouri River into Kansas in the border troubles prior to the Civil War. Although it did not begin as such this became the peopling of the prairies, the founding and forming of the actual Midwest.

The Homestead Act came pretty late in the settlement of the interior. Land had been given free of cost to many, as outlined in earlier chapters. It had been sold at nominal prices and on easy terms by public land offices and by canal and railroad companies. The squatter who settled without title was generously protected by preemption rights and practices that grew stronger. Many millions of acres had been deeded as homesteads before the act and many more continued to be acquired by other means afterwards. Land was long available in great abundance. The price in money of the wild land was the least cost of making it into a farm. Public land offices were set up to get land into private hands quickly, simply, and cheaply. Under the Graduation Act lands were reduced in price according to the length of time they had been on the market, the last cut being to twelve and one-half cents an acre. Canal and railroad lands were priced to sell. The railroads were well aware that revenue from farm traffic would be their largest return. The land seeker was induced to buy railroad land because he knew that he was given facility of transportation. The theme that land was a commodity for speculation is certainly true, yet it may be overstressed and oversimplified. The settler knew that the price of the farm was mainly in the work of all the family, in making out or doing without, in minimizing wants and spending. Largely our farms could not be reproduced from wild land at present prices, wages, and standards.

Advantage of location was of first importance in selecting the home site. The original entry of a tract was because of its immediate suitability as a homestead rather than because it would continue to be most desirable; locational advantages change as might productive capacity. Settlers were in process of regrouping themselves in neighborhoods of their liking. The drawbacks of one place having been experienced, a better location might be sought farther on. Property passed from one hand to another at a price reflecting, perhaps, the improvements made more than rise in land value. The term land speculation is not fully adequate or appropriate. The relinquisher was paid for the worth he had put in, the purchaser received a partially improved farm. The early succession of owners largely was a passing from weaker to stronger hands financially. The border was pretty fluid in its first years. Those who moved on are forgotten, or appear only as names of patentees and first conveyors of title. Those who remained and took root became the Old Settlers. There were various kinds and conditions of people who moved into or across the Middle Border, the restless and the sedentary, the overflow from older settlements farther east and the immigrants from Europe for whom this was a first opportunity to live on land of their own.

The famous frontier thesis of Professor Turner was adapted

from a theory of social evolution that was popular late in the nineteenth century. According to it, mankind everywhere has gone through the same series of stages of progress from simpler to more advanced skills and societies. The succession is held to be the same, the rate to differ with the environment. It was an attractive, simple theory of history, not borne out by the facts anywhere. Turner picked up the general idea and thought to reproduce the whole supposed history of human experience in the short span of the American frontier. Thus he saw our frontier as a "field for comparative study of social development," beginning (1) with Indian and white hunter, followed by (2) the "disintegration of savagery by the entrance of the trader, the pathfinder of civilization," then by (3) the pastoral stage (4) the raising of unrotated crops of corn and wheat in sparsely settled farming communities (5) intensive agriculture, and finally (6) the industrial society. He saw each stage present "in the march toward the West, impelled by an irresistible attraction. Each passed in successive waves across the continent." This plot of a westward-moving pageant in six scenes was good drama but was not our history.

As corollary to this theory of cultural succession he proposed one of cultural regression, namely that whoever entered a new scene or stage reverted from his former ways to accept those of the "stage" he was joining. Thus, the wilderness "takes him from the railroad car and puts him in the birch canoe and arrays him in the hunting shirt and moccasin. It puts him in the log cabin of the Cherokee and Iroquois and runs an Indian palisade around him . . . he shouts the war cry and takes the scalp." A half truth. Every migrant group loses some of the elements of its previous culture in fitting itself into a new environment, whether wilderness or city. It may also introduce some traits of its own. The spell of a uniformly determinate course of social evolution as cast by the anthropologist Lewis Morgan and the sociologist Herbert Spencer took hold of Turner, who passed it on to his pupils.

The first three stages or waves of Turner did not exist in the Middle Border. The next two were not stages but the entry of differing cultures.

The American settler acquired learning that was important

for his survival and well-being from the Indian, mainly as to agricultural ways. The settler was still a European in culture who had the good sense to make use of what was serviceable to him in the knowledge of the Indians of the eastern woodlands. This learning began at Jamestown and Plymouth and was pretty well completed before the Appalachians were crossed. It contributed Indian corn, along with beans and squash, as the basis of frontier sustenance. The seed corn the settler took west with him was dent corn from Indians of the Middle Seaboard and flint corn from those of the Northeast. Mainly he appears to have grown yellow dent, presumably acquired from Indians in Pennsylvania. A preferred parent in breeding our races of hybrid corn has been the Lancaster Surecropper, an old kind from eastern Pennsylvania. The Indian corn, beans, and squash of the East were well suited to western climate and soils until settlement got well beyond the Missouri River. The settler took over Indian ways of woodland clearing and planting. He prepared corn for his staple food in Indian ways, from succotash and hominy to corn cakes. He had learned back east to make maple syrup and sugar after the Indian fashion and continued thus to supply himself as far west as sugar maples grew. He brought with him the Indian art of dressing buckskins and making apparel. These were new learnings. Professor Turner possibly was right in attributing the stockade to Indian example but if so it too was learned from Indians of the Atlantic states. The Indians, of course, did not have log cabins.

Little seems to have passed from the Indians of the interior to the settlers. The Indian culture west of the Appalachians was still significantly based on cultivation, more largely so than is thought popularly to have been the case. Whether the western Indians contributed any strains of cultivated plants had little attention until we get much farther west, to the Mandans of the Upper Missouri and the Pueblo tribes of the Southwest. The Pawnee were a numerous village-dwelling people living toward the western margin of the humid country. One might expect that some strains of plants they cultivated passed on to the white settlers. Did their earth lodges suggest the dugout house of the pioneer, a curious and unusual form of dwelling? The Caddoan tribes to which the Pawnee and Wichita Indians belonged were anciently established farmers as well as hunters living between the prairies and high plains (witness the Coronado expedition) and might have had something to add to the trans-Missouri frontier.

The American entry into the Mississippi Valley encountered the Indian tribes in an advanced condition of disturbance, dislodgement, and dissolution. In most of our early accounts they are described in terms of disdain, deprecation, and disgust, without awareness that what was being witnessed was the breakdown of a native society. The Delawares, Wyandots, and Shawnees had been driven far from their homes. The Spanish government in Upper Louisiana invited them to a haven west of the Mississippi. Briefly they built and occupied farming villages there, but the Louisiana Purchase soon dislodged them again to drift west beyond the borders of Missouri. The Illini tribes were broken early, beginning with Iroquois raids that stemmed from French and English rivalries. American penetration about the Great Lakes pushed Pottawatomis, Kickapoos, Sacs, and Foxes to pressing upon tribes that lived beyond the Mississippi. The old resident tribes did not like the new ones, the whites liked neither. The Missourians in particular, carrying on the Indian hating of the Kentuckians and Tennesseans would have none of them. The remnants of a score of tribes were piled west beyond the Missouri line, some from as far east as Pennsylvania and New York. In the territories that were to become Kansas and Nebraska they were given reservations between the native Osages, Kansas, and Pawnees until most of them in a last remove were taken into the Indian Territory. (The original Kansas City, Kansas, was named Wyandot and began as a village of those Indians.)

Dispossessed of title to home, deprived of their economy, and losing hope that there might be another start, many were reduced to beggary or lived as pariahs about the white settlements. Their debauch was completed by alcohol, a thing wholly foreign to their ways, which became for them a last escape. Objects of despair to each other, and of contempt and annoyance to the whites, the time was missed when the two races might have learned from each other and lived together.

The French settlements, nearly all in river villages, were the meager reality of a vast colonial design of a New France that was planned to reach from the St. Lawrence to the Gulf of Mexico. The French habitants contributed little to the ways of the Middle Border. Some of their villages remained as enclaves in the American land. They were indifferent farmers. Despite the rich alluvial lands by the side of which they lived, they were often short of food. Some were fur traders in season, ranging far up the rivers, and instructing a few Americans in the fur trade, but this had precious little to do with the settlement of the interior. Some showed Americans, such as Moses Austin, a very primitive way to mine and smelt lead. The Americans got the word "prairie" from them to replace the name "barrens," which had been given to grassy uplands in Kentucky and was still used in Missouri around the time of the Louisiana Purchase. The French were easygoing, amiable people who did a little of various things and some of these well but they were not the pathfinders of a French, much less an American, civilization, nor did they think of themselves as such. The romantic attribution to the trader of being the pathfinder has its proper place in the western mountains and beaver streams, not in the interior prairies and woodlands.

Most of the earlier American pioneers of the Mississippi Valley came by a southerly approach. They were known as Virginians and Carolinians, later as Kentuckians and Tennesseans, and in final attenuation as Missourians. They came on foot and horseback across the Cumberlands and Alleghanies, usually to settle for a while in Kentucky or Tennessee and thence to move on by land or river and cross the Ohio and Mississippi rivers. The relocations of the Lincoln and Boone families are familiar examples. Turner's stages are not properly descriptive of the order or manner of their coming. By his scheme they would need to be distributed through his four first stages, least apparent in the second. Actually, they do not sort out as such separate waves.

The border had an element that came in for unfavorable comment in almost every early account, of persons who had taken to the backwoods because they did not fit into an ordered society, because of their indolence, perhaps for some misdemeanor or crime. They were the shiftless and the reckless, sometimes called drifters in the language of the West, the flotsam carried on the advancing wave of settlement, but not the first, nor a distinct wave. Violence was not marked in the history of this border except for Kansas where ruffians enjoyed a license through the approaching civil conflict. Some such "out" groups became lodged permanently in the poor corners of the Midwest. But largely they drifted on into the farther Southwest and Far West. Some got stranded on the overflow lands of the Missouri and Mississippi, others in the "hollers" of the hill lands adjacent. They were early in the history of settlement and chose to live segregated from the rest, usually marrying among their own kind. Of all settlers these were the most fully self-sufficient. A patch of cleared ground was in the woman's care; a litter of hogs ranged free. The men fished and hunted and loafed and kept hound dogs. In the steamboat days money could be had by cutting and loading firewood. When the railroads came there were ties to be hacked. They would work to sell something when they wanted money, employment they avoided. They were indifferent to increasing their income or to owning property. Some were defectors from civilization; I knew two of the most famous names of Virginia among them. They were considered to be predominantly a farther fringe of the Southern poor whites, usually bearing English surnames, in part a residue from the least fit part of those shipped to the Colonies. I do not think that Turner's view of cultural regression on the frontier applies; the frontier gave room for antisocial elements as well as for the builders of society.

The main contingent of pioneer settlers were a different breed. Theodore Roosevelt hailed them as Scotch-Irish, Mencken stressed their Celtic tone and temperament, Ellen Semple saw them as Anglo-Saxons of the Appalachians. Whatever their origins, and they were multiple, those were the backwoodsmen who brought and developed the American frontier way of life. They were woodland farmers, hunters, and raisers of livestock in combination, and very skilled in the use of axe and rifle. Trees were raw material for their log cabins and worm fences, and also an encumbrance of the ground, to be deadened, burned, or felled. The planting ground was enclosed by a rail fence, the livestock ranged free in wood or prairie. When the New Englander Albert Richardson reported life in eastern Kansas in the time of border troubles (*Beyond the Mississippi*) he said he could tell the home of a settler from Missouri by three things: The (log) house had the chimney built on the outside and at the end of the house; the house was located by a spring which served for keeping food in place of a cellar, and one was given buttermilk to drink. He might have added that there would be corn whiskey on hand and that if the family was really Southern the corn bread would be white.

This colonization was early and massive, beginning by 1800 and having the new West almost to itself until into the 1830's. At the time of the Louisiana Purchase American settlers already held Spanish titles to a million acres in Missouri alone, mainly along the Mississippi and lower Missouri rivers. They moved up the northern tributaries of the Ohio River as far as these were wooded; they filled the river valleys of Illinois and those of eastern Iowa and even penetrated north somewhat into Wisconsin and Minnesota. Their homes and fields were confined to wooded valleys, their stock pastured on the upland prairies. Nebraska alone of the mid-continent remained almost wholly beyond the limits of their settlement.

Viewed ecologically, their occupation of the land was pretty indifferent to permanence. Trees were gotten rid of by any means, the grasslands were overgrazed, game was hunted out. They were farmers after the Indian fashion of woods-deadening, clearing, and planting, and made little and late use of plow or wagon. The impression is that they gave more heed to animal husbandry than to the care of their fields or to the improvement of crops. Central and northwest Missouri for example, the best flowering of this "Southern" frontier, developed the Missouri mule early in the Sante Fe trade, and later bred saddle, as well as trotting, horses, and beef cattle. I do not know that it contributed anything to crop improvement, unless it was in bluegrass pastures.

There was self-sufficiency of food to this frontier but also there was a well-marked commercial side. It had things to sell or exchange for merchandise, above all tobacco, not a little corn whiskey, hogs on the hoof, in some cases hemp or cotton, all items that could be put on boat or horseback or driven to more or less distant markets. The settlers brought with them knowledge as to how tobacco should be grown, harvested, cured, and packed for shipment.

Corn and tobacco were the two crops planted in the new clearings in the woods, and they continued to be grown on the same land so long as its fertility lasted. Several acres of tobacco gave the needed purchasing power to the small farmer. Tobacco growing also attracted slave-owning planters north across the Ohio and especially west across the Mississippi, beginning with the Spanish government that freely granted land and sanction of slavery. From the beginning, the backwoods farmer, the hunter of the long rifle, and the slave-holding planter mingled in this stream of American Colonists; they might indeed be the same individuals. When the corn and tobacco fields began to fail under the clean cultivation these crops required, more virgin woodland was at hand or farther on. The effects of soil exposure to slope-wash by continued planting of corn and tobacco in early days may still be seen from the Muskingum Valley across Missouri to the Kansas border in surfaces of light color and tight texture that reveal the loss of the original top soil (A horizon).

This migration of the early nineteenth century came without benefit of constructed facilities of transportation, of public or private capital, or of most of the products of the newly begun machine age, except for the river steamboat. The people came in bands of kindred and friendship to settle in contiguity that was less than close clustering and more than wide dispersal. Their locations bore the name of a "settlement" quite properly, identified perhaps by the name of the leader, or of the stream along which their homesteads were strung. Thus, the group Daniel Boone led to Missouri was known both as the Boone Settlement and as the Femme Osage Settlement, the French name of the principal creek. The colony of families the senior Bollinger led from North Carolina across the Mississippi to Missouri was known by his name and as the Whitewater Settlement. Largely such transplanted communities were of kith and kin that maintained close connections even though each household lived on its own homestead. The lonely family cabin, removed far from and isolated from its neighbors is mostly a myth, even as to Daniel Boone himself. Sociability, not aloofness, was the quality of life sought. Much of the work was done by mutual aid; leisure time was time for meeting, a word of special meaning in the verna-cular of the frontier. Such were the people and the life that Mark Twain knew so well and portrayed with affection. They enjoyed discourse in all forms and on all occasions, respected those who excelled in it, and produced an able lot of politicians, lawyers, ministers of the gospel, and schoolteachers.

The great northern immigration began in the 1830's and depended from the beginning on improved transportation, the Erie Canal, steamships on the Great Lakes, stout and capacious wagons. It continued to demand internal improvements (the term of the time for public aid to communication), first canals and soon railroads, only rarely, constructed and surfaced roads. Wagon transport, however, was important and a wagon-making industry sprang up in the hardwoods south of the Great Lakes. It may be recalled that the automobile industry later took form in the same centers and by using the same skills and organiza-tion of distribution. Canals, most significantly the Illinois and Michigan Canal completed in 1848, linked the Great Lakes to rivers of the Mississippi system for shipping farm products to the East. Railroads were first projected as feeder lines to navig-able waters. The first important construction, that of the Illinois Central, was chartered in 1850 to build a railroad from Cairo, at the junction of the Ohio and Mississippi rivers, to La Salle, on the Illinois and Michigan Canal and on the Illinois River. It was given a grant by Congress of two million acres of land. Its principal early support was by the sale of lands, in tracts from forty acres up; its continued success depended on the produce of the farms and the goods needed to be shipped in. The pattern was adopted and given an East-West orientation by other rail lines that quickly spread their ribbons of steel westward, often in advance of the farm homesteads.

This last great movement of land settlement was out onto the prairies and it differed largely in manner of life and kind of people from the settlement of the woodlands. It depended on industry and capital for the provision of transportation. It was based from the start on plow farming, cast-iron or steel plows to cut and turn the sod: plows that needed stout draft animals, either oxen or heavy horses. By 1850, agricultural machinery had been developed for cultivating corn and harvesting small grains and was responsible for the gradual replacement of oxen by horses as motive power.

The prairie homestead differed from that of the woodlands in the first instance by depending on plow, draft animals, and wagon. It, too, grew corn as the most important crop. In part the corn was used for work stock but largely it was converted into meat and lard by new, large breeds of swine developed in the West. Stock was penned and fed. Fences were needed, not to fence stock out of the fields but to confine it. The livestock was provided with feed and housing. The farm was subdivided into fields, alternately planted to corn, wheat, oats, clover, and grass, arranged in a rotation that grew the feed for the work animals and for the stock to be marketed. A barn was necessary for storage and stables. This mixed economy, its cash income from animals and wheat, spread the work time through the seasons, and maintained the fertility of the land. It was a self-sustaining ecologic system capable of continuing and improving indefinitely and it was established by the process of prairie settlement. There was no stage of extractive or exhaustive cultivation.

By the time of the Civil War—in a span of twenty years or so—the prairie country east of the Mississippi, the eastern half of Iowa, and north Missouri were well settled. Some counties had reached their highest population by then. My native Missouri county had twice its current population in 1860. More people were needed to improve the land and to build the houses and barns than it took to keep the farms going. Some of the surplus sought new lands farther west, much of it went into building the cities. These people who settled the prairies were farmers, born and reared, out of the Northeast or from overseas, first and in largest number Germans and thereafter Scandinavians. They knew how to plow and work the soil to keep it in good tilth, how to care for livestock, how to arrange and fill their working time. They needed money for their houses and barns, which were not of logs but frame structures with board siding. The

lumber was mainly white pine shipped in from the Great Lakes,
long the main inbound freight source. These settlers needed
money, as well as their own labor, to dig wells and drain fields.
The price of the land again was the lesser part of the cost of
acquiring a farm. The hard pull was to get enough capital to
improve and equip the homestead and this was done by hard
labor and iron thrift. This is a sufficient explanation of the work
ethic and thrift habits of the Midwest, often stressed in disparagement of its farm life. In order to have and hold the good land it
was necessary to keep to a discipline of work and to defer the
satisfactions of ease and comforts. The price seemed reasonable
to the first generation who had wrested a living from scant acres
in New England or to those who had come from Europe where
land of one's own was out of reach.

Dispersed living, the isolated family home, became most characteristic of the "Northern" folk on the frontier. In Europe,
nearly everyone had lived in a village or town; in this country,
the rural village disappeared or never existed. Our farmers lived
in the "country" and went to "town" on business or pleasure.
The word "village," like "brook" was one that poets might use;
it was strange to our western language. The nature of frontier
life has often been ascribed to the ways of the Scotch-Irish who
have been credited with or held responsible for almost anything
that took form or place there. Thus, the dispersed farmsteads
have been credited to the fact that some lived on small tracts in
Scotland, as so-called cotters. Over here, they were conspicuous
in the forward fringe of settlement but it cannot be said that it
was the Scotch-Irish who broke the conventionally ordered pattern of rural living in villages. The nucleated New England town
early acquired outlying farm homes in number. The Pennsylvania German settlements early included farm as well as village
habitation. Land was available to the individual over here in
tracts of a size beyond any holdings he might ever have had
overseas. The village pattern was retained almost only where
religious bonds or social planning prescribed living in close
congregation.

Normally, the land holding was the place where the family
lived and this identification became recognized in the establish-

ment of title. The act of living on the occupied land was part of the process of gaining possession. As time went on, prior occupation and improvement of a tract gave more and more weight to preemption rights; living on the land protected against eviction and gave a first right to purchase or contract for warranty of ownership. The Homestead Act was a late extension of the much earlier codes of preemption by which possession by residence on the land and improvement could be used to secure full and unrestricted title.

The General Land Survey established the rectangular pattern of land description and subdivision for the public domain. Rural land holdings took the form of a square or sums of squares, in fractions or multiples of the mile-square section of land. The quarter section gradually came into greatest favor as the desired size of a farm and became the standard unit for the family farm in the Homestead Act. Thus, four families per square mile, a score or so of persons, were thought to give a desirable density of rural population. The reservation of one school section out of the thirty-six in a township, for the support of primary public schools, provided an incentive for the only kind of public building contemplated in the disposal of public lands. Four homes to the square mile and about four schools to the six-mile-square townships gave the simple general pattern for the rural geography of the Midwest. The pattern was most faithfully put into effect on the smooth upland prairies. Here the roads followed section lines and therefore ran either north-south or east-west and the farmsteads were strung at nearly equal intervals upon one or the other strand of the grid. It is curious that this monotony was so generally accepted, even a clustering of homes at the four corners where the sections met (and giving the same density) being exceptional.

Little attention has been given to the site where the house was placed, or to the assemblage of the structures that belonged to the farm. The choice of location was greatly important, as in exposure to wind and sun, for example. We may take a largely forgotten instance, malaria. Presumably, malaria came with the French, carried up the Mississippi from the south. The French were subject to chills and fever but kept on living in the river bottoms. The Americans also suffered thus, but soon began to select their living sites accordingly. The general idea was that the sickness came from the miasmas forming from stagnant water, the answer was to build the house on a ridge where the wind would sweep the miasmatic air away. The river bottoms long had a bad reputation. The Illinois Valley was malarial through most of its length, the early settlement of Bureau at the southward bend of the upper river for instance having been relocated for that reason. It would be of interest to determine the distribution of malaria at various times, the flare-ups and gradual recession, and the effects on living sites.

The logistics of home location is an attractive and hardly investigated field of study, as is indeed the whole question of the rural landscape and its changes. The location of house and farm buildings involved conservation of energy in the work on the farm, cultural preferences of different colonizing groups, microclimatic adjustments, and esthetic satisfactions. The relation of water, drainage, and sanitation was unrecognized, the toll paid in typhoid and "summer complaint."

Building was starkly utilitarian and unadorned. Neither the log cabin of the woodlands, nor the box-shaped frame house of the prairies, nor yet the sod house of the Transmissouri country (made possible by the sod-cutting plow) was more than compact and economical shelter, varying but little in each form. Ready-cut houses of standard simple patterns were already offered by railroads to buyers of their land, an early form of tract housing. Quality of house and quality of land seem to be in no relation. The embellishment of the home and the planting of the yard were left mostly to the second generation, for country town as well as farm. The history of the dissemination of ornamental trees and shrubs might be revealing, perhaps to be documented through the nurseries that sprung up from Ohio to Nebraska (mainly post Civil War?).

The economy from its beginnings was based on marketing products, but it also maintained a high measure of self-sufficiency. Smokehouse, cellar, and pantry stored the food that was produced and processed on the farm. The farm acquired its own potato patch, orchard, berry and vegetable gardens, diversified as to kind from early to late maturity, for different flavors and uses, selected for qualities other than shipping or precocious bearing. The farm orchards now are largely gone and the gardens are going. Many varieties of fruits that were familiar and appreciated have been lost. A family orchard was stocked with diverse sorts of apple trees for early and midsummer applesauce, for making apple butter and cider in the fall, for laying down in cool bins in the cellar to be used, one kind after another, until the russets closed out the season late in winter. The agricultural bulletins and yearbooks of the past century invited attention to new kinds of fruits and vegetables that might be added to the home orchard and garden, with diversification, not standardization in view. Exhibits in the county and state fairs similarly stressed excellence in the variety of things grown, as well as giving a prize for the fattest hog and the largest pumpkin.

The Mason jar became a major facility by which fruit and vegetables were "put up" for home use in time of abundance against winter or a possible season of failure in a later year. The well-found home kept itself insured against want of food at all times by producing its own and storing a lot of it. The family, of ample size and age gradation, was able to provide most of the skills and services for self-sufficiency by maintaining diversified production and well-knit social organization. This competence and unity was maintained long after the necessity had disappeared. As time is measured in American history the life of this society, and its vitality, was extraordinary.

Looking back from the ease of present days these elder days may seem to have been a time of lonely and hard isolation. It was only toward the end of the period that the telephone and rural mail delivery were added. The prairie lacked wet-weather roads. In the hill sections, ridge roads might be passable at most times, on the plains, winter was likely to be the season of easiest travel, spring, that of immobilization by mud. The country doctor was expected to, and did rise above any emergency of weather. Life was so arranged that one did not need to go into town at any particular time. When the weather was bad the activities of the family took place indoors or about the farmyard. In our restrospect of the family farm as it was, we may incline to overstress its isolation. The American farmstead did not have the sociality of the rural villages of Europe or of Latin America, but the entire family had duties to learn and perform and times of rest and diversion. It depended on a work morale and competence in which all participated and in which its members found satisfaction. Perhaps it suffered fewer social tensions and disruptions than any other part of our society.

Though living dispersed, the farm families were part of a larger community which might be a contiguous neighborhood or one of wider association. The community, in some cases, got started on the Boone pattern of a settlement of kith and kin. A sense of belonging together was present to begin with or it soon developed. The start may have been as a closed community; it was likely to continue in gradual admission of others by some manner of acceptance. Consanguinity, common customs, faith, or speech were such bonds that formed and maintained viable communities through good times and bad. The Mennonite colonies are outstanding examples. The absence of such qualities of cooption is shown in the Cherokee strip, opened as a random aggregation of strangers.

The bond of common customs and language showed up strongly in the German settlements made between 1830 and the Civil War, and in the Scandinavian settlements of somewhat later origin. Both were attracted to districts where some of their people had chanced to locate and tended to increase about such nuclei. This clustering, a partial segregation, gave protection from cultural alienation and loss and afforded time to adjust and contribute to the common ways of life. Although the Germans were sharply divided as to confession, they were drawn into areas where German speech was used, however strong the difference in creed or dialect. Most of their settlement took place before 1870 and included people not only from the states that were to join the German empire, but from Switzerland, Austria, and later from Russia.

The country church played a leading part in social communication, differing again according to the particular confession. Catholic and Lutheran communicants perhaps had more of their social life determined by their church than did the others.

Their priests and pastors were most likely to remain in one community and to exercise and merit influence on it. Parochial schools extended the social connections. Church festivals were numerous and attractive. Sunday observance was less austere. The Methodist church on the other hand shifted its ministers, usually every two years. In a half century of service my grandfather was moved through a score of charges in five states. The high periods of the Methodist year were the winter revival meetings and the camp meetings in summer after the corn was laid by. For some, these were religious experiences, for others, especially for the young people, they were sociable times, particularly the camp meeting, held in an attractive, wooded campground where one lived in cabins or tents on an extended picnic. Almost everyone belonged to some church and in them found a wide range of social contacts and satisfaction.

The churches also pioneered higher education, founding colleges and academies across the Middle West from Ohio into Kansas before the Civil War and before the Morrill Act fathered the tax-supported colleges. These church-supported small colleges, about fifty of which still exist, first afforded education in the liberal arts to the youth of the prairie states and they did so by coeducation. Their students were drawn by their church affiliations, not only from nearby but from distant places. In these colleges, humane learning was cultivated and disseminated. Their campuses today are the Midwest's most gracious early monuments of the civilization aspired to by its pioneers.

Country and town were interdependent, of the same way of life, and mostly of the same people. By a tradition that may go back to the town markets of Europe, Saturday was the weekday for coming to town to transact business (note the pioneer implications in the term "to trade") and to visit. The town provided the services, goods, and entertainment which the farm family required. In time, it also became home for the retired farmer. Farmstead and its particular town were linked in community by factors beyond the one of economy of distance. When the railroads were building across the prairie, they laid out what seemed a most rational spacing of town sites for shipping and trading centers. Some grew, some withered away, and some never got started. Quantitative measurement of radius of trade never has been enough. The choice of direction and destination in going to town had other reasons than economy of energy expended. One liked it better in one town than in another, a matter of social values and affinities which are ponderable but not measurable.*

The era of the Middle Border ended with World War I. Hamlin Garland introduced the name in 1917 in his *Sons of the Middle Border,* a retrospect he made in middle age. Willa Cather, growing up on the westernmost fringe of Nebraska, drew its life in quiet appreciation in her two books written before the war. Then she saw her world swept away. Some of us have lived in its Indian summer, and almost no one was aware how soon and suddenly it was to end.† A quarter section was still a good size for a family farm and the farm was still engaged in provisioning itself as well as in shipping grain and livestock. It was still growing a good crop of lusty offspring. The place of the family in the community was not significantly determined by its income, nor had we heard of standard of living.

The outbreak of the war in 1914 brought rapidly rising demand and prices for supplies to the Allies and to American industry. Our intervention in 1917 urged the farmer to still more production: "Food will win the War"—in the war that was to end all wars. He made more money than ever before, he had less help, he was encouraged to buy more equipment and more land. The end of the war saw a strongly industrialized country that continued to draw labor from the rural sections. Improved roads,

---

*Lewis Atherton, *Mainstreet of the Middle Border* (1960) has a large documentation and itemization of life in the country towns. His composite picture is later and less attractve than are my own recollections. He stated that he was not relying on his own memories or family tradition. I, however, have done so, not knowing a nearer approach to objectivity than by putting such recall to reflective scrutiny. This is not sociologic method but do systems of analysis bring enough understanding of what we are, or of what we were? A literary genre in disparagement of rural life and country town originated towards the end of the period with its ugly geography of Winesburg, Spoon River, Zenith, and Main Street.

†I made field studies in northern Illinois and in Missouri from 1910 to 1914, when rural life was much more like that of Civil War time than of the present.

cars, tractors, and trucks made the horse unnecessary and thereby the old crop rotation broke down. Farming became less a way of of life and more a highly competitive business for which the agricultural colleges trained specialists, engineers, chemists, economists, to aid fewer and fewer farmers to produce more market goods, to widen their incomes against the rising cost of labor, taxes, and capital needs. This became known as "freeing people from the land," so that now we have about a tenth of our population living on farms (among the lowest ratios in the world) and these are not reproducing themselves.

The Middle Border now belongs to a lost past, a past in which different ways and ends of life went on side by side. We have since defined the common welfare in terms of a society organized for directed material progress. For the present at least, we control the means to produce goods at will. We have not learned how to find equivalent satisfactions in jobs well done by simple means, and by the independent judgment that gave competence and dignity to rural work. The family farm prepared youth well for life—there or elsewhere. It enriched the quality of American life and it will be missed.

JOHN M. BREWSTER

# The Relevance of the
# Jeffersonian Dream Today

IT IS TIMELY to take a current look at Griswold's *Farming and Democracy*. In this way we may gain improved understanding and appreciation of long-standing and deeply motivating beliefs in our rural traditions, and their role as policy directives from Colonial times up to now.

As Griswold observed, Jefferson's devotion to the family farm stemmed from his belief in a "casual relationship between [family] farming and the political system of democracy."[1] A prime concern of Griswold was with the validity of this belief. He devoted two chapters to disproving it. We shall not belabor this issue further; a more fruitful question is why such a belief became so much a part of our folklore in the first place.

As we interpret him, Griswold's concern with the supposed casual relationship between farming and democracy grew out of his observation that the New Deal "revived the Jeffersonian Ideal and made the family farm an explicit goal of farm policy."[2] He might have added that this revival, like revivals in general, did not include a definition of what was being revived; in this way it generated one of the greatest definitional blizzards of all time. Why this was unavoidable will become apparent.

I take the Jeffersonian Dream to mean Jefferson's affection for and desire to establish and preserve an agriculture of freeholders—full-owner operators, debt-free, unrestricted by any contractual obligations to anyone—all in all, pretty much the monarchs of all they survey.

The freehold concept of the family farm was an unusually effective policy directive throughout most of the settlement era. Then the worm turned. An appreciable transformation of freeholders into debtors and tenants was noticeable by 1880. But since that date, the relevance of the Jeffersonian Ideal to present problems has continued to decline in the sense that it has failed to generate the kinds of policies and programs required to maintain a high approximation of a freeholder agriculture.

But we know that a predominantly family-farm agriculture has not disappeared; that the fostering of this institution remains an important objective of farm policy. In my judgment this will be the case for many years because the family farm is not on the way out, although some dangers confront it now as in the past. Naturally in taking this position I have in mind a definition, a concept, of the family farm. It is my gauge for what facts are relevant and what facts are not relevant to the issue.

As used here, a family farm is an agricultural business in which the operating family does most of the work and is a *manager* of ongoing operations of the business as well as a *risk-taker* in the outcome (financial returns) of the business venture. In this definition, *operatorship is equated with varying degrees of managerial power and with risk-taking involving management and production inputs, including labor.* As used here, managerial power is equated with the operator's prerogative to negotiate contracts and to make decisions concerning the combination of resources.

This definition applies to the Jeffersonian freeholder and the modern family farmer alike. In both cases, most of the farm work is done by the operating family who is a risk-taking manager in the outcome of the business. However, in the usual case, they differ substantially in their degree of risk-taking managerial power. The Jeffersonian freehold was a very high approximation of the self-sufficient firm. By this we mean a firm from which the will and interest of all conceivable participants in the business, except those of the operator, are totally excluded. In the self-sufficient firm, the operator alone is the sole risk-taker in the outcome of production activities he is guiding and coordinating. Thus the managerial power of the Jeffersonian freeholder was absolute, since he was totally independent of all commitments to outside parties concerning the way he used the resources of the firm and the kind of products it produced. In his managerial decisions, it was unnecessary to take account of the will or interest of another living soul. The Ages had always equated managers of self-sufficient firms as lords, the monarchs of all they surveyed.

But in industry, this self-sufficient firm disappeared as a representative institution with the close of the handicraft era, and agriculture has been making departures from it since about 1870. And each step in its progressive extinction has aroused new anxieties concerning the future of the family farm.

Yet farms on which operating families are risk-taking managers and do most of the work are not losing their relative position in American agriculture. I regard these as family farms. But usually the managerial power of their operators is not absolute; it is limited in varying degrees by contractual commitments of the operators with outside participants in the farm business, such as the landlord, the banker, the contractor seeking products of specified qualities, and even the government. Committing certain of their services to the operator, these outsiders seek legally binding commitments of the operator to follow certain lines of behavior as means of protecting them against loss of their stakes in the operator's business. The operator enters into these commitments because he believes the services of the outsiders will enable him to achieve a more profitable business than otherwise. Whether this proves to be the case turns on his abilities to guide and coordinate the operations of his business to a successful issue. No one would assume a modern road-builder not to be an independent operator simply because he agrees to produce a product that meets the specifications of his customers who send out inspectors to see if he is complying with the specifications he agreed to meet. We do not do so because his contract specifications do not negate the fact that he remains to some degree a risk-taking manager in the outcome of a business. The same principle applies to farming.

It may be that much of the confusion about what is meant by the family farm stems from the lack of a clear image of the operator's degree of risk-taking managerial power under the contractual foundations of modern farming. We know it lies somewhere between two extremes. It lies to the left of that absolute lordship which belonged to the self-sufficient firm that excludes all participants in the business except the operator, as did the Jeffersonian freeholder. It also lies to the right of the "directed worker" with whom the farm operator is sometimes equated in literature on

"vertical integration." In line with this fact, I equate farm operators with managers and risk-takers in the outcome of their business undertakings, and then equate a family farm with a business
in which the operating family does most of the farm work. By a
larger-than-family farm, I mean any agricultural business whose
total labor requirement is too great for the usual farm operating
family to supply most of it.

One further definitional matter. In this paper I commonly
use the term "proficient family farm." By this I mean a family
business in agriculture with sufficient resources and productivity
to yield income to meet expenses for (a) family living (b) farm
expenses including depreciation, maintenance of the livestock
herd, equipment, land, buildings, and interest on borrowed capital (c) enough capital growth for new farm investments required
to keep in step with technological advance and rising levels of
living. Farms without this level of resources and productivity are
inadequate farms, and they are either disappearing or being supplemented by income from nonfarm sources, usually off-farm
employment.

Proficient family farms may come into being through the
reorganization of inadequate units or through hitherto larger-
than-family farms falling into the category of family farms as a
result of substituting capital for labor to the point where the
operating family is able to do most of the farm work.

In using these concepts, I do not mean that they are *the*
true ones—their status in this respect will turn on how useful
they may prove to be as guides in measuring and interpreting
the kinds and directions of changes now occurring among the
business units of American agriculture. I expect to modify the
concepts I am here using whenever further research investigations warrant it.

In these terms, we will have a family-farm agriculture so long
as most of our farm production is done by business units in
which operating families are risk-taking managers who do most
of the work. In keeping with his times, Jefferson thought of the
family farm in terms of the restricted freeholder meaning of the
term. However, I believe it is in keeping with his larger spirit
to expand his Dream to include contractual as well as highly

self-sufficient firms like the freehold. In Jefferson's time, there was no conflict between an agriculture of proficient family farms and the need of opportunities for farm people. There is a severe conflict today, since only around one million such farms would be needed to supply all the foods and fibers which society wants at reasonable prices.

With these preliminary remarks in mind, these five major themes will be elaborated:

*First:* Since Colonial times, two distinct personal and policy-guiding beliefs have been indigenous to the farm and nonfarm sectors of our society. First is a deeply moving commitment to proficient work as the hallmark of praiseworthy character; the second is an equally firm belief in the natural or moral right of men to acquire all the property they can from the earnings of their work. The first of these commitments stemmed from the revolutionary interpretation of the ethical significance of proficient work by the religious reformers of the late sixteenth and seventeenth centuries, and was a complete reversal of ancient and medieval attitudes toward economic work. In line with this new sense of obligation, people soon found themselves producing beyond the limit required to support their customary needs. But in doing so, they ran into head-on conflict with the age-old belief that the natural or moral right of men to acquire property, as a fair reward for work, is limited to the amount required to produce their customary needs. John Locke, the greatest of the natural rights philosophers, resolved this conflict by demonstrating that the older belief was true only in very primitive, savage societies in which a money economy was totally absent.

*Second:* From early Colonial times, American settlers carried the radical belief in proficient work, as the badge of superior merit, alongside the equally radical Lockean belief in the natural or moral right of individuals to acquire as much property as they can from the earnings of their work. These directives have been stable motivations throughout both the settlement and post-settlement phases of our history.

Throughout the era of cheap land and relatively inexpensive farm technologies, these directives were a powerful generator of the Freeholder ideal to which the name of Jefferson is attached.

For, if land is free or very cheap, obviously farm families can achieve a greater reward for their proficient work as debt-free, full-owner operators, than as renters, or as owners with varying degrees of credit obligations. This is not necessarily the case, however, if land is increasingly scarce and capital requirements of proficient farms are growing larger. As these conditions came to pass with the close of the settlement era, the same directives called for departures from the freeholds to contractual relationships with creditors, landlords, and others as means of achieving proficient farms. This separation between the farmer's actual status of limited managerial power and his hitherto absolute power was made sufferable by the new idea of an "agricultural ladder" that enabled farm people to envision their departures from the Freeholder Ideal as actual stepping stones to its fulfillment.

*Third:* Working hand in hand with the foregoing directives to a freeholder agriculture in the settlement era, was the carryover of the feudal aversion to tenantry and wage status as a badge of inferior character. More specifically, farmers demanded freeholds as the best means of enabling them to earn as much as they could as a fair reward for working as proficiently as they could, and they also demanded freeholds as the best possible means of escaping the ancient onus of tenantry and wage status as a badge of inferior character. But this "marriage of convenience" began disintegrating with the disappearance of cheap land and the increasing capital requirements of proficient farms. These conditions generated increasing conflict between the ancient devotion to the Freeholder Ideal with the more modern devotions to proficient work as a badge of personal excellence and to acquisition of as much earnings and property as one can get as fair reward for his proficiency. In this conflict, the age-old devotion to a freehold agriculture, as a citadel of superior virtue, proved an increasingly weak competitor.

*Fourth:* In developing the foregoing themes, emphasis is placed on the economic or materialistic implications of the ethical directive to proficient work at the expense of its larger humanitarian or idealistic implications. To correct this imbalance, we shall point out that the operation of this directive in American life not only has led the whole nation along remarkable paths of material progress, but has also enkindled a "practical idealism" which has long distinguished our people, and has infused the higher reaches of the spirit with the promise of the American Dream of what lies in store for men devoted to proficient use of their creative power. Furthermore, our historic commitment to proficient work, as tangible evidence of personal excellencies, includes commitments to distributive as well as commutative justice, both of which the plain man calls the "justice of equal opportunity." If we fail to counterbalance the economic import of our historic commitment to proficient work with its equally idealistic import, then with our own voice we convict ourselves of the common but false charge that America is the most materialistic civilization on earth. We shall seek to avoid this error.

*Fifth:* Our fifth theme concerns the current status and prospects of the family farm, considered as a business in which the operating (management and risk-taking) family does most of the work of the business they operate.

## SALIENT FEATURES OF THE MEDIEVAL LANDLORD CIVILIZATION OUT OF WHICH OUR FARM AND NONFARM SOCIETY EMERGED

Of all our major economic institutions, the family farm alone has a life span which connects our atomic age with the ancient and medieval landlord civilization out of which America and modern Europe emerged. To know and understand the belief-forming role of the family farm in the life of the nation is to be wiser men concerning our whole American civilization, especially since our fathers were mostly family farmers throughout our two-hundred-year settlement era when our national character and institutions were in their most formative period.

In keeping with this fact, Griswold found it necessary to step back into the older landlord civilization out of which our rural society and modern Europe emerged in order to find the proper point of departure in understanding the Freehold Ideal. We need to follow the same procedure, especially since, in our judgment, there is more in this ideal than is disclosed in Griswold's analysis. There is no other way of determining which of the deeply motivating beliefs underlying this Ideal were carry-overs from the

older landlord civilization of Europe, and which ones were pro-
foundly revolutionary breaks with this older order. To make
this clear, six strategic features of this older culture need to be
identified. In substance, they are as follows:

(1) Commonly called feudalism, but more accurately known
as a traditionalism, this precapitalistic landlord civilization was
distinguished by a system of master-servant beliefs and correlative
institutions that distinctly segregated the managerial and labor
roles of life into separate classes, called lords and serfs. The nobil-
ity were viewed as essentially personifications of divine-like managerial wisdom and power to know and administer an impartial
justice for all classes. Those saddled with the work of the world
were viewed as so lacking in managerial intelligence and other
virtues that they were essentially personifications of turbulent
passions and labor capacities, fit only for producing subsistence
for the whole community.

(2) This master-servant hierarchy both nurtured and rested
on the equation of proprietorship with the spirit of self-mastery
and other virtues, and on the correlative equation of tenantry
and wage status with subservience, turbulent passions, and mental
and moral incompetence.

(3) This older culture necessarily included a Self-Sufficiency
Ideal of Freedom. For within the master-servant relationship, the
free man can be envisioned only as the one who has absolute
command over all the personal services and other resources
required to meet his needs. To the feudal lords, for example, it
was self-contradictory to say in one breath that one is a free man
and in the next say that his living depends on market exchange
between producers and consumers.

(4) This older hierarchy of superiors and inferiors both generated and rested on the belief that exemption from economic
employments is prima facie evidence that one possesses the praise-
deserving qualities of mind and character, and that dependence
on such employments proves that one is so deficient in meritor-
ious capacities that he deserves only the lower stations, even
servility.

(5) This aversion to economic work as a badge of disrepute
went hand in hand with the further belief that capital accumu-

lation should be limited to the amount of goods and services required to support the customary needs of people in their various social roles or life stations. Acquiring property in excess of these limits was equated with greed and miserliness. Thus, this older culture would have been shocked by James Madison's axiom, widely shared by the founding fathers, that the chief object of good government was the protection of men in their "different and unequal faculties for acquiring property."[3]

(6) Finally, this older landed hierarchy of superiors and inferiors was the outward institutional expression of the belief that natural inequality is the proper guide to use in relating man to man with reciprocal rights and duties in all spheres of life. In line with this belief, the good society was viewed as one which invests the individual with only those rights and duties which mark him as an instance of a particular class. In one man it lodges the rights and duties of all serfs; in another, the rights and duties of all artisans; in another, the rights and duties of all landlords, and so on. In this way, the common sense of this older civilization tossed aside as nonsense the democratic belief that all men have a common nature in virtue of which they deserve an equal status that entitles each to the same bundle of rights and duties, whatever his particular social (class) roles may be.

## PROPRIETORSHIP AS BADGE OF GOOD REPUTE AND TENANTRY AS A BADGE OF SERVILITY

A striving for personal significance is apparently so universal that we assume men the world over share a profound *aversion* to being identified with status symbols which their age and civilization deem sure proof of servile attitudes and other vices. From Plymouth Rock and Jamestown on, the driving power of this tremendous urge for personal significance was a potent generator of the dream of an agrarian America of freeholders long before it was named the Jeffersonian Dream. For, in permitting the hitherto separate roles of lords and serfs to be recombined within the same skin, the two billion acres of virgin continent gave working people the chance to escape the age-old equation of tenantry and wage status with servility through becoming freeholders, and in this way to identify themselves with the dignity—the esteem and proud sense of independence—which the ages had always posited in the lords of the land. The emerging agriculture of family farms along the moving frontier of the New World thus generated within everyday people an envisioned realm of equal dignity and worth, which all America soon enshrined within her national self-image much before Jefferson's day. Jefferson did not invent the Jeffersonian Ideal; he merely identified his name with an Ideal which freeholders themselves already had embedded in their very bones.

By enabling plain people to view themselves as equally lords of the land, our earlier expanding agriculture of freeholders generated the aspiration for democracy long before even the brightest minds of the Age were able to liberate themselves from the inherited equation of proprietorship with civic virtue, and nonproprietorship with civic vices. Two observations illustrate this fact. The founding fathers were still so guided by the carry-over of this ancient equation that they were unable to envision the possibility of a democratic society in terms of a predominantly wage-earner and salaried population. At the Constitutional convention, James Madison expressed this state of mind in these blunt words:

> In future times a great majority of the people will not only be without land, but any other sort of property. These will either combine under the influence of their common situation, in which case property and liberty, will not be secure in their hands: or what is more probable, they will become the tool of opulence and ambition, in which case there will be equal danger from the other side.[4]

In similar vein, Daniel Webster declared:

> A republican form of government rests not more on political constitutions, than in those laws which regulate the descent and transmission of property. Government like ours could not have been maintained, where property was holden according to the principles of the feudal system; nor on the other hand, could the feudal constitution exist with us. Our New England ancestors brought hitherto no great capitals from Europe. They left behind them the whole feudal policy of the other continent. They came to a new country. There were,

as yet, no lands yielding rent, and no tenants rendering service. The whole soil was unreclaimed from barbarism. They were themselves nearly on a general level in respect to property. Their situation demanded a parceling out and division of the lands, and it may be fairly said, that this necessary act fixed the future frame of their government. The character of their political institutions was determined by fundamental laws respecting property.[5]

As our earlier expanding agriculture of freeholders was the prime generator of an increasingly strong demand for political democracy, so this political objective, in turn, generated powerful demands for public land policies that would strengthen democratic government through enabling people with little or no capital except their labor to become freeholders. This strategy was expressed with uncommon clarity and eloquence by Thomas Hart Benton in the great land policy debates of the 1840's:

Tenantry is unfavorable to freedom. It lays the foundation for separate orders in society, annihilates the love of country, and weakens the spirit of independence. The farming tenant has, in fact, no country, no hearth, no domestic altar, no household god. The freeholder, on the contrary, is the natural supporter of a free government; and it should be the policy of republics to multiply their freeholders, as it is the policy of monarchies to multiply tenants. We are a republic, and we wish to continue so: then multiply the class of freeholders; pass the public lands cheaply and easily into the hands of the people; sell, for a reasonable price, to those who are able to pay; and give, without price, to those who are not. I say give, without price, to those who are not able to pay; and that which is so given, I consider as sold for the best of prices; for a price above gold and silver; a price which cannot be carried away by delinquent officers, nor lost in failing banks, nor stolen by thieves, nor squandered by an improvident and extravagant administration. It brings a price above rubies— a race of virtuous and independent laborers, the true supporters of their country, and the stock from which its best defenders must be drawn.[6]

While this reasoning enabled early America to turn her inherited equation of proprietorship and civic virtues to the service of democratic ends, it did so at the high cost of an invidious distinction between proprietors and nonproprietors with respect to moral excellencies. The longevity of this distinction is astonishing. For example, in an address not many years ago the head of one of our more conservative trade associations spoke as follows:

> Today the greatest threat to democratic institutions ... and ultimately to freedom itself, lies in our big cities. They are populated for the most part with the mass of men, devoid of intelligence, and devoid of civic responsibility. He will vote for anyone who offers him something for nothing, whether it be subway fares for half price or public housing at one-third price. ... Our one hope of survival as a free country is that rural and semi-rural areas will dominate most of the State legislatures through their representatives and still dominate the House of Representatives at Washington.[7]

## JEFFERSON'S CONTRIBUTION TO THE FREEHOLDER IDEAL

Jefferson is distinguished by his sharp differentiation of all proprietors with respect to civic virtues. He did so with a neat logic which sets up a casual relationship between freeholders and democracy. Here is the logic. (1) "Corruption of morals ... is the mark set on those, who ... depend for their subsistence on the caprice of customers. Such dependence begets subservience and venality, suffocates the germ of virtue and prepares fit tools for the designs of ambition."[8] Holding precisely the same belief, the feudal lord would have declared that Jefferson took these words right out of his mouth. In both cases, the conclusion follows from a Self-Sufficiency Ideal of Freedom which is actually incompatible with market dependence.

(2) Owing to its relatively noncommerciality in Jefferson's time, farming enabled people to produce most of their own subsistence and in this way liberated them from dependence on "the caprice of customers" for a living; thus generating a proud spirit of personal independence which brooked no outside interference with the sense of self-mastery. Thus, the really significant output of family farming is not food and fiber, but the brick and mortar of democratic society. In Jefferson's words:

Those who labor in the earth are God's chosen people . . . whose breasts He has made His peculiar deposit for substantial and genuine virtue. It is the focus in which He keeps alive the sacred fire, which otherwise might escape from the face of the earth.[9]

(3) From the premise that farming and nonfarm employments produce opposite types of character, Jefferson deduced his third premise of political science. Here it is: The possibility of a democratic society diminishes directly with the increase of the ratio of nonfarmers to farmers. He expressed this deduction in these words:

> . . . generally speaking, the proportion which the aggregate of the other classes of citizens bears in any State to that of its husbandmen, is the proportion of its unsound to its healthy parts, and is a good enough barometer whereby to measure its degree of corruption . . . The mobs of the great cities add just so much to the support of pure government, as sores do to the strength of the body.[10]

Throughout this reasoning, Jefferson, as Griswold observed, claimed a virtual monopoly of "good morals for farmers."[11] So completely different is the spirit of his disquisitions on farmers and nonfarmers from the spirit of the Declaration that it is difficult to realize that they were both composed by the same man. Lincoln, a farm boy and as matchless a politician as Jefferson, referred to the Declaration as containing "the true axioms of democracy." But in speaking to a large gathering of farmers at the Wisconsin State Agricultural Society at its annual fair on September 30, 1859, he referred to the equation of farmers with superior excellencies as a device for flattering farmers. Said he:

> I presume I am not expected to employ the time assigned me in the mere flattering of farmers, as a class. My opinion of them is that, in proportion to their numbers, they are neither better nor worse than any other people. In the nature of things they are more numerous than any other class; and I believe there are really more attempts at flattering them than any other; the reason of which I cannot perceive, unless it be that they cast more votes than any other.

There is no question but that Jefferson served the already indigenous devotion of rural America to an agriculture of free-holders with singular distinction. But other than creating an ingenious device for flattering farmers, no useful purpose is served through imputing to them a virtual monopoly of good morals. Yet, there is no mystery concerning the survival power of this myth. For any group is most happy to be singled out and assured by high authority that they are "the chosen people of God" in "whose breasts He ... keeps alive the sacred fire, which otherwise might escape from the face of the earth."[12] It would be less than human to expect farmers to stand up and deny it, and its oratorical potential is obviously too great to be overlooked by alert politicians and others seeking the good graces of the countryside.

## REVOLUTIONARY INTERPRETATION OF THE ETHICAL SIGNIFICANCE OF PROFICIENT WORK

Attention is now directed to the fact that the carry-over of the ancient aversion to tenantry and wage status as the badge of inferior character was by no means the only directive to a free-holder agriculture throughout the settlement era. Equally potent directives were a revolutionary interpretation of the ethical significance of proficient work, which stemmed from the sixteenth and seventeenth century religious reformers, and a correspondingly revolutionary interpretation of the natural or moral right to acquire property, which stems from John Locke, the greatest of the natural rights philosophers.

The revolutionary interpretations of the ethical significance of proficient work, as sure evidence of highest personal worth, came into Western society in substantially the following manner.[13] In their break from the Mother Church, the religious reformers of the sixteenth and seventeenth centuries had to face the question of what occupation is most truly appropriate for the upright man. According to the traditional view, such employment was boxed up in the monasteries where every moment of the twenty-four-hour day was organized into a systematic series of routines known as the Holy Callings. So long as the reformers left this view unchallenged, it was impossible for them to complete their break from the Mother Church. They completed the break by taking the position that all employments, whether composing sermons, painting pictures, making mousetraps, or growing corn, were equally appropriate ways of showing that one possessed qualities of mind and character that deserved his own highest respect and esteem and the respect and esteem of others as well.

The following are typical illustrations of this revolutionary belief. Richard Baxter, an exceptionally able minister, put it this way:

> God doth call every man and woman . . . to serve him in some peculiar employment in this world, both for their own and the common good . . . the great Governor of the world hath appointed to every man his proper post and province, and . . . he will be at a great loss if he does not keep his own vineyard and mind his own business. [Therefore] be wholly taken up in diligent business of your lawful calling, when you are not exercised in the more immediate service of God.[14]

Again he clothes the same belief in these poetic lines:

> How is it that ye stand all the day idle . . . Your trade is your proper province . . . Your own vineyard you should keep . . . Your fancies, your understandings, your memories are all to be laid out therein.[15]

As a guide to the use of time, Cotton Mather expressed the same belief in these words:

> There should be . . . some Settled Business, wherein a Christian should for the most part spend the most of his Time, and this, that he may glorify God, by doing of Good for *others,* and getting of Good for *himself.*[16]

And Baxter, with his usual lucidity, emphasized the same point in more detail:

> Keep up a high esteem of time and be every day more careful that you lose none of your time, that you lose none of your gold and silver. And if vain recreation, dressings, feastings, idle talk, unprofitable company, or sleep be any of them

temptations to rob you of any of your time, accordingly heighten your watchfulness.[17]

Under the guidance of this new belief, the profound need of achieving proofs of personal significance required ceaseless action, and an end to "taking it easy." In the words of Baxter:

> It is for action that God maintaineth us in our activities; work is the moral as well as the natural end of power. . . . It is action that God is most served and honored by . . . the public welfare or the good of the many is to be valued above our own.[18]

This expanding concept of God's work to include all occupations released an avalanche of productive aspirations that literally reshaped the world. Vast energies that hitherto found release in building great cathedrals now found new expressions of the heavenward urge in sailing the seven seas, turning deserts into gardens, conquering pests and disease, breeding scrub stock into fine herds, transforming hovels into firesides of good cheer, and building new social worlds: new churches, new schools, new governments—new ways of living and of making a living in all spheres of human endeavor. These were the new songs of salvation.

No amount of riches ever exempts one from a responsibility for further expression of his powers in productive employment— a fact which the able Baxter put this way:[19]

> If God shew you a way in which you may lawfully get more than in another way (without wrong to your soul, or to any other), if you refuse this and you choose the less gainful way . . . you refuse to be God's steward . . . you may labor to be rich for God, though not for flesh and sin.

Then he continues:

> Will not riches excuse one man from laboring in a calling? No; but rather bind them to it the more; for he that hath more wages from God, should do Him most work. Though they have no outward want or urge to them, they have great a necessity for obeying God, and doing good to others, as any other men have that are poor.

In thus placing proficient work in any employment within the category of tangible evidence of character which most deserves emulation and esteem, this new breed of minister was obliterating the sharp and clear line which the Ages had hitherto drawn between secular and religious employments. No one has ever expressed this new attitude toward the ethical significance of work more truly than did Hiram Goff, a simple shoemaker, in a conversation with his minister, John Jessig. To strike up pleasant chatter Goff remarked:

> I believe in honest work. Work is the law of nature and the secret of human happiness.

His minister replied:

> I am glad to see a man who can use the humblest vocation to the glory of God as you are doing.

This made the shoemaker's hair stand on end. Said he:

> There ain't no such thing in this wide world, pastor, as a humble vocation. Listen, you are a minister by the grace of God . . . I am a shoemaker by the grace of God. You'll carry up to the judgment seat a fair sample of the sermons you preach, and I'll carry up a fair sample of the shoes I've been making. If your sermons are your best, and my shoes are my best, He'll say John and Hiram, you have used your talents about equally well. It's just as necessary for people to have good shoes as it is good sermons.[20]

No greater incentive to proficiency is conceivable than this identification of the services of any employment with sure evidences (proofs) of character which most deserves emulation, respect, and esteem for its own sake. For, whether it takes a religious or a secular form, this belief diverts the insatiable striving for evidences of personal worth from the "easy ways" into a ceaseless striving for being proficient, even far beyond one's actual abilities. Any amount of earnings one can ever generate from his work will always fall short of the amount he needs for the sake of showing he has all the initiative, genius, imagination, knowledge of right policy, and other virtues which entitle him to as much approbation and esteem as he would like to deserve and enjoy. Thus no achieved level of proficiency, however high, can ever release him from the felt obligation to strive for a still higher level. If he succeeds in making two blades of grass grow where only one had grown before, his thirst for a still finer image of himself then obliges him to find a way of making three blades grow where only two had grown before.

This deeply motivating belief not only directs people in their working activities, but also in their leisure employments—activities done without pay, such as vacations, club activities, and the like. As many writers have pointed out, we work as hard to generate evidence of personal worth through use of our "vacation time" as we do of our "work time."[21] Energized by this directive, people seldom find any rest and would be bored if they did; always they are on the move and never are they so taut as when everything gets quiet and there is nothing to do except sit. In a passage previously cited, the great minister Baxter declared, "It is action that God is most served and honored by." By and large, American people, both farmers and nonfarmers, have long since tended to lose the older feeling that the proper purpose of proficient action, whether in "leisure" or "work" time, is to serve and honor God, but this has scarcely weakened their devotion to proficient action as the best way to serve and honor themselves and others.

## CONFLICT BETWEEN PROFICIENT WORK AND THE PRECAPITALISTIC CONCEPT OF RIGHT TO ACQUIRE PROPERTY

Attention is now directed to the fact that the revolutionary commitment to proficient work, as a badge of character deserving highest emulation and esteem for its own sake, threw people into head-on conflict with the precapitalist (traditionalist) concept of the right to acquire property.

There were two aspects of this older concept. The first was that a man had a natural or moral right to "the full product of his hands." This belief was tied into the further belief that one's natural or moral right to acquire property is limited to what he can work with his own labor and use the products from. The justifying ground for this limitation was the belief that if one acquired more property than needed for this purpose, he deprived others of that land and other property which they needed for making a living.

Both aspects of this concept harmonize wonderfully well so long as people limit their work to the amount required to support their customary needs. But they were thrown into sharp conflict with each other as soon as people took to themselves the judgment that proficient work is sure evidence of character most deserving of respect and esteem for its own sake. For under the guidance of this belief, the striving to justify the highest possible valuations of one's personal worth becomes a motivation to work as much as one is able and to receive the full product of his hands as the just reward of his proficient work.

In line with this directive, people found themselves producing in excess of their customary needs. To put this excess product of their work to proficient use, they exchanged it for money, which they invested in additional land, shops, stores, and the like. In this way, they expanded their possessions far beyond the amount they could work with their own labor, and also beyond what they needed for their own subsistence. This subjected them to the charge of depriving others of their natural and moral right to as much property as they needed for making a living.

Here was a conflict of ethical beliefs that was the very heart of the serious policy problem of seventeenth-century England. Government was on the spot. If it took the position that men could not acquire more property than they could work themselves and use the products from, it would thereby deny the individual his natural or moral right to the full product of his work whenever he was proficient enough to produce more than he needed for his own living. This didn't make sense. On the other hand, if government protected the individual in his natural right to the equivalent of his productive contributions whenever he produced more than he could use, then the government enabled some men to acquire more property than they needed for a living through depriving others of their right to acquire as much property as they needed. This alternative made as little sense as the first.

These conflicting meanings of the older concept of property generated the fundamental policy question of what is the primary responsibility of government to the governed, anyway. This kind of "value problem" can easily lead to civil war.

## JOHN LOCKE TO THE RESCUE

The answer which John Locke worked out for this question was no less a revolutionary departure from the past than was the religious reformers' identification of proficient work with sure evidence of character deserving of emulation and esteem. For, in using widely accepted presuppositions, Locke demonstrated that the traditionalist concept of the moral right to acquire property held true only within exceedingly primitive societies where a money economy was totally absent. But whenever men consent to treat money as the exchange equivalent of all other forms of property, their nature-given right to acquire property as fair reward for proficient work, expands to the limit of their abilities to contribute an equivalent amount of goods and services to society. This revolutionary concept worked hand in hand with the equally revolutionary belief in proficient work as the sure evidence of supremely praiseworthy character.[22]

### PRESUPPOSITIONS

Locke derived his radical theory of property from the following widely held presuppositions concerning the prepolitical societies, which he called the "state of nature":

*Postulate 1:* In negative terms, the state of nature is characterized by a total lack of central political authority. This means three things. First, it lacks

> an established, settled, known law, received and allowed by common consent to be the standard of right and wrong, and the common measure to decide all controversies between them.[23]

Again it lacks

> ... a known and indifferent judge, with authority to determine all differences according to the established law.[24]

Finally it lacks

> a central 'power to back and support the sentence when right, and to give it due execution.'[25]

Expressed positively, the state of nature is characterized by men who are "equally kings," each being:

> ...absolute lord of his own person and possessions, equal to the greatest and subject to nobody...without a common superior on earth with authority to judge between them.[26]

*Postulate II:* In the state of nature (prepolitical society) men are directed by reason to observe the "law of nature." This rational or moral directive

> ...teaches all mankind who will but consult it, that being all equal and independent, no one ought to harm another in his life, health, liberty, or possession; for men being all the workmanship of an omnipotent and infinitely wise Maker, ... are His property...sharing all in one community of Nature, there cannot be supposed any such subordination among us that may authorize us to destroy one another.... Everyone as he is bound to preserve himself...so, by the like reason when his own preservation comes not in competition, ought as much as he can, to preserve the rest of mankind, and not... take away or impair the life, or what tends to be the preservation of the life, liberty, health, limb, or goods of another.[27]

Not only is each man obligated to observe this law of nature but also to use force if necessary in requiring others to observe it.

> ...that all men may be restrained from invading other's rights, and from doing hurt to one another, and the law of nature be observed, which willeth the peace and preservation of mankind, the execution of the law of nature is in that state put into every man's hands, whereby everyone has a right to punish the transgressors of that law to such a degree as may hinder its violation. For the law of nature would...be in vain if there were nobody that in the state of nature had a power to execute that law, and thereby preserve the innocent and restrain offenders; and if anyone in the state of nature may punish another for any evil he has done, everyone may do so. For in that state of perfect equality, where naturally there is no superiority or jurisdiction of one over another, what any may do in the prosecution of that law, everyone must have a right to do.[28]

*Postulate III:* Transcending "the law of nature," in case of conflict, men in the state of nature are directed by the law of "self-preservation."

> ... the first and strongest desire God planted in men, and wrought into the very principles of their nature, is that of self-preservation.[29]

Rightful concern and responsibility for self thus takes precedence over concern and responsibility for others, in case of conflict. This means that nature endows men with absolute rights but only relative duties, as duties stand on the same footing as rights only when their observance requires no sacrifice of one's own right to life and pursuit of happiness.[30]

*Postulate IV:* By the very act of birth, nature, and not civil society, confers on all men a rightful ownership claim to their labor or productive capacities:

> ... every man has a property in his own 'person.' This nobody has any right to but himself. The 'labor' of his body and the 'work' of his hands ... are properly his.[31]

*Postulate V:* Earliest societies were characterized by an absence of money as well as a central political authority. Locke describes this condition as

> ... the first ages of the world, when men were more in danger to be lost, by wandering from their company, in the then vast wilderness of the earth then to be straitened for want of room to plant in.[32]

Though characterized by abundance of natural resources—potential plenty—this sparsely settled, highly undeveloped, primitive society is actually a state of "penury" in terms of useable goods:[33] "Nature and the earth affords only the almost worthless materials as in themselves" such as acorns, berries, leaves, or skins. Existence is thus close to the bone; and no one can secure more than the bare necessities for self-preservation.

From these postulates Locke deduces his theory of property.

THE RIGHT TO ONLY LIMITED PROPERTY IN A PRE-MONEY ECONOMY

In the first part of his theory, Locke demonstrates that within a pre-money economy, the "law of self-preservation" invests each man with a natural or moral right to acquire as much property as he needs for making a living, and that the "law of nature" (reason) denies him the right to acquire more. For if he did, he would be depriving others of their right to enough resources to support their survival needs.

Locke felt obliged to demonstrate this concept of limited right because traditional reflections on the "beginning ages" of the world had long raised doubt as to whether there can be any justification of the so-called right to private appropriation of natural resources. This doubt had its roots in the biblical dictate that the earth and its fruits were originally given to mankind in common.[34] As Locke says:

> ... this being supposed, it seems to some a very great difficulty how anyone should ever come to have a property in anything.

Then he continues:

> But I shall endeavor to show how men come to have a property in several parts of that might God gave to mankind in common, and that without any express compact of all the commoners.

His proofs are as follows:

> (a) ... every man has a "property" in his own "person" ... Whatsoever, then, ... he hath mixed his labor with, and joined it to something that is his own, [he] thereby makes it his property ... it hath by this labor something annexed to it that excludes the common right of other men. For this "labor" being the unquestionable property of the laborer, no man but he can have a right to what that is once joined to, at least where there is enough, as good in the common for others.[35]

Locke then applies this labor method of rightful appropriation to the "parts of nature which God gave to mankind in common."

The first part are the perishables such as acorns, berries, wild fruit, and wild game. When and why do such "fruits of the earth" become the rightful and exclusive possession of anyone? He answers:

> 'Tis plain, if the first gathering made them not his nothing could. That labor put a distinction between them and the

common. That added something to them more than nature ...
had done, and so they became his private right. ... And taking this or that part does not depend on the express consent
of all the commoners. ... The labor that was mine removing
them out of that common state they were in, hath fixed by
property in them.[36]

(b) Locke next shows that the same principle applies to precious metals and wild lands.[37] For if men did not have some
means of appropriating to their private uses that which "God
gave mankind in common," they would soon perish. The only fair
way of doing so is through their own work; otherwise one would
have to get his subsistence by robbery.

(c) Locke next shows that within a pre-money economy, the
amount of property one may rightfully acquire, is limited to the
amount required to support his necessary needs.

First, a man may appropriate only as much as leaves "enough
and as good" for others.[38] This limitation is imposed by the similar right of others to have enough resources to support their
survival needs.

Second, with respect to perishables, one's right to appropriate
is limited to the amount he can use before it spoils. If he picks
more wild berries than he can use before they spoil, he wastes
what others need for their subsistence.

Third, in a pre-money economy, the right to appropriate land
is limited to what one can use with his own labor by the fact
that any larger amount is worthless. In Locke's words:

> As much land as a man tills, plants, improves, and cultivates,
> and can use the products of, so much is his property. He by
> his labor does, as it were, enclose it from the common. Nor
> will it invalidate his right to say everybody has equal title
> to it, and therefore he cannot appropriate, he cannot enclose
> without the consent of all his fellow-commoners, all mankind.
> God, when he gave the world in common to all mankind,
> commanded man also to labor, and the penury of his condi-
> tion required it of him. ... He that, in obedience to this
> command of God, subdued, tilled, and sowed any part of it,
> thereby annexed to it something that was his property, which
> another had no title to, nor could without injury take from
> him.[39]

Enlarging one's possession beyond this point is a sheer waste of effort.

> For supposing an island, separate from all possible commerce with the rest of the world ... what reason could anyone have there to enlarge his possessions beyond the use of his family, and a plentiful supply to its consumption, either in what their own industry produced, or they could barter for like perishable, useful commodities with others ... What would a man value ten thousand or a hundred thousand acres of excellent land ... where he had no hopes of commerce with other parts of the world, to draw money to him by the sale of the product? It would not be worth the enclosing, and we should see him give up again to the wild common of nature whatever was more than would supply the conveniences of life, to be had there for him and his family.[40]

### Introduction of Money Removes Older Limitation on Right to Acquire Property

Having shown why the right to acquire property in a pre-money economy is limited to the amount each needs to support his survival requirements, Locke next shows that this limitation ceases to hold true as quickly as a money economy emerges. The major steps in his reasoning are as follows:

(a) Prior to consent to the introduction of money, "labor gave a right to property."[41] but not afterward. For in the process of introducing money, men agreed to divide among themselves all the hitherto unappropriated lands and other resources, thus wiping out the earlier natural right to acquire property from what "God gave all in common" by merely mixing his labor with raw resource.

> ... in some parts of the world (where the increase of people and stock, with the use of money, had made land scarce, and so of some value), the several communities settled the bounds of their distinct territories, and by laws, within themselves, regulated the properties of the private men of their society, and so by compact and agreement, settled the property which labor and industry began. And ... either expressly or tacitly disowning all claim and right to the land in the other's possession, have by common consent, given up their pretenses to

their natural common right . . . and so have, by positive agreement, settled a property amongst themselves in distinct parts
of the world.[42]

Wherever this agreement to use money has not been made,
much of nature's resources remain unappropriated and in a state
of waste:

> . . . there are still great tracts of ground to be found, which
> the inhabitants thereof, not having joined with the rest of
> mankind in the consent of the use of their common money,
> lie waste . . . and so still lie in common; though this can
> scarcely happen amongst that part of mankind that have con-
> sented to the use of money.[43]

(b) Again, according to Locke, the consent to the introduction of money included consent to unequal possessions:

> . . . since gold and silver . . . has its value only from the con-
> sent of men . . . it is plain that the consent of men have agreed
> to a disproportionate and unequal possession of the earth . . .
> I mean out of the bounds of society and compact; for in gov-
> ernments the laws regulate it; they, having by consent found
> out and agreed in a way how a man may rightfully and with-
> out injury, possess more than he himself can make use of by
> receiving gold and silver, which may continue long in a man's
> possession, without decaying for the overplus, and agreeing
> those metals should have a value.[44]

(c) Again, in Locke's view, consent to the introduction of
money included consent to the wage relationship, based on the
contract of individuals involved:

> . . . a free man makes himself a servant to another by selling
> him for a certain time the service he undertakes to do in
> exchange for wages he is to receive; and though this com-
> monly puts him into the family of his master, and under the
> ordinary discipline thereof, yet it gives the master but a
> temporary power over him, and no greater than that is con-
> tained in the contract between them.[45]

(d) Again, in consenting to treat money as the exchange
equivalent of all other properties, men intended that money
was not merely a medium of exchange, but capital in that it

rightfully earns its owner interest just as land earns rent. Its earning power stems from mutual agreements among those having unequal possessions.

> ... by compact [money] transfers that profit, that was the reward of one man's labor, into another man's pocket. That which occasions this, is the unequal distribution of money; which inequality has the same effect too upon land, that it has upon money.... For the unequal distributions of land, (you having more than you can, or will measure and another less) brings you a tenant to the land ... the same unequal distribution of money (I having more than I can, or will employ, and another less) brings me a tenant for my money....[46]

## Locke Turns the Tables on the Traditionalists

In this reasoning, Locke neatly turned the tables on the precapitalistic concept of appropriation according to which the individual had a natural or moral right to the full product of his labor, but a right limited to only as much property as was necessary for his customary needs. The advent of money removed this restriction for two reasons:

First, it removed all limits on the possessions individuals may seek to acquire. For if one can acquire more land than he can work himself, others will pay him rent for the privilege of using it, or he can exchange it for money and then loan out the money for interest, or invest it in a business and reap a profit from it. Thus, as Locke said:

> Find out something that hath the use and value of money amongst his neighbors, and you shall see the same man will begin presently to enlarge his possessions.[47]

Second, in addition to thus releasing each man's desires to expand his possessions without limit, money provided society with the means of returning to the individual the full equivalent of all he could possibly produce, however much this might exceed the amount required to support his customary needs. Therefore, if, for any reason, the individual was motivated to produce more goods and services than required to support his customary wants, then the ancient justice of receiving "the full product of his labor" gave him a natural and moral right to more money than required for his customary needs. Since the difference between his total product and his subsistence needs (savings) was his to use as he pleased, he had a perfect right to exchange it for more property than he could work with his own labor. Thus, the more proficiently each man works, the more he gets riches for himself in return for equivalent riches he gives to society—a fact which Locke pointed out through a comparison of the pre-money economy of the Indian tribes with that of his native England. The former, said he,

> . . . are rich in land and poor in all the comforts of life . . . for want of improving it by labor, [they] have not one hundredth part of the conveniences we enjoy; and a king of a large and fruitful territory there feeds, lodges, and is clad worse than a day laborer in England.[48]

LOCKE'S THEORY OF PROPERTY AS RE-ENFORCEMENT OF THE RADICAL ETHICAL INTERPRETATION OF WORK

In thus using the traditionalist's own presuppositions as a means of proving that the natural right to the full product (or money equivalent) of one's labor also included the right to acquire more property than required to support one's customary needs, Locke rescued the religious reformers from devastating attack. For, while ministers might use the Scriptures in supporting their radical belief that men fail in their moral responsibility if they choose the less gainful way when "God shows them more gainful ways," they were intellectually defenseless against the charge that they were actually teaching people to enrich themselves through exploiting their brothers. Locke relieved them of this embarrassment by showing how it follows from the money linkage of commodities with each other that society is most enriched when each man receives the full product (or money equivalent) of his labor even though he may acquire more property than he can work with his own labor.

## COMMITMENTS TO PROFICIENT WORK AND RIGHT TO ACQUIRE UNLIMITED PROPERTY AS DOMINANT DIRECTIVES OF SETTLERS

The older landlord civilization could provide no home for radicals who were committed to the beliefs, first, that proficient work is the true mark of upright men, and second, that there is no justifiable limit on the amount of property which any individual has a natural or moral right to acquire from the earnings of his work, except the limit of his abilities to produce goods and services for society. These presuppositions pointed to a new destiny and were a different faith from that which the older landlord civilization had trusted and guided its feet by for a hundred years. So the new radicals had no choice but to tear up this older order or get out. They did both. American settlers stemmed mainly from those who got out.[49]

Attention is now directed to five main ways in which their heritage of radical commitments led them to revolutionary departures from ways of life and social organization generated by older traditionalist beliefs, some of which they also shared.

(1) In line with their directive to proficient work, settlers demanded a freeholder agriculture. For within their virgin continent of cheap land, a system of debt-free, full-owner operated businesses gave each individual a better chance to earn and accumulate more property from proficient work than could any other system. Settlers also demanded a freehold agriculture because full-owner operatorship enabled them to escape the onus of "subservience and venality" which the Ages had imputed to tenants and wage workers.

This traditionalist motivation reenforced the proficiency directive for a freeholder agriculture, but it was not the dominant factor. For the desire for freeholder status as a means of escaping the onus of tenantry could be met by public land policies which limited farm sizes to what the usual family could handle with its own labor and management, except perhaps for relatively short seasonal labor peaks. But such policies were incompatible with the Lockean belief that each man's natural or moral right to a fair reward for his industry is violated by any state-made limit on the amount of possessions he may acquire.

To be sure, in their long struggle for equitable land policies, settlers did limit their *request* for land from the government to the amount a man and his family could handle with their own labor. But this limited request did not arise from any belief that this was all the land one had a moral right to acquire; it stemmed from the fact that under any alternative policy, settlers were fleeced by absentee speculators. If, for example, the government sold only large tracts, it gave monied men a monopoly of first opportunities to acquire title to public land, which they could turn to a speculative profit by resale in small tracts to settlers. As a protection against such exploitations, settlers demanded policies whereby the government would give the man with little or no capital, except his labor, the first opportunity to acquire at least as much public land as he and his family could work themselves. But they wanted no limit on any additional amount which they might acquire through their own initiative and industry. In this spirit, the settlers, like John Locke, were a highly capitalistic-minded people.

Griswold argues that Locke's concept of natural right to only limited property was "confirmation, if not inspiration for his [Jefferson's] ideal community of small land holders."[50] This may be correct. But it is appropriate to add that Locke's whole aim was to show that this traditionalist concept of right to only limited possessions applied only to pre-money societies and not to money economies like those of the settler. Under such conditions, the heart of Locke's theory is that each man has a natural and moral right to acquire as much property as his initiative and industry will enable him to acquire, however much his possessions may exceed the amount he can work with his own labor. In this belief, Locke never had more kindred disciples than the settlers themselves.

(2) With respect to improving prevailing ways of living and making a living, the settlers' directive to proficient work comes into clear dominance over traditionalist biases in favor of old methods handed down from father to son. To be sure, there are many instances of their resistance to change. A classic example is the often cited hesitation of pioneering prairie farmers to use the steel plow for fear it would "pizin the land." In reasoning from such cases, and their number is legion, the impression is sometimes given that settlers were fundamentally "tradition bound," and that present-day agriculture resulted from the fact that scientific and technological leadership of the Land Grant Colleges and commercial pressures of modern industry simply

*engulfed* our older rural society with a tidal wave of proficiency beliefs and values which were never indigenous to farm people.

This puts the cart before the horse. It overlooks the fact that long before the rise of agronomists and agricultural engineers, the settlers, by and large, were well known for their belief that one fails in his duty to earn the respect and esteem of himself and others unless he is on the alert for improved ways of removing drudgery and relieving want and privation from his own household, his country, and even the whole world. From earliest times, this belief bore good fruit. For, however slow the settlers may have been to change their ways, the fact remains that innovators were their heroes. In emulating such heroes, they became "tinkerers" long before the rise of agricultural specialists. Out of their tinkering, prior to the 1860's, came most of the basic machines and implements which entered into the mechanization of agriculture during the late nineteenth century. Widespread agricultural fairs centered around their interest in improved farming. It is thus no accident that the so-called "captains of industry" who guided the building of industrial America from the Civil War to around 1900, were mostly migrants from family farms of premachine America.[51] Viewed in this light, our Machine Age, including modern scientific agriculture, is the cumulative expression of the prior commitment of farm and nonfarm people alike to increasingly proficient endeavor as the hallmark of praiseworthy character, and not the other way around.

To be sure, the spectacular advance of the last hundred years in either industry or agriculture would be inconceivable without the cooperation of scientists and technological leaders with businessmen and farmers alike. But it does not follow that they were a sufficient condition. From the very beginning, they couldn't have gotten their foot in the door, as it were, except for the fact that farmers and businessmen were already seeking ways of working more proficiently. Both yesterday and today, biases of farmers for the old ways have often impeded a faster rate of progress than was actually achieved. But we know of no reason for supposing that such biases have been more pronounced among farmers than nonfarmers, especially in view of the fact that for a century the gain in output per worker has been nearly as rapid in agriculture as in industry, and in the last decade it has been appreciably faster.

(3) The dominance of the proficiency directive among settlers is especially evident with respect to what is commonly called "quietism" and "activism." Quietism is the technical term used in denoting such traditionalist commitments as the belief that work is the badge of inferior worth, and that no sensible person will do no more of it than is necessary to support his customary needs so as to have ample time for good fishing, picnics, festivals, wholesome loafing, delightful companionship of coon dogs, and the like. Activism is the technical term used in characterizing people in whom the proficiency directive is so urgent as to be a well-nigh insatiable need for ceaseless action as means of earning favorable valuations of their worth.[52]

In these terms, it is questionable if any people were ever so completely energized by the proficiency directive as American farmers and others of the settlement era. Historians picture this fact in many ways. For example, in their account of America from 1820 to 1850, Morrison and Commager observed that this period

> ... was America's busy age.... Each Northern community was an ant hill, intensely active within, and constantly exchanging ants with other hills. Every man worked ... the few who wished to idle, and could afford idleness, fled from the approbrium of 'loafing' to Europe where they swelled the chorus of complaints against democratic institutions.... The Northern American had not learned how to employ leisure; his pleasure came from doing things.[53]

Such zeal for industry is far in excess of that which we would expect of a people cherishing ancient ways and whose *summum bonum* was a freehold big enough to support their customary needs and provide escape from the ancient onus of tenantry as a badge of subservience. This traditionalist motivation characterized French peasants who finally succeeded in achieving their Freeholder Ideal through the French Revolution. But for this very reason they differed from the American settlers as night from day. DeTocqueville pointed out this fact in a memorable passage:

In certain corners of the Old World. . . . The inhabitants are, for the most part, extremely ignorant and poor; they take no part in the business of their country, and are frequently oppressed by the government; yet the countenances are generally placid and their spirits light.

In America I saw the freest and most enlightened men placed in the happiest circumstances which the world affords; it seemed to me as if a cloud habitually hung upon their brow, and I thought them serious, and almost sad, even in their pleasures.

The chief reason for this contrast is, that the former do not think of the ills they endure, while the latter are forever brooding over advantages they do not possess. It is strange to see with what feverish ardor the Americans pursue their own welfare; and to watch the vague dread that constantly torments them, lest they should not have chosen the shortest path which may lead to it.

A native of the United States clings to the world's goods as if he were certain never to die; and he is so hasty in grasping at all within his reach, that one would suppose he was constantly afraid of not living long enough to enjoy them. . . . A man builds a house in which to spend his old age, and he sells it before the roof is on; he plants a garden and lets it just as the trees are coming into bearing; he brings a field into tillage, and leaves other men to gather the crops; he embraces a profession, and gives it up; he settles in a place, which he soon afterwards leaves to carry his changeable longings elsewhere. If his private affairs leave him any leisure, he instantly plunges into the vortex of politics; and if, at the end of the year of unremitting labor, he finds he has a few days vacation, his eager curiosity whirls him over the vast extent of the United States, and he will travel fifteen hundred miles in a few days, to shake off his happiness. Death at length overtakes him, but it is before he is weary of his bootless chase of that complete felicity which forever escapes him.

At first sight, there is something surprising in this strange unrest of so many happy men, restless in the midst of abundance. The spectacle is, however, as old as the world; the novelty is, to see the whole people furnish an exemplification of it.[54]

Thus energized by an insatiable hunger for proficient action, it is questionable whether the settlers' thirst for innovations was any less intense than that of modern farmers. The safe conclusion appears to be that the settlers' quest for novelty could not be gratified nearly so rapidly as that of modern farmers since they had no vast system of research institutions and agricultural specialists to feed them an ever-hastening stream of new farm know-how. But this handicap does not obscure the fact that from earliest time until now the driving power of typical farmer's proficiency image of worthwhile life so keeps him on the move that what he most dreads is the arrival of the day when he must retire and "take it easy."

(4) The same belief in the ethical significance of work, which thus energized settlers with a boundless activism, also generated a peculiar brand of practical idealism which has always distinguished our people. In virtue of this belief, the settlers were seeking a workbench on which to prove themselves. This they found in a virgin continent of potential plenty. But this realm of potential plenty was a hard world, especially so for a people with little or no capital except their bare hands. But however severe the privations and cruelties of the new continent, it would nonetheless turn into marvelous shapes and forms under the touch of patient industry; and soon there emerged the inspiring vision of a whole wide wilderness transforming into farms, homes, and thriving cities in response to diligence and creative toil. As men saw the oak in the acorn, so they envisioned farms in swamps and thickets, ports and thriving cities on river bends, paths of commerce along the wild-game trails. In this way the poetry of the spirit joined the sinews of the hand with the stuff that dreams are made of. Thus was born the American Dream as the felt assurance of nature and providence alike that, in the capacities for superior industry, men have ample means to bring their actual circumstances increasingly in line with their aspirations. As Santayana observed, the typical American is "an idealist working on matter."[55] This fact accounts for his skittishness toward either visionary idealism or crass materialism, and of no one is this more true than the usual farmer. Few things so get on his nerves as the preaching of "ideals" that are without tangible promise of such materialistic outcomes as conquering

disease or unlocking the secrets of photosynthesis. Thus his "idealism" and "materialism" are like the sides of a coin. The one is inconceivable without the other, although neither is identical with the other. Accordingly, if one calls him a materialist, he scowls. Call him an idealist, and he wonders if you think he is softheaded. But call him a practical idealist, and he dilates with good feeling. Add that he is a self-made man, and he bursts with pride. His "practical idealism" is thus only another name for his work-ethic faith that, in their capacities for proficient industry, men have ample means for bringing their actual conditions increasingly in line with their dreams or visions through an ever-greater mastery of nature, both human and physical.

(5) Finally, the same directive for proficient work which generated the settlers' demand for a freeholder agriculture, his thirst for innovations, his ceaseless activism and practical idealism, also included unique concepts of equity. For the belief that the key responsibility of the individual to himself and society is to earn high standing through increasing competence in any useful employment of his choice obviously includes the further belief that society owes three reciprocal debts to individuals. These debts are the obligations to (a) provide all its members with opportunity or access to the means (e.g., public schools) necessary for developing his potential to the fullest extent possible; (b) offer opportunities for productive roles in keeping with his abilities; and (c) give each a fair return for his contributions. Thus the directive to proficient work places society under duties to the individual which are no less binding than those which it places on the individual to himself and society. Accordingly, it is impossible for the individual not to resent the unfairness of a society which fails to do its best to discharge all of these debts to the individual and at the same time expects him to earn good repute through proficient work. It is equally impossible for society not to resent the unfairness of the individual who seeks a living and a favorable valuation of himself, but is unwilling to earn these goods through superior industry.

These three concepts of equity are all caught up in what is commonly called "the justice of equal opportunity." The first two debts are called distributive justice, and the second is called commutative justice. That is, distributive justice includes the belief that society owes to each (a) access to the means necessary for developing his potential as fully as possible and also (b) the opportunity for a productive role in keeping with his abilities. Commutative justice includes the belief that society is obliged to return each a fair reward for his contributions.

There is no "natural harmony" between these beliefs. Individual capabilities are themselves largely the function of goods and services that are within society's power to extend or withhold. Therefore, distributive justice may require severe limitations on income inequalities that many might regard as incompatible with the right of each to a fair return for his contributions.

It is interesting to observe that the settlers rejected the medival method of resolving this conflict; yet, thanks to the abundance of cheap land, the resolution they actually achieved closely approximated the one called for by the medieval theory of natural right to only limited possessions. As previously stated, the heart of this theory is the belief that each man has a natural or moral right to the "full product of his labor" but that his right to acquire property is limited to the amount which he can work with his own labor in supporting his customary needs. Obviously this limitation precludes the possibility of inequalties of income ever becoming so great as to throw the just demand for equal opportunities for personal development and creative roles into conflict with the equally just demand for each to receive the equivalent of his contribution.

But the settlers held this limitation would rob the industrious of their just deserts. They did so because of their Lockean belief that, if the individual produces more than he needs for a living, he has a natural and moral right to exchange the surplus for money, which he may invest in additional property that yields additional money, which he has a right to invest in still more income-producing property. There is no conceivable limit on the income inequalities which this process may generate. For there is no assignable limit to the diverse and unequal capacities of men for proficient industry and wise investment.

As Madison ably stated, this means that protection of [different and unequal faculties for acquiring property] is the first object of government,[56] however great may be the income inequalities which are generated by their unequal capabilities. But no government can be totally committed to this objective and also totally committed to (1) providing all its citizens with access to the means necessary for developing their potential as fully as possible; and (2) offering them opportunities for productive roles in keeping with their abilities.

This contradiction was resolved in early America by the abundance of land. For with relatively inexpensive farm technologies and enough "dirt-cheap" land available for everyone, no one would work another's land because he could earn more by acquiring title to a farm big enough to fully utilize his own labor. Thus, the abundance of land held income inequalities within very narrow limits, and in this way prevented any conflict that would have otherwise arisen between the competitive requirements of commutative and distributive justice.[57]

But today the conflict is serious, made so by high-priced land, highly productive farm technologies, limited outlets for farm products, and a national economy with five to six million unemployed. Under these conditions, price-depressing surpluses siphon off to the rest of society a disproportionate share of the cost-reducing benefits of the farmer's increasingly superior industry. Thus, commutative justice is disturbed. Seeking to rectify this inequity through programs designed to cut back production to the level at which total supply balances total demand at reasonable prices, improves incomes for agriculture as a whole. However, such programs may worsen the inequality of opportunity to productive roles and fair incomes among the relatively few families who are on proficient farms and the great bulk who are on inadequate farms. Seeking to rectify this inequity through credit programs designed to accelerate growth in the total number of proficient farms generates additional price-depressing surpluses, thus worsening the lack of fair returns to farmers as a whole. Seeking to get out of all these boxes through programs designed to move surplus workers out of agriculture expands the national pool of unemployed. This further infringes on the natural and moral right of all citizens to productive and fairly rewarding roles in keeping with their abilities.

Thus, all our genius and wit are far less effective than was the abundance of cheap land of the settlement era in limiting income inequalities to the point of harmonizing the otherwise seriously conflicting demands of distributive and commutative justice.

## THE WIDENING GAP BETWEEN THE FREEHOLDER IDEAL AND PROFICIENT PRACTICE

As previously explained, the Freeholder Ideal was an agriculture of businesses in which the will and interest of all participants are totally excluded except those of the operating families who do most if not all the work of their businesses. In such self-sufficient firms, the managerial and risk-taking role of the operator is that of absolute lord and master over all conceivable operations of his business. Divested of all commitments to any outsider, such as creditor, landlord, government, or others, the freeholder was truly the monarch of all he surveyed.

Furthermore, until the late nineteenth century, the actual status of farm families and their Ideal status as freeholders were identical. The Actual and the Ideal were not hooked together by an "agricultural ladder" in which a would-be freeholder started out as a farm hand, worked a few years until he saved enough from his wages to buy a line of equipment; then became a tenant until he could save enough to buy a farm with the help of creditors, then worked and saved a few more years until he could pay off all his creditors; and then live out the evening of his life in the proud feeling that he was absolute lord and master of all that lay within his fence lines. Farmers of the settlement era would have regarded this separation of the Ideal from the Actual (Theory and Practice) as a monstrosity. For their Ideal was an agriculture in which the young man began the race of life as a freeholder—a debt-free, full-owner operator—and the ladder of his dreams extended from that point up.

Thus, the concept of the "agricultural ladder" is wholly the product of the post-settlement era and stemmed from the need for assurances that continual departures from dying Ideals are in fact merely steppingstones to their fulfillment. Four observations bear out this point:

*First:* As cheap land gave out and farm technologies became increasingly expensive, the amount of land and other resources required for proficient farming quickly exceeded the amount which the usual farm family could acquire with its own limited assets. In line with this fact, increasing numbers of family operators departed from their freeholder status by seeking the help of creditors who would supplement their limited resources with real estate as well as capital loans on reasonable terms. Both public and private lenders responded to this invitation. But, the price of their doing so was a debt contract that limited the farmer's absolute managerial power over his own equity until creditor liens were satisfied. In this way, a wedge was driven between his actual status and his Ideal status as a freeholder. But sufference of the gap was made easy by the faith that, within a few years of diligent industry and thrift, debtor operators would accumulate enough savings to pay off their creditors and wind up their later years as the absolute sovereigns of a Jeffersonian freehold.

Two innovations in practices of farm lenders in recent years indicates that the essential function of agriculture credit today is to enable operators to acquire operating control over proficient farms through perpetual credit. First, this fact is implicit in the establishment of forty-year real estate loans. For the lifetime of such loans substantially exceeds the productive lifespan of the usual farmer. Second, the same fact is implicit in the use of loan renewals and lengthening the lifespan of chattel loans. It is also implicit in a small increase in incorporated family farms.

*Second:* As increasing numbers of family farmers sought the help of creditors in purchasing farms, so they likewise sought the help of landlords who would supplement their working capital by lending them the use of their land and buildings. Landlords responded, but the price of their response was a rental contract that limited the operator's absolute managerial power. For example, to protect his contribution to the operator's business, the landowner might require commitments of the operator to follow a specified rotation system, and make no alterations in fixed improvements without the landowner's approval. In this way, a second wedge was driven between the actual status of increasing numbers of family farmers and their Ideal status as freeholders. But again the sufferance of this gap was made easy by the faith that with a few years of diligent industry and thrift the usual tenant operator would eventually save enough to achieve a debt-free, full-ownership status.

*Third:* Since the 1930's, farmers have sought government assistance in helping them to balance their output to total demand at fair prices. Government has responded with price-support guarantees. But the cost of this response has been production contracts which again limit the hitherto absolute managerial power of the farmer to produce whatever amounts of commodities he chooses. In this way, a third wedge has been driven between the farmer's actual managerial status and his Ideal status as a freeholder.

*Fourth:* In recent years, merchandisers of a very limited number of foods like poultry, table eggs, and certain fruits and vegetables began bypassing wholesalers and warehouses and going to first processors in the marketing chain with contracts which specified the prices they would pay for specified volumes, delivery dates, and quality characteristics of given products. First processors in turn translated their contracts into corresponding production contracts with farmers—the first producers. Thus, in addition to creditors, landlords, and the government, contractors, including feed dealers, have entered into the farmer's business with contractual arrangements that further limit the historic Ideal of himself as the absolute master of a self-sufficient firm. Today, the farmer is only a relative master of a contractual firm.

It is often said that "the family farm as we have known it is on the way out." Right. But this has been true for nearly one hundred years. It first became true when the family operator allowed creditors, especially real estate creditors, to be participants in his business, thus limiting his absolute managerial power with contractual commitments to comply with specified rules which his creditors deem necessary for the protection of their interest in the farmer's business. Again the family farm, "as we have known it," disappeared when the operator consented to the landowner's becoming a participant in his business, limiting his absolute managerial power with commitments whereby the landowner could send out the sheriff if he didn't live up to this agreement.

Still again, the family farm "as we have known it" disappeared when family operators, by the millions, sought for their government to become a participant in their business by guaranteeing them price floors in exchange for commitments which limited the farmer's hitherto absolute power to produce any amount of whatever products he pleased. Finally, in some sectors of agriculture, the family farm "as we have known it" has disappeared because the operator has allowed contractors to become participants in his firm through contracts which specify both the price and the product he may produce. In return, the farmer limits his absolute power to produce as he pleases with commitments to comply with certain specified practices which will meet the specifications of the contract.

In following their three-century directive to be proficient farmers, actual family operators over the last one hundred years have steadily shifted their operations from self-sufficient firms to contractual firms. I see no possibility of turning the clock back. If this be true, the Jeffersonian Dream in the strict sense of the word is dead.

But is it realistic to be this strict?

## PROSPECT

An agriculture, in which operating families do most of the work and have varying degrees of risk-taking and managerial power, is very much alive and on the go. Otherwise, an increasing proportion of total farm work would be accounted for by hired labor, and also an increasing proportion of total farm output would be accounted for by larger-than-family farms, that is, farms using more hired labor than can be supplied by an ordinary farm family, which is approximately 1.5 man-years. Unless both of these changes were definitely underway, an agriculture of predominantly family farms could not be going down the drain. They do not appear to be underway.

Throughout the 1950's, work done by both family and hired workers declined rapidly but both declined at about the same rate, although the rate decline in hired work was somewhat faster.[58] Again, family operated farms accounted for over 74 per cent of total farm marketings in 1954 as compared with nearly 67 per cent in 1949.[59] Preliminary indications are that approximately the same relationships obtained for the 1954–59 period as for the 1949–54 period. (The figures cited were unaffected by changes in farm wage rates or prices received by farmers.)

But the fact that the family farm is not going down the drain does not mean that the road ahead is clear of danger. My chief apprehension stems from two areas; one pertains to the nature of future farm technologies, the other to the increasing capital requirements of proficient farms.

In the visible future, will scientists and engineers develop farm technologies that make possible the widespread introduction of the factory process into food and fiber production, as was done in industrial production at the beginning of the Industrial Revolution?

Before the rise of the machine process, agriculture and industry were characterized by a sequential pattern of operations in which the various production steps were separated by time intervals, so that the same individual could perform one production step after another until the final product was the embodiment of his own planning and effort. The shift from hand to machine methods quickly wiped out this pre-machine similarity of agriculture and industry. But the shift to machine production in farming, by and large, does not transform the age-old sequential pattern of operations into a simultaneous pattern. If it did, plowing, cultivating, and harvesting would need to be done concurrently. But nature does not permit this; she separates these operations by very wide time intervals.

Were this not the case, the shift to machine farming would quickly multiply the number of things that must be done at the same time far beyond the number of workers in any family. In this way, it would destroy the pre-machine institution of family farms (or businesses) and replace them with factories. For a factory is simply a production organization in which the many steps involved in making a product, such as an automobile, are divided into different places along a production line and done concurrently with the input-output rate of each operation controlled by the flow-rate of materials between operations. No family could possibly operate a factory. The number of things that need to be done concurrently is far greater than the number of workers in many, many families.

In some agricultural processes, nature separates production steps by very short intervals. This is true of the timespans between animal feedings, for example, and milking cows. Approximation of the factory process in farming has been achieved to some extent in these situations. In such instances, the family farm becomes a physical impossibility for the same reason that a family factory is unthinkable in industry. In the main, however, the "Industrial Revolution" in agriculture is mainly a spectacular change in the implements with which operations are performed, whereas in industry it is a further revolution in the sequence of productive operations.

The age-old sequential pattern of operation is the physical basis of the family production unit, in either industry or agriculture. It is long since gone in industry. Can it be expected to continue much longer in agriculture? There is reason to suspect it will not. The family farm would go out like a light, if the secrets of photosynthesis were unlocked, as it seems they surely will be. It is said we are now closer to this achievement than we were to the atomic bomb in 1905 when Einstein opened up the possibility of it with his famous formula for the equivalence of matter and energy.

Even much before this event, scientists and engineers may go far in wiping out the physical possibility of the family farm through discovering profitable ways of separating the production of crops and livestock on the same farm throughout the Corn Belt and elsewhere. Should this happen, there probably would not be much left of family farming. From a physical standpoint, livestock feeding can now be organized into an approximate factory process. Although my foresight is very limited, the day may not be far off when specialists will bring forth profitable farm technologies that will wipe out the wide time intervals between the many operations on given farm products.

In addition, many fear the family farm is on the verge of being wiped out by its expanding investment requirement. It is not uncommon for proficient farms to represent real investments from $75,000 to over $200,000, and non-real estate investments of an additional $35,000 to $75,000.

How can individual families with assets of this magnitude pass them on intact to the next generation? The ready answer is that the farm real estate owners may combine into relatively large corporations, convert their assets into stock shares, and then protect the value of their assets and assure reasonable dividends by appointing boards of directors who will hire professional farm managers to see that farming is carried on in a proficient manner. By witholding rental privileges, and offering stock shares in exchange for renters' investments in working capital, the corporation would be able to induce family farmers now on a rental basis to become shareholders in the corporation. At their option, they might remain on the same farms as before, but as wage or salaried workers of the corporation under the direction of professional managers.

This may happen, but there is an obstacle that may prevent it from happening very soon. As I see it, the obstacle is this: the relationship between prices received and prices paid by farmers has seldom been sufficiently favorable to make possible a return to labor comparable to that of workers of similar capacities in non-farm employment. If agriculture had to compete with industry for workers in the same general labor market, then to take over in great numbers in any given area, large farming corporations would have to pay workers as much as they can earn in other employment, else they would choose industrial employment. Furthermore, from early times up to now, really large agricultural businesses have become the dominant institution in American agriculture only in those regions, such as the Far West and the plantation areas of the South, where peculiar institutional arrangements have enabled agriculture to secure large supplies of relatively cheap labor outside the general labor market, and in this way escape the necessity of competing with industry for labor services. No similar institutions prevail throughout all the major regions in which family farming has long been the dominant business unit of American agriculture, and, as I see it, there is little possibility of such institutional developments in these areas.

Therefore, my guess is that investment requirements of proficient farms will fail to proceed to the point of wiping out a predominantly family farm agriculture in the visible future.

Expanding investment requirements may become incompatible with the family farm without leading to big stock-share corporations. The trend in farm mechanization is in the steady direction of larger capacity machinery and equipment which decreases labor per unit of output. Fuel, oil, and other machine costs might be cut appreciably by larger business which enables operators to purchase supplies in wholesale, rather than retail, lots. Savings might also be achieved in farm marketing costs. Such factors suggest that we may be reaching a point where increasing numbers of operators, by expanding their business to four- or five-man farms, may be able to achieve enough savings in costs to compete with industry for labor. This eventually might or might not involve large stock-share corporations, but in either case it would wipe out the family farm. The main obstacle to this development, as I see it, is high risk on large investments which stems from uncertainty of farm prices and incomes. I do not expect these obstacles to be overcome in the near future, but I may be mistaken.

## CONCLUSIONS

The foregoing analysis leads to five main conclusions:

(1) Considered as a business in which the operating family is a risk-taking manager of an undertaking in which it does most of the work, the family farm is no less a dominant institution of American agriculture now than it was in Jefferson's day. The difference lies in the fact that the typical family farm of his day was a highly self-sufficient firm in which the will of the operator was absolute; his power to run his business as he pleased was not limited by outside participants, such as his creditor, his landlord, his government, or buyers of his products, or his suppliers, such as the feed dealer. Furthermore, in Jefferson's day of cheap land and low capital requirements per farm, there was a high correlation between this concept of a self-sufficient firm, in which the operator's will was absolute, and the requirements of a proficient farm—that is, a farm with sufficient resources and

productivity to utilize a "full line of equipment" and generate
at least enough income to meet expenses for operating costs,
fixed charges, family living expenses, and enough capital growth
for new investments to keep in step with technological advance
and rising levels of living. Under modern conditions, this older
concept of the self-sufficient firm has long ceased to coincide with
the requirements of a proficient farm. In the actual life of farm
people, requirements of proficient farming have taken precedence
over values which may attach to their image of themselves as absolute masters of their businesses. As a result, the typical family
farm of today is a contractual firm in which the operator's managerial power and risk-taking are limited in varying degrees by
his commitment to follow certain rules under which others are
willing to extend him services that enable him to operate a more
proficient farm than he could otherwise do.

(2) In Jefferson's time no one did more than he to advance
the cause of scientific agriculture. From this fact, we may infer
that he sought, above all else, an agriculture of proficient family
farms. Such an agriculture is not possible today except as the
usual family seeks and secures the help of other owners of production and marketing services. In light of this fact, we may infer
that Jefferson would expand his agricultural Ideal to include
contractual firms in which families consent to limit their otherwise absolute managerial power with commitments under which
others are willing to extend them the production and marketing
services they need for becoming operators of proficient farms.

(3) In these terms, the traditional Ideal of a predominantly
family agriculture of proficient farms remains as relevant to
present-day policy considerations as in the settlement era. In that
era, implementation of the Ideal merely called for equitable land
policies that gave families with little or no capital except their
labor, first opportunities to acquire fee simple ownership to
enough public lands for a proficient farm. Today, the lines of
implementation are quite different. At least four deserve mention.

Achievement of an agriculture of proficient family farms calls
for continual improvement in agricultural credit policies and
programs to enable competent operators of inadequate farms to
expand their resources and productivity to farms of sufficient

size to effectively utilize a full line of equipment. As this is done, we approximate an agriculture of farms able to produce foods and fibers for society at minimum cost per unit of out put. Limited available data on the economies of farm sizes indicates that under conditions of reasonable prices for farm products, such an agriculture will enable operating families to have earnings for their labor and management comparable to earnings of people of similar capacities in nonfarm employments. The data also indicate that in most types of farming, farms larger than proficient family farms would not be able to produce foods and fibers at less cost per unit of output, although they would return greater profits to management because of their larger volume of output.

Again, achievement of the traditional agricultural Ideal of proficient family farms calls for continual effort to establish and maintain equitable contracts between tenants and landlords; between operators and contractors seeking products of specified grades and quality; and between government and farmers seeking ways to bring total farm output in line with total demand at reasonable prices.

Third, in connection with new land developments, such as large reclamation projects, implementation of the family farm Ideal calls for policies that keep the door of opportunity open to families seeking to become established as operators of proficient farms.

Finally, implementation of the Ideal calls for continual scrutiny of tax laws to see that these do not take unfair advantage of proficient family farm operators.

(4) But the striving to achieve this Jeffersonian agriculture of proficient family farms runs into conflict with another historic Ideal of ample opportunities for farm people for productive work in return for which they earn decent incomes and the high standing they seek in their own eyes and in the eyes of others. When land was so abundant as to be "dirt cheap," there was room enough in agriculture for every family to have a proficient farm that wanted one.

Today, this is far from true. In 1959, there were over 2.4 million commercial farms. Depending on what assumptions are used, one may reach somewhat different estimates of the number of proficient family farms that would be needed to provide society with all the foods and fibers it wants at reasonable prices. But all the "educated guesses" I know indicate about one million proficient farms would be enough to do this job.

Achieving an agriculture of proficient family farms comes at a very high price when the cost of it is the uprooting of well over half the present commercial farm population. It will not do to say they will shift into higher-paying nonfarm employments. This alternative is limited by a lack of over five million opportunities for the needs of the national labor force. It also is severely limited by the fact that farm families commonly lack the training and skills required to take advantage of nonfarm opportunities and also by the fact that anyone's occupational mobility is definitely circumscribed, once he has trained and geared himself for a particular career such as farming, mining, teaching, or research.

Above all, the clash between the drive for proficiency and the need of opportunities for farm families is not basically a knock-down-drag-out struggle between an agriculture of family farms and an agriculture of larger farms. For, as previously explained, in terms of the proportion of total farm work and total farm output accounted for by farms on which operating families do most of the farm work, family farming is not losing out. This means that the drive for achieving the historic agricultural Ideal of proficient family farms is in fundamental conflict with the equally historic Ideal of providing ample opportunities for farm people; and this conflict cannot be resolved by "programs to save the family farm."

(5) This does not mean surrender of the family farm Ideal, but it does mean that policies and programs to achieve it must be incorporated within the larger objective of finding opportunities for farm people who are otherwise sacrificed by an overwrought dedication to the agricultural Ideal of proficient family farms. The overriding concern of Jefferson was with policies that would provide abundant opportunities for people; and his interest in an agriculture of proficient family farms was incidental to his larger concern with the need of people for opportunities.

If this be a correct estimate of the man, the first requisite of Jeffersonian principles bids us turn attention more directly to ways of expanding educational opportunities for rural areas and of creating more new nonfarm employment opportunities in both rural and urban sectors of the nation. Only as we move toward this objective of more abundant opportunities for all people do we open a realistic road to more rapid achievement of an agriculture of proficient family farms for all who remain in farming. That, as I understand it, is the true relevance of the Jeffersonian Dream today.

## NOTES

1. A. Whitney Griswold, *Farming and Democracy* (New Haven, Conn.: Yale University Press) (Published in 1948 by Harcourt, Brace & Co., Inc.), pp. 19, 47.

2. *Ibid.,* p. 163; also see pp. 4–5; 14–16.

3. Federalist Paper No. 10.

4. "Documents Illustrative of the Formation of the Union," Government Printing Office, Washington, D.C., 1927, pp. 489–90.

5. "First Settlement of New England," 1820, address at the celebration of the two-hundredth anniversary of the landing of the Pilgrims at Plymouth Rock, in *The Works of Daniel Webster*, Vol. I, 5–6.

6. From a speech by Thomas Hart Benton, *Thirty Years' View: A History of the American Government for Thirty Years, from 1820 to 1850*, Vol. I, Chap. IV, pp. 11–12.

7. Cited by Andrew Hacker, *New York Times Magazine*, March 4, 1962, p. 84.

8. Thomas Jefferson, *Notes on the State of Virginia*, Query XIX, first published in 1782.

9. *Ibid.*

10. *Ibid.*

11. Griswold, *op. cit.,* p. 31.

12. Thomas Jefferson, *loc. cit.*

13. The pioneerng works on this subject are: Max Weber, *The Protestant Ethic and the Spirit of Capitalism* (Frome and London: Butler and Tanner Ltd., 1948); Ernst Troeltsch, *Prostestantism and Progress* (Beacon Hill, Boston: Beacon Press, 1958); R. H. Tawney, *Religion and the Rise of Capitalism* (New York: Harcourt, Brace & Co., Inc., 1926); Georgia Harkness, *John Calvin: The Man and his Ethics* (New York, Nashville: Abington Press, 1958); see especially Chap. VII.

14. Cited by Tawney, *op. cit.,* p. 240.

15. *Ibid.*, p. 245.

16. Cited by Ralph Barton Perry, *Puritanism and Democracy* (New York: Vanguard Press, 1944), p. 312.

17. Cited by Weber, *op. cit.*, p. 261.

18. *Ibid.*, p. 260.

19. Cited by Perry, *op. cit.*, pp. 314–15.

20. Cited by Fredrick Brown Harris, *Washington Star*, editorial page, October 30, 1955.

21. See, for example: David Dempsey, "Myth of the New Leisure Class," *New York Times Magazine*, January 26, 1958; Frank W. Abrams, "The Dangers and Delights of Unlimited Leisure," *Saturday Review*, October 14, 1961.

22. In the development of the following summary of Locke's theory of property, the author is especially indebted to two highly original and able interpretations of Locke's theory of property, C. B. MacPherson, "Locke on Capitalistic Appropriation," the *Western Political Quarterly*, 1951, pp. 550–66; and Leo Strauss, *Natural Right and History* (University of Chicago Press, 1953), pp. 234–51.

23. John Locke, *Second Treatise on Civil Government*, first published in 1690, Sec. 124.

24. *Ibid.*, Sec. 125.

25. *Ibid.*, Sec. 126.

26. *Ibid.*, Sec. 19 and 123.

27. *Ibid.*, Sec. 6.

28. *Ibid.*, Sec. 7.

29. Cited by Leo Strauss, *op. cit.*, p. 227.

30. *Ibid.*, pp. 225 and 227.

31. John Locke, *op. cit.*, Sec. 27.

32. *Ibid.*, Sec. 35.

33. *Ibid.*, Sec. 31 and 32.

34. *Ibid.*, Sec. 25.

35. *Ibid.*, Sec. 26.

36. *Ibid.*, Sec. 27.

37. *Ibid.*, Sec. 32 and 37.

38. *Ibid.*, Sec. 26.

39. *Ibid.*, Sec. 31.

40. *Ibid.*, Sec. 48.

41. *Ibid.*, Sec. 45.

42. *Ibid.*

43. *Ibid.*

44. *Ibid.*, Sec. 50.

45. *Ibid.*, Sec. 85.

46. John Locke, "Some Considerations of the Lowering of Interest and Raising the Value of Money" (1691), *Works*, 1759 edition, Vol. II, 22–23. Cited by MacPherson, *op. cit.*, 557.

47. John Locke, "Second Treatise on Civil Government," first published in 1690, Sec. 49.

48. Ibid., Sec. 41.

49. This fact is apparent in Perry's account of the waves of immigrants through the eighteenth century: Ralph Barton Perry, Puritanism and Democracy (New York: Vanguard Press, 1944), pp. 62–81.

50. Griswold, op. cit., p. 41.

51. Louis M. Hacker, The Triumph of Business Enterprise (New York: Simon & Schuster, Inc., 1950), pp. 265–66.

52. Sebastian DeGrazia, The Political Community: A Study of Anomie (Chicago: University of Chicago Press, 1948), pp. 59–71.

53. Samuel Eliot Morrison and Henry Steel Commager, The Growth of the Republic (New York: Oxford University Press, 1937), Vol. I, 391–92.

54. Alexis DeTocqueville, Democracy in America, Tr. by Henry Reever (New York: Century & Co., 1898), Vol. 11, 163–64.

55. George Santayana, Character and Opinion in the United States (Garden City, New York: Anchor Books), p. 108.

56. Federalist Paper No. 10.

57. To be sure, "the abundance of land" was able to do this only through the assistance of government land policies which did a fairly effective job of meeting the settlers' minimum request for first opportunities to acquire title to as much land as the usual family could handle with its own labor and the most productive technologies available.

58. Radoje Nikolitch, "Family and Larger Than Family Farms: Their Relative Position in American Agriculture," Agricultural Economic Report No. 4, Economic Research Service, USDA, Washington, D.C., January, 1962, Fig. 6, p. 23, Table 21, p. 40.

59. Ibid, Table 16, p. 29.

ROSS B. TALBOT

# The Political Forces

EVERY POLITICAL SYSTEM is a fusion, an interaction, of theories and conditions. Theories concerning the nature of man, the "good life" which man does or should seek, and the legitimacy of the methods to be used in the process of achieving those goals, are intrinsic to any political system. The conditions are those of time, place, and environment. Ideals are confronted by economic and social realities. The vision of the politician and political man needs to stretch forth and proclaim the hopes and expectations of the future, but the imagery must not reach beyond our abilities, not at least if we wish to live within a free, orderly, and progressive society.

## THE CONSTITUTIONAL CONVENTION OF 1787

Such at least were the beliefs, with very few exceptions, of those who were in attendance at the Constitutional Convention of 1787. The enduring quality of that momentous conclave was its shrewd sense of realism combined with the desire to make this nation more powerful, its people more prosperous, its individuals freer, and its institutions more stable and orderly. Whether one is an adherent or admirer of the Fiske, the Jensen, Beard, or McDonald thesis is beside the point here. Rather the contention is that the United States Constitution sets up the structure, allocates and denies certain powers, and determines general procedures within our political system. Time and man have molded and modified the basic document but in a discourse on the political forces giving rise to land policy within the United States it seems to be the essence of political logic to begin the presentation with a brief statement concerning the political system itself. Indeed, all of our political conflicts have been resolved more or less peacefully (with one gigantic exception), within this constitutional framework.

Perhaps familiarity breeds pedantry but let us reflect for one moment on the Constitutional Convention of 1787 and the product thereof—the Constitution of the United States. The delegates to that convention wanted to bring forth a national government which would have the power and therefore the resources to help build a prosperous, free, and dynamic nation. This must be done, however, with a clear understanding that man's nature was selfish, if not depraved.[1] Federalist Paper Number 10 is still our most penetrating exposition of this point of view. Because of this human condition, power must be made to counteract power, and it must be understood that "the accumulation of all powers, legislative, executive, and judiciary, in the same hands, whether of one, a few, or many, and whether hereditary, self-appointed, or elective, may justly be pronounced the very definition of tyranny."[2] In truth, these men were generally concerned about the abuses of power, but, specifically, they were more perturbed about the abuses of majority rule. They believed, perhaps too readily, that the ordinary processes of democratic government would check minorities. What must be done was to prevent a rash, precipitate, even vulgar majority from acting so as to deny "justice" and bring about "anarchy."

The result was an anomaly; a democratic republic in which policy and programs (legislation) would be the outgrowth of decisions made by a concurrence of minorities. Internally, ". . . the legislative, executive, and judiciary departments ought to be separate and distinct."[3] While, "in the extended republic of the United States, and among the great varieties of interests, parties, and sects which it embraces, a coalition of a majority of the whole society could seldom take place on any other principles than those of justice and the general good."[4]

Rather than elaborate the obvious, I shall state in capsule form what you already know. The product of this Convention was a written Constitution which: (1) limited the powers of the national and state governments; (2) created a federal system in that certain governmental powers were allocated to both governments; (3) established a separation of powers so that the executive, legislative, and judicial would each have "a will of its own"; (4) further divided the Congress because in "republican government, the legislative authority necessarily predominates," and there is needed "a remedy for this inconvenience"; (5) by implication, at least as interpreted by Hamilton and, later, Chief Justice Marshall, Article 3 gave the Supreme Court the power of judicial review; (6) provided for an amending process which if not torturous was certainly formidable; and (7) showed their contempt of political parties by all the foregoing arrangements.

A recent and most persuasive article by John Roche indicates that very practical political considerations forced Madison and others into accepting a political instrument which checked and divided power quite beyond their choosing.[5] In other words, the Virginia Plan (fathered by Madison, although first presented by Randolph) would have given us a stronger national government, more chastened state government, and perhaps, a parliamentary system. Even if one finds Roche's analysis convincing—and I do—the fact still remains that the art of politics called for the acceptance of a partial loaf rather than no bread at all. The less powerful states simply pushed the Nationalists into a federal system and presidential government, so to speak—somewhat exaggeratedly. From political necessity, if not from philosophic preference, our political system is one in which power is diffused and distributed in a most complex manner.

## THE STATICS AND DYNAMICS OF AMERICAN POLITICAL INSTITUTIONS, RELATIVE TO LAND POLICIES

It is now further contended that this political system has really given us many forms of "government," and that each of these so-called "governments" constitutes a center, or core, of political power. True, no one of these power centers will probably be able to perform each of the traditional functions of government alone: nevertheless, it may be strong enough to thwart the acceptance of a policy which it cannot accept, or which places its own power position in jeopardy. Here again, my generalizations will proceed substantially beyond the evidence offered but there seems to be no viable alternative.

### Constitutional Government

A somewhat tattered axiom in political science says that constitutional government means, by definition, that the powers of government are limited. Thus, those who declare the scope and extent of the limitations become power-holders in our political system. Our acceptance of the doctrine of judicial review lends much credence to Chief Justice Hughes' dictum that "the Constitution is what the Supreme Court says it is." When Chief Justice Marshall observed that "it is a Constitution we are expounding," and began to permit some considerable stretch in the necessary and proper clause, it became evident that the United States Supreme Court, in particular, had assumed the role of a powerful policy maker in the American political system.

What will be the Court's role in the future development of public and private land policies? An answer depends on the courses of action taken by other political forces—private interest groups, state governments, federal departments, and the like. Our federal courts do not initiate action, rather they attempt to arbitrate conflicts within the provisions of the Constitution.

The Hoosac Mills Case,[6] although not directly aimed at the use of private farm land, showed the impact the Court had, and could again have, in the area of farm policy. True, the Court's rather narrow interpretation of the taxing-power clause and its strong emphasis on the doctrine of reserved powers was later reversed in the *Mulford* v. *Smith* decision, and the elastic clause was given a full stretching in the decision of *Wickard* v. *Filburn*.[7] Congress leaned on the spending power in the passage of the Soil Conservation and Domestic Allotment Act of 1936 and the constitutionality of the act has not been questioned, partly because of the difficulty of taxpayers' suits. Provided that due process procedures have been carefully adhered to, it would seem that the Supreme Court would uphold in the future the use of the power of eminent domain and of legislation based on the commerce and spending power, as all of these affected private lands. Private property can only be taken for public use through due process, and with just compensation, therefore constitutional questions might arise if the national government should engage in large-scale land retirement programs.

As to the public lands, the Supreme Court ruled in 1941 that the federal government's power of eminent domain extended to state lands, even when the taking interfered with the states' water and conservation projects.[8] The constitutional questions pertaining to water have posed much more complex and, even yet, baffling problems for the Court. These issues will not be reviewed here but they do affect public and private land policies. Such legal conflicts pertain to contests between the national government and the states, the states themselves, and individuals— including corporations versus the national and state governments. The "water problem" in the United States is only beginning; the legal headaches in this area are by no means all behind us.

More pertinent to public land policy, however, will be the mentioned problems of procedural due process. Legal difficulties will surely arise from the administration of the new Cape Cod seashore because the National Park Service will be administering an area in which substantial development of private property already exists. Zoning restrictions, for example, will probably be intricate and tedious.

In summary, constitutional government will throw few roadblocks in the path of the national government if it watches how it proceeds in the enforcement of public and private land policies. Water is quite another matter, let it be noted.

FEDERAL GOVERNMENT

By definition, federal government is a form of political system which requires a formal division of powers between national and state governments. The division cannot be precise, therefore conflict situations do arise. Consequently, unique political controversies occur within a federally organized nation-state.

During the nineteenth century the prevailing doctrine seemed to be dual federalism. That is, the national government had certain powers; the state governments had others, and ne'er the twain shall meet. Dual federalism was, however, more theoretical than real. The Homestead Act itself is a splendid example of what has come to be called cooperative, or functional, federalism.

The federal grants-in-aid system came about because state governments would not, or could not, act to meet the rising demands and expectations of the ever-increasing interest groups. Morton Grodzins and the University of Chicago's Center for the Study of American Federalism have developed what Grodzins refers to as "the marble-cake theory" of American federalism.[9] That is, he believes the cooperative aspects of national-state relations were prevalent even in the nineteenth century and that dual federalism (a sort of two-layer cake idea) was an erroneous concept because the exercise of governmental powers has historically been intertwined and interwoven into the actions of both these governments. Certainly the Morrill Act of 1862 and the Hatch Act of 1887 lend credence to his thesis.

More recently, the Clarke-McNary Act of 1924 brought cooperative federalism into play in the area of fire protection on national, state, and even private forest lands. In 1935, the Soil Conservation Act, and subsequent enabling legislation by the states, permitted the formation of soil conservation districts.

On the administrative side too, there are many examples of national-state-local cooperation in the area of public and private land policies concerning such matters as parks, reservoir planning and management, recreational facilities, and zoning.

There are those who view the whole grants-in-aid scheme as a form of bribery and intimidation by the national government. The majority opinion seems to be that the system works well, for the most part, because it enables the national government to inspire, or at least to induce, the states to do some thirty-seven different kinds of tasks which, without the inducement, they would either not perform at all or at a reduced pace.

The federal government is more an instrument through which political forces bring to bear their own interests than a political force itself. The push-and-tug that these interests exert on the federal concept is, however, important to the development of land policies in the United States, and will be even more so in the future. Furthermore, and importantly, the federal system is a symbol too—a symbol which conveys a belief in the American tradition of local self-government and in the integrity of the idea of statehood.

## CONGRESSIONAL GOVERNMENT

Recently Senator Mike Mansfield, majority floor leader of the United States Senate, is reported to have remarked: "The brains are in the committees."[10] It is my further contention that a good deal of the political brawn is there also. More explicitly, the major congressional decisions concerning public and private lands are made in committees. Since the passage of the Legislative Reorganization Act of 1946, there has been an increase in the influence of the Senate policy committees of both parties. Nevertheless, it seems fair to generalize that the more streamlined, concentrated, and better-staffed standing (permanent) committees have retained their potency and prestige. "Congressional government," writes George Galloway, "is in large part, government by committee."[11] The inconstancy of party responsibility has meant that the necessity for the exercise of power has brought along with it additional accretions of authority for the House and Senate standing committees.

Even a general analysis of the structure and functions of these committees cannot be entered into here. Table 1 indicates the committees and subcommittees in the 87th Congress (1961–62) which are most powerful in the development of national land policies. Furthermore, the table is designed to show the geographic, or sectional, strength of the committees. Also, it reveals but does not explain, the wider diversity of membership on the appropriations subcommittees (II). Seniority governs, for the most part, in matters of appointment to the committee and certainly for promotions to chairmanship of the committee. As Senator Humphrey recently quipped: "The longer I'm in the Senate the more I admire the seniority rule."

There are certainly exceptions to the rule but committee action generally controls congressional decisions. A study by the writer of the House and Senate Committees on Agriculture (and Forestry, in the Senate) in the 86th Congress (1959–60) indicated that only one bill out of ten is reported out of committee but nine times out of ten that bill will then pass in the respective house.[12] With regard to appropriations, the recommendations of the committee are seldom changed by floor debate and in fact, the subcommittee action is usually crucial in the appropriations process. The data in Table 1 (III) uphold this contention.

## TABLE 1

### HOUSE AND SENATE COMMITTEES AND SUBCOMMITTEES CONCERNED WITH LAND POLICIES (87TH CONGRESS, 2ND SESSION, 1961)

| House | Senate |
|---|---|
| *I. House Committee on Agriculture* | *I. Senate Committee on Agriculture and Forestry* |
| 1. Committee membership: 21 Demo., 14 Rep. | 1. Committee membership: 11 Demo., 6 Rep. |
| 2. Committee chairman: Harold Cooley (N.C.) | 2. Committee chairman: Allen Ellender (La.) |
| 3. Sectional basis of the majority of membership: | 3. Sectional basis of the majority of membership: |
|   a. *Demo.*    b. *Rep.*<br>  South—14    North Central—9 |   a. *Demo.*    b. *Rep.*<br>  South—6    North Central—3 |
| 4. Chairman of subcommittees—14 (all Demo.)<br>  a. South—10    North Central—4 | 4. Chairman of subcommittees—4 (all Demo.)<br>  a. South—4 |
| *II. House Committee on Appropriations* | *II. Senate Committee on Appropriations* |
| 1. Committee membership: 30 Demo., 20 Rep. | 1. Committee membership: 17 Demo., 10 Rep. |
| 2. Committee chairman: Clarence Cannon (Mo.) | 2. Committee chairman: Carl Hayden (Ariz.) |
| 3. Subcommittees: | 3. Subcommittees: |
|   a. Department of Agriculture and related agencies Whitten (Miss.) Chairman |   a. Department of Agriculture and related agencies Russell (Ga.) Chairman |
| *Demo.*    *Rep.*<br>Natcher (Ky.)    Anderson (Minn.)<br>Santangelo (N.Y.)    Horan (Wash.)<br>Slack (W.Va.)    Michel (Ill.) | *Demo.*    *Rep.*<br>Hayden (Ariz.)    Young (N.D.)<br>Hill (Ala.)    Mundt (S.D.)<br>Robertson (Va.)    Dworshak (Idaho)<br>Holland (Fla.)    Hruska (Neb.)<br>Stennis (Miss.)    Case (S.D.)<br>McGee (Wyo.)    Aiken (ex officio) (Ver.)<br>Humphrey (Minn.)<br>Ellender (ex officio) (La.)<br>Johnston (ex officio) (S.C.) |
|   b. Department of Interior and related agencies Kirwan (Ohio) Chairman |   b. Department of Interior and related agencies Hayden (Ariz.) Chairman |

# TABLE 1 (CONT.)

| House | Senate |
|---|---|

**House**

| Demo. | Rep. |
|---|---|
| Magnuson (Wash.) | Jensen (Iowa) |
| Denton (Ind.) | Fenton (Pa.) |

c. Public Works
Cannon (Mo.) Chairman

| Demo. | Rep. |
|---|---|
| Kirwan (Ohio) | Jensen (Iowa) |
| Fogarty (R.I.) | Taber (N.Y.) |
| Evans (Tenn.) | Fenton (Pa.) |
| Boland (Miss.) | Andersen (Minn.) |
| Magnuson (Wash.) | Pillion (N.Y.) |
| Whitten (Miss.) | |

III. *House Committee on Interior and Insular Affairs*
1. Committee membership: 18 Demo., 13 Rep.
2. Committee chairman: Wayne Aspinall (Colo.)
3. Sectional basis of the majority of membership

| a. *Demo.* | b. *Rep.* |
|---|---|
| West—11 | West—6 |

4. Chairman of subcommittees—(All Demo.)
a. South—4
West—1
East—1

**Senate**

| Demo. | Rep. |
|---|---|
| Chavez (N.M.) | Mundt (S.D.) |
| Russell (Ga.) | Young (N.D.) |
| McClellan (Ark.) | Dworshak (Idaho) |
| Kefauver (Tenn.) | Kuchel (Calif.) |
| Bible (Nev.) | |
| Byrd (W.Va.) | |
| McGee (Wyo.) | |
| Humphrey (Minn.) | |

c. Bureau of Reclamation and Interior Marketing Power Agencies (a unit of the Public Works Subcommittee)

| Demo. | Rep. |
|---|---|
| Hayden (Ariz.) | Mundt (S.D.) |
| Ellender (La.) | Young (N.D.) |
| Magnuson (Wash.) | Dworshak (Idaho) |
| Russell (Ga.) | |
| McClellan (Ark.) | |
| Holland (Fla.) | |

III. *Senate Committee on Interior and Insular Affairs*
1. Committee membership—11 Demo., 6 Rep.
2. Committee chairman—Clinton Anderson (N. Mex.)
3. Sectional basis of the majority of membership

| a. *Demo.* | b. *Rep.* |
|---|---|
| West—10 | West—3 |

4. Chairman of subcommittees—5 (all Demo.)
a. West—5

Source: Congressional Quarterly, *Weekly Report*, "Special Report," March 2, 1962.

145

## Party Government

A favorite pastime at meetings of political scientists is to debate the merits and demerits of our decentralized party system. In the concluding section of this paper the controversy will be developed, at least at its core. For the moment let us simply note that we have a conglomeration of political parties in the United States. David Truman's essay, "Federalism and the Party system," points up the condition.[13] We have two major presidential parties which are somewhat in prominence at all times but notably on even-numbered years at four-year intervals, and congressional parties, House and Senate, with subparties (factions) within each party. Individual senatorial parties, state parties, and constituency parties add to the length of the list and magnitude of the confusion.

Political parties are clearly political forces and are involved in the determination of land policies. However, the diffused and decentralized nature of the nomination and election processes means that the congressional politician is, in a real sense, his own party—Democratic or Republican. He must fight for his state or constituency interests or he may well not be re-elected; he must seek appointment to the "right" committees in the House or Senate so that he will be in a position to fight effectively for those interests. As the old saying goes, a Senator has two years, after re-election, during which he can be a statesman, but a Representative must always be a politician because he is always running for re-election.

The impact that this decentralized party system and the geographically oriented congressional committees have on the development of land policies is considerable indeed. In coalition with other "governments," the Midwest, Great Plains, and South have determined national private land policies, while the western states have written the public land policies. The political structure of power is in the process of change and the possible outcome of these shifts will be referred to later on.

## Presidential Government

Among the numerous and prescient insights of Alexis de Tocqueville was his observation that "executive power" would increase in the United States as we moved from an isolated nation to a world power. The history of "strong" Presidents in the United States is also a history of crisis situations. Some contend that Theodore Roosevelt created his own crisis. Others observe that not only has the nagging and awesome issue of war or peace—now, hot war or cold war—been a major cause in the growth of presidential leadership but so has the internal issue of prosperity versus recession and depression. We have been able to overcome some of the dispersive effects of congressional weak-party interest-group government through dynamic presidential leadership.

However, Richard Neustadt's study points out the limitations of presidential power.[14] A President does not order and then the army engineers obey. His continuing and ever-challenging task is to guide the nation along the road of national interest, as he sees that interest, all the while pulling, cajoling, needling, pleading, and jabbing those who are inclined to veer in a different direction or move at too slow a pace. Because of his limited resources the President has to establish priorities, and adjust his strategy to accomplish his objectives.

Theodore Roosevelt made masterful strides forward in the area of public land policy. Franklin Roosevelt was able to do likewise because of his avid interest in conservation, the depression, and his astute political abilities. He also strongly influenced the first large-scale conservation efforts for private lands. Since 1941 the nation has not been at peace and this condition has clearly affected public land policy. Presidents Truman and Eisenhower were primarily involved in matters of foreign relations and the nation's economic health. President Kennedy has assumed the role of the "new frontiersman" and seems to be pressing for a revival of the spirit and vigor of the Roosevelts in the areas of public and private land policy.

GOVERNMENT BY INTEREST GROUPS

A recent volume entitled *National Organizations of the United States* contains the names of something over nineteen thousand groups.[15] All of them are potentially or actively engaged in influencing policy, and often they are involved in more direct forms of partisan political activity. Political scientists are engrossed in a debate of at least minor magnitude as to the effectiveness of these organizations. In the late 1920's, Peter Odegard and Pendleton Herring called them pressure groups and the fad came to be: the "pressure boys" really run the government. Then, with the later studies of these groups by V. O. Key, David Truman, and E. E. Schattschneider, we began to see them in more balanced proportion. Now the fashion seems to be to depreciate interest groups ("interest" presumably being a less value-oriented term than "pressure") because of their lack of representativeness, narrow base of constituent support, and the like.

This recent trend appears to be close to the realities of American politics but no student, I believe, of our Congress would deny the influence and sometimes control of these groups in, or over, the policy-making process. The controversy centers around such relative matters of degree as efficacy, intensity, frequency, and latency—sort of a modern version of the old Benthamite calculus.

A few more generalizations will have to suffice here. First, we need to see that the orientation and alignments of interest groups are different for private land policies as contrasted to those for public lands, although some organizations such as the American Farm Bureau Federation and the National Farmers Union are involved in both. Next, most of these groups are of the "self-oriented" variety.[16] All of them will proclaim the dominence of the national interest over an obvious special interest, but their policies invariably reveal that the rationalizations of organized groups are at least as prevalent as those of harried individuals.

Third, and importantly in the area of public land policies, there are "promotional" interest groups: those who do not have a direct economic interest in the area of their concern but do feel strongly that their goals should be promoted.[17] The Izaak Walton League of America and the National Audubon Society, among many others, are in this category. As this nation becomes more metropolitan, these promotional groups, particularly the recreational and nature-loving varieties, will become more powerful in the arena of American politics.

Also, there are clientele groups such as the National Rural Electric Cooperative Association, the National Association of Soil Conservation Districts, and the National Reclamation Association. Their "clients" are the Rural Electrification Administration (REA), the Soil Conservation Service, and the Bureau of Reclamation, respectively. The National Reclamation Association may be, in fact, the creation of the Bureau of Reclamation.[18] There is a mutual "back-scratching" which goes on between such public and private interest groups and, when fused with the "proper" crannies of power in Congress, these alliances are formidable.

Finally, we must realize these interest groups are often in conflict with one another. David Riesman's thesis is that these conflicts have brought about a new form of "veto" power.[19] In other words, no powerful group, or segment of groups, can get what it wants but does have the strength to prevent the balance of power from being moved against its real or avowed interests. I do not quite accept Riesman's concept for reasons which I shall advance, but his thesis does provide us with useful insights into the condition of interest groups in the United States today.

GOVERNMENT BY BUREAUCRACY

The core of modern government is bureaucracy, according to Carl Friedrich.[20] That is, the power and necessity of modern government mean that public policies need to be administered by professionals who will, at least so long as they maintain their professional competence and personal integrity, be certain of tenure and assured of promotion. One thinks immediately of the SCS, BLM, Forest Service, National Park Service, Bureau of Reclamation, and the Agricultural Research Service. The Agricultural Stabilization and Conservation Service (ASCS) is a somewhat different breed—an amalgam of professional bureaucrats and political administrators at the national level, along with political, professional, and some patronage appointees at the state level, and elected and semiprofessional officials at the county and local levels.

The professional forester, engineer, conservationist, and economist are vital to the success of modern government. That point hardly seems debatable, but we should raise an issue or two concerning the role of the professional public bureaucrat. What should be the power of the professional in the development of public policies? Do watershed projects which are financed under the provisions of the Watershed Act of 1954 (Public Law 566) come about because of the desires and demands of the local constituents; or is the steering committee actually under the guidance and direction of the "grass roots" bureaucrat? Do not the activities of the ASCS and the Bureau of Reclamation lend credence, at least in some instances, to the usefulness of Parkinson's law—that is, a little bureaucracy continuously grows in numbers and appropriations, and produces more and more of what we need less and less? To ask a question is not to foreordain an answer but surely we can say that reclamation projects, the ACP program (Agricultural Conservation Payments), small watersheds, and other such programs are clear examples of the importance of government by bureaucracy.

## Government by "the Public" and "the Publics"

One important piece of political mythology in the United States is the idea of government by public opinion, to use Lord Bryce's phrase. As with most myths perhaps, its usefulness comes from the idealism and sense of aspiration and hope which are imbedded within it. Recent studies of American politics indicate rather sharply that the American, as a voter, has only a general notion of tendencies in regard to the matter of ideologies and issues. Table 2 has been extracted from *The American Voter* study and speaks to this point.[21] It denotes the superficial level of understanding and interest of the individual voter in a mass society. To talk about "what society wants," and "what the public thinks," is both useless and hopeless in terms of specific issues.

TABLE 2
LEVELS OF UNDERSTANDING OF MAJOR PARTIES AND
CANDIDATES WITH RESPECT TO DOMESTIC POLICY, 1956

| Level of Understanding | Proportion of Voters |
| --- | --- |
| I. Ideology | 3% |
| II. Near Ideology | 9 |
| III. Group Benefits | 42 |
| IV. Nature of the Times | 24 |
| V. No Issue or Policy Content | 22 |
| Total | 100% |

John Dewey's concept of the pluralistic publics is much more helpful. There is no general public opinion in regard to the programs of the Forest Service or the Bureau of Reclamation. There are many publics composed of substantial numbers of farmers and ranchers, private utility companies, hunters and fishermen, small town businessmen, and others who, concerned about the policies of those bureaucratic organizations, will try to influence those policies in varying fashion and with relative effectiveness.

The congressman from Iowa's Fourth Congressional District will be definitely concerned about the reactions of certain publics in his district relative to the impact of a soil bank program. Neither he nor they will be noticeably moved about the King's River project in California or the allocation of water from the Upper Colorado River program. The parochial nature of American politics transforms these publics into political forces. The function of the congressional politician is to understand not public opinion but the opinion of publics in his district or state. Interest groups are an indicator for him but he has come to treat their protestations and threats with respectful skepticism.

## GOVERNMENT BY OPINION-MAKERS AND OPINION-SAMPLERS

The public relations expert and the professional pollster are somewhat recent additions to the political scene. It is safe to say they have become political forces in our system of government but hazardous to estimate the extent of their influence. From Smokey the Bear to Associate Justice Douglas is quite a jump in appearance and intellect, but not so much in terms of outlook.[22] The Forest Service and the National Wildlife Federation have made Smokey into a symbol which connotes certain desires for the conservation of the forests and their natural inhabitants. Justice Douglas, although speaking to a different audience in a much more intellectual fashion, is still trying to make us realize why modern man needs the wilderness, and lots of it.

The pollsters have become a fixed cost in all major political campaigns. The candidates want to know what we are thinking and what we plan to do, in terms of issues and candidates. The opinion-sampler's job is to find out. We need not probe into the advantages and deficiencies of this new profession. However, we can say that Samuel Lubell and Louis Harris have become a modern version of a political divining rod.

In summary, public and private land policies in the United States are an outgrowth of the demands and denials of an aggregation of "governments." Pluralism and diversity characterize the American political system, and policy and program are the outgrowth of these many "governments" in conflict. One importance of the case-study method in the area of public policy is that it enables us, when the skill of the analyst is equal to his task, to see how these many forces operate in the arena of partisan politics. Political scientists are not able to contribute much to such important matters as maximum allowable soil losses, sustained yields, flow-rates, and biological controls, but we should be of some value in analyzing the power struggles and value conflicts which occur in those and many other decision-making areas involving land policies, public and private.

## THE APPROPRIATIONS PROCESS AND LAND POLICIES

Table 3 is an attempt at political shorthand. Each of the five bureaus and services—Bureau of Land Management, Bureau of Reclamation, and the National Park Service in the Department of Interior; the Forest Service and the Soil Conservation Service in the Department of Agriculture—have a particular, even peculiar, structure of power.

Each of these bureaucratic organizations has become, within the last few decades, a center of political power in itself—a sun, to use Lubell's term, which other satellites hover over, strike at, or break away from.[23] The over all strategy of each of these subdepartments has come to be one of increasing the "governments" which can be of assistance as it seeks to broaden the scope of its orbit.

The magic formula in each instance, although to varying degrees, is the multiple-purpose concept—flood control; soil conservation; recreation facilities; preservation of certain animal and plant life; water management for farm, city and industry; electric power; and aesthetic improvements. Each of these ends becomes a means and the bureaucracy comes to be an instrument which seeks to create and foster different forms of "the good life."

Each of these bureaucracies is immersed in the political process; therefore political techniques are a necessary tool for the protection and advancement of the organization. One might look upon the whole scene as a sort of serpentine continuum. Begin with the initiation of the legislation (possibly by a private interest group, probably by the public interest group), then the tussle with the Bureau of the Budget, over to the authorization committee in the House and Senate (that is, the Committees on Agriculture and Interior Affairs) and not overlooking at this stage the importance of subcommittees, on to the House Rules Committee, then later the rather unimportant—but occasionally volatile—floor action by the House and Senate, finally the compromising, split-the-difference conference committees whose decisions just about have to be accepted by their respective house.[24] Then, assuming the President signs the bill, the process starts all over again for the funds needed to implement the legislation. An authorization, need it be stated, is not an appropriation.

If we highlight the political forces which are brought to bear on and by these bureaucracies, the picture looks, in very general terms, as follows:

*The Bureau of Land Management.*—In late 1960, the BLM brought into public view its Project 2012. By the year 2012, $4.1 billion will be needed for some 470 million acres of public land under BLM jurisdiction in order to advance significantly conservation practices, forage production, timber yields, roads, and recreational facilities on those lands. To do this job, the BLM will need to have about $79 million in appropriations, on a yearly average and assuming constant dollar values, for 52 years.[25] The appropriations for fiscal 1962 was nearly $33.4 million, the highest in BLM history.

The principal political force in opposition to the BLM seems to be the cattle interests. The Taylor Grazing Act of 1934, the advisory boards with their built-in dominance by the cattlemen, the inability or lack of desire of the members of Congress from the western states to thwart the will of the livestock producers, the divisions within the BLM of the "disposers" (those who want to assist in bringing about the transfer of public lands to private

## TABLE 3

### The Appropriations Process

(Regular annual appropriations for certain Bureaus and Services in the Departments of Agriculture and Interior for fiscal years 1954 through 1962 in dollars.)

| Name of Department and Bureaus | Fiscal Year | Budget Requests | House Appropriations Committee | House Floor Action | Senate Appropriations Committee | Senate Floor Action | Conference Committee Reports | Final Appropriation[a] |
|---|---|---|---|---|---|---|---|---|
| *Department of Interior* | | 15,085,000[b] | | | | | | |
| (1) Bureau of Land Management | 1954 | 13,746,000 | 13,000,000 | 13,000,000 | 13,746,000 | 13,746,000 | 13,483,000 | 13,483,000 |
| | 1955 | 14,625,000 | 13,483,000 | 13,483,000 | 15,413,000 | 15,413,000 | 14,413,000 | 14,413,000 |
| | 1956 | 16,487,000 | 15,700,000 | 15,700,000 | 15,800,000 | 15,800,000 | 15,750,000 | 15,750,000 |
| | 1957 | 23,278,000 | 22,500,000 | 22,500,000 | 23,238,600 | 23,238,600 | 22,969,300 | 22,969,300 |
| | 1958 | 28,720,000 | 28,500,000 | 28,500,000 | 27,480,000 | 27,480,000 | 27,480,000 | 27,480,000 |
| | 1959 | 25,375,000 | 25,375,000 | 25,375,000 | 27,625,000 | 27,625,000 | 26,875,000 | 26,875,000 |
| | 1960 | 29,577,000 | 29,523,000 | 29,523,000 | 25,077,000 | 25,077,000 | 25,602,000 | 25,602,000 |
| | 1961 | 24,875,000 | 24,875,000 | 24,875,000 | 28,904,000 | 28,904,000 | 26,300,000 | 26,300,000 |
| | | 31,092,000[c] | | | | | | |
| | 1962 | 34,050,000 | 33,250,000 | 33,250,000 | 35,494,000 | 35,494,000 | 33,350,000 | 33,350,000 |
| (2) Bureau of Reclamation | | 231,188,000[b] | | | | | | |
| | 1954 | 177,350,000 | 133,146,675 | 133,146,675 | 153,279,450 | 153,279,450 | 143,669,660 | 143,669,660 |
| | 1955 | 155,410,000 | 140,179,700 | 140,179,700 | 164,190,127 | 164,190,127 | 155,687,000 | 155,687,000 |
| | 1956 | 179,616,000 | 145,090,442 | 178,745,000 | 180,095,000 | 180,095,000 | 179,995,000 | 179,995,000 |
| | 1957 | 174,170,000 | 174,668,223 | 174,668,223 | 183,624,223 | 183,624,223 | 179,974,223 | 179,974,223 |
| | 1958 | 199,312,000 | 174,688,223 | 167,612,000 | 183,624,223 | 188,850,000 | 181,114,500 | 181,114,500 |
| | 1959 | 269,101,000 | 245,739,200 | 246,739,200 | 263,730,335 | 263,730,335 | 255,577,335 | 255,577,335 |
| | 1960 | 251,196,000 | 253,409,500 | 253,409,500 | 263,872,500 | 263,872,500 | 256,250,250 | 256,250,250 |
| | 1961 | 301,314,000 | 277,362,705 | 277,362,705 | 292,559,025 | 292,559,025 | 280,113,705 | 280,113,705 |
| | 1962 | 296,910,000 | 274,983,500 | 274,983,500 | 278,751,000 | 278,751,000 | 274,408,100 | 274,408,100 |
| (3) National Park Service | | 40,019,000[b] | | | | | | |
| | 1954 | 36,169,000 | 32,971,550 | 32,971,550 | 34,070,850 | 34,070,850 | 33,770,850 | 33,770,850 |
| | 1955 | 28,468,000 | 25,956,099 | 25,956,099 | 27,880,099 | 27,880,099 | 26,663,489 | 26,663,489 |
| | 1956 | 44,650,000 | 43,350,000 | 43,304,300 | 45,380,700 | 45,380,700 | 45,029,300 | 45,029,300 |

154

TABLE 3 (CONT.)

| Name of Department and Bureaus | Fiscal Year | Budget Requests | House Appropriations Committee | House Floor Action | Senate Appropriations Committee | Senate Floor Action | Conference Committee Reports | Final Appropriation[a] |
|---|---|---|---|---|---|---|---|---|
| (3) National Park Service (cont.) | 1957 | 71,713,000 | 67,688,000 | 67,680,000 | 67,995,000 | 68,020,000 | 68,020,000 | 68,020,000 |
| | 1958 | 78,651,000 | 77,580,000 | 77,580,000 | 75,423,000 | 75,423,000 | 75,480,000 | 75,480,000 |
| | 1959 | 62,362,000 | 61,480,000 | 61,480,000 | 74,712,000 | 74,712,000 | 70,137,000 | 70,137,000 |
| | 1960 | 80,075,000 | 73,254,000 | 73,254,000 | 79,722,000 | 79,722,000 | 79,722,000 | 79,722,000 |
| | 1961 | 86,311,000 / 100,608,000[c] | 82,985,000 | 82,985,000 | 88,149,125 | 88,149,125 | 83,060,000 | 83,060,000 |
| | 1962 | 111,608,000 | 103,771,000 | 104,771,000 | 112,413,000 | 112,413,000 | 105,712,500 | 105,712,500 |
| USDA (1) Forest Service | 1954 | 65,136,000 | 65,429,408 | 65,429,408 | 67,985,708 | 67,985,708 | 66,433,408 | 66,433,408 |
| | 1955 | 71,601,500 | 72,400,000 | 74,427,671 | 75,662,190 | 75,662,190 | 74,774,890 | 74,774,890 |
| | 1956 | 84,623,000 | 84,536,890 | 84,536,890 | 93,826,690 | 93,826,690 | 90,315,129 | 90,315,129 |
| | 1957 | 96,773,000 | 96,773,000 | 96,773,000 | 106,348,500 | 106,348,500 | 100,960,750 | 100,960,750 |
| | 1958 | 126,896,000 | 118,456,000 | 118,456,000 | 119,206,000 | 119,206,000 | 118,956,000 | 118,956,000 |
| | 1959 | 116,129,000 | 116,980,000 | 116,980,000 | 140,280,000 | 140,280,000 | 129,555,000 | 129,555,000 |
| | 1960 | 128,200,000 | 129,813,000 | 129,813,000 | 128,220,000 | 128,220,000 | 130,220,000 | 130,220,000 |
| | 1961 | 149,536,500 | 149,286,500 | 149,286,500 | 169,096,000 | 169,096,000 | 153,576,500 | 153,576,500 |
| | 1962 | 198,764,000 | 194,438,000 | 194,438,000 | 233,273,200 | 233,573,200 | 208,418,000 | 208,418,000 |
| (2) Soil Conservation Service | 1954 | 66,491,000 | 61,269,514 | 61,269,514 | 61,629,014 | 61,629,014 | 61,629,014 | 61,629,014 |
| | 1955 | 66,117,000 | 70,600,000 | 71,427,671 | 73,047,671 | 73,047,671 | 72,547,671 | 72,547,671 |
| | 1956 | 75,396,200 | 80,612,579 | 80,612,579 | 82,000,000 | 82,000,000 | 81,300,000 | 81,300,000 |
| | 1957 | 92,147,000 | 97,232,000 | 97,232,000 | 97,232,000 | 97,232,000 | 97,232,000 | 97,232,000 |
| | 1958 | 112,615,000 | (d) | (d) | 112,615,000 | 112,615,000 | 111,615,000 | 111,615,000 |
| | 1959 | 124,615,000 | 128,615,000 | 128,615,000 | 128,615,000 | 128,615,000 | 128,615,000 | 128,615,000 |
| | 1960 | 128,647,000 | 133,397,000 | 133,397,000 | 127,397,000 | 127,397,000 | 133,147,000 | 133,147,000 |
| | 1961 | 135,632,000 | 143,132,000 | 143,132,000 | 143,132,000 | 146,132,000 | 146,132,000 | 146,132,000 |
| | 1962 | 173,143,000 | 178,680,000 | 178,680,000 | 175,911,500 | 175,911,500 | 178,680,000 | 178,680,000 |

[a] Does *not* include supplemental appropriations.
[b] Top line=Truman's budget.
Bottom line=Eisenhower's budget.
[c] Top line=Eisenhower's budget.
Bottom line=Kennedy's budget.
[d] A lump sum appropriation was made for SCS and the Soil Bank ррrogram. House action was reversed by the conference committee.
Source: (1) Senate and House Appropriations Committees, *Committee Reports* and *Conference Reports*, 1954–62 fiscal years.
(2) *Congressional Quarterly Almanac*, 1953–1961.

owners) versus the "managers" (those who want to maintain and advance the public administration of these lands)[26] are all conditions, among several others which the Calef and Foss studies set forth, that point to the political impotence of the BLM.[27]

In view of this weakness, the Department of Interior, under Secretary Udall, has developed a strategy of seeking a new structure of power in order that BLM public lands can be used and developed for more varied and more broadly public purposes. The advisory committees are being reorganized in order to bring in the diverse interests of recreation, irrigation, power, and wildlife. The grazing fee scale will probably be increased so that it will be more in line with that of the Forest Service, and part of the proceeds therefrom could then be used to increase the grants-in-lieu of taxes to local units of government in those areas. Political opposition to this new strategy was less than might have been anticipated. The American Farm Bureau Federation took credit for slowing down, if not impeding some of these program changes, but the tone and substance of the Farm Bureau's criticism was one of quite modest belligerency.[28]

The short-run fate of the 2012 project will be fairly well determined by the appropriations which will be forthcoming within the next two or three years. The issue, in political terms, is this: can the Secretary of Interior and the BLM develop positions of strength which will enable the BLM to acquire those desired appropriations?

*The Bureau of Reclamation.*—A different constellation of power is evident in the Bureau of Reclamation. The strident demands for the development of the arid and semiarid western lands by farm and business interests, the strength of these "publics" within our "committee governments," and the potency of the public and private interest groups in their efforts to protect the Bureau from political damage by adverse groups have transformed this organization into a political success story. Table 3 indicates that the Senate gives considerably more support to the Bureau than does the not-so-western-oriented Subcommittee on Public Works Appropriations in the House. Also, the Bureau of the Budget under Presidents Eisenhower and Kennedy has tried to halt, or slow down, the "new starts" of Bureau projects but, as Table 4 indicates, with no, or only modest, success.

TABLE 4

"New Starts" and the Bureau of Reclamation

| Fiscal Year | President's Budget | Congressional Action | Estimated Ultimate Cost | Funds Provided for Fiscal Year | Authorized Starts Deferred During Year |
|---|---|---|---|---|---|
| 1959 | 0 | 11 | $212,600,000 | $ 6,860,000 | 2 |
| 1960 | 0 | 9 | 114,800,000 | 6,728,000 | 1 |
| 1961[a] | 8 | 8 | 199,700,000 | 13,912,000 | — |
| 1962 | 7 | 9 | 630,500,000[b] | 11,996,000 | — |

[a]Includes "new starts" deferred from previous years.
[b] Includes $483,080,000 for San Luis Unit of the Central Valley project to be constructed in cooperation with the state of California.
Source: Bureau of Reclamation, letter to the author, May 4, 1962.

There does seem to be a good deal of friction between the Bureau and its now prodigal son, the National Reclamation Association, over the public power issue. Also, the Secretary, as well as the Bureau, constantly is asked about the ostensible political illogic of not letting the left hand know what the right hand is doing in regard to land policy—in other words, a Feed Grains Act in 1961 coupled with "new starts" for the Bureau seems to convey a certain amount of inconsistency to the inquisitive. All the while, the Bureau carries on its perennial feud with the Army Engineers. Albeit, this is a success story: shotgun marriages reconcile most of the interorganizational feuding; marriages of convenience keep the private and public power and water interests tolerably happy; and several times each year the Secretary of Interior and the Chief of the Bureau of Reclamation assure the public that no surplus foods are produced on the public-reclaimed lands, and insert a full-page chart in the *1961 Annual Report* of the Department of Interior to prove they are right.[29] Regarding the last contention, Charles Hardin claims he knows of only one agricultural economist who agrees[30] (there must be more!); the editor of Wallaces Farmer says the Bureau is talking "nonsense,"[31] and this political scientist from the Midwest hurriedly observes that sectionalism and localism are more primary forces than logic and the criterion of economic efficiency in the arena of American politics.

However, the strategy of the Bureau is to bring more diversity of political forces within its own orbit. An increasing stress on recreation and wildlife programs in and around the Bureau projects; the maintenance of the preference-customer policy but also placation of the private utility interests (as in the Upper Colorado Basin project); the use of a kind of Malthusian argument, particularly as we look at 1975 and beyond and ask about the availability of adequate food supplies—all these are among the elements of the ongoing strategy of the Bureau of Reclamation.

*The National Park Service.*—In 1956, the condition of the public lands and facilities of the National Park Service were portrayed as follows: "... roads were unsafe, camp grounds run-down and overcrowded and most conditions at a substandard level."[32] Mission 66—a plan for large-scale improvements in the services and facilities of the Service by 1966—was initiated that year. Table 3 indicates that Congress was at least somewhat responsive by 1957 to the demands for increased appropriations.

Other than the Everglades National Park, which attained that status in 1947, no national parks had been added to the domain of the National Park Service from the end of World War II to the establishment of the Cape Cod Seashore in 1961. Our national parks are teeming with citizens and other visitors, and the predictions are for almost fantastic increases in the future, but the NPS appears to be lacking in political support. Promotional interest groups do not seem to have the political acumen and drive that is evident in the self-oriented groups. There are many consumers, so to speak, but a lack of politically effective consumer groups.

On the other hand, one should not underestimate the political strength of the conservation and recreation groups along with the ever-growing "publics." Freeman Tilden's judgment is that "the Service has the backing of hundreds of thousands of organized and ardent conservationists, who swarm forth like wasps when someone throws stones at the nest."[33]

The 85th Congress provided in 1958 for the establishment of the Outdoor Recreation Resources Review Commission (ORRRC) and that commission reported to President Kennedy and the 87th Congress on January 31, 1962.[34] In political terms, the strategy of the present administration is to broaden its base in regard to constituent groups. The challenge to Congress is clear; there is an obvious and rapidly growing need for the expansion of acreage and facilities for our national parks. The national interest, as difficult as the concept is to define, seems apparent, but Congress has thus far displayed considerable reluctance to move forward in this area, although the tempo of advancement is accelerating. State and local governments are faced with the same burgeoning numbers within their own park facilities. General public opinion, even if rather irresolute and amorphous, will call for more positive and orderly legislative action. In some instances— such as the proposed Indiana Dunes Park—the National Park Service is caught between powerful and conflicting interests. Those who want to utilize the contested area for industrial purposes appear to be the more potent politically, but this condition also makes many of us look to the future. The ORRRC study proves the need for immediate and increasing improvements in outdoor recreation facilities. Are our political institutions geared so that we may realize those cultural demands?

*The Forest Service.*—Certainly one of the most powerful bureaus within any of the national departments is the Forest Service. In terms of the scope and magnitude of operations, quality and prestige personnel, and number of "governments" which are involved, the Forest Service is unique.[35] Budget requests, after minor accretions by Congress, are customarily translated into appropriations, as exhibited by Table 3. There are, of course, political forces opposed to the Forest Service. Differences have arisen between it and some of the other federal bureaucracies; grazing and timber interests have protested regulations pertaining to fees, cutting practices, and land use; local governments complain about the loss of tax base. But the political strength of the Forest Service comes from its prudent adaptability to the multiple-use concept. So many interests are concerned with the administration of these nearly 186 million acres of public land that the principal task of the Forest Service, politically speaking, is to achieve and maintain a high degree of diplomatic skill. Many interests have to be taken into account, adjusted, and accommodated.

One example, among many, would be the passage of the National Forests Act of 1960 (PL 86-517, 86th Congress, 2nd Session). This legislation was neither novel in conception nor notable for its controversy. Rather it gave congressional confirmation to existing administrative practices. The multiple-use sustained-yield strategy of the Forest Service in the areas of timber management, watershed practices, range procedures, recreation, and fish and wildlife practices was affirmed. However, the balance of power was not to be disturbed: there was to be no restriction of existing practices and regulations concerning mining, prospecting, water development, jurisdiction of states over fish and wildlife, and grazing of the ranges. The bill passed both the House and Senate by voice votes.

Intense controversy centers upon the National Wilderness Preservation System bill (S. 174), which passed the Senate by a 78–8 vote in 1961. This issue poses a threat to the prevailing structure of power and is, therefore, highly controversial. The final Senate vote hides the real conflict. On the first proposed amendment by Senator Allott (Colorado) to the bill on the Senate floor the vote was 32–53:

| | | |
|---|---|---|
| Democrats: | For—12; | Against—43 |
| Republicans: | For—20; | Against—10 |

The amendment was to the effect that all wilderness areas of 5,000 acres or more would have to be approved by concurrent resolution (that is, a majority vote in both houses). Passage of the amendment would have considerably weakened the administration's bill but would have aided those who favor the present land use patterns in order to protect their position. Much of the 50–55 million acres of land would have come from Department of Interior lands but the Forest Service displayed its usual political aptitude by ruling in 1962 that within certain forest lands in Oregon and Washington, "... timber cutting will be limited to that needed for recreational purposes, or to maintain thrifty healthy forest cover that is aesthetically pleasing."[36]

It is also of interest that the promotional interest groups were those who favored S. 174; with perhaps one or two exceptions, the self-oriented groups were solidly opposed to it.[37] Also, I should note Justice Douglas' opposition to the current land use practices of the Forest Service and certain private, self-oriented interest groups. Referring to the Glacier Park area, he observes that "those bent on exploiting it...have a great advantage. They [lumbermen and mining interests] hope to perfect their plans before the public is aware of the great treasure that is here. The Forest Service is under pressure from these powerful interests to do their bidding."[38] In his latest book—also intended to further the cause of more wilderness areas—he states: "Men running for public office in cattle or sheep country seldom, if ever, campaign against overgrazing. The weight of the federal bureaucracy in cattle or sheep country is, with few exceptions, on the side of the ranchers. The newcomer in the Forest Service or BLM who sees what overgrazing is doing to the high country in Wyoming and who speaks up may not last long. He is the dangerous non-conformist."[39]

Forest Service diplomacy seems to be strongly affected by the spirit of "cooptation," to use Philip Selznick's term.[40] That is, "if you can't beat 'em, join 'em," and try to achieve your goals at a slower pace.

*The Soil Conservation Service (SCS).*—This bureau was established under the authority of the Soil Conservation Act of 1935. It had certain antecedents, but from that date on, soil conservation ranked as one of the powerful myths in American life, and the myth became institutionalized. Circumstances for such a course of action were highly propitious. Terrible farm prices, gruesome dust storms, dynamic leadership in the person of Hugh Hammond Bennett, a conservation-minded President, and a distraught Congress, made the inauguration of the SCS almost a political certainty.

Since that time, the SCS has spread its word and deed throughout the nation. State legislatures provided the necessary enabling acts and by January 1, 1961, there were 2,879 soil conservation districts, covering some 1,677,612,000 acres and 4,608,000 farms. Conservation plans have been drawn up for well over one-third of those farms, although it should be observed that a plan of action does not necessarily mean that action is taken.[41]

The SCS has been alert to its political problems. The state extension services and the AFBF have had their differences with this new bureaucracy.[42] Secretary of Agriculture Ezra Benson accommodated the AFBF by abolishing the regional offices of the SCS in 1953. The AAA, PMA, CSS, and the ASCS (all one bureau but the alphabet changes with each new President) have developed areas of disagreement with the SCS. A clientele interest group, the National Association of Soil Conservation Districts, has come on the political scene to assist the SCS, with both more and less political fortune.

The SCS's position of strength, however, seems to come from the deep-seated national belief that soil is one of the dearest of our natural resources and must be preserved, and the full-hearted acceptance of this belief by the members of Congress who dominate the agriculture committees and agricultural appropriations subcommittees in Congress. Agronomists and economists may debate warmly, even in oral examinations of Ph.D. candidates, the issue of maximum-allowable soil losses, but the myth has overwhelmed their skepticism.

Table 3 indicates that the House Appropriations Committee has been even more zealous than has the SCS, at least in terms of the desired quantity of appropriations. The substantial increases in appropriations since fiscal 1956 reflect the passage of the Watershed Protection and Flood Prevention Act of 1954 (PL 84-566). Table 5 points to the growing amount of appropriations for watershed projects during the last several years.

### TABLE 5
Funds for Watershed Protection Projects (Soil Conservation Service)
(President's Budget)

| Requests | | Appropriations | |
|---|---|---|---|
| 1955 | $ 7,955,150 | 1954 | $ 5,000,000 |
| 1956 | 10,994,243 | 1955 | 77,205,150 |
| 1957 | 16,000,000 | 1956 | 11,994,243 |
| 1958 | 25,500,000 | 1957 | 17,500,000 |
| 1959 | 24,000,000 | 1958 | 25,500,000 |
| 1960 | 20,000,000 | 1959 | 25,500,000 |
| 1961 | 27,704,313 | 1960 | 22,750,000 |
| 1962 | 53,746,000 | 1961 | 36,754,313 |
| 1963 | 59,635,000 | 1962 | 53,746,000 |

Source: Office of Budget and Finance, U.S. Department of Agriculture.

The "catch-the-rain-where-it-falls" theory may well be prescient and wise. This matter is for others to debate. Herein, it seems necessary to point out that the small watershed program offers remarkable opportunity for a new form of political pork-barreling. The federal subsidy involved in each watershed project is usually quite handsome. As of February 1, 1962, the box-score is as given in Table 6.

**TABLE 6**

STATUS OF PL566 WATERSHED PROJECTS (AS OF FEBRUARY, 1962)

| | |
|---|---|
| Applications Received | 1,637 |
| Authorized for Planning Assistance | 720 |
| Authorized for Operations | 370 |
| Under Construction | 184 |
| Construction Completed | 43 |

Source: Soil Conservation Service, USDA.

The political potentialities of this program are well-nigh inexhaustible. The SCS has shrugged off its setback in the early years of the Benson administration, has adopted the multiple-use strategy of the Forest Service, and is now offering watershed projects for purposes of municipal water supply, recreation, and fish and wildlife preservation as well as soil conservation and flood control.

*The Agricultural Conservation Program (ACP).*—The future of the Agricultural Conservation Program is much less certain than that of the SCS. ACP payments began in 1936 as a form of a "gentle rain of Treasury checks" upon improvident farmers. The Supreme Court had nullified the first AAA so an alternative form of federal assistance for the destitute farmers had to be devised. Congress made the transition by passing the Soil Conservation and Domestic Allotment Act of 1936. Federal subsidies to farmers for certain soil-conserving practices have been with us ever since.

Table 7 gets at the center of the controversy over ACP payments. The program uses a calendar, not a fiscal, year approach so when a Congress appropriates for the coming fiscal year it also authorizes for the succeeding calendar year.

A growing agitation against the program has been coming from some urban congressmen, the AFBF, certain agricultural

## TABLE 7
### ADVANCE AUTHORIZATIONS FOR THE AGRICULTURAL CONSERVATION PROGRAM

| Program Year | Requests (President's Budget) | Authorization (by Congress) |
|---|---|---|
| 1954 | $140,000,000 | $195,000,000 |
| 1955 | 250,000,000 | 250,000,000[a] |
| 1956 | 175,000,000 | 250,000,000 |
| 1957 | 250,000,000 | 250,000,000 |
| 1958 | 250,000,000 | 250,000,000 |
| 1959 | 125,000,000 | 250,000,000 |
| 1960 | 100,000,000 | 250,000,000 |
| 1961 | 100,000,000 | 250,000,000 |
| 1962 | 150,000,000 | 250,000,000 |
| 1963 | 150,000,000 | |

[a]$55,000,000 earmarked for use under diverted acres program.
Source: Office of Budget and U.S. Dept of Agriculture.

economists, and several journalists because of the lack of logic (so they contend) in retiring land with one legislative hand while improving it with the other. Some charge that the National Limestone Institute is the principal beneficiary, and one could hardly charge that interest group with nonpartisanship so far as the ACP program is concerned.

For the last five program years, Presidents Eisenhower and Kennedy, and particularly the Bureau of the Budget, have been attempting to reduce considerably the advance appropriations for the program, but to no avail. The committees mentioned have thus far returned to the magic figure of $250 million.

However, the program is being seriously challenged on the floor of the House and Senate and its demise seems certain, although political certainty has a much lower priority than death and taxes.

During the 1961 (87th) Congress, Representative Henry Reuss (Dem., Wis.) moved to reduce ACP payments from the committee-recommended $250 million to President Kennedy's requested $150 million. His motion was first accepted, by a standing vote; then rejected by a roll-call vote of 184–196:

| | | |
|---|---|---|
| Democrats: | For— 80; | Against—148 |
| Republicans: | For—104; | Against— 48 |

We cannot review the arrangement of political forces in this vote but it does indicate a strong discontent with the existing situation. A like amendment was introduced in the Senate by Senators Douglas (Dem., Ill.) and Williams (Rep., Del.), and it was also defeated, 35–54.

*The Soil Bank Programs.*—Since the passage of the "Soil Bank" Act of 1956, the policy of the national government has been to attack the dual "evils" of excess farm production and decreased farm income through the retirement of large amounts of farm land. The program was an outgrowth of expediency born of frustration. Neither President Eisenhower and Secretary Benson, nor the Democratically controlled Congress, could pass the kind of election-year legislation that each desired. Boles and Talbot studied the political forces involved in the origin and development of the Soil Bank programs from 1956 through 1960.[43] In capsule form this was the gist of the findings: small town businessmen, congressmen who did not like to lose constituents, and the National Farmers Union brought an end to the continuation of the acreage and conservation reserve programs, that is, no acreage reserve program after 1958 or new conservation reserve contracts after 1960. Certain malpractices in the administration of the program were disclosed by the General Accounting Office and then came the coup de grâce, aided by metropolitan newspapers.

The programs have been and will be costly, as Table 8 indicates, but the merits and demerits need not be evaluated here.

TABLE 8

SOIL BANK PROGRAMS

(Estimated Total Costs, Fiscal Years 1956–70)

| Program and Fiscal Year | Cost |
|---|---|
| 1. Acreage Reserve Program: 1956–59 (actual) | $1,639,130,987 |
| 2. Conservation Reserve Program: | |
| 1956–60 (actual) | 634,354,462 |
| 1961–70 (estimated) | 2,203,347,975 |
| Total | 2,837,702,437 |
| 3. Total, Both Soil Bank Programs | $4,476,833,424 |

Source: Hearings of the Subcommittee of the House Committee on Appropriations, *Department of Agriculture Appropriations For 1962*, Part 2, p. 683

The Kennedy administration attacked the surplus problem first in the form of the Emergency Feed Grains Act of 1961, and then the Agriculture Act of 1961. The first was a voluntary land retirement program; the second, as sent to Congress, would have permitted the use of marketing orders to attack the surplus/income problem, but the end result was the extension of the feed grains legislation and the inclusion of a voluntary wheat-acreage reduction program for 1962.

At the time of this writing, Secretary Freeman was doggedly and skillfully attempting to persuade a reluctant Congress to accept the Food and Agriculture Act of 1962 and all its compulsory features; the Farm Bureau was striving to combine certain God-made natural laws with voluntary federal subsidies for land retirement, all in the form of the Land Retirement Act of 1962 (H.R. 10060 and others); and the members of the House and Senate committees on agriculture were searching for a compromise which would not make too many people unhappy in November, 1962, especially farmers.

Freeman did try to expand his constituencies in the Food and Agriculture Act of 1962 by including provisions which might prove attractive to the recreationists and the conservationists.

It is certainly safe and accurate to state that as of April, 1962, all proposals regarding the retirement of private farm land are in a condition of uncertainty and flux. Apparently, the President and the Bureau of the Budget have made it clear to the USDA that the budget costs of the farm programs must be pared. To carry out this slicing operation, the secretary of agriculture must convince the Congress, and especially the agriculture committees, that the President's directive is a form of a mandamus and not just a mandatory gesture. Then he must persuade the farmers that a favorable referendum vote, and the compulsory actions which would follow therefrom, are in their own best interests. In the words of a happily unknown bard: why would anyone who wants to be sane and natural, have anything to do with legislation agricultural!

## POLITICAL FORCES AND FUTURE LAND POLICIES

This final section begins with the assumption that any major problem area, such as land policies, which has existed over any considerable period of time, has brought forth a few persons who desire major changes in political institutions, others who intend

to use the existing arrangements to bring about important policy
shifts, some who seek to maintain the status quo, a limited number who believe that administrative reorganization can achieve
the stated goals with more efficiency and dispatch, and several
who want to return to a bygone and avowedly halcyon era. Let
us take a rapid look at each position.

### THE NEED FOR A POLITICAL REFORMATION

For some thirty years now there have been those, especially
in the political science discipline, who have argued vigorously,
even vehemently, for a political reformation. Their argument
goes as follows: our political party system and the Congress need
a genuine overhaul. That is, we must have political institutions
which will be truly responsive to the will of the majority,
although reasons do vary as to the necessity of such a reformation.

Schattschneider and Bailey want a truly liberal/conservative
orientation to American political parties. Parties should "stand
for something." When victorious at the polls, the program of the
winning party should be transformed into policy—an American
version, so to speak, of the British parliamentary system.[44]

Charles Hardin views the international crisis as one which
bodes ill for the United States if we do not alter our Constitution
and its arrangement of offices to meet the global, if not inter-
global, threats of Soviet and Chinese Communism.[45] The parochial, provincial, and pork-barreling aspects of American politics must be overcome through constitutional reform. To do
less, he believes, is to deprive this nation of the political means
which are necessary in order to cope with an increasingly dangerous international situation.

If the Schattschneider-Bailey-Hardin school should prevail
(which it will not!) the resultant changes in land policies might
well be quite considerable. The ACP program would quickly
vanish; the SCS would have a much more difficult job of budget
justification to contend with; the Bureau of Reclamation would
face an even more serious challenge than the SCS; while the
Forest Service, BLM, and National Park Service would prosper,
policy- and dollar-wise.

## THE APPROACH OF THE NEW FRONTIER

James Burns has analyzed President Kennedy as a rhetorical radical, a policy liberal, a fiscal moderate, and a conservative in regard to matters of organization, party, and administration.[46] His call to action has been brilliant and resounding, but the instruments at hand mean that Machiavelli must be joined with Elijah. Forward movement is not impossible, but only probable in modest amounts.

What does the "new frontier" approach mean relative to national land policies? One primary consideration is the President's own priority list. So long as international policy must be his major concern, then land policy will have a lesser priority ranking. And cabinet leadership is not a substitute for presidential leadership in our political system. The secretaries of agriculture and interior can achieve national publicity by climbing mountains, drinking milk, being ordered off private property, reasoning with housewives and retired colonels at checkout counters, and cutting underwater ribbons. Congress may well be impressed by their qualities of showmanship, but plaudits are not necessarily followed by legislation. What Congress does with "The Water Resource Planning Act of 1961" and "The Food and Agriculture Act of 1962" will provide us with authentic tests of executive leadership.

It needs to be said that both departments have acted in a manner which would indicate that departmental policies are being pursued rather than a conglomeration of bureau policies. Secretary Freeman resurrected, in a somewhat new form, the Bureau of Agricultural Economics; Secretary Udall has set up a central office of Science Adviser, has established a Bureau of Outdoor Recreation, and seems intent on bringing into reality some of the administrative changes recommended by the staff of Resources for the Future. This RFF study observes that "there is a strong tendency for the Department [of Interior] to be little more than a holding company, a loose confederation of Bureaus."[47] The same could be said, I would suggest, for the Department of Agriculture, so the recent endeavors toward departmental unification need to be viewed with interested skepticism.

Also, both departments have recently moved toward the formulation and coordination of certain interdepartmental policies, which is both a novel and hopeful innovation.

Perhaps a new "Commission of Organization of the Executive Branch of the Government"—co-chairmaned by former Presidents Truman and Eisenhower—is needed. What would this mean in terms of national land policy? Such a commission would surely have prominence and importance. It might well be able to convince Congress that this is the proper moment to transform some of the recommendations of the two Hoover Commissions, the President's (Truman) Water Resources Policy Commission, and the Missouri Basin Survey Commission (1952) into functional and organizational changes.[48]

## THE SHIFTING SANDS OF CONGRESSIONAL POWER

What appears to be happening within the congressional structure of power is that the Senate is becoming more responsive to the interests and demands of the urban-metropolitan constituencies while the House is being converted into a conservative organ because of, in part, the gerrymandered, one-party congressional districts.

The recent Supreme Court decision (*Baker* v. *Carr*, 369 U.S. 186) may, in the long pull, cause the House to be redistricted on the basis of equal population but this day will be far in the future, and there are those who defend the existing situation.[49] Also, it should be noted that the balance of urban-rural power in the House does respond somewhat to Bureau of Census returns. A recent census report states: "The 1960 Census data shows that of the 437 Congressional Districts, as constituted for the present session, those with population more than 50 percent urban, numbered 300."[50] Some twenty-five states have gone through the process of reapportioning within the last year or more, so these alterations may further swing the balance in favor of the cities, but early indications do not point to much of a change.

The strong tendency for Congress to look at land policy as a sort of pork-barrel activity is evidenced in the recent reapportionment which occurred in Mississippi. Representative Whitten, Chairman of the House Agriculture Appropriations Subcommittee, is being challenged by Representative Frank Smith, a member of the House Public Works Subcommittee on Watershed Development. Recently Whitten made this statement on the House floor: "My membership on this committee has contributed greatly in my own state to the boll weevil laboratory, the many flood control and watershed projects, soil conservation, REA, extension and 4-H club programs, the Greenville and Pascagoula Harbor projects, the Agricultural Conservation Program, and many others which I have been able to promote."[51]

Smith has not yet made public his list of "all the things I've done for my district," but that disclosure will surely be forthcoming very soon.

Congress is plagued with a business-as-usual attitude and resolutely refuses to become, what has been called, a twentieth-century Congress.

If Congress should later accept the President's proposed Department of Urban Affairs the outcome might well have a considerable impact on land policies, particularly in and around the urban fringe areas. Urban "sprawl" is converting some excellent farm land into an ever-growing suburbia. State legislatures—possibly some forty-two of them—are so rurally and small-town dominated that they tend to either ignore or treat superficially this new condition. A Department of Urban Affairs might, with congressional assistance, develop a program of federal grants-in-aid to assist the cities and surrounding counties in coming to grips with this disturbing situation. If the states should refuse to gear themselves into this program then direct federal aid would need to be offered to the metropolitan areas. Indeed, this arrangement has already come about on a quite limited scale.

THE "RADICAL RIGHT"

This new breed—probably just another name for an old variant—has become a recent force in American politics. Their persistent efforts are directed, at least on the surface, against the domestic Reds, the "fellow-traveling" liberals, the "misguided" conservatives, and any other fairly rational types they might encounter. If one takes this breed's unique, not to say peculiar, form of political logic into the arena of land policy the results become incredibly macabre. Their brand of historical retrogression would presumably abolish all land retirement programs that are directed toward private land; the public lands would somehow be disposed of, although the racial prejudices of the Radical Right would hardly permit these lands to be returned to the Indians!

Such groups, however, do constitute a political force which must be treated seriously. Land policy calls for the application of intelligent, long-range planning. The Radical Right brings into the political arena a form of "looney-gooney" thinking which makes rational action difficult, and systematic planning by the agencies of government suspect. Liberals have become more conservative; conservatives even more timid than is customary, and the indigenous Radical Left is only faintly heard. All this does not portend will for the forces of change, and that is the kind of atmosphere the Radical Right really wants to foster.

To conclude: when one takes a longing look into the political, plexiglass ball the images makes one mindful of what Madison termed the "...indistinctness of the object, imperfection of the organ of conception, and inadequateness of the vehicle of ideas."[52] We can hope for more emphasis on the public interest, because the decade calls for major political decisions. Nevertheless, American political institutions are, by design, stubborn and unruly. Change comes about gradually, perceptibly, but with rather a low order of predictability. Surely we can believe that the changes to be wrought in land policies by 2062 will be even greater than those that we have witnessed since 1862.

## NOTES

1. Benjamin F. Wright, "The Federalist on the Nature of Political Man," *Ethics*, No. 2, Part II, January, 1949.

2. Ralph H. Gabriel (Ed.), *Hamilton, Madison and Jay on the Constitution, Selections from the Federalist Papers* (New York: The Liberal Arts Press, 1954), Federalist No. 47, pp. 68–69.

3. *Ibid.*, p. 68.

4. *Ibid.*, Federalist No. 51, p. 77.

5. John P. Roche, "The Founding Fathers: A Reform Caucus in Action," *The American Political Science Review,* Vol. LV, No. 4, December, 1961, 799–817.

6. United States v. Butler, 297 U.S. 1 (1936).

7. 307 U.S. 38 (1938), and 317 U.S. 111 (1942), respectively.

8. Oklahoma v. Atkinson Co., 313 U.S. 508.

9. Morton Grodzins, "The Federal System," in The Report of the President's Commission on National Goals, *Goals for Americans* (New York: Prentice-Hall, Inc., 1960), Chap. 12.

10. *New York Times,* July 17, 1961, quoted in James A. Robinson, *Congress and Foreign Policy-Making* (Homewood, Ill.: The Dorsey Press, Inc., 1962), p. 216.

11. George B. Galloway, *History of the United States House of Representatives* (Washington, D. C.; U.S. Government Printing Office, 1962), House Doc. No. 246, 87th Congress, 1st Session, p. 86. Also see Donald R. Matthews, *U.S. Senators and Their World* (Chapel Hill: University of North Carolina Press, 1960), Chap. VII.

12. Ross B. Talbot, "Farm Legislation in the 86th Congress," *Journal of Farm Economics,* Vol. XLIII, No. 3, August, 1961, 582–605.

13. David B. Truman, "Federalism and the Party System," Arthur W. MacMahon (Ed.), *Federalism: Mature and Emergent,* (New York: Doubleday & Co., Inc., 1955), pp. 115–37.

14. Richard E. Neustadt, *Presidential Government* (New York: John Wiley & Sons, Inc., 1960).

15. *National Organziations of the U.S.,* Vol. I, (Detroit: Gale Research Co., 1961).

16. S. E. Finer, *Anonymous Empire: A Study of the Lobby in Great Britain* (London: Pall Mall Press, 1958), p. 3.

17. Finer, *Ibid.*

18. Charles McKinley, *Uncle Sam in the Pacific Northwest* (Berkeley: University of California Press, 1952), pp. 619–26.

19. David Riesman, *The Lonely Crowd* (New York: Doubleday & Co., Inc., 1953), Anchor A16, pp. 246–60.

20. Carl J. Friedrich, *Constitutional Government and Democracy* (New York: Ginn and Co., 1950), Chap. II.

21. Angus Campbell, *et al., The American Voter* (New York: John Wiley & Sons, Inc., 1960), Chap. 10. Table 2 is an abbreviated version of Table 17 in Warren Miller's chapter, "The Political Behavior of the Electorate," *American Government Annual, 1960–61* (New York: Holt, Rinehart and Winston, Inc., 1960). Miller was one of the authors of *The American Voter* study.

22. Associate Justice William O. Douglas, of the U.S. Supreme Court, has provided an eloquent and learned defense of the "wilderness area" concept in his *My Wilderness—The Pacific West* (New York: Doubleday & Co., Inc., 1960), and *My Wilderness—East to Katahdin* (New York: Doubleday & Co., Inc., 1961).

23. Samuel Lubell, *The Future of American Politics* (Garden City, N. Y.: Doubleday & Co., Inc., 1956), Chap. 10.

24. A very useful description and analyses of the appropriations process is found in a study by Marion Clawson and Burnell Held, *The Federal Lands: Their Use and Management* (Baltimore: The Johns Hopkins Press, 1957), pp. 150–65.

25. Congressional Quarterly, Inc., *Weekly Report,* "On Project 2012," Dec. 23, 1960, pp. 1990–91.

26. Wesley Calef, *Private Grazing and Public Lands* (Chicago: The University of Chicago Press, 1960), p. 251.

27. Phillip O. Foss, *Politics and Grass* (Seattle: University of Washington Press, 1960), and Calef, *Ibid.,* Chap. IV.

28. American Farm Bureau Federation, *Official Newsletter,* January 1, 1962, p. 1.

29. Secretary of Interior Stewart L. Udall, *Resources for Tomorrow,* 1961 Annual Report of the Department of Interior (Washington, D. C.: U.S. Government Printing Office, 1962), p. 86. Also, see the news release of the Department of Interior for Oct. 19, 1961, which is an address delivered by Secretary Udall on that date to the National Reclamation Association Convention.

30. Charles M. Hardin, "Land Policy and the Development of the West," in Franklin S. Pollak (Ed.), *Resources Development: Frontiers for Research* (Boulder: University of Colorado Press, 1960), p. 9. More precisely, Hardin states, "Few agricultural experts now believe that we need to irrigate additional arid acreage at high costs in the foreseeable future..." and he cites Roy E. Huffman as "...a distinguished, but lonely exception."

31. *Wallaces Farmer,* April 7, 1962, p. 15.

32. Congressional Quarterly, Inc., *Weekly Report,* "On National Parks," December 2, 1960, p. 1938.

33. Freeman Tilden, *The National Parks* (New York: Alfred A. Knopf, Inc., 1955), p. 21.

34. Outdoor Recreation Resources Review Commission, *Outdoor Recreation for America,* a report to the President and Congress (Washington, D. C.: U.S. Government Printing Office, January, 1962).

35. See the excellent study by Herbert Kaufman, *The Forest Ranger* (Baltimore: The Johns Hopkins Press, 1960).

36. U.S. Department of Agriculture, *The Daily Summary,* March 29, 1962.

37. *Congressional Quarterly Almanac*—1961, pp. 442–44.

38. Douglas, *My Wilderness—The Pacific West, op. cit.,* pp. 158–59. A well-balanced presentation of the wilderness controversy is found in: John Ise, *Our National Park Policy* (Baltimore: The Johns Hopkins Press, 1961), Chap. XXX. He explains why, in his opinion, "it is impossible to make a fair appraisal of the merits of this controversy." (p. 647). Also see the press release of the Department of Interior Information Service, "Secretary Udall Approves Basic Wilderness Preservation Policies of National Park Service," April 2, 1961, and especially the memorandum attached thereto.

39. Douglas, *My Wilderness—East to Katahdin, op. cit.,* p. 45.

40. Phillip Selznick, *TVA and the Grass Roots* (Berkeley: University of California Press, 1949), pp. 219–26.

41. W. Robert Parks, *Soil Conservation Districts in Action* (Ames: Iowa State University Press, 1952).

42. Charles M. Hardin, *The Politics of Agriculture,* (Glencoe, Ill.: The Free Press, 1952), Part I.

43. Donald E. Boles and Ross B. Talbot, "Governmental Framework for Achieving National Land Use Adjustments," in *Dynamics of Land Use: Needed Adjustment* (Ames: Iowa State University Press, 1961), pp. 278–98.

44. See E. E. Schattschneider, *Party Government* (New York: Farrar, Rinehart, and Co., 1942), and Stephen K. Bailey, *The Condition of our National Parties,* "An Occasional Paper on the Role of the Political Process in the Free Society," (New York: Fund for the Republic, Inc., 1959), for two examples of this point of view.

45. Charles M. Hardin, "Constitutional Reform in the United States," January 15, 1958, expanded from an address given at Oregon State University, December 10, 1957. Unfortunately, this paper has not been published.

46. James Burns, "The 4 Kennedys of the 1st Year," *New York Times Magazine,* January 14, 1962, p. 9.

47. Resources for the Future, Inc., *A Report on Planning, Policy Making and Research Activities—U.S. Department of Interior,* May, 1961, p. 26.

48. A summarization of these proposals and others is found in Clawson and Held, *op. cit.* pp. 364–75.

49. For example, Andrew Hacker, "Voice of Ninety Million Americans," *New York Times Magazine,* March 4, 1962, pp. 11, 80, 82, 84.

50. U.S. Department of Commerce, (Census), CB 62–23, February 24, 1962. However, for a different calculation, due to another set of definitions, see Congressional Quarterly, Inc., *Weekly Report,* "On Rural-Urban Representation," February 2, 1962, pp. 153–78.

51. *Congressional Record,* September 18, 1961, Vol. 107, 87th Congress, 1st Session, p. A7391.

52. Gabriel (Ed.), *op. cit.,* Federalist Number 37, p. 43.

# The Economic and
# Institutional Forces

A MOST HAZARDOUS UNDERTAKING for a social scientist is to write
on a subject deficient in scientifically valid propositions and principles. Land policy is such a subject. In a discussion such as this,
we expose our individual philosophies and viewpoints. We can
agree on the facts or the events in U.S. land policy as reported
in the first two chapters of this book. However, in the interpretation of such facts, or in stating the reasons for them, our minds
encounter conflict, and we wage "intellectual battles" to rationalize our individual beliefs and values. Why? Because a settled
science of human behavior does not exist nor does a related
science of ethics, to challenge seriously our individual social
philosophies and prejudices. Furthermore, we are making meager
if any progress in developing these subjects into sciences.[1]

Having presented a warning that an objective analysis of
the economic and institutional forces giving rise to U.S. land
policy may not be forthcoming, I will proceed with the subject at
hand. I interpret my assignment to be two-fold: (1) to explain the
relation among economic forces, institutional forces, and U.S.
Land Policy, and (2) to appraise our land policy in terms of
influences upon past and future economic development, distribution of property and income, and efficiency in agricultural
production.

## ECONOMIC FORCES, INSTITUTIONAL FORCES,
## AND LAND POLICY

I believe an appropriate point of departure into my assignment would be to define economic forces, institutional forces,
and what constitutes our land policy.

Economic forces will be interpreted to mean the influences
of materialistic wants or desires of individuals and society upon
actions and policy. Much has been said against treating man as

an economic machine, a creature with no motives or purposes other than what the economic textbooks say he has. But, can we assert that such motivations of man are not important, that people do not prefer more of the scarce items used in our living to less, or that our actions are influenced only by other purposes? Perhaps money income, property, or other means to material well-being are also means to such higher-level purposes as happiness, satisfaction, prestige, or social status, but, if so, materialism may be a necessary condition for attending these high-level purposes.[2] Francis Hackett, an Irishman, expresses the role of materialism (economics) as follows:

> I believe in materialism. I believe in all the proceeds of a healthy materialism—good cooking, dry houses, dry feet, sewers, drain pipes, hot water, baths, electric lights, automobiles, good roads, bright streets, long vacations away from the village pump, new ideas, fast horses, swift conversation, theatres, operas, orchestras, bands—I believe in them all for everybody. The man who dies without knowing these things may be as exquisite as a saint, and as rich as a poet; but it is in spite of, not because of, his deprivation.[3]

Why does every community, every state, and the nation, judge its institutions and policies in terms of influence upon economic development? Why do we judge our congressmen primarily upon the basis of their degree of success in enlarging federal expenditures in our home territories? Why was economic development a major campaign issue in the last presidential election? Because people do have materialistic motives that influence their behavior, including their voting behavior; I do not believe this phenomenon is something new to the American scene. This is not to deny that, in a hierarchy of values, materialism would necessarily rank first. Many of us fail to see any conflict between our materialistic and other objectives, but, rather, we view them as complements. And because of this, as well as the fact that our economic activity is such a large part of our total activity, we appear to be predominantly materialists by our actions.

The feudal system of land tenure from which we descended put restraints on the pursuit of individual economic objectives for all except the lords. Was our break with this system due to the force of individual economic motives which came into being as an active force with the new land becoming available for settlement? This seems to me to be as reasonable as the hypothesis that desire for freedom by the serfs was the motivation underlying this change in tenure systems. Freedom could be considered merely a means to the exercising of individual pursuit of economic objectives. Democracy as interpreted by our forefathers also could be considered a means whereby individuals could pursue economic objectives *as individuals*.[4]

Institutional forces are more difficult to describe than the economic. The subject of institutions is vast, complex, and vague. What are institutions? First, institutions are formal and informal rules prescribing our individual rights and conduct in groups or society. By this definition, institutions would encompass laws, administrative regulations and procedures, rights and obligations by common assent, customs and traditions adhered to, etc. How economic opportunities were distributed among individuals would be determined by institutions. A second meaning of institutions in social science usuage is that they are organizational attributes of groups or society. These would be market institutions, institutions of higher education, political organizations, economic systems, family farms, public agencies, etc. Perhaps the organizational attributes of groups or society are merely manifestations of institutions by the first definition. However, organizations can exert a force upon our actions independently of the institutions from which they spring.

Institutions arise from group rather than individual action, and they exist to serve the common purposes among individuals. They may act as a force to enlarge the opportunities of individuals to pursue purely individual objectives. Also, the force may be the opposite—to restrict actions of some individuals in order to increase achievement of group purposes. Whether institutions themselves, when once established, can be considered to have additional forces depends upon whether we associate ideologies or valuations of people with their institutions. I do. The force is a perpetuating influence over time. We place values upon our institutions as means to ends, and institutions which reflect traditional values, or come to have value only to politically powerful interest groups, are difficult to change. This kind of force affects the way we try to solve new group or society problems as they arise; we merely graft onto existing institutions rather than initiate wholly new ones more fitted to current conditions. As a result, our institutions frequently are inconsistent, and they reflect various interests over time and at a single point in time. Also, grafting onto existing institutions often fails to solve the problems the grafting was intended to solve.

United States land policy is a set of publicly sponsored institutions relating to farm land, although it is not necessarily the whole of our land institutions. Land policy up to about 1900 was a set of "guiding principles" about as follows:[5]

(1) Settlement of the public domain as rapidly as possible in "family-sized units of land, and encouragement of individual or family ownership of these units;

(2) Equal opportunity among individuals in gaining control of land;

(3) Freedom of individuals or families to change size of units and form of tenure from that intended by settlement policy;

(4) Freedom of individuals to manage the soil resources in their possession as they please; and

(5) Right of testate succession, or prohibition of primogeniture and entail (Ordinance of 1787).

After 1900, other public policies related to farm land came into being, the more prominent being (1) credit policy to implement the goal of ownership of land in "family-sized" units; (2) irrigation of arid areas to expand settlement under secure conditions (Reclamation); (3) specification of private grazing rights on the public lands (Taylor Grazing Act); and (4) a policy to achieve conservation of privately owned lands. Our land policy also includes rights reserved by society such as rights to tax, power of eminent domain, police power, and right of the public to improve the conditions under which farmers hold their land.[6]

Even though our land policy is composed mainly of rather broad general principles, possible inconsistencies in these principles are evident. The intent is to encourage individual ownership of land in "family-sized" units, but there are no restrictions to the development of other sizes and other forms of tenure.

Although it is the "public" intent to bring about a high degree of conservation on privately held farm land, the policy also is to permit individual owners to manage the soil as they please. The social costs of these inconsistencies are not small. We have spent substantial portions of our resources trying to reverse the growing deviation between the owner-operated family farm ideal and what exists in reality. Likewise, public expenditures to achieve conservation on privately held lands are mounting year by year, but tangible results of a permanent nature are difficult to verify.

Even though inconsistencies in our land institutions have consequences of considerable magnitude, of more significance are the conflicts in effects of land policy and other farm policies. I have classed settlement policy, credit policy, and conservation policy as the main ingredients of our land policy. Other farm policies are research and education, and price or income policy. A major ideological thread in all these policies is the family-farm philosophy, a guiding principle in the formation of our land institutions, particularly in reference to settlement. Our land institutions as they actually exist comprise a mechanism of major influence in the distribution of the effects of the other farm programs. As I shall try to demonstrate later, the actual effects of the nonland farm policies are opposite to the intended effect of making the traditional ideal of family farming conform more to reality.

## THE FAMILY-FARM PHILOSOPHY AND
## RELATED ECONOMIC FORCES

Ideologies are conceptions of what would be an ideal or perfect reality. An ideology never corresponds exactly with reality (what actually exists) for two major reasons: (1) people in a given society differ in their ideas about what constitutes perfect reality, thus conflicting ideologies temper the influence of any one, and (2) there are forces other than ideologies determining what actually exists. Nevertheless, ideologies can influence reality, and evidence of this influence is a positive association in time, however small, among ideology, policy, or action, and results of policy or action. When these diverge over time, (negative correlations), the ideology may well be a myth. In my view, the family-farm ideology as held by our forefathers did have an influence upon reality for a considerable period of time, particularly in the settlement period of our history, but, in recent decades, its degree of correspondence with reality would cause many to question its usefulness as a guide to policy.

Generally, we associate the ideology of family farms with Jefferson, but Jefferson is a mere symbol of the viewpoint. Philosophical support of the view precedes Jefferson, for we know John Locke wrote on the subject. Jefferson did much writing on philosophy relating to family farming, and he took some leadership, as did many others, in the formation of our settlement policy. What was the ideology? It was an ideal land tenure system, a division of the land into private holdings of a size corresponding to the needs of individual families for employing their labor. Why was it applied in policy mainly in settlement of the public domain? Because, in the Colonial period of America, other land tenure systems gained prominence and existed in the thirteen original Colonies at the time settlement policy was being formulated. We had the township system in New England, the plantations and large estates in the South, and mixed systems, but strongly influenced by holdings of the Dutch patrons, in the Middle Colonies. Thus, the family farm ideology at the time was not a universal viewpoint. Practically, however, it could provide a guide to policy for settling lands west of the thirteen original Colonies. The choice of our founding fathers seemed to be either a free land system based upon family farms, or semi-feudal system with the accompanying danger of nondemocratic political institutions. After all, about 90 per cent of the people inhabiting the country at that time were farmers, and any serious thought about political institutions naturally brought the rural institutions into consideration.

We know the actual settlement policy deviated from a free-land policy until the Homestead Act. The federal government needed revenue, and the sale of the public lands was a major way the needed revenue could be obtained. Although the price generally ranged up to about two dollars per acre to settlers, this amounted to a significant sum to pioneers who had limited means of producing beyond family subsistence requirements. Prior to the Homestead Act the size of the holdings acquired by the families probably may have been more influenced by the acreage they could afford to pay for than actual policy in this respect.

The Homestead Act more nearly exemplified the family-farm ideology than any other piece of land legislation. Free land simplified the acquisition of ownership for settlers. The 160-acre unit corresponded reasonably well to the labor supply of a family in areas of general crop farming. Later modifications of the act to permit larger acreages in ranching areas were in accordance with the ideology.

It is difficult to determine the point at which an institution, independently of the ideology underlying it, becomes a major force in policy formation. Perhaps this is when the institution gains a status in society. The people most affected by an institution such as the family farm, which, in this case, would be the farmers, place values upon it based upon experienced or observed results. In the pre-machine age of farming, or prior to about 1880, there could be little reason to suspect farmer dissatisfaction with family farming as traditionally conceived. Labor and land were the only two factors of any major significance in farm production. The economic objective of combining these in optimum proportions was reasonably consistent with the family-farm ideal. Freedom, independence, equality in economic opportunity, and other traditional values were consistent with the family-farm ideal in the pre-machine age. Farm mechanization and other technological developments affecting farm output in the period 1880–1900 were not the only disturbing factors in that situation. Output also had expanded through increase in acreage farmed. There was a growing scarcity of free land, and, as such a resource becomes scarce, its price increases. Farmers' income was not keeping pace with costs, and economic insecurity ensued. Farmers blamed their plight upon high freight rates, hard money policy (the green-back controversy), and monopoly in nonfarm businesses. Many farmers lost their farms; by 1880, about 25 per cent of the operators of farms in the United States were tenants, and tenancy was on the increase. My interpretation of the difficulty of the period is that economic forces were contributing to the growing commercialization of agriculture; there was an increasing economic interdependence of farming with other sectors of the economy; and a shifting of economic power from agriculture to nonagricultural sectors of the economy. These economic forces created insecurity in the traditional family-farm tenure system. Farmers turned to government for help in attacking the economic forces, but the end in view appeared to be the protection of the family-farm organization. Thus, I believe it was in this period that the family-farm institution first experienced a major test for survival. It had gained sufficient status to become an institutional force operating as a resistance to change.

Farmers' unrest in the period was at least in part responsible for the birth of farm organizations, agricultural economics, and the agricultural experiment stations. There also were some "delayed" effects upon policy formation. The Reclamation Act was enacted in 1902, but this creation could have been due more to the desire of western legislators for an instrument for "pork-barreling" activity than a serious desire to solve the farm problem. Nevertheless, Reclamation did add to settlement policy. President Theodore Roosevelt appointed a country life commission to study rural problems, and this commission produced findings influential in the Smith-Lever Act of 1914 (agricultural extension), the Smith-Hughes Act of 1917 (vocational agricultural education), and the Federal Land Bank Act of 1916. Of these three pieces of legislation, only the Federal Land Bank Act could be considered an addition to land policy—the purpose was to contribute directly to security in the family-farm tenure system through extension of low-cost, long-term federal credit to farmers for purchasing land.

After 1900, farmers became more prosperous and remained so until 1920. Farm prices rose through increased exports of farm products and the effects of World War I. After 1920, another period of economic distress for farmers ensued, which reached a peak in intensity during the depression of the 1930's. Again, insecurity in ownership of farm land by families was a major part of the situation. The farm debate in the 1920's centered upon price and income policy rather than upon land policy. But, in the 1930's, the insecurity of the family-farm system had become acute, and additions to tenure policy was included in the package of broad federal legislative attacks on farmer problems. One addition was the Resettlement Administration, which later became the Farm Security Administration, and, subsequently, the Farmers Home Administration. Some major purposes of policy were to resettle farmers residing on submarginal land onto more productive lands, adjust debts of farmers, provide intermediate credit and grants to those most insecure on the land, and aid low-income tenants into becoming owners through long-term, low-cost loans for purchasing land.

World War II brought forth to many farmers a period of unprecedented prosperity that lasted more than a decade. It also initiated major technical, institutional, and economic changes in our farming that persisted through the period of declining net farm income in the decade of the 1950's. These continue to persist. The machine age in farming has come of age. Non-real estate assets of farmers more than doubled in the postwar period. Farming has become more specialized. Tenure systems have increased in complexity. Farming has become a small sector of that portion of the total economy contributing to the production of food and fiber products. What about the status of the family farm? In the strict, traditional meaning of the family farm, we have very few of them left. We have remnants of the system nearly everywhere, but predominately in the areas where settlement policy applied.

The decline in the proportion of owner-operator farms of a size corresponding approximately to the family labor supply has created semantical problems in defining a family farm. Clearly, the traditional definition will not do if we want to characterize our farming as predominately an organization of family farms. For some unexplained reason, many of us want to characterize our farming as such. The term has emotive connotations arising from our heritage. The semantic argument began as early as the 1930's, but more formal arguments occurred in a farm tenure conference of social scientists in 1946.[7] The more prominent definition today seems to be a farm in which the operating family does most of the work and is manager of the business.[8] This definition removes the traditional connection between the family farm and land tenure. Many of our current policy makers have other ideas; for example, I present two quotations—one from Cochrane, author of the gospel underlying current tendencies in farm policy, and the other from a speech by Secretary of Agriculture, Orville Freeman.

From Cochrane, we find the following:

> ... there is one institution I value particularly, one that is currently undergoing rapid change and may be in danger.... It is the family farm.... What I want to say here is that I think our country will be losing something vital if it loses the institution of the owner-operated family farm.[9]

From Secretary Freeman:

> ... the family farm is a unit of agricultural production characterized by the fact that the owner or operator who manages the farm is the farmer himself.... Its distinguishing feature is the incentive and enterprise that comes with individual ownership.[10]

In my view, there can be no definition of a family farm which can apply simultaneously to most of our farms and provide operational guidance to farm policy. Our farming is too diverse for this. A wide range of tenure systems and tenure arrangements exist. Development of this diversity in tenure is not entirely new nor was it ever prohibited by land policy. In fact, the great amount of variability in tenure permitted by our land policy has permitted development of wide variability in other attributes of our farming. We have a wide range in sizes of farms, regardless of how we measure size. Labor used on farms varies from nearly none provided by the operating family to all provided by the family. Variability in family incomes and efficiency in use of farm resources is extensive. The proportion of total income by families on the land derived from farming varies from nearly none to all. The proportion of total inputs in farming which are off-farm produced varies widely among our farms. And, of course, what is produced on individual farms is highly variable among farms. It seems to me that any tracing of the effects of particular farm policies within the population of farmers and within the economy would require more facts about this diversity in our farming than have been assembled.

Henceforth, I shall consider the family farm in the traditional sense to be a myth, and the family farm by any new definitions to be too arbitrary and general for usefulness. Later, I shall discuss our farm policy in relation to some related current and prospective future problems of tenure, efficiency in the use of resources in agricultural production and incomes of families on the land. Some institutional forces associated with our land institutions, but not identified in this section, will be discussed in connection with the subsequent discussion of problems of tenure.

## SOIL CONSERVATION AND RELATED ECONOMIC FORCES IN LAND POLICY

Earlier it was pointed out that land policy until about 1900 permitted owners to manage the soil resources in their possession as they pleased. This policy permitted exploitation for private gain in the short-run, and deterioration, maintenance, or development of soil, in accordance with individual interests. Generally speaking, this still is the policy, but it now is public policy to exercise an influence on owners in the management of soil and to provide technical and other assistance in carrying out measures deemed to be soil-conserving in effects.

Public concern about individual exploitation of natural resources long preceded establishment of the Soil Erosion Service in 1933. Rapid disappearance of our forest resources by settlement was dramatized by Gifford Pinchot in the latter part of the nineteenth century. This started the progressive conservation movement, which gained national status in public consciousness during the Theodore Roosevelt era of 1901–1908. Direct public action to conserve soil on privately held farm land did not materialize during the early years of the conservation movement, although it was talked about. The Agricultural Extension Service, which began in 1914, did carry on some activity in influencing farmers to conserve soil. However, the activity of this service lacked the missionary spirit contained in the conservation movement and thus it was unsatisfactory to conservationists.

Soil conservation was given a major status in the revived conservation movement during the 1930's. Hugh Bennett had performed studies of the soil erosion problems during 1929–1932. The results of these studies did much to arouse public consciousness about soil losses, and they set the stage for action at the federal level beginning in 1933. First, the Soil Erosion Service was established in the Department of Interior with Hugh Bennett as head to do pilot work on erosion preventive measures. This service concentrated on activity in the dust bowl areas of the Southern Plains, but it worked cooperatively with the Civilian Conservation Corps (another newly established agency) on erosion problems elsewhere. In the meantime, Hugh Bennett continued to preach the gospel of conservation as applied to farm land with the objective of expanding public action in this field. The creation of the Soil Conservation Service as an agency of the Department of Agriculture in 1935 to replace the Soil Erosion Service, provided the means for an expanded program sought by Dr. Bennett. In accordance with the provisions of the Act, the various states soon followed with enabling legislation for creation of soil conservation and soil conservancy districts.

Each of the federal agencies operating in the field of conservation has its own interpretation of the ideology of conservation. For the Soil Conservation Service, it is treatment of each acre of farm land in accordance with its needs, and use of each acre in accordance with its capability. Thus, the philosophy encompasses both development of agricultural land to maximum physical productivity, and use consistent with maintenance of this productive capacity. Hugh Bennett, who headed the Service for many years, mainly was responsible for firmly ingraining the ideology in the minds of employees of the Service and others. Our army of "soil doctors," in alliance with local soil conservation districts, now constitute one of the major institutional forces in agriculture. It is a political force to be reckoned with in all matters of policy directly affecting the use of farm land. The upstream flood prevention acts of 1944 and 1954 added to the political power of the Soil Conservation Service.[11]

The program of the SCS from the beginning was based in part upon the natural sciences, particularly soil science. However, there is little evidence of any significant influence of economics. Scattered pieces of economic research on soil conservation contain conflicting results in respect to whether soil treatments and uses in accordance with the ideology would result in increases in individual net farm incomes. One complicating factor in research of this kind is the many opportunities on individual farms to increase net incomes under any given price-cost conditions and independently of conservation. It is easy to confound some of these opportunities with budgeted changes in income with conservation farming. Nevertheless, a major "sales pitch" of the SCS is that conservation pays for the individual as well as for society. Lack of complete individual farmer acceptance of soil management plans devised by SCS technicians is evidence of some suspicion by farmers as to whether complete conservation farming pays. Furthermore, it is difficult to assess the actual influence of the SCS in the trend of decreasing amount of exploitation and deterioration of soils on farms in the United States. There have been economic and technological forces associated with this trend. Consumer demand has been shifting to favor less production of soil depleting crops. Also, technical progress has permitted the production of any given output of soil depleting crops on fewer acres, and this trend is continuing. Unquestionably, the SCS has contributed to this technological trend in farming.

It appears to this writer that the major consequence of the technical assistance program of the Soil Conservation Service has been an acceleration of technical progress in farming. Its soil management service also is a farm management service with emphasis on encouraging farmer adoption of new technology in combination with recommended land treatments and uses. Thus, the program has contributed to our current problems with excess productive capacity in the farm sector of our economy. We like to believe that technological progress in farming contributes to efficiency and economic development, both in the farm sector and nationally. In 1947, Theodore W. Schultz raised a question about this belief by the following statement:

It may well be that one of the main causes for the economic

inefficiency of agriculture in Western countries is to be found in the very advances in farm technology and the researches that have made this possible, coupled with the forward strides that have been made in farm management as it is now conceived and applied.[12]

Some analysis is required to disentangle the issues about the contributions of developments in our farming to economic development and efficiency in agricultural resource use. Much of the remainder of this chapter will focus on these issues, but with emphasis on the role of our land institutions in the developments to date.

## ROLE OF LAND INSTITUTIONS IN ECONOMIC DEVELOPMENT AND EFFICIENCY

Earlier, I quoted from a recent speech by Secretary Freeman in my discussion of the family farm. I now will present other statements from that speech depicting the rather popular view by the strong adherents of the family-farm ideology that this institution was responsible for the development of a highly efficient modern agriculture:

> The family farm economy has proved its superiority by developing the world's most efficient and productive agriculture. ... [p. 6]
> Recently I was told by one of the leaders in India that they were not nearly as impressed with America's ability to produce automobiles and appliances and ICBMs as they were with our ability to produce *more than enough* food with only 9 per cent of our working force. ... [p. 7]
> As we recognize the efficiency and productivity of American farmers, as we recognize the great asset that we have in the family farms of this Nation, we must make sure of their opportunity to gain adequate rewards for their achievement. ... [p. 10]
> Are we going to say that within our democratic system we cannot solve the social and economic problems that are related to our abundant productivity? ... [p. 17]
> ... so many of the sincere, liberal, and usually well informed analysts of economic problems are actually *not* well informed about the farm problem. ... [p. 2][13]

As one of those sincere, liberal, and (I hope) informed analysts of economic problems with some ideas about the farm problem I am condemned in advance by the Secretary if I choose to disagree with him, which I do. The statements quoted do raise some basic questions about efficiency, economic development, and the role of a land institution such as the family farm in our agricultural and national progress. Can we have the world's most efficient agriculture, which I believe we have, but still have a marked degree of inefficiency in farm resource use? I believe so. The meaning of efficiency is a crucial element in this belief. Is our food supply produced by 9 per cent, or less, of our work force? No, there are many more contributors to this production than those actually employed on farms. Does the presence of social and economic problems in our agricultural sector, as, for example, low incomes of many farmers, reflect an inefficiency of our farm economy? I believe so, and this was the major thesis of Professor Schultz in his article on this subject a decade and a half ago.[14] Is the family-farm institution really responsible for the technical progress we have experienced in our farming? At best, it could be one of the contributing conditions for the kind of progress we have experienced. But, there are other aspects of our land institutions, and conditions unrelated to land tenure, which have contributed to technological advance in farming.

Economic development occurs when there is an increase in real per capita incomes in a nation. According to history, no nation can experience the kind of economic development that has occurred in many countries of the western world while remaining primarily agrarian in economic organization. Thus, a necessary condition for economic development in the United States was a transformation from the agrarian economy of our pioneer period to an economy primarily nonagricultural in orientation. What has been the contribution of our land policy, and land institutions, to this transformation?

The policy of rapid settlement of the public domain prevented the development of population pressure on the land resources in any areas of the kind we now observe in many underdeveloped countries of the world. Having vast quantities of land resources in relation to population was prerequisite to this policy.

Acreages settled per family were large enough for adoption of the labor-saving machine technology that was to come prior to the end of the settlement period. The policy of no restrictions on acreages that may be acquired by families following settlement added to the ability (and incentive) of the families to adopt labor-saving technology when available. The point often is made that the family farm tenure system was more consistent with adoption of labor-saving technology than others due to the shortage of labor relative to other factors of production on family farms. This may have been the situation during the early period of the machine age. Plantations in the South did have less reason for desiring labor-saving technology—they had a plentiful supply of labor—slaves prior to the Civil War, and sharecroppers after the Civil War. But this argument does not necessarily apply in case of other nonfamily farms, particularly in the West. The larger-than-family farmers in the West (e.g., ranchers) may have had more reason than the family farmers to desire labor-saving technology.

The potential demand for technology by farmers, particularly labor-saving machinery, was a necessary but insufficient condition for technological advance. The technology had to be produced at a cost farmers could afford to pay. This production came at an opportune time in our history. First, there was machinery and equipment to combine with horse power to substitute for human effort. The tractor and associated equipment did not become prominent until after the turn of the century. The adoption of these permitted the release of rural population for nonfarm employment. Another necessary condition for economic development was the creation of nonfarm job opportunities at a rate sufficient for employing the released rural labor. Except for the depression period during the 1930's, these off-farm employment opportunities did expand.

Settlement policy indirectly contributed to the expansion of nonfarm employment opportunities. The geographical expansion of farming brought forth demands for additional transportation facilities, service establishments for new communities, public services, etc.

Farm families are contributing a small and decreasing proportion of the total resources going into our agricultural production. In addition to the farm sector, our agricultural industry includes the agri-businesses carrying out the functions of producing inputs (including services) used by farmers in production, and processing and marketing products of farms. Also, the industry includes the firms producing and marketing inputs used by the agri-businesses, and public employees in agricultural research and education and in administration of the various agricultural policies and programs. About 40 per cent of total consumer expenditure for goods and services is for the end products of the agri-businesses. Thus, as a rough approximation, 40 per cent or more of our national resources are devoted to agricultural production. Expressions indicating the efficiency of our agriculture by pointing out the number of on-farm workers in relation to total national work force or population are, at best, misleading. Technological and other developments have resulted in the movement of many functions once performed on farms into agri-businesses. This has resulted in increased specialization in production by the farm sector and a decrease in its functions in agricultural production. This process is continuing.[15]

The process of transfer of functions in agricultural production off the land has put a major burden on the farm sector to adjust. Capital, technology, and off-farm labor has substituted for on-farm land and labor. Any lag in adjusting on-farm resource use consistent with "optimum" substitution of this kind reflects inefficiency in agricultural production. This is not to say that farmers as individuals bear all the responsibility for existing inefficiency in the agricultural industry or in the farm sector thereof. The organizational setup, original settlement pattern, land institutions, and other factors have an influence. However, any unfavorable consequences of inefficiency in agriculture do tend to fall primarily upon farm people in the form of low incomes in relation to incomes of other Americans. Also, these unfavorable consequences tend to be distributed unevenly among farm families due primarily to differences in their potential for economic adjustment. I shall pick on two related problems in adjustment by farm families to current and prospective technological and economic conditions: (1) acquisition and intergeneration transfer of sufficient assets per farm to meet "acceptable" standards of efficiency and of incomes to farm families for their labor and management, and (2) the wide variations in potential of farm families to adjust.

Most of our farms as businesses have life cycles corresponding to the life cycles of families. This means the assets of these businesses are refinanced each generation. At present, it requires $100,000 to $200,000 in capital assets, including the value of land, for a family to achieve a reasonable degree of efficiency in farming and to obtain labor and management income comparable to income standards of nonfarm families. This price is going up. Obviously, few potential beginning farmers of today can start with an operating unit of this size, and few can accumulate to an efficient size of business in a lifetime of farming. The ideal of individual family ownership of farms is in trouble. Furthermore, this situation likely will grow worse instead of better.

A major factor in the high capital requirements for farming is the price of land. The price of farm real estate has about doubled since 1950,[16] yet, in this period, aggregate net farm income has declined. Why? Are these inflated land prices which will fall when everybody (particularly farmers) realize they are inflated? The answer is not this simple. The economic importance of farm land as a contributor to farm output has declined as reported by Professor Schultz in some of his writings.[17] This is due to the increase in off-farm production of inputs which have substituted for farm land. However, the farm real estate market is not reflecting this decline in importance of farm land. In defiance of our marginal productivity theory in economics, land's share of the total farm output is increasing, and this increase puts pressure on the earnings of labor and management used in farming.

It is my thesis that changes in aggregate net incomes of farmers have come to be poor predictors of changes in farm real estate prices. Technological progress has pushed back the limits on farm size faster than the realized increase in acreages per farm, and this has increased the potential demand for farm land by farmers. Effective demand by farmers for farm land as reflected in the market depends only on the buying power of a small proportion of the farmers. Only about 3 per cent of the farm land is in bona fide sales each year, and a relatively small number of farmers and others active in the market determine the price of all farm land. Who are these participants in the land market? Mainly, they are the higher-income farmers who are making the larger farms larger, urban people who are making investments, and a few beginning farmers who are risking much to gain a foothold in the occupation of farming.[18] The "typical" farm operator is not an important participant in the land market on the buying side. He needs all his income for maintenance of the farm as a going concern and for family consumption. The resistance or inability of farm families to adjust out of farming adds pressure to farm real estate prices on the supply side.

The income and wealth inequality of farm families contributes to the pressure on farm real estate prices and perpetuates additional inequality via the results of the land market. Additional contributing influences to this process are the federal farm programs. Farm land has come to be a major resting place for the income transfers to the farm sector of the economy. Such programs as acreage allotments with price supports, research and education, soil conservation, ACP payments, etc., all add to the pressure on farm real estate prices.[19] That is, ownership of land is prerequisite to gaining a major portion of the beneficial effects of these income transfers. A new generation of farmers who actually purchase land are not beneficiaries of these programs; they pay for the benefits via the land market. However, once a new-generation farmer pays the price, he has a vested economic interest in retaining the programs. Unless there is a continuous increase in income transfers to farmers into perpetuity with resulting continuous increases in land values, the cost of the farm programs tend to be borne by new-generation landowners as well as by the taxpayers.[20] The land institutions provide the mechanism for these kinds of distributive effects.[21]

There appears to be small hope for a beginning farmer with few resources to climb an agricultural ladder of bygone days to ownership of a farm of efficient size. Intergeneration transfers of large aggregates of resources as going businesses may be the solution, but many problems associated with this procedure remain unsolved. Acquisition and intergeneration transfer of large aggre-gates of capital are not new problems—they simply have become acute in recent years.

The potential for adjusting going farm businesses to techno-logical and economic change varies widely among farmers. Gen-erally, the larger farm businesses have the greater potential for upward adjustments in size. This is where the greater amount of adjustment is taking place, and the result is a continuous widen-ing of the property and income distribution within the farm sector. The process has the effect of enlarging our areas of rural poverty and reducing the potential of families in those areas to adjust.[22]

Did our land institutions or policy contribute to the develop-ment of large areas of rural poverty in this country? According to a hypothesis by Galbraith, and research results by Booth, the answer appears to be yes.[23] Galbraith's hypothesis is that the settlement pattern initiated inequality in incomes among farm families. That is, where the land-man ratio was greatest initially the greater degree of adjustment and progress took place. For this thesis, one must measure land in productive capacity as well as in acres. Booth found agreement of the facts with the hypo-thesis in his study of a 24-county area in Eastern Oklahoma.

The relevance of the settlement pattern hypothesis for explaining variation in adjustment potential of farm families appears to be its perpetuating influence. Land institutions influence the nature of other institutions in a local area, which, in turn, influence the economic development and adjustment potential of a local area. Where too many people initially settled in a local area, a greater amount of adjustment was needed accompanying technological and economic change, yet this also is where the local institutional setup had the greater degree of adjustment necessary for achieving economic development poten-tial comparable with areas less heavily populated initially. Apparently, this influence of local institutions now is a problem in some of our more prosperous rural areas. Karl Fox expresses the idea that county institutions in Iowa are inadequate for local economic development; the need is for a larger matrix upon which to focus economic development policy.[24]

It is not my intention to blame land institutions or policy for all the ills of our farm economy. Many other factors contribute to our current rural social problems. However, generally, I conclude that our current programs have different effects than intended, and this is due partly to the influence of land institutions in determining these effects.

## ECONOMIC FORCES AND LAND INSTITUTIONS OF THE FUTURE

Wisdom often has been associated with foresight, or ability to predict the future. The end objective of science is to make valid predictions. There are many limitations of economics in this respect, and too often the predictions of economists are the opposite of the realized state of affairs. Nevertheless, the public expects economists to make predictions, and I will fulfill this obligation cautiously.

During the past two decades, we have observed much change in our farm economy due primarily to technological and economic forces. My image of the future is that these forces will become more intense with accompanying increases in intensity of adjustment problems and adjustments made in our farm economy. Changes in our land institutions likely will come about only by the force of technological and economic circumstances instead of by deliberate acts through public policy. Some recent and current trends with direct or indirect consequences in land tenure are (1) more farmer acceptance of tenure systems and arrangements other than the ideal of owner-operator family farms; (2) increase in contract farming and vertical integration; (3) increase in dependence of farm families upon nonfarm sources of income; and (4) more interest by farm families in means of transfering farm businesses to oncoming generations.

Currently, about 40 per cent of the farm land is owned by people other than operating farmers. Although many of these people are retired farmers, the trend toward more ownership by urban people is evident. The increase in farm tenancy has been more prevalent in the more commercial, crop-farming areas. Part-ownership has become a major tenure pattern, particularly in the Great Plains.

Contract farming is not of recent origin, but it has increased recently in importance. Federal acreage allotments and marketing agreements represent a form of contract farming. We have had contract farming in our vegetable and fruit production for many years. A more important recent trend is the transition of this arrangement into integration of farm production with the agri-businesses.

An important adjustment by farm families to the low earnings from farming is acquisition of income from nonfarm sources while remaining in farming. Nonfarm sources of income amount to about a third of the total net incomes of farm families. It is difficult to assess the significance of part-time farming—whether it mainly amounts to a transition of families out of farming, or whether it represents a permanent and growing source of income for farm families. I am inclined to believe it is the former, even though it has increased in recent years and will likely continue to do so in the immediate future.

More interest of farm families in transferring farm businesses intact to oncoming generations is reflected mainly by the growth in farm family corporations. So far, however, these corporations represent a small proportion of our farms.

During recent years, the United States Department of Agriculture has come forth with projections of land requirements to meet our projected food and fiber needs for about fifty years into the future.[25] The picture presented is opposite to the Malthusian thesis of growing pressure of a population on its food supply. Notably absent in these projections are the number and sizes of farm businesses of the future for efficiency in production. There have been guesses that the major part of our farming twenty-five to fifty years hence will be organized into units representing asset values of one-quarter to one-half million dollars. I am unable to present a better guess than this of the sizes which would be consistent with a reasonable degree of efficiency in farming during the latter part of this century. However, I believe such a change in our farming businesses will require some major changes in our land tenure systems, particularly in areas where the family-farm tradition has been strongest.

Lindsay suggests that the trend of vertical integration of

farms with agri-businesses will be the predominant development of the future, and, by the end of this century, nearly all of our commercial farming will be fully integrated with the firms producing farm inputs and providing market outlets for farm products.[26] This means farm families will provide labor and some management in farm production, but not necessarily the land and capital. This development, if it materializes, would solve the asset acquisition and transfer problem of farm families by drastically changing the existing tenure systems. Whether it does become a reality will depend upon whether workable alternative means are created for solving the tenure problem which are more acceptable to the farmers and to the public. That is, I am inclined to agree with Lindsay if we assume such alternatives will not be forthcoming.

As a possible alternative, Dorner suggests a particular form of corporate farming, where stocks representing farm assets, particularly land, are managed by a public holding company or a federal agency such as the Farm Credit Administration.[27] Farmers could obtain equity in the businesses by purchasing the stocks, but such purchases by the farmers would not be prerequisite to their employment in farming. Development of this alternative would require federal legislation, and this likely would encounter insurmountable opposition from the family-farm philosophers and adherents.

Another recent proposal is the idea of permanent mortgages on farm land. This would amount to public leasing of farm land to operators where public ownership would be in the form of mortgages held by the federal credit agencies, and financial terms of the leases would be annual payments of interest on the loans by the farmers. By this procedure, beginning farmers never would have to obtain equity in the land they operated, although they could do so by choosing to make some principal payments on the loans.

There may be other alternatives in public land policy which would contribute to the solution of the tenure problem, but no drastic changes in our tenure policy likely will be forthcoming. Our tenure policy is too firmly engrained in traditional values to be changed. This means what develops likely will depend upon the technological and economic forces of the future and upon what is possible under current policy. I expect the recent trends in farm tenancy, ownership of farm land by urban people, and vertical integration to continue. There likely will be marginal adjustments by farm families such as more attention to transfer of farming assets to oncoming generations, including more family corporations. However, vertical integration of farming with agri-businesses eventually could become the dominant trend under these conditions. Its development is not excluded by current land policy.

A major force which may contribute to vertical integration, other than the problem of intergeneration transfer of large aggregates of resources in farming, is the growing economic power of agri-businesses providing market outlets for farm products. These agri-businesses already have much influence upon the location and degree of specialization in farm production. The advantage of integration to the agri-businesses will increase as the gap between potential and actual efficiency and scale of farming operations increases. I am not proposing that a development such as vertical integration necessarily means our farms will be organized into corporations. They still could retain many of the characteristics of family enterprises, even though much labor would be hired and some limits on family contribution of capital and management could be expected.

In my effort to be realistic, I have experienced a poverty of relevant facts for handling the problem of prospective changes in the organization of our farming. This poverty could be reduced by research, at least to the extent that the public could be made more aware of problems associated with our farm land tenure structure. Such research also may reveal some presently unknown shortcomings of current and prospective farm policies having major purposes of increasing farm income and preserving the family farm. It seems to me what is most needed is less tradition and more realism in our farm policies. This can be accomplished only through research.

## NOTES

1. For an alternative view, see Glenn L. Johnson and Lewis K. Zerby, "Values in the Solution of Credit Problems," in E. L. Baum, *et al.* (Eds.), *Capital and Credit Needs in a Changing Agriculture* (Iowa State, 1961), Chap. 19. My views in this respect are nearly consistent with those of C. West Churchman as presented in *Prediction and Optimal Decision* (Prentice-Hall, 1961).

2. For an alternative view, see John M. Brewster, "Beliefs, Values and Economic Development," *Journal of Farm Economics*, November, 1961, pp. 779–96.

3. Quoted by Paul A. Samuelson, *Economics: An Introductory Analysis*, 5th Ed. (New York: McGraw-Hill, 1961), p. 775.

4. To this writer, there does not appear to be agreement upon the meaning of democracy. For expressions of several different meanings of the term, some of which are inconsistent, see Robert Parks, "The Meaning of Democracy," *Farm Policy Forum* (Winter, 1955), pp. 2–8.

5. For more detailed accounts of our land policy, particularly up to 1900, see Joseph Ackerman and Marshall Harris (Eds.), *Family Farm Policy* (Chicago, 1947), Ch. 2; and Murray R. Benedict, *Farm Policies of the United States, 1790–1950* (The Twentieth Century Fund, 1953), Chap. 1. The above statement of land policy mainly is an abstraction of the discussion by Ackerman and Harris.

6. Public rights in respect to privately held land will not be included in the analysis of forces giving rise to our land policy.

7. Ackerman and Harris, *op. cit.*, Chaps. 3 and 15.

8. See John M. Brewster's paper in this book.

9. Willard W. Cochrane, *Farm Prices, Myth and Reality* (Minnesota, 1958), p. 131. One may wonder about the degree of sincerity of Cochrane in this statement, for his next sentence is as follows: "As far as I know, I am indifferent to the question of government ownership and operation of productive resources."

10. Orville L. Freeman, "Sustaining the Values of the Family Farm." Address at annual banquet of the Farmers Union Central Exchange, St. Paul, Minnesota, Mar. 13, 1962, USDA 949–62, p. 4.

11. See Ross Talbot's discussion of the political force of the Soil Conservation Service in Chapter 6.

12. "How Efficient Is American Agriculture," *Journal of Farm Economics*, August, 1947, p. 658.

13. Orville L. Freeman, "Sustaining the Values of the Family Farm," *op. cit.* I interpret Secretary Freeman's conception of the farm problem, from statements in this speech, to be the lack of sufficient economic power by farmers in the market place to achieve the economic rewards they deserve.

14. "How Efficient Is American Agriculture," *op. cit.*, pp. 644–58.

15. For a more formal discussion of the organization of our agriculture, see Quentin W. Lindsay, "The Problem of Periodic Reorganization in Ameri-

can Agriculture," *Journal of Agricultural Economics* (English), May, 1961, esp. pp. 360–61.

16. Cf. Elton B. Hill and Marshall Harris, *Family Farm Transfers and Some Tax Consideration,* North Central Regional Publication 127 and Michigan Agricultural Experiment Station Special Bulletin 436, 1961, esp. pp. 8–9.

17. e.g., Theodore W. Schultz, "Land in Economic Growth," in Harold G. Halcrow, *et al.* (Eds.), *Modern Land Policy* (University of Illinois Press, 1960), pp. 17–40.

18. For some empirical evidence of this hypothesis about the farm real estate market, see Don Kanel, *Opportunities for Beginning Farmers,* North Central Regional Publication 102 and Nebraska Agricultural Experiment Station Bulletin 452, 1960; and, Roger W. Strohbehn and John F. Timmons, *Ownership of Iowa's Farm Land,* Iowa Agricultural Experiment Station Research Bulletin 489, 1960.

19. Detailed analysis of the incidence of costs and benefits of federal farm programs is being prepared for publication by an interregional land tenure subcommittee.

20. Possible beneficial effects of the programs, such as achieving a greater degree of balance of supply and demand at reasonable prices to farmers, creation of a reserve capacity to produce farm products, etc., are not considered in the above statement of the incidence of costs and benefits of the federal farm programs.

21. Cf. Walter E. Chryst and John F. Timmons, "The Economic Role of Land Resource Institutions in Agricultural Adjustment," in *Dynamics of Land Use—Needed Adjustment* (Iowa State University Press, 1961), pp. 238–52.

22. Cf. W. B. Back and Verner G. Burt, *Potential for Agricultural Adjustment and Development in the Ouachita Highland of Oklahoma,* Oklahoma Agricultural Experiment Station Bulletin B-582, 1961.

23. John Kenneth Galbraith, "Inequality in Agriculture—Problems and Program," First J. J. Morrison Memorial Lecture, Department of Agricultural Economics, Ontario Agricultural College, 1956 (Mimeograph); and, E. J. R. Booth, *"Economic Development in Eastern Oklahoma until 1950,"* Ph.D. thesis submitted to the faculty of the Graduate School of Vanderbilt University, 1961.

24. Karl Fox, "The Study of Interactions Between Agriculture and the Nonfarm Economy: Local, Regional and National," *Journal of Farm Economics,* February, 1962, pp. 1–34.

25. Cf. *Resource Requirements for Meeting Projected Needs for Agricultural Production, Texas River Basins,* Prepared for United States Study Commission—Texas, Farm Economics Division, Economic Research Service, 1961, (Mimeograph).

26. "The Problem of Periodic Reorganization in American Agriculture," *op. cit.*

27. Peter Dorner, "The Farm Problem: A Challenge to Social Invention," *Journal of Farm Economics,* November, 1960, esp. pp. 822–24.

PAST, PRESENT, AND FUTURE
DEMANDS FOR LAND
IN THE U. S.

HARRY A. STEELE
and NORMAN E. LANDGREN

# Land for Agriculture

THE LAND AREA OF THE UNITED STATES must fulfill increasing
demands from a growing population and a continuously developing economy. Demands for land and its products and services will
change in form and intensity as they have in the past. The
supply of agricultural land is likely to be subject to increasing
pressure from urbanization and greatly expanded public installations and facilities. Such uses are creating demands for land
which, to a large extent, were nonexistent or insignificant
throughout much of our history.

The demand for land is made up of a multitude of demands
from various segments of the economy. Some of these are for
land for direct consumption uses, such as use for a home site.
Other demands are derived from the need for products that must
go through many steps of additional processing before reaching
the ultimate consumer. On the supply side, there are many
unique characteristics of land, water, and other natural resources:
relatively limited quantity, relatively fixed productive capacity
under a given state of technology, and immobility as to location. Decisions regarding land use are often irreversible. The
sequence of use and timing are extremely important. Since many
of the demands for land are derived and because the characteristics of land supply are unique, it is difficult to analyze the
demand for land in the sense that one might analyze the demand
for an agricultural commodity or an industrial product.

Agriculture—the production of food and fiber for domestic
consumption and export—is the most important claimant upon
land. From early settlement of the United States until the
present there has, in general, been sufficient land available to
satisfy the agricultural needs of the nation with more than
enough left over to fulfill the nonagricultural needs. Aided by
the availability, conquest, and development of frontier lands,

and technological revolutions in production techniques, our agriculture has forcefully repudiated the predicted Malthusian consequences of population growth.

But what about the future? Will more land be needed to produce the increased food and fiber requirements of an expanding population, thereby causing increased agricultural demand to compete with an expected increased nonagricultural demand for land? Or will we be able to meet future agricultural requirements with less land than now used, thereby releasing to nonagricultural uses some land currently in agricultural uses? Answers to questions such as these are requisite to the formulation of land policy.

This paper focuses on the past, present, and future use of land for agriculture in the United States. Historical trends in use and the expansion of agriculture through new land settlement are briefly reviewed. The changing structure of modern agriculture is examined in some detail. Factors determining future demands for the products of land are appraised. Based upon a set of assumptions about these factors and about resource productivity, estimates of land requirements for agriculture in 1980 are presented. The potential for meeting demands for agricultural products further in the future is briefly discussed.

## NATIVE VEGETATION—AN INDICATOR OF LAND USE

Native vegetation reflects environment and is the product of past and present climatic and soils factors. As such, it is a good indicator of the inherent suitability of land for agriculture. A look at the native vegetation of the United States reveals the high quality and broad extent of the land resource base.

In its natural state, about half (48 per cent) of the land area of the continental United States was forested (Fig. 8.1). The forests formed two belts, one inland from the Atlantic coast and the other inland from the Pacific coast. The eastern forest was predominantly broad-leaved, but with extensive areas of pine in the Southeast and of spruce, fir, and other conifers in the Northeast. This forest was distributed over both valleys and mountains; it covered nearly all of the humid East, except the prairies, extending into parts of the present states of Minnesota,

NATIVE VEGETATION

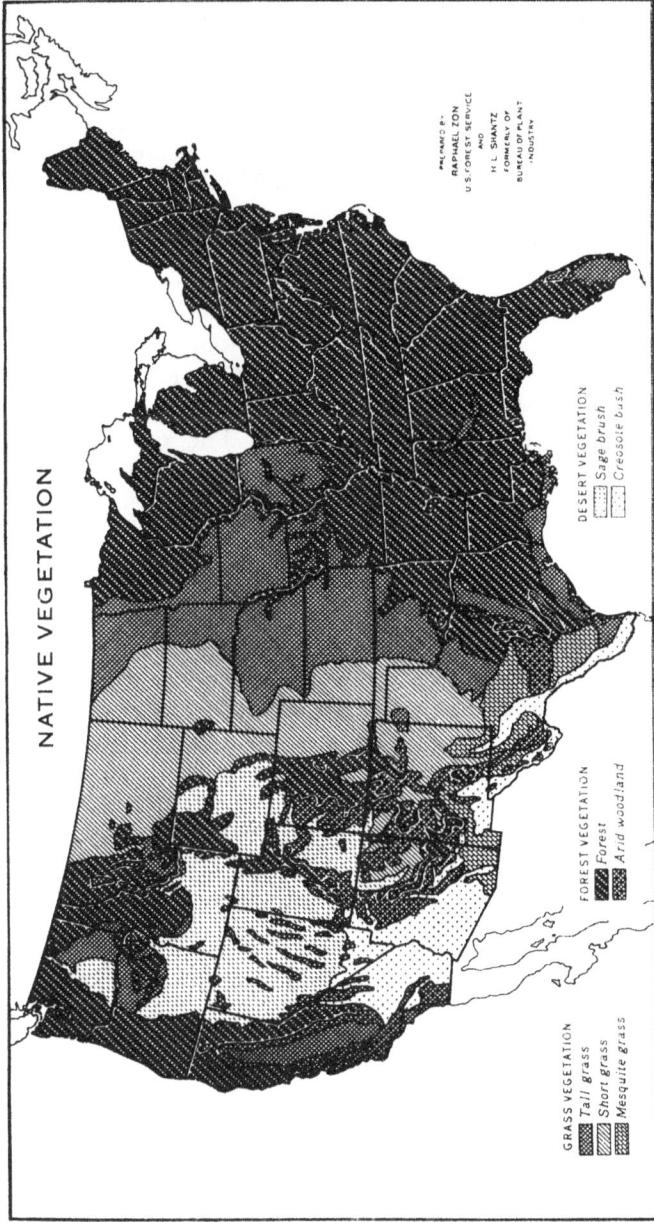

GRASS VEGETATION
Tall grass
Short grass
Mesquite grass

FOREST VEGETATION
Forest
Arid woodland

DESERT VEGETATION
Sage brush
Creosote bush

PREPARED BY
RAPHAEL ZON
U.S. FOREST SERVICE
AND
H.L. SHANTZ
FORMERLY OF
BUREAU OF PLANT
INDUSTRY

U.S. DEPARTMENT OF AGRICULTURE

FIG. 8.1

NEG. 58(5)-2499 AGRICULTURAL RESEARCH SERVICE

Iowa, Missouri, Oklahoma, and Texas. The western forest was principally coniferous, and was concentrated along the Pacific coast with scattered segments throughout the mountain areas west of the Great Plains.

Nearly two-fifths (38 per cent) of the land area was covered with grasses. The bulk of the grasslands was located in a broad belt separating the eastern and western forests. This central grasslands area was divided into two parts, the tall grass (prairie grassland) and the short grass (plains grassland) areas. The tall grass area was characterized by a plentiful supply of rainfall. It occupied 16 per cent of the present total land area of the United States. Tall grasses east of the Mississippi River principally were located in Illinois, the black-belt of Mississippi and Alabama, and the Florida Everglades. The short grass area, characaterized by more limited rainfall, began at about the one-hundredth meridian and extended westward to the mountains, accounting for about 14 per cent of the total land area. Other grasses, such as mesquite, bunchgrass and marshgrass, covered 8 per cent of the United States.

Desert shrub vegetation grew over the remaining 14 per cent of the United States. These shrubs were adapted to limited rainfall and grew throughout the intermountain region where rainfall or other environmental factors were not conducive to other types of vegetal growth.

## EXPANSION OF LAND SETTLEMENT AND DEVELOPMENT

Although the natural characteristics of land have strongly influenced both the pattern of settlement and the use of land, geographic location was perhaps the greatest single factor affecting the growth of the earliest settlements in the United States. The first settlement along the Atlantic coast at St. Augustine, Florida, in 1565 was slow to grow. The second settlement at Jamestown, Virginia, in 1607, and subsequent settlements along the Chesapeake Bay also grew slowly. After the initial arrival of settlers in the North Atlantic Colonies, however, their numbers grew more rapidly. Good harbors and a somewhat shorter sailing distance across the North Atlantic to Europe gave impetus to a steady stream of European immigrants into these Colonies.

The development of agricultural lands in the United States resulted from the conquest of the frontier by an expanding, westward-bound population. Since a population census was never taken in the Colonies, it is possible to trace population movements accurately only after 1790, the year of the first census. In 1790, the population of the thirteen states and unorganized territory was estimated as approximately 3.9 million people. Settlement extended from Maine to southern Georgia but was confined almost entirely within the Atlantic Plain, reaching an average depth of penetration from the Atlantic coast of 255 miles.[1] The Alleghany and Appalachian Mountains were natural barriers to the westward movement, but by 1790, settlement had begun to penetrate beyond them. More than twenty isolated settlements in the "western wilderness," however, accounted for less than 5 per cent of the population.[2]

Although hunters and trappers in search of game led the way, early settlement inland from the Atlantic coast was principally agricultural. In most cases settlement took place on the more productive soils. Transportation access to the Atlantic seaboard was important and thus inland population movements also tended to follow navigable streams.

As the population moved westward, forest lands were cleared and converted to agricultural uses. It has been estimated that there were 30 million acres of improved lands in the United States in 1790, of which 8 million were tilled or in gardens and orchards, 8 million were devoted to meadow and fallow, and 14 million were improved pasturelands.[3] Agricultural products produced on these lands were more than sufficient to meet domestic requirements and the surplus was exported in exchange for commodities or articles not produced in the United States. Principal agricultural exports included wheat, flour, corn, cornmeal, and raw tobacco; other important exports were rice, beef, pork, manufactured tobacco products, cotton, and flaxseed.[4]

Heavy immigration continued into the nineteenth century and the ever-increasing population pushed westward beyond the mountains. This westward population thrust was not uniform

and, in general, did not represent a directed or organized effort
to settle the land. Pioneers chose their own routes and usually,
after crossing the mountains, followed rivers and settled in the
valleys. Large pockets of unsettled lands to the rear of the frontier were bypassed and left for later settlement.

By 1850, the population of the United States had increased
to about 23.3 million inhabitants. The frontier had been extended

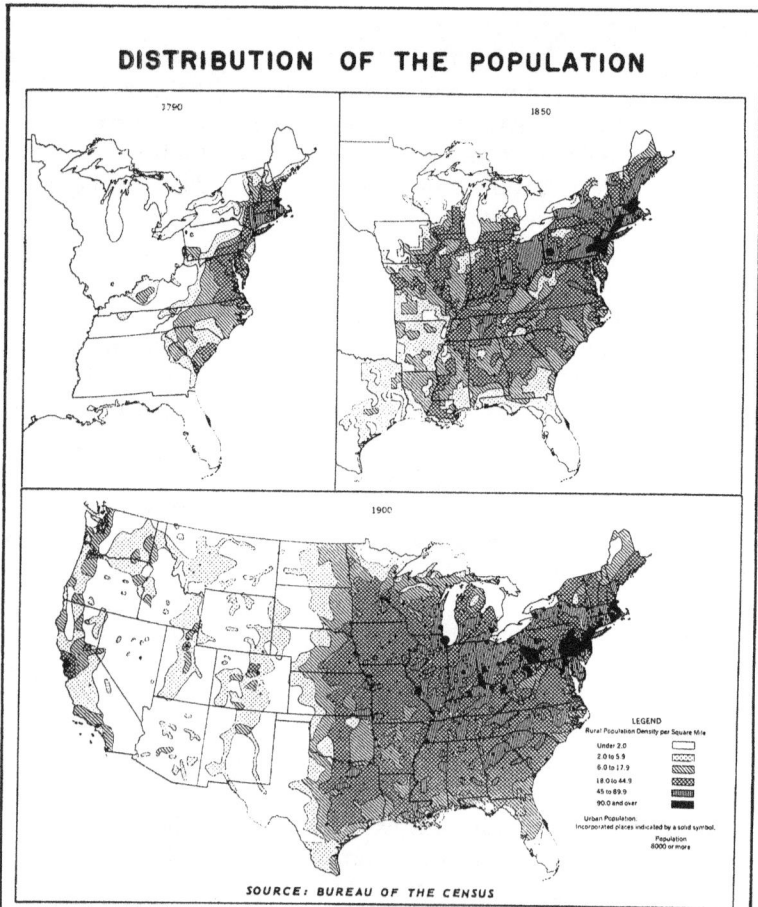

DISTRIBUTION OF THE POPULATION

LEGEND
Rural Population Density per Square Mile

Under 2.0
2.0 to 5.9
6.0 to 17.9
18.0 to 44.9
45 to 89.9
90.0 and over

Urban Population:
Incorporated places indicated by a solid symbol.
Population
8000 or more

SOURCE: BUREAU OF THE CENSUS

U. S. DEPARTMENT OF AGRICULTURE     NEG. ERS 1147-62(5)     ECONOMIC RESEARCH SERVICE

Fig. 8.2

to eastern Minnesota, central Iowa, the western borders of Missouri and Arkansas, and eastern Texas, a line roughly coinciding with the western limit of the Eastern forest area (Fig. 8.2). Having advanced through the forested lands, agricultural settlement was beginning to spread on to the prairies. A few pioneers had penetrated farther west to settle in Oregon, Utah, and California.

Since the United States economy was principally agrarian

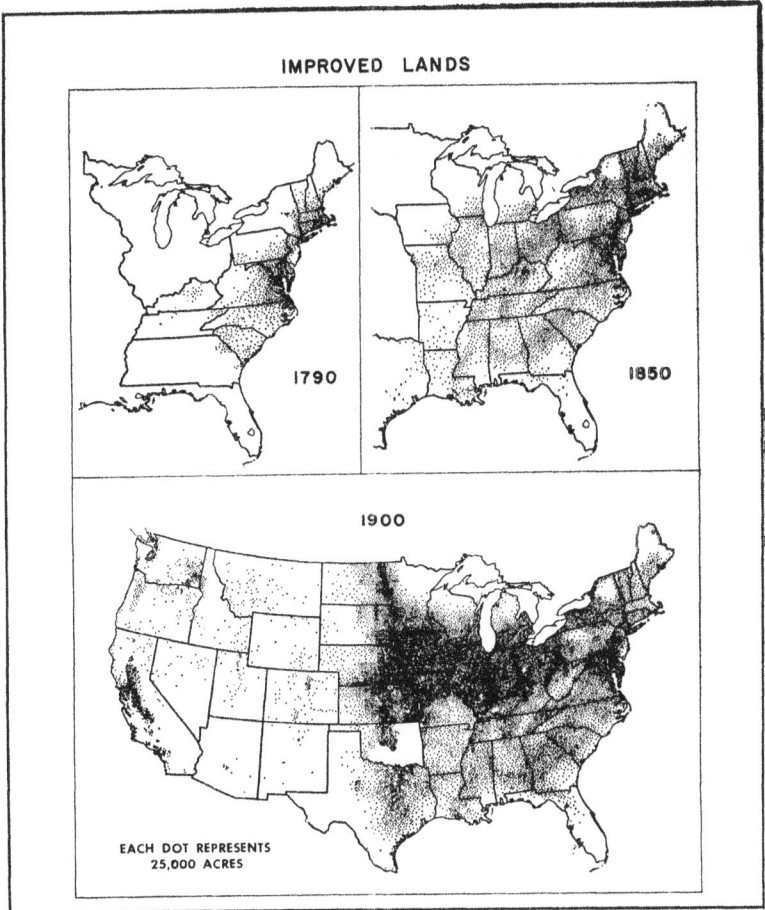

IMPROVED LANDS

1790

1850

1900

EACH DOT REPRESENTS
25,000 ACRES

U.S. DEPARTMENT OF AGRICULTURE     NEG. ERS 1146-62(5) ECONOMIC RESEARCH SERVICE

Fig. 8.3

during the first half of the nineteenth century, the development of agricultural lands accompanied, and corresponded to, the westward population migration (Fig. 8.3). By 1850, lands in farms embraced 294 million acres, of which 113 million acres were cropped and 181 million acres were farm woodlands, some of which were used for grazing.[5] The extent of land development between 1790 and 1850 is particularly impressive when it is remembered that the virgin forests had to be cleared before much of the land could be used for crops.

Throughout the last half of the nineteenth century, the strong current of westward migration continued. This population movement was facilitated by completion of the transcontinental railroad in 1869 and was encouraged by public policy which sought to dispose of the public domain and bring about concomitant economic development of the West through such devices as the Homestead Act of 1862 and the Desert Land Act of 1877. By the turn of the century settlement was fairly general to the Pacific coast (Fig. 8.2). The expansion of dry land farming coupled with irrigation of about 7.5 million acres in the West[6] had increased the amount of cropland in the United States to 319 million acres.[7] The Corn Belt had already assumed its role as the dominant agricultural area in the nation (Fig. 8.3).

The conquest of arid and semiarid lands extended into the twentieth century. The Enlarged Homestead Act of 1910 and the Stock-raising Homestead Act of 1916 stimulated the increased agricultural use of arid and semiarid lands. By 1920, dry land farming in the Great Plains region and irrigation in the West had been greatly expanded, and total cropland in the United States had been increased to 402 million acres.[8]

But although the population of the United States numbered only about 106 million people in 1920, the real expansion of agriculture was nearly completed. Agricultural migration to the West had practically ceased even though there was still a heavy migration to West Coast cities. There were signs that agriculture was beginning to contract in some areas. A decrease in improved lands was apparent in the northeastern states and locally in some South Atlantic states. The United States had been settled and young people were beginning to migrate from farms to cities.

The stage was set for structural changes producing the agricultural industry that we have today.

## THE CHANGING STRUCTURE OF AGRICULTURE

During the period 1920 to 1960 the population of the United States increased by 73 million people, or by 69 per cent. The average rate of increase in national income was much more rapid —these four decades were a period of great economic growth. If we accept the likelihood of continued economic progress, a review of the impact of these changing conditions on agriculture, and its response to them, provides insight into the probable future requirements for land for agriculture.

TREND IN LAND UTILIZATION

Perhaps the most significant observation relating to trends in land use since 1920 is that the needs of the nation for agricultural products have been met with a relatively stable, or slightly declining, cropland base (Fig. 8.4). From a peak of 480 million

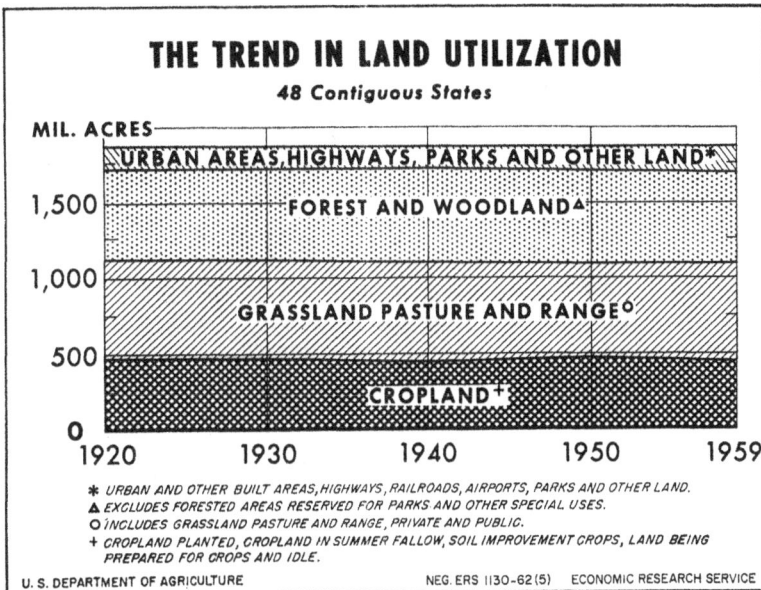

**THE TREND IN LAND UTILIZATION**

**48 Contiguous States**

MIL. ACRES

URBAN AREAS, HIGHWAYS, PARKS AND OTHER LAND*

1,500 — FOREST AND WOODLAND▲

1,000

GRASSLAND PASTURE AND RANGE○

500

CROPLAND+

0
1920    1930    1940    1950    1959

\* URBAN AND OTHER BUILT AREAS, HIGHWAYS, RAILROADS, AIRPORTS, PARKS AND OTHER LAND.
▲ EXCLUDES FORESTED AREAS RESERVED FOR PARKS AND OTHER SPECIAL USES.
○ INCLUDES GRASSLAND PASTURE AND RANGE, PRIVATE AND PUBLIC.
+ CROPLAND PLANTED, CROPLAND IN SUMMER FALLOW, SOIL IMPROVEMENT CROPS, LAND BEING PREPARED FOR CROPS AND IDLE.

U. S. DEPARTMENT OF AGRICULTURE          NEG. ERS 1130-62 (5)    ECONOMIC RESEARCH SERVICE

FIG. 8.4

acres reached between 1920 and 1930, cropland in the 48 contiguous states had declined to 457 million acres by 1959. During the
1950's alone, cropland decreased by 4 per cent. The decrease
since 1920 has not been at a uniform rate. In the late 1930's there
was a decline in cropland of about 13 million acres, with a regain
prior to 1950 of about 11 million acres. The decline in the acreage of cropland harvested during the decade of the 1950's was
even sharper—a drop of about 10 per cent.

Aggregate figures tend to obscure important regional shifts
in cropland use. For example, from 1950 to 1960, approximately
10 per cent of the agricultural counties showed significant
increases in cropland acreage. These increases were more than
offset, however, by decreases in other counties, sometimes within
the same state or region. In general, there has been a tendency
for the amount of cropland to decrease in the East, increase in
the West, and remain relatively stable in the Central States.
Regional shifts reflect the concentration of crops in the more
productive areas, the reversion of marginal lands to grass or
forests, and the continued development of arid and other potentially productive lands. Recent cropland development, however,
has not kept pace with reversion of cropland to other uses,
including nonagricultural uses. Only twelve of the forty-eight
contiguous states showed significant increases in cropland from
1950 to 1959. Nine of these states were in the West and three in
the Corn Belt. A number of northeastern and southeastern states
lost cropland acreage.

It may also be noted from Figure 8.4 that the acreages of pasture and nonforested range, and forests and woodlands, have
been relatively stable during the past four decades. Pasture and
nonforested range has gradually declined from 652 million acres
in 1920 to 630 million acres in 1959. This decrease has resulted
principally from reversion of grassland to forest in the forest
areas, or absorption by nonagricultural uses. Excluding reserved
forest areas, forest and woodlands have increased by 12 million
acres since 1920.[9]

In both absolute and percentage terms the greatest change
in land use since 1920 has been the increase in special-purpose
uses such as urban areas, highways and roads, farmsteads, parks,

and wildlife refuges. During the 1950's, the average rate of absorption of rural land by special-purpose uses was about 2 million acres per year. Approximately 40 per cent of the land shifted to special-purpose uses consisted of cropland and grassland pasture, and about 40 per cent was obtained from forest and 20 per cent from idle land.

GROWTH OF FARM OUTPUT

In spite of the lesser amounts of cropland devoted to agricultural production, gross farm output has been trending upward during the past four decades (Fig. 8.5). In 1960, it was 83 per cent greater than in 1920, compared with the population increase of 69 per cent during the same period. As illustrated in Figure 8.5, since the early 1940's gross farm output has exceeded the domestic requirements of the growing population. Breaking down the composition of gross farm output, we find that the production of livestock and livestock products has increased somewhat more than crops.

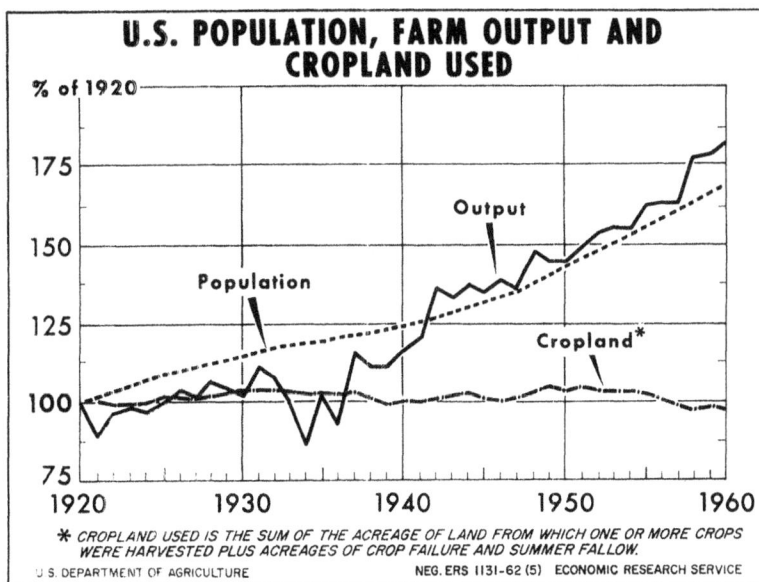

FIG. 8.5

PRODUCTIVITY OF LAND

The great increase in farm output from a relatively constant cropland base has been achieved principally through increased application of nonland capital inputs to land, including the development of highly productive land through irrigation, flood control, and drainage. These inputs have been made available and their costs lowered through technological advances. Although absolutely essential, land is but one of several resources necessary in the production process. Within physical capabilities and economic limits, many resource mixes may be combined with land to achieve a given level of output. Undoubtedly, the increased application of capital inputs to land has been stimulated by production control programs for some crops which have limited acreages but have not limited capital inputs or quantities produced.

With acreage controls, the amount of the land resource that may be used is fixed, and the extent to which capital inputs are applied to land depends upon their prices relative to the prices of the commodities they produce. During World War II, the price structure encouraged adoption of new technologies. Although the parity ratio has been declining since the war, the costs of production-increasing technologies relative to product prices have continued to make it profitable to increase the application of capital inputs to land.

Increased application of capital inputs to land has also taken place in the production of crops not restricted by acreage controls. The extent to which capital inputs are applied depends not only upon the price of the product but also upon the relative prices of land and capital resources. Frequently, farmers have found it profitable to apply additional capital resources, for example, fertilizer, in the production of nonsupported crops rather than to expand their acreages.

The impact of technological innovations on land use requirements is not necessarily confined to innovations directly effecting the productivity of land. For example, a development in animal nutrition that improves the feeding efficiency of livestock permits a given output of product from less feed. Since less feed is required, less land is required to produce it. Hence, such a development indirectly increases the productivity of land. Excepting broilers and turkeys, no spectacular breakthroughs in feeding efficiency have occurred during the past forty years. But some progress has been made and the technical possibilities for major advances are known.

Thus the technological developments which have increased agricultural productivity are many and varied. They are biological as well as mechanical and include fertilizers, power machinery, mechanical equipment, pesticides, herbicides, and insecticides, to name only a few. Although necessarily limited in the number of resources shown, Figure 8.6 illustrates the nature of the revolution in the adoption of technology which has produced a large increase in output per acre and an even greater increase in output per man-hour.

From Figure 8.6 we may observe that since 1920 we have moved rapidly from the "horse age" to mechanized power. This transition was most rapid during the Forties and by now it is

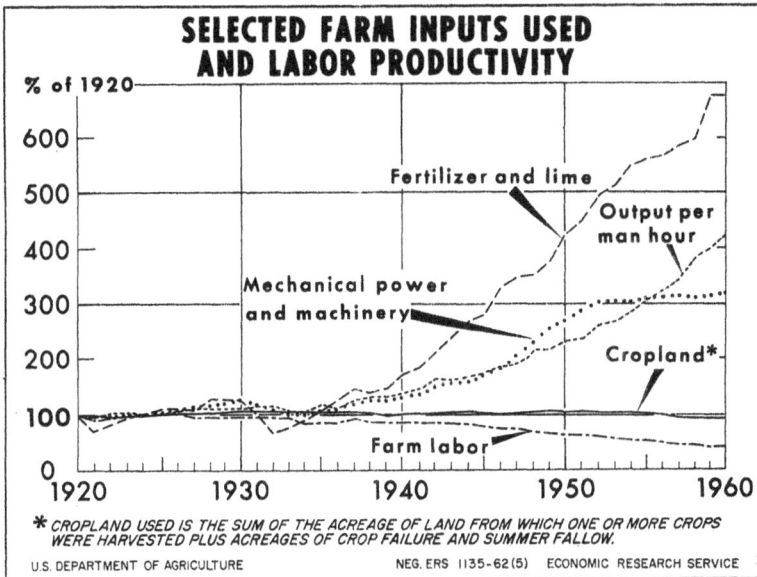

SELECTED FARM INPUTS USED AND LABOR PRODUCTIVITY

* CROPLAND USED IS THE SUM OF THE ACREAGE OF LAND FROM WHICH ONE OR MORE CROPS WERE HARVESTED PLUS ACREAGES OF CROP FAILURE AND SUMMER FALLOW.

U.S. DEPARTMENT OF AGRICULTURE        NEG. ERS 1135-62(5)   ECONOMIC RESEARCH SERVICE

FIG. 8.6

nearly complete. The increasing use of commercial fertilizers and lime has been no less dramatic, and it seems that we are still far from achieving an economic optimum with respect to these inputs. In 1960, farmers used about 575 per cent more fertilizer and lime than in 1920. Most of the increase in fertilizer use came during the latter half of this period. Associated with the adoption of power and mechanical equipment has been a decline of more than 50 per cent in the man-hours of labor used in agriculture. This, coupled with the increase in farm output, has resulted in a more than quadrupled output per man-hour since 1920.

In addition to reducing labor requirements in agriculture, mechanization has released for production for human consumption much cropland formerly required to produce feed for horses and mules. The 83 per cent increase in farm output illustrated in Figure 8.5 represents farm production available for eventual human use and, therefore, excludes the production required to furnish the energy requirements of draft and riding animals. Hence, a part of the increase in output is attributable to the decrease over time of feed requirements of horses and mules. It has been estimated that about 51 per cent of the increase in farm output realized during the 1920's and 1930's and about 23 per cent of the increase achieved from 1940 to 1955 is attributable to the reduction in farm-produced power.[10] Cropland as shown in Figure 8.5, however, includes those acres used for production of feed for draft and riding animals and, therefore, does not accurately picture over time the acreage used to produce products for human use.

The importance of the decline in numbers of horses and mules and the consequential release of cropland to production of products for human consumption is revealed in Figure 8.7. Whereas in 1920, 90 million acres of harvested crops, or one in every four, produced feed for horses and mules, in 1960 only 5 million acres, or one in every sixty-five, produced feed for these animals. The net effect has been that although 36 million fewer acres of cropland were harvested in 1960 than in 1920, the amount of land used for producing products for human use was greater by 49 million acres, an increase of about 18 per cent.

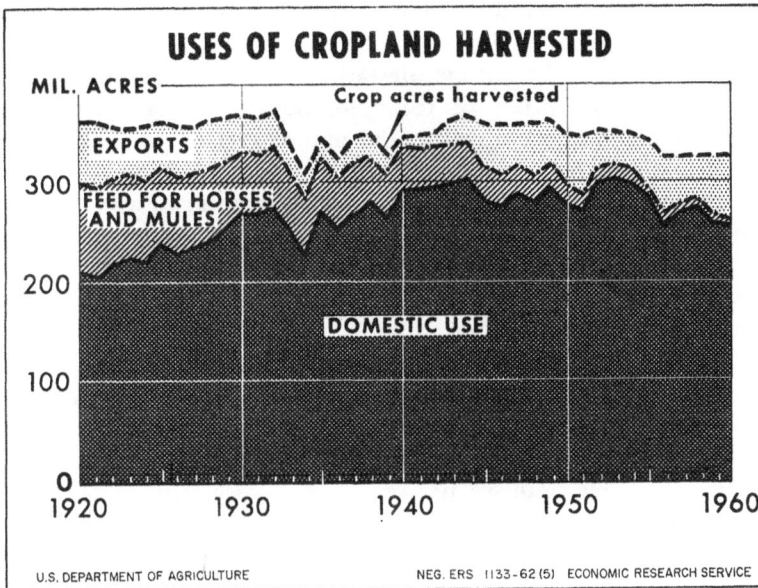

**USES OF CROPLAND HARVESTED**

FIG. 8.7

Most of the released acreage has been used for producing products for domestic consumption. In 1960 this acreage was up 45 million acres from 1920, an increase of 21 per cent. Acreage producing products for export has fluctuated widely during this period, with no perceptible trend. In 1920, one of every six acres of crops harvested produced export products as compared with about one of five in 1960, but within this interval the relative importance of export requirements varied substantially.

IMPACT ON AGRICULTURE

We are all well aware that the structure of agriculture has undergone tremendous adjustments since 1920. In general, these adjustments have been in response to the adoption of technological innovations which have tended to create surplus land and labor resources in agriculture. That land and labor are currently in surplus does not mean that these resources have not reacted to the impact of technological developments; rather, their movement out of agriculture to new uses has not kept pace with increases in productivity.

To discuss at length manifestations of the impact on agriculture of the adoption of technological innovations would be redundant, but to emphasize the nature and magnitude of the adjustments a few observations are made. In 1920, 30.1 per cent of the population of the United States lived on farms; in 1960, the comparable figure was 11.4 per cent. In absolute numbers, farms claimed more than 11 million fewer residents in 1960.[11] During this 40-year period the number of farms declined from nearly 6.5 million to less than 4 million, and the remaining farms have tended to become larger. Whereas in 1920 only 10.7 per cent of the farms were larger than 259 acres, 21.8 per cent exceeded this size in 1959. Also in 1959, 9.1 per cent of the farms were larger than 499 acres and 3.7 per cent larger than 999 acres, compared with 3.4 per cent and 1.1 per cent, respectively, in 1920.

## Agricultural Land Use in Relation to Economic Growth

Economic growth is principally characterized by an increase in real national income that exceeds the rate of population growth. The result is that more people have more purchasing power to satisfy their wants. This is reflected in increased demands for goods and services which derive not only from the added numbers of people, but importantly also from the additional real income that each person has to spend.

Although agriculture has contributed substantially to economic growth through the adoption of technological innovations which have increased the productivity of labor in agriculture, released labor to other productive segments of the economy, and supplied food at moderate cost, agriculture has not generally shared proportionately in the benefits of this growth. The increase in demand for agricultural commodities has not kept pace with the increases in demand for the products of most other industries. Agricultural surpluses have accumulated and farm incomes have been relatively low. This situation stems from the price and income elasticities of demand for agricultural commodities relative to other products, important factors in explaining why agricultural acreages have remained relatively constant over the past four decades and why some agricultural lands have been shifting to nonagricultural uses.

Between 1920 and 1960 disposable personal real income per capita about doubled, yet the per capita consumption of food was down from 1,542 to 1,465 pounds. Without regard to the composition of the diet, the aggregate demand for the physical volume (poundage) of food increases only at about the same rate as population. If aggregate productivity per unit of land used increases more rapidly than population, a characteristic of agriculture during the past twenty years, land use adjustments must take place or excess supplies will be produced. Because of the extremely low price elasticity of demand for agricultural products, small excesses of supply reduce prices, and thereby farm incomes more than proportionately. To maintain prices, government storage programs have siphoned excess supplies off the market, but the need for basic land use adjustments to eliminate the production of excess supplies remains with us.

In a progressive economy, land use adjustments within agriculture should reflect differences in income elasticities of demand for the various commodities. As consumer incomes increase, expenditure patterns change with regard both to the distribution of expenditures for food among the major food groups and expenditures for food relative to nonfood items. The aggregate income elasticity of demand for food is probably less than 0.2. Thus, the rate of increase in food expenditures would lag far behind the rate of increase in national income. But among the different agricultural commodities, the income elasticities of demand are vastly different. For example, recent estimates of income elasticities of demand for major food groups include meat animals, 0.48; dairy products, 0.09; poultry, 0.62; eggs, 0.04; fruits and vegetables, 0.16; and cereals, potatoes, and beans, —0.23.[12] The nature of the changing composition of the average American diet, perhaps largely in response to increased incomes, is shown in Figure 8.8.

Reading from Figure 8.8, we may note that relative to 1920, in 1958 on a per capita basis we consumed 22 per cent more meats, poultry, and fish; 10 per cent more dairy products; 7 per

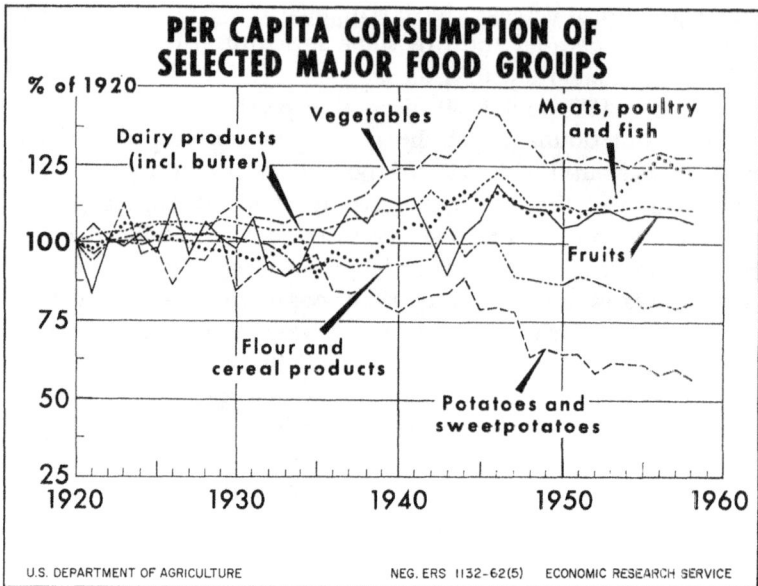

FIG. 8.8

cent more fruits; and 27 per cent more vegetables. But we consumed 44 per cent fewer potatoes and sweet potatoes, and 20 per cent less flour and cereal products. Dietary changes of these magnitudes obviously dictate a dynamic land use pattern within agriculture. Over the past forty years changes in the composition of our diets appear to be only imperfectly reflected in changes in the composition of the agricultural output.

As contrasted with the low income elasticity of demand for food, the elasticities are much higher for many other products of land. These include, among others, demands for recreation, industrial sites, urban dwellings, and highways. Demand for these nonagricultural uses of land will grow, not only in proportion to population, but also as a function of national income.

## FOREST LANDS

The foregoing discussion has dealt mainly with farmland. Let us turn for a moment to the trends in forest land use.

As indicated in the map of natural vegetation (Fig. 8.1), a large part of the farmlands of the United States were once virgin forests. The settlers dealt with these forests as an obstacle. Later, as the demand for lumber grew, the remaining forests were exploited and cut over by timber companies. It has been estimated that in the eastern part of the United States an original forest area of over 680 million acres was reduced to a present commercial timber area of about 370 million acres. The reduction in the timber resource was much greater. The original volume of about 5,400 billion board feet was reduced to about 625 billion board feet.[13]

In the western part of the United States, forest lands were not usually suitable for farmland and national forest reservations came early enough to save more of the forests. From an original area of 145 million acres, forest lands were reduced to 117 million acres. Volume was reduced from 2,240 billion board feet to 1,400 billion board feet.[14]

Forest management outside the national forests was not seriously attempted until after 1920. Indeed, some authorities indicate that most large private industrial ownerships have been brought under continuous forest administration since World War II.[15] On the smaller ownerships that together account for more than half the commercial forest land in the United States, progress has been slow.

Studies of the competition of forestry and crop production on land capability classes I–III indicate that usually crops have the advantage. Therefore, timber will be grown on about the present forest area plus some lands not needed for crop production. As pointed out in the timber resources review of the USDA, "forestry is a long-time undertaking."[16] Action taken during the next ten to twenty years will determine where the nation stands in timber supply fifty to seventy years from now. This makes it imperative that programs be undertaken to improve the productivity of forest land in farm and other small ownerships where productivity is far below potential. Substandard stocking following harvest cutting is especially serious on these small ownerships, and they are the least adequately protected from fire, insects, or other losses. Timber quality is generally poor. We now face a serious problem of rehabilitating the small private forests of the nation.

## FUTURE DEMAND FOR LAND

To illustrate the future demand for land we will use projections to 1980 recently prepared by the USDA Land and Water Policy Committee.[17] Although the committee projected requirements for all land uses, including nonagricultural, our subsequent discussion in keeping with the assignment of this paper, is focused mainly on projected requirements for agricultural purposes. A more complete discussion of the projected requirements and the assumptions underlying them is contained in the report by the committee.

### PRINCIPAL ASSUMPTIONS

The principal factors that will affect the future demand for products of land are the rate of population growth, the level of economic activity, consumer expenditure patterns, and the composition and level of exports and imports. Moreover, the availability and adoption of technological innovations as reflected through yields and feeding efficiencies will determine the transformation of demands for agricultural products into use requirements for land.

The rate of population growth is the most important factor affecting future demand for products of land. The population for the United States was projected at 261 million for 1980, an increase of about 48 per cent over that of 1959. This projection is in accordance with recent trends in population growth.

Demand for the products of land also will be affected by consumer incomes, which are a function of the level of economic activity of the nation. Measured in constant dollars so that the increases represent real gains, total disposable personal income was projected in 1980 to increase by 132 per cent above that of 1959. This represents an increase of about 57 per cent in disposable personal incomes per capita.

Per capita consumption of all farm products was projected to increase 2 per cent by 1980, relative to 1959. Per capita consumption of all foods was projected to be up by 4 per cent, representing an increase of 8 per cent in consumption of livestock products and a decrease of 2 per cent in consumption of crops. Per capita consumption of nonfood agricultural products was projected to be down 19 per cent. These projected consumption estimates reflect anticipated upgrading of diets accompanying increased consumer incomes, and a continued increase in the use of such products as synthetic fibers and detergents, although at a slower rate than during the past decade.

The 1980 export goal for farm products was set at 30 to 35 per cent above 1960 exports. This goal would include exports of 750 to 800 million bushels of wheat, 7.5 to 8.0 million bales of cotton, and 15 to 17 million tons of feed grains.

Based upon the foregoing assumptions regarding factors influencing the demand for farm products, the following increases over 1959 in farm output would be necessary to meet 1980 requirements: total farm output, 46 per cent; total crop production, 42 per cent; pasture production, 41 per cent; and livestock production, 55 per cent. Demand for timber in 1980 was projected at 16 billion cubic feet, an increase of about one-third over current annual consumption.

Assumptions about the availability and adoption of technological innovations are reflected in projected yields and livestock feeding efficiency. These projections are based mainly upon trends during the 1950's. Relative to 1959, per-acre yields of all crops were projected to increase by 56 per cent by 1980. Pasture yields were projected to increase 35 per cent. Timber growth, on the basis of recent trends, was projected to increase about 22 per cent. The efficiency of livestock in converting grain and forage into meat was projected at 8 per cent above that of 1959.

LAND REQUIREMENTS

Demand for the products of land was computed from estimates of the future magnitudes of principal demand determinants. Based upon projected estimates of yields and feeding efficiency, product demands were then transformed into major land use requirements. Figure 8.9 illustrates diagramatically the general projection scheme used, the breakdown of demand for agricultural products into its several constituents, the merger of

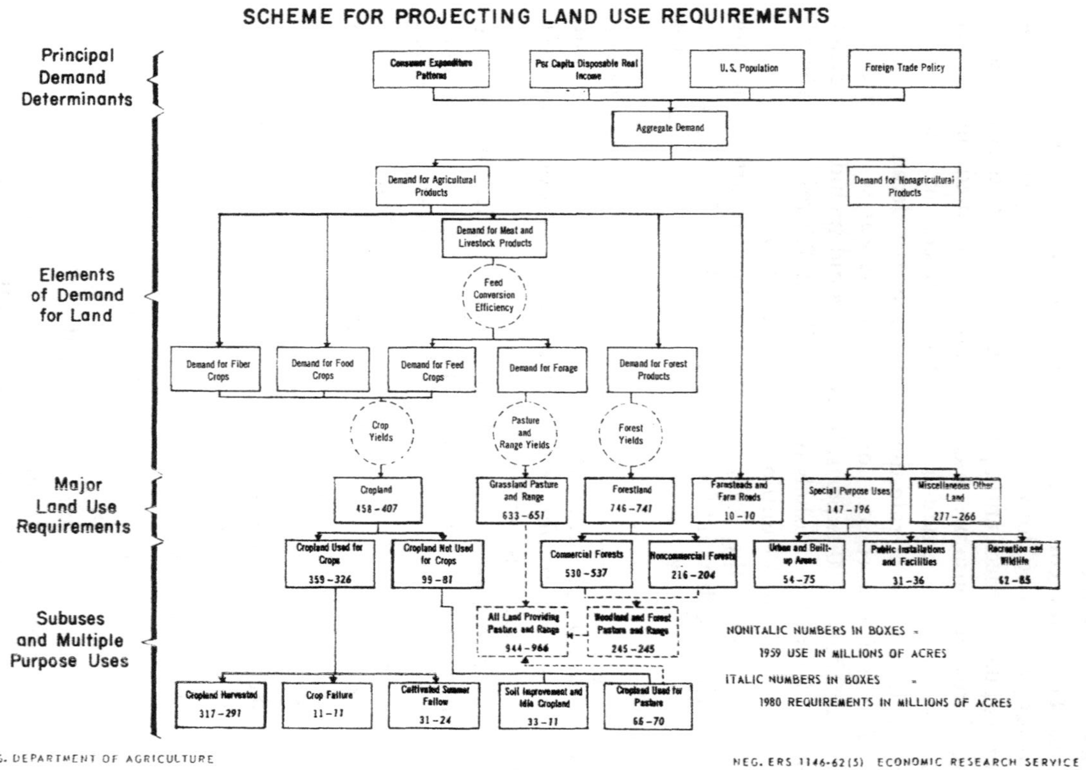

SCHEME FOR PROJECTING LAND USE REQUIREMENTS

Principal Demand Determinants

Consumer Expenditure Patterns | Per Capita Disposable Real Income | U.S. Population | Foreign Trade Policy

Aggregate Demand

Demand for Agricultural Products | Demand for Nonagricultural Products

Elements of Demand for Land

Demand for Fiber Crops | Demand for Food Crops | Demand for Feed Crops | Demand for Forage | Demand for Forest Products

Demand for Meat and Livestock Products

Feed Conversion Efficiency

Crop Yields | Pasture and Range Yields | Forest Yields

Major Land Use Requirements

Cropland 458–407 | Grassland Pasture and Range 633–651 | Forested Land 746–741 | Farmsteads and Farm Roads 10–10 | Special Purpose Uses 147–196 | Miscellaneous Other Land 277–266

Cropland Net Used for Crops 99–87 | Commercial Forests 530–537 | Noncommercial Forests 216–204 | Urban and Built-up Areas 54–75 | Public Installations and Facilities 31–36 | Recreation and Wildlife 62–83

Woodland and Forest Pasture and Range 245–245 | All Land Providing Pasture and Range 944–966

Subuses and Multiple Purpose Uses

Cropland Harvested 317–291 | Cropland Used for Crops 355–326 | Crop Failure 11–11 | Cultivated Summer Fallow 31–24 | Soil Improvement and Idle Cropland 33–71 | Cropland Used for Pasture 66–70

NONITALIC NUMBERS IN BOXES –
1959 USE IN MILLIONS OF ACRES

ITALIC NUMBERS IN BOXES  –
1980 REQUIREMENTS IN MILLIONS OF ACRES

NEG. ERS 1146-62(5) ECONOMIC RESEARCH SERVICE

U.S. DEPARTMENT OF AGRICULTURE

Fig. 8.9

224

constituent product demands to form requirements for major land uses and subordinate or multiple-purpose uses.

Total cropland required in 1980 to meet projected demands was estimated at 407 million acres, a decrease of 51 million from the 1959 acreage. Assuming that the acreage of crop failure remained constant and that the acreage of cultivated summer fallow declined by 7 million, cropland needed for crops in 1980 was estimated as 326 million acres, a decline of 33 million from that used in 1959. Harvested cropland requirements would total 291 million acres as compared with the 317 million harvested in 1959. The 33-million-acre reduction in cropland needed for crops, a decrease of 22 million acres in the amount of cropland idle or in soil improvement crops, and an increase of 4 million acres in cropland used for pasture is equal to a projected net reduction of 51 million acres in total cropland requirements.

Less substantial adjustments than those required from 1959 are implied when the 1980 projected requirements are compared with 1961 cropland use. The Feed Grain and Conservation Reserve programs brought the amount of cropland harvested within 6 million acres and cropland used for crops within 12 million acres of projected requirements.

The demand for forage as reflected in increased demand for livestock products was projected to be greater than would be met from increased yields, requiring an increase of 22 million acres in pastureland. It was assumed that this requirement would be met by shifting 4 million acres of better cropland to cropland pasture and by shifting 18 million acres of less suitable cropland to permanent pasture. Since yields are higher on rotation pasture than on permanent pasture, the entire increased pasture requirement also could be obtained by increasing cropland pasture by 10 to 11 million acres. On the other hand, if the expanded demand for forage were met by permanent pasture alone, an increase in permanent pasture of between 60 and 70 million acres would be needed.

Needed growth to meet the projected demand for timber is estimated at about 68 billion board feet, or about 44 per cent above present production. Projected growth based on the continuation of recent trends would fall short of needed growth by 14 per cent. This deficit could be partially met by a small net increase in the acreage of commercial forest land but more would have to come from improved management. The deficit in timber production is expected to become increasingly serious after 1980. Prompt and very substantial expansion and intensification of forestry in the United States will be necessary if timber requirements after that date are to be met.

The greatest increase in requirements for land during the next two decades is expected to come from nonagricultural uses (Fig. 8.10). Requirements in 1980 for special-purpose uses,

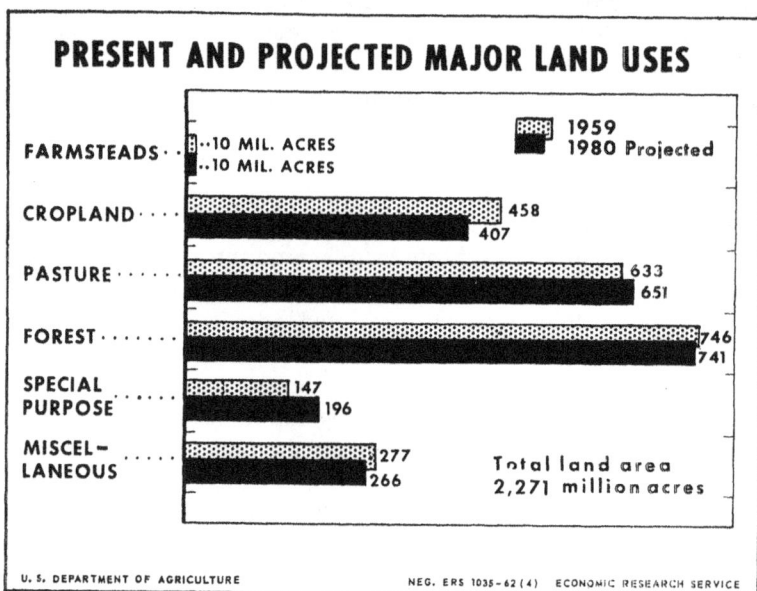

Fig. 8.10

which include urban and built-up areas, areas principally used for recreation or wildlife, and areas used for public installations and facilities, are projected as 196 million acres, an increase of 49 million acres from 1959 use. Miscellaneous other lands, which include desert, bare rock, swamp and other similar types of land, will supply part of the requirements for urban and other nonagricultural uses, and are projected to decline by 11 million acres.

## RELIABILITY OF LAND USE PROJECTIONS

To project land use requirements, specific estimates must be made of the future values of many variables. Variation of actual future conditions above or below these estimates would modify accordingly the requirements for cropland or other land uses. For example, a 1980 population projection 15 million below the 261 million projected by the Land and Water Policy Committee would reduce cropland requirements by about 20 million acres. If the level of exports realized in 1960 or 1920 should prevail in 1980, cropland requirements would be reduced by about 15 million acres. A breakthrough in livestock feeding efficiency would further reduce cropland requirements. Projections of future land requirements, therefore, at best can be considered only as indicating probably directions rather than as absolute quantities.

The sensitivity of projections of agricultural demands for land to estimates of future demand determinants and resource productivities has been stressed elsewhere.[18] The degree of sensitivity is indicated by the amount of variation in the several recent projections of cropland requirements in 1980. As contrasted with the projection of 407 million acres discussed in this paper, the medium level estimate of a recent study by Resources for the Future is 437 million acres.[19] In the 1959 studies by the Senate Select Committee on National Water Resources, cropland requirements based upon a 1980 population estimate of 244 million were projected at 480 million acres, or about the total acreage in use in 1950.[20] This projection reflected much lower crop yields than the 1962 study by the Land and Water Policy Committee on which this discussion has been based.

## POTENTIAL USE OF LAND FOR CROPS

In closing this discussion, we will go a step beyond our assigned topic to briefly examine the amount of land potentially available for crop production. It has been estimated that

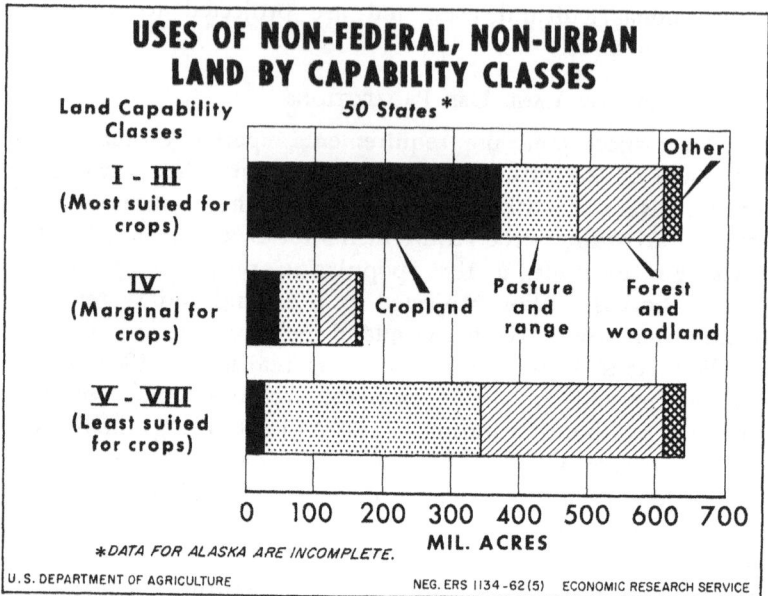

FIG. 8.11

crop production needed in 1980 could be produced on 407 million acres. There are 638 million acres of nonfederal nonurban
land in capability classes I, II and III (Fig. 8.11). Land in these
capability classes is physically suitable for regular cultivation.
Currently, about 113 million acres of this land is in pasture
and range and could be fairly easily converted to crop uses if
necessary, although some might require draining or other
improvements. Clearing and other improvement likewise could
make available for crop production about 125 million acres of
forested land in these capability classes.

Approximately 169 million acres of Class IV land is suited
for occasional cultivation at high cost and with intensive conservation treatment. Only about 49 million acres of Class IV
land is currently used for crops. Thus, in extreme need, considerable additional crop production could be obtained from
these lands.

As a nation we are fortunate to have such a large cropland

potential. It is a valuable national asset which must be con-
served for the future. As projections of future demands and
requirements cannot have a high degree of accuracy the nation
should make provision for adequate land reserves which could
be shifted to crop use in case of need.

Analysis of the future demand for land has now become a
part of our procedure in developing land use policy. We must
improve our data and methods so that farmers, the general
public, and legislative and administrative policymakers will
have a better basis upon which to make their decisions.

## NOTES

1. U.S. Bureau of the Census, *Statistical Atlas of the United States*. U.S.
Government Printing Office, Washington, D.C., 1914, p. 13.

2. *Ibid.*

3. Samuel Blodgett, Jr., *Economica: A Statistical Manual for the United
States of America* (City of Washington, printed for the Author, 1806), p. 60.

4. Timothy Pitkin, *A Statistical View of the Commerce of the United
States of America* (New York: James Eastburn and Co., 1817), pp. 109–43.

5. U.S. Bureau of the Census, *Historical Statistics of the United States,
Colonial Times to 1957* (Washington, D.C., 1960), p. 239.

6. O. E. Baker, "Rural-Urban Migration and the National Welfare,"
*Annals of the Association of American Geographers*, Vol. XXIII, 63.

7. U.S. Bureau of the Census, *Historical Statistics of the United States,
Colonial Times to 1957*, p. 239.

8. *Ibid.*

9. Forest and woodlands have increased from 614 million acres in 1920
to 639 million acres in 1959 if areas reserved for parks, wildlife refuges, and
other special uses are not excluded.

10. Donald D. Durost and Glen T. Barton, "Changing Sources of Farm
Output." USDA, Production Research Report 36, February, 1960, p. 17.

11. Figures relating to farm population are based on the old census
definition of a farm residence. The new definition which is intended to
remove from the farm population families who live in the open country but
sell little or no farm produce would decrease the number of farm residents
in 1960 by nearly 5 million, and would decrease the farm population as a
percentage of the total population to 8.7.

12. Nathan M. Koffsky, "Potential Demand for Farm Products," *Dynamics
of Land Use—Needed Adjustment* (Ames: Iowa State University Press, 1961),
p. 44.

13. Marion Clawson, R. Burnell Held, and Charles H. Stoddard, *Land for the Future* (Washington, D.C.: Resources for the Future, Inc., 1961), pp. 286 and 297.

14. *Ibid.*

15. Charles H. Stoddard, *The Small Private Forest in the United States* (Washington, D.C.: Resources for the Future, Inc., 1961).

16. Forest Service, USDA, "Timber Resources for America's Future," Forest Resource Report No. 14, Washington, D.C., January, 1958, p. 1.

17. On August 24, 1961, the Secretary of Agriculture formed a USDA Land and Water Policy Committee and directed it to prepare a preliminary report to "review the present and prospective land, forest and water resource situation, analyze its implications for Department policies and give program recommendations." This report was transmitted to the Secretary, January 8, 1962. The preliminary report was subsequently revised and has recently appeared in its final version, "Land and Water Resources—A Policy Guide," U.S. Government Printing Office, May, 1962.

18. George S. Tolley, "Interrelated Land Development Possibilities," *Modern Land Policy* (University of Illinois Press, Urbana, Ill., 1960), pp. 121–40.

19. Joseph L. Fisher and Hans. H. Landsberg, *Natural Resources Projections and Their Contribution to Technological Planning* (Reprint No. 32, Washington, D.C.: Resources for the Future, Inc., January, 1962), p. 123.

20. U.S. Senate Select Committee on National Water Resources. "Land and Water Potentials and Future Requirements for Water," 86th Cong., 1st Sess., Comm. Print No. 12, U.S. Government Printing Office, 1960, p. 16.

LOWDON WINGO, JR.

# The Use of Urban Land

AMONG ITS PURPOSES the Homestead Centennial Symposium has sought "to develop a perspective of national land policy from the vantage point of a hundred years." What kind of a vantage point does this hundred years yield? Our national population has increased sixfold; our urban population has expanded twenty-fold—from 30 per cent in 1860—and now numbers seven out of every ten persons in the nation.[1] Our annual gross private product has grown from $11 billion to $212 billion (constant dollars), and 96 per cent of the growth has taken place in the private, nonfarm sector.[2] Fifty-five million people now make their homes in the vast expanse of the continent west of the Mississippi where scarcely 3.5 million people lived in 1860.[3] Then, as now, three out of four members of the labor force were engaged either in agriculture or in services, but in 1870, two-thirds of these were on the farm, compared to one-fifth in 1950: the 1950 agricultural labor force was almost exactly the same size it was in 1870, while the labor force in services had increased twelvefold.[4]

There are many other ways of summarizing what has happened in this century, but these changes in population, income, and employment rough-in its salient features. Against such a setting the issues surrounding the use of urban land take on a special importance.* Luther Halsey Gulick summed this up recently:

> Once a nation has grown together, knit into a modern, integrated, industrial, financial, transportational, and managerial structure, the efficiency level of the great urban complexes is an inseparable part of the total national structure.[5]

Within the theme of a *national* land policy two arguments resist the development of an *urban* land perspective: first, urban land takes up an insignificant amount of our national space;

* In the interest of comprehensiveness, transportation and industrial uses of the land are subsumed in "urban land."

Wooten has estimated it at an order of magnitude of one per cent.[6] Then, too, public policy governing urban land has traditionally been the responsibility of state and local governments— there are many policies, but no Policy. Nevertheless, urban uses of the land generate some of the most difficult policy consequences of the urban revolution which is reshaping our economics, our society, our politics, and the whole future direction of our culture. Although the land *supporting* our cities is a petty fraction of the spatial wealth of the nation, the land *affected* by cities is not. Cities' needs for water, for example, comprehend entire river basins: Chicago would lower the level of the Great Lakes to handle its requirements, while in the arid, rapidly growing Southwest the issue is already joined between thirsty people and industries and thirsty acres.

But to get closer to home, cities are growing and changing rapidly—taking up more space, using it differently, shaping and reshaping the geography of its employment. The dynamics of these changes throw a long speculative shadow over the urban hinterlands which is as much a consequence of the physical and institutional phenomenon we call the city as is the central business district. Tomorrow, the umbra of this shadow will be massive investment in real property serving urban needs. Thus there is a need to shift from a static, short-run viewpoint to one which is concerned with the long-run dynamics of urban land requirements and the more extensive effects on river basins and natural recreation resources.

Further, the petty fraction of land in urban use will not remain petty. Donald Bogue satisfied himself several years ago that farmland in metropolitan areas was converted to urban use during the 1940's at a rate of approximately one acre to every four to six persons added to the urban population.[7] Marion Clawson's careful analysis of the 1950 Census and supporting data led to a more conservative estimate of six persons per acre.[8] If these rates held across the nation in the Fifties, some five to eight million acres were converted to urban use. Today, on opposite sides of the nation, two great metropolitan regions—the northeastern megalopolis[9] and the urban region of southern California —afford us a preview of a future reflecting a new scale and pattern of relationships between urban and nonurban components of the nation.

The lack of formal national policy governing the use of urban land obscures the increasing interaction of national policy and metropolitan problems. This growing political interdependency has engendered such a web of intergovernmental relationships focused on the spatial organization and land use structure of urban regions, that the features of a more coherent national perspective about urban land are clearly visible. For better or worse the politics of urbanization have implicated every level of government. One consequence of this new set of relationships is the tendency for spill-over problems of urban land use to be "kicked upstairs" from one level to the next. In this process, discretion is surrendered, standards get set, methods of analysis and decision making become uniform, and, without warning, someday, we will wake to the consciousness of a national urban policy, with spatial and land use implications.

Large choices stemming from urbanization and its attendant consequences confront us in the management of our national space. Increasingly they are identified with policy issues at all levels of government. These issues involve massive public investments, the rapid growth of administrative regulation, and developmental decisions looking ahead to the next century. These choices will be wise in the degree to which they rest on a firm base of knowledge about the quantity and geography of the spatial requirements of a metropolitan economy. Ultimately, the significant demand and supply characteristics of urban space— and the forces working to modify them—will define the areas within which we must seek strategies by which the high priority goals of a metropolitan society can be addressed.

## URBANIZATION: PATTERN AND PROCESS

First, urban land use is rooted in the complex national and regional dimensions of urbanization. Clearly the likelihood that a parcel of land will be used for urban purposes depends essentially on the way in which the national economy grows and becomes distributed over the national space. Consider what has happened to the regional structure of the nation during the last century, as the U.S. population increased from 81 million in 1860 to 179 million in 1960. The historical stability of the regional pattern during the century is demonstrated in Table 1; to recreate the 1860 distribution of population would require a

TABLE 1

REGIONAL DISTRIBUTION OF U.S. POPULATION

| Region[a] | 1860 (per cent) | 1960 (per cent) | Gain (+) Loss (−) (per cent) |
|---|---|---|---|
| U.S. total | 100 | 100 | 0 |
| New England | 9.97 | 5.86 | − 4.11 |
| Middle Atlantic | 26.50 | 21.90 | − 4.60 |
| Great Lakes | 22.04 | 20.15 | − 1.89 |
| Plains | 6.90 | 8.56 | 1.66 |
| Southeast | 30.70 | 21.30 | − 9.40 |
| Southwest | 2.22 | 7.98 | 5.76 |
| Mountain | .24 | 2.40 | 2.16 |
| Far West | 1.43 | 11.95 | 10.52 |
| Sum of gains and losses | | | 40.10 |
| Index of redistribution | | | 20.05 |

Source: U.S. Bureau of the Census, *Historical Statistics of the United States, Colonial Times to 1957*, Washington, D.C., 1960, Series A 123–180, p. 12, and *Advance Reports, General Social and Economic Characteristics, United States*, PC (A3)-1, Table 105, p. 8.
[a] Regions are those used in Harvey S. Perloff, Edgar S. Dunn, Jr., Eric E. Lampard, and Richard F. Muth, *Regions, Resources, and Economic Growth* (Baltimore: The Johns Hopkins Press, 1960), p. 6.

reshuffling of only one-fifth of the population in 1960—of the 148 million people we have added during the century, a mere 29.6 million have brought about the shift in the regional structure of the population. This shift has taken place across the Mississippi with half of the total shift coming from the Southeast and half of it ending up in the Far West. More significantly, as agriculture's relative role in the economy declined, the regional distribution of total population increasingly resembled that of the urban population (See Table 2).

TABLE 2

| Date | Relative Distribution Index | Per cent of Labor Force in Agriculture |
|---|---|---|
| 1870 | 25.8 | 51.2 |
| 1910 | 20.7 | 32.5 |
| 1950 | 10.2 | 11.7 |

Source: Perloff *et al., op. cit.*
*Note:*The relative distribution index is calculated by summing the absolute differences of regional shares in urban and total population and dividing by two.

This historical stability has concealed a significant shift in the dynamics of relative regional growth: as the agricultural sector has declined to a minor fraction of the total economy, free play is given to the redistributional tendencies of the urban sector of the economy. These tendencies are demonstrated by the regional structures of national and of urban population during the period 1870–1950, for which the index of regional redistribution* for the urban population works out to 23.1 per cent—half again as great as that of the total population at 14.8 per cent. As the urban sector increases its dominance, the national economy will be reorganized to reflect the needs of a metropolitan civilization.

Consider how recent population flows are influencing differentially the development of our urban regions. In 1960, a sizable 6.5 million persons† were living in different states than in 1950, largely as the result of the search for happier job-hunting grounds.[10] Such flows are rarely geographically neutral: half of the people who moved across state lines between 1950 and 1960 moved into California; another fourth moved into Florida; one-third of all migrants originated in the Southeast.[11] Finally, one out of every twenty-three people who lived in standard metropolitan statistical areas in March 1960 had lived in a different county one year previously.[12] This was not even an extraordinarily mobile period; the rate at which people migrate across state and county lines holds remarkably constant year by year at approximately 3 per cent and 6.5 per cent of the population respectively.[13] The net results of these flows can be measured against the 18 per cent growth of the nation as a whole between 1950 and 1960. The population of *all* metropolitan areas grew 26.4 per cent, but those in the Far West expanded 48.5 per cent. The class of metropolitan areas having populations between 500,000 and 1,000,000 grew most rapidly of all size classes—36 per cent over the ten-year period. The bias in these flows of population is changing the aspect of urban America.[14]

The changes in the regional housing stocks have special sig-

* See Table 1.

† Computed by adding the absolute values of net migration by states and divided by two.

nificance because residential land use makes up about 80 per cent of the total private use of urban lands. Relating the percentage changes in the regional housing stocks by metropolitan status during the period 1950–1956[15] to the percentage changes in interpolated population[16] indicates that the site of the housing stock for each region does increase with population on a rough one-to-one basis, while constant population was identified with roughly a 10 per cent expansion of the stock. In short, the flow of housing investment and the quantity of urban land needed to support it are intimately related to population flows.

As the economic relations among the urban regions work themselves out, they tend to develop specialized roles within the national economy. Comparative advantages and disadvantages in resource endowment, in access to markets, and in human resources create relationships of dominance and subordination among urban regions. New York is so highly specialized with respect to financial activities that it is the financial capital of the nation. The specializations of Miami, Pittsburgh, Detroit, and Washington are only slightly less dramatic.

A focus on urban scale reveals two additional facets of urban-industrial organization. As cities grow, their own markets for locally produced goods expand and, concurrently, the share of their resources allocated to export kinds of activities declines. Serving the local markets becomes the dominant economic activity; the local consumer market and local capital investment supplant export activities as the mainsprings of the metropolitan economy. Cities seem to reach an economic "takeoff" point when their sheer size creates markets affording local scale economies in almost any economic activity for which inputs are available. The profitable substitution of local production for imports elicits investment in new plant and equipment, expands employment, and further deepens the local market. This "filling in" process which comes with growth prepares the ground for the emergence of metropolitan functions.

Powerful functional and developmental relationships are involved in the interplay between the size of an urban region, the degree of its specialization, and the extent to which it manifests a metropolitan character. The *metropolitan* region stands out as a distinct entity in this complex of interregional relations: it is the richly diverse labor market necessary to a technologically advanced economy, the fountainhead of investment funds and financial services, the "hothouse" for new industry, the administrative point of control of the national economy. The goods it produces for the nation become less important than the services it produces; more crucial than both are the integrative functions it performs between consumer, producer, and public economies across the nation. Here the decisions which count in our national economic life are made. The moral of this story clearly follows: these relationships and processes generate the mix of economic activities around which a community is organized and which, in turn, set up the basic demand conditions for the amount and character of the urban land needed to support these activities.

These processes change, if slowly, in response to large shifts in the direction in which the national economy moves. During the last century, the shift from agriculture toward manufacturing accelerated the rate of urbanization. Now, a new shift is underway toward consumer and business services. New production technologies reshuffle regional and local advantages for the production of goods and services. Innovations in transportation and communications technologies reduce the frictions of space releasing economic activities from their bonds to places. Meanwhile, productive populations with growing discretionary incomes have become the powerful economic magnets attracting the new activities. Forces such as these are constantly redistributing national economic activity and reshaping regional growth and development. The needs for urban land shift among the component regions in similar fashion, creating policy issues as they encounter unique circumstances of time and place. Rapid growth can generate crises in public investment in land-serving capital facilities; land may be wastefully idled by speculative forces; valuable agricultural capital may be inundated by waves of urbanization. Polluted rivers, denuded watersheds, and toxic atmospheres may jeopardize the viability of the city. Where and how these issues emerge depend on the unfolding regional structure of the national economy.

## URBAN STRUCTURE AS A VARIABLE

The decentralizing city in twentieth-century America is a well documented fact. Schnore calculated that 96.7 per cent of metropolitan growth during the period 1950–1960 occurred outside the central city boundaries of 1950.[17] Bogue has shown that the 6 million migrants into SMSA's during the Forties really represented a net *gain* to the surrounding area of 7.2 million and a net *loss* to the central city of 1.3 million people.[18] Such an occurrence suggests that generally the central city is full, its vacant land is used up, and intensification of residential land use is uneconomical. True though this may be generally, it does not explain fully the changes which are taking place. The 1.3 million *net* loss to the central city was compounded of the outmigration of two and a half million whites who were replaced by a million and a quarter nonwhites.[19] Schnore found these trends continuing into the 1950–1960 period.[20] The suburban rings are growing not only because the new metropolitan growth is settling there, but because activities in the core of the metropolitan region are deconcentrating to the outer areas.

The development of space-extensive production technologies and the automobile have participated powerfully, if not exclusively, in these structural changes. Some population has been pushed out by expansion of activities at the metropolitan core. The loss of resident population on Manhattan in the last census period resulted in part from the demolition of dwelling units in the path of the unprecedented surge in office-building construction in the post-war period. The 1950's have seen widespread demolition of dwelling units by public programs. The razing of "the Hill" in Pittsburgh and of Washington's Southwest by urban renewal programs supplanted large numbers of low-income families with middle- and upper-income groups at substantially lower gross densities. The federal interstate highway system has begun to take its toll of the dwelling stock of the core area. Finally, at certain income levels and family stages, central city households become very volatile and boil off to the suburbs either to seek better schools and the other public services which the middle class values highly or to escape the increasingly difficult problems of the older core.

The selective decentralization of employment poses the largest threat to the future of the metropolitan core through its induced acceleration of the centrifugal population movement. We have ample evidence of the shift of retailing to the suburbs. Manufacturing firms also show signs of decentralizing.

New, land-extensive industries have little choice but to locate on the urban fringes; at the same time, a continual pressure for modernization and expansion dislodges older firms from the center. In one case, older firms in obsolete, inefficient plants find their market positions threatened by competitors using new production technologies which favor the one-story, site-extensive plant. Even at small scales the site costs to accommodate such a plant in the central city are generally exorbitant; large-scale plants have little choice but to find locations in the outlying areas.

The secular rise of consumer demand in most industries constantly presses successful firms to expand their output. In the central city, plant expansion frequently entails complicated, time-consuming, and costly assembly of land, clearance, and reconstruction of plant. Thus, the large tracts of undeveloped suburban lands present an almost irresistible appeal to the expanding firm. The revolution in suburban land uses triggered by the completion of Boston's circumferential Route 128[21] is a dramatic example of these relocational processes at work. The belt of modern plants which sprang up along the new route finds its source largely in the relocational decisions of local firms carrying out modernization or expansion programs. The joint impact of the automobile and the expansion of space requirements for new production technologies are manifest in this revolution in land use.

Urban organization and processes clearly take place around a center. For many dimensions of the urban economy, distance from the urban core is a significant variable, but urban organization is much more complex than such a simple model would suggest. The radial structure of transportation imposes some special characteristics on the way in which urban regions develop. Typically, the highways and railroads converging on the urban core pass through the hinterlands as developmental corridors. In a static sense they relate the intense concentration of economic activities at the core to the dispersed populations in the suburbs which represent, on the one hand, the region's pool of highly skilled and professional manpower, and, on the other hand, the most lucrative consumer markets in the region.

The dynamic rather than the structural role of these radial transportation corridors exerts a powerful influence on the evolving form and structure of the region.

New urban development tends to nucleate at points along these corridors and to expand outwardly away from them as growth continues, gradually filling in the intervening rural wedges. Suburban development is attracted to the areas along the transportation corridors which are highly accessible to the urban core; at the same time, new residential development tends to proceed at points where indispensable social overhead facilities—schools, shopping centers, and utilities, for example—are already in place. The intersection of transportation corridors with areas having some surplus capacity in these services provides a powerful impetus for new development.

Industrial location needs are more specialized. The availability of utilities, including water and sewer, may be important, but industrial firms have greater leverage in bringing about extension of such services to appropriate sites. Transportation needs depend on the form of the plant's inputs and products, and particular constellations of rail, highway, and even pipeline facilities can rigorously pinpoint the opportunities for a plant site. From the vantage point of urban development, industrial location can be a more capricious process than residential development.

Turning now to the structure of urban land use, we must acknowledge the lamentable state of the data. We do have some clues, however, to the allocations of land to urban uses. Harland Bartholomew's analysis of some reasonably consistent data on the land uses among a select group of American cities[22] reveals that residential site makes up a fairly uniform 80 per cent* of

* Mean 81.3 per cent with standard deviation 7.2 per cent.

the land used by private sector activities among fifty-three central cities. Streets occupy a somewhat less regular 60 per cent* of the nonprivate land use. Approximately 70 per cent† of the land area in any American city is confined to streets and residential site, and the real differences in how these cities occupy their space occur in only 30 per cent of their total developed areas.

John Hamburg identified some characteristics of the land use organization in Chicago which are generally consistent with Bartholomew's figures.[23] Again the strongest regularities show up with respect to residential site and streets; residential site as a proportion of *all* land in use beyond five miles from the Loop approximated 40 per cent, while streets quite uniformly occupied 30 to 35 per cent of the land area in the same zone. From the standpoint of sheer area the suburban land use patterns dominate the total picture and yield the kinds of aggregate consistency suggested by Bartholomew's figures, simply because only 5 per cent of the land area of the Chicago region falls within the five-mile zone.

These are cross-sectional figures, true, but there is little evidence that the composition of land use varies considerably over time. The inertia of sunk capital in real estate seems to exert a powerful brake on the rates of land use conversion, as our urban renewal experience can richly testify. Some structure conversion takes place, especially between industrial and commercial uses, but this involves a small fraction of the land in private uses. A substantial conversion of land from *residential* to *nonresidential* uses would be needed to make a perceptible difference in the mix. Data from the 1956 National Housing Inventory show, on the contrary, that from 1950 to 1956 the rate of conversion was minute and netted out in favor of the housing stock (see Table 3). Conversion of improved properties is a slow and thin process at best, and cannot be expected to alter radically the sunk capital inertia of the developed urban plant. Changes in the composition of *private* land uses among developed urban lands are likely to take place almost glacially at this level of aggregation. The

---

* Mean 58.3 per cent with standard deviation 12.3 per cent.
† Mean 68.4 per cent with standard deviation 9.6 per cent.

TABLE 3

| | |
|---|---:|
| Total housing stock, 1956 | 55,342,000 |
| Net additions to stock, 1950–1956 | 9,355,000 |
| Net conversions, 1950–1956 | 708,000 |
| Net conversions as per cent of net additions | 7.60% |
| Net conversions as per cent of 1956 housing stock | 1.28% |
| Average annual per cent contribution of conversions to 1956 housing stock | .21% |

Source: U.S. Bureau of the Census, *1956 National Housing Inventory*, Vol. I, Components of Change, 1950–56, Part 1, United States and Regions, Washington, D.C., 1958, Table C, p. 15.

sunk capital effect is reinforced by urban land use regulation—and especially zoning—which militates strongly against conversion of existing land uses to uses in other private use classes and which tends to be conservative in its sensitivity to existing interests and the status quo.

Among the nonprivate uses some substantial conversion is likely as the federal interstate highway program's urban portion unfolds. The demolition of existing structures in the built-up urban core for new urban freeway systems can increase perceptibly the proportion of existing urban land in streets, at the expense largely of residential uses. This effect seems to be the only potential source of large-scale land use conversions, although in the longer run and for the region as a whole the new areas brought into urban development may redress the balance.

Our present information does not refute beyond doubt the possibility that the urban land use mix is being altered in rapidly growing metropolitan areas by radically different compositions among the new increments to development. Hamburg's data do not suggest this with respect to Chicago: the composition of land uses in the six-mile ring differs little from that in the sixteen-mile ring. True, suburban housing is becoming more and more land extensive, but the automobile has made this true of commercial and industrial uses, also. Transportation has kept up with the tendencies to land extensiveness in the developing margins: here, highway interchanges using forty acres are taking the place of highway grade intersections which take up a quarter acre; three-hundred-foot freeway rights-of-way are replacing the 80-foot rights-of-way of the past. In short, the differential land extensiveness of activities at the margin does not promise to change the overall concentric mix substantially even among the most rapidly growing metropolitan regions.

The spatial organization of economic activities is most likely to change. Decentralization, suburbanization, deconcentration—all these terms have been used to suggest the powerful centrifugal drift of many economic activities away from the urban center. The terms "urban sprawl," "scatteration," "blight," and "grey areas" have been coined to describe symptoms of this drift. The new increments to the housing stock grow up on the outer boundaries of the old. As they grow, new market opportunities emerge for the distribution of consumer goods and services, so that an increasing bundle of commercial activities follows. New industrial investment seeking the freedom of large sites and finding labor markets nearby join the drift, and a new urban spatial structure is in the making.

## THE CHANGING PARAMETERS

The *how much, where,* and *when* dimensions of urban land use depend heavily on the great variables surrounding social and economic change in a nation as a whole. Political and economic institutions, evolving technologies, population characteristics, income distributions, and tastes—each delimits in its own particular way the course along which cities will evolve.

The interplay between our economic and political institutions has been instrumental in the changing character of our cities. The allocation of land to urban uses takes place through a set of markets—markets in land, in housing, in industrial and commercial structures, in mortgages—functioning within a fluid policy environment. Why the allocation takes place the way it does derives from the nature of this interaction.

Consider some contrasts. Industrial location plays a strategic role in urban growth and organization. In the United States, a business firm bases its locational decision on a specified set of private costs, while another set of costs is absorbed by the community at large in the forms of unpriced public services and spillover effects on other private interests. In the Soviet economies, by contrast, plant location is a central decision calculated upon both private and social costs and within a context of *industry* efficiency and *national* policy. In the United Kingdom, industrial location decisions are centralized, also, to serve national objectives such as the containment of London, the New Towns policies, and the relief of economically stagnant areas. These centralized forms for allocating producers to locations and land to plants based on some higher level efficiency conditions necessarily engender differing forms of urban organization compared to those resulting from the effects of the decentralized decisions of firms and individuals built into our institutions.[24]

The indiscriminate sprawl of urban uses over the metropolitan countryside is a very clear product of the way in which our market and political institutions interact. Stockholm, by contrast, has girded itself with a broad greenbelt to contain the city in compact form, while the rigorous shortage of space in the Netherlands has made it necessary to protect its valuable reservoir of agricultural land from wasteful urban development.

The balance of the public and private in the allocation of land is perhaps less influential than the content of the policy constraints which circumscribe the markets. Zoning—a complex element in this interaction—has clearly not been able to prevent the scatter of new developments over the urban hinterlands because legal institutions restrain it. As a policy tool it is used for diverse ends. Stanley Tankel recently described very low density zoning around New York as an inconceivable extravagance with a scarce resource.[25] Charles Haar several years ago pointed out how such zoning has been used as a tool of social and economic exclusion.[26] What kinds of control are available, and to whom, can make all the difference in how urban organization evolves.

Haar has set out the thesis that "this country's legal climate is such that any strong and persistent pressure or need will find or make accommodation for itself."[27] Anyone looking back over the generation and a half that separates us from the validation of zoning in the Euclid Village case can detect this in the drift toward increasing discretion in the allocative processes by local governments. While it is not clear that this adds up consistently to a more intensive use of urban lands by the shaping of more compact urban forms, a more circumscribed role for the market factors appears in the offing. On the other hand, powerful controls wielded by parochial local governments may generate such conflict in the metropolitan region that land use control would gravitate to appropriate region-wide institutions simply because such a situation is inherently unstable.

Behind the interaction of political and economic institutions is the ever-present dynamism of technological change. At the regional scale the coming of the railroad created the geography of cities in the vast inner regions of the nation; at the urban scale, the curtain wall and the elevator made possible the modern city.

Transportation supplies the most dramatic illustration of technological impacts on urban form and land use. The pedestrian city was either small or extensively decentralized simply by the small scale of economic activities and because the speed of walking set the boundaries of the labor market. The commuter and street railroads pushed these boundaries out along the main lines into the hinterland, and now sixty years later the automobile—and the extensive road and street system which it has elicited—are spreading the city out thinly between and beyond the commuter railroad corridors. Every stage in this development has extended the limits of the urban land market radically, reducing values and bringing about lower and lower densities at the margins. We can now actually identify a group of "auto age" cities in the South, Southwest, and Pacific Coast area which have accrued the major portion of their population growth since, say, 1920, so that their form and organization has been largely structured by the automobile. Los Angeles is certainly the capital, but Miami, Houston, San Antonio, and Phoenix follow closely in recent growth rates. The inverse relationship between recent growth rates and densities of urbanized areas of cities with 100,000 population in 1950 suggests that the margins of the urbanized areas of the auto age cities are developing population densities of approximately 2,500 persons per square mile.[28]

The current phase of that revolution—typified by the vast metropolitan freeway systems engineered to high speed, high volume auto travel—is again radically altering the pattern of urban accessibility. An increase in average travel speeds from twenty to forty miles per hour will quadruple the area within an hour's drive from the CBD and increase the developable land supply by a much greater factor. An additional five minutes of driving to work can be trivial, but at forty miles per hour, five minutes can push one three and a half miles farther out into the hinterlands. Highly developed speeds seem clearly associated with increasing sprawl at the edges of urban development. This association is reinforced by the declining propensities to travel resulting from work-week changes, more efficient distribution techniques for consumer goods and services, and changing preferences for the utilization of discretionary leisure and income.

Simultaneously, the congestion associated with the high concentration of activities at the urban core—which the new freeway systems compound—is spurring the deconcentration of activities from the central business district. The direct and indirect congestion costs which have contributed to the outward migration of merchandising and service activities are the target for the next major technological breakthrough in urban transportation: improved mass transit facilities, new monitoring and pricing techniques seeking more intensive use of automobiles, and automated traffic flows at the core. Any such development would permit the evolution of a low-density urban region focusing on a strongly centered urban core; otherwise, a diffuse, scattered, weakly centered urban region with homogenized activities and land uses may become the characteristic form of our urban future.

Other technological forces are changing the conditions of production and distribution. The cybernetic revolution continues to supplant human control in production processes. Laborless, automated refineries, machine tools which can learn their tasks, and automatic inventory controls handling millions of stock records are the visible signs of the revolutionary changes which are changing the operating requirements of American industry. Several consequences are immediately perceptible. Accessibility to the central business district becomes less important for automated activities: transportation links are increasingly supplanted by communication technology; plants become oriented to a high skill level of technicians and professionals concentrated in the suburbs; the heavy proportion of capital to total inputs emphasizes technical and design factors over land costs and labor market position. All of these add up to an increase in the suburban orientation of goods production and distribution.

Technology is changing the consumer's world in other respects than transportation. Economic services are being internalized within the home, reducing the transportation linkages between the home and the centers of distribution: television, home freezers, laundry appliances all reduce the needs for externally produced services. The per capita consumption of services is increasing, of course, but the shift is away from household-supporting services and in the direction of those with the high income elasticity of demand associated with leisure time activities—recreation, entertainment, and education.

Residential location is still tied to the complex of public services, however: houses must have local streets, and connect with water and waste disposal systems. Here, outer space technology may have an impact on urban space: solution of the waste reduction-water conservation requirements of space travel may point the way to dissolving the crucial water-sewerage link that contains the development of residential activity within the service areas of these public facilities.

In short, technology seems to be working for more extensive utilization of urban space and indeed for an even more exaggerated diffuseness of urban structure and form than even present epithets such as scatteration, sprawl, and slurbs suggest.

The effects of tastes and secularly rising family incomes on housing and land use derive from the increasing productivity of urban populations and the array of consumption opportunities being generated by the economy. The gains from productivity show up in rising incomes and expanding leisure of the urban population. All the signs suggest that people will have more time and more money to do the things which are important to them at the margin. The behavior of consumers on the housing market to date suggests that the single family dwelling on a large suburban lot may rank very high to upwardly mobile families.

There is another powerful potential here also. The Negro population of our major metropolitan areas has been growing at a very rapid rate for two generations. Economic discrimination has dammed this growing group in the central cities while the growth of the white population was absorbed in the metropolitan fringes. As this pressure has mounted, more and more of the white population has fled to the suburbs accelerating the shift in the central city racial proportions. Parts of this group have shared in the productivity gains of the last generation and they have developed identification with the middle-class tastes which have impelled the suburban explosion.

Growing forces are working to break down these market barriers. A strong likelihood exists that the middle-class Negro will soon swell the migration to the suburbs, reducing core densities, competing for suburban housing, and leaving behind in the center a growing concentration of dependent lower-income groups. One round of the consequences of rising income and leisure is already working itself out in urban organization. The second round, triggered by the collapse of economic discrimination against minority groups, can be equally dramatic in its effects on the form and organization of the city.

Population changes lie at the heart of these processes of change. Virtually the whole of the population increment occurring during the 1940 to 1960 census period shows up in the urban column, a major portion of this in the major metropolitan areas: for example, Donald Bogue pointed out that almost 6.5 million people migrated into metropolitan areas during the 1940–50 census period.[29] These trends will change in the future as the nonurban and nonmetropolitan sectors of the population become a small fraction of the total.

Pickard has projected a U.S. population of 320,000,000 people by 2,000 A.D., an increase of almost 100 per cent for the 44-year period between 1956 and 2,000. Looking at trends in metropolitan growth, he estimated that 96 per cent of the 152,000,000 additions to the population will find themselves living in metropolitan areas, and 60 per cent of these in Atlantic Northeast, Great Lakes, and California metropolitan areas.

Urban land use changes exhibit two distinct components over time: one is the *growth effect* which reflects the sheer increase in the number of land-using units—persons and activities; the other I call the *amplifier effect,* the combined impact of all of the factors working toward changes in the per unit utilization of space. Population change is a good proxy for the growth effect, and this brief examination points up the powerful thrust we can expect from it. The contributions of institutional changes, technological developments, and consumption forces are not free from ambiguity because of movement to enlarge the role of public policy at the expense of market in allocating urban land. However, the powerful market forces unleashed by the spiraling rate of technological change and the growing consumption power of urban populations can be counted on to resist.

For the next generation, at any rate, the amplifier effects appear to net out strongly positive: the amount of urban space per person promises to continue to expand, and nowhere short of some institutional revolution can countering effects of any strength be detected. Pickard's 150 per cent increase of metropolitan population may well be accompanied by a tripling of the national space devoted to urban activities in metropolitan areas purely as a consequence of the changes in the great parameters which make up the social, political, and economic environment in which American urbanization is taking place.

## SOME REFLECTIONS ON POLICY

These regional, evolutional, and environmental facts of urban life in the United States may be impelling us toward a *de facto* national urban land policy. In a nation of 300 million people three-fourths of whom will follow urban pursuits in giant metropolitan regions, defective accommodations in the urban sector will be amplified throughout the social, economic, and political structure of the nation. In this sense, national policy can emerge from the integration of those activities and programs of all levels of government working to relate public and private activities to the inescapable realities of a metropolitan society.

I find little reason to doubt that the role of the federal government in the evolution of national urban land policy will continue to expand. Already federal programs are deeply involved in all of the major dimensions of urban growth and change.

The intricate net of urban transportation activities has become closely geared to federal programs: the federal interstate highway program will spend a major portion of its billions on urban transportation facilities, while the underwriting of urban mass transportation systems is now an accepted, if untested, federal urban policy. The growth and disposition of the urban housing stock are almost inconceivable in the absence of the Federal Housing Administration, whose administrative standards have powerfully influenced the pattern of suburban development, while the federal urban renewal program is our prime weapon against deterioration of the older housing stock.

The federal government has now embraced the preservation of open spaces for recreation, conservation, and the shaping and containment of urban growth. It has underwritten urban and regional planning activities. It has supported the development of community facilities.

Federal urban activities ranging from airports to flood control in urban areas point up how thoroughly the federal government has become a willing party to an urban policy partnership. In fact, the conduct of local policy-making independent of federal policy in urban areas is no longer a feasible choice for any but the smaller cities. A marriage of necessity has taken place for better or worse; there is no alternative but that it endure.

The recent unsuccessful campaign to create a Department of Urban Affairs in the President's Cabinet placed some importance on the role of the Department to coordinate the urban-oriented programs of the federal government. However merited the move itself was, the objective of coordination struck only a glancing blow at the core issue which its partnership with the city has posed. Federal urban policies urgently need to develop around a clear and consistent view of the nature of a metropolitan civilization, the conditions essential to its viability in the face of these powerful trends, and the human, fiscal, and natural resources which can be marshalled to meet them. Coordination of a multitude of independent agency policies presents an ineffectual substitute for so demanding a task: the problem is not one of preventing federal agencies from stepping on each others toes, but of assuring that the varied federal policies which touch upon metropolitan development proceed from a consistent set of objectives and postulates. This first step toward a national set of urban policies is the indispensable contribution which the federal government can now make to the partnership.

Federal leadership can help to fashion new institutions for planning and development to implement the partnership. We have now agreed, for example, that urban transportation is a regional problem which cannot be subdivided by local political boundaries; for all of our predilection for local control, urban economic activities—and the lands they use—have characteristics of a regional system, also. An opportunity for such leadership exists wherever federal policies affect land use in the urban region. Integration of federal urban policies at the center needs to be reiterated at the region, if the impact of the policies is to be consistent with some authoritative conception of the region's development; federal programs have as much need to be regionally integrated as other regional functions.

Third, the partnership needs an urban intelligence system to work well. Following military intelligence, the objective is maximum anticipation of critical changes in the urban environment for effective deployment of resources. From the national level the system would monitor, interpret, and project the regional dimensions of national trends while at the regional level a continual intelligence check would be maintained on the factors influencing the evolution of urban form and organization. The sensitivity and appropriateness of policy responses to new conditions will depend on such information.

Responsibilities and opportunities exist for the other party to this partnership, also. Where the federal government needs a consistent national image of a metropolitan society, local governments and their constituents will require an equally forceful conception of a developing region embodying the broad conditions of efficiency and amenity which dominate the community's consciousness of itself and its future. This is the task of regional planning—to develop the authoritative image within which national and regional interests can coalesce.

If history should be kind to Pickard's projections, the year 2,000 will find the population of the Atlantic Northeast exactly doubled over 1956, and 30 million more people will live in Metropolitan California. But this is not the crucial issue. Implied by all of these figures is a tremendous pressure upon the whole superstructure of institutions which we have built upon the institution of private property in the land.

The response to this pressure will undoubtedly be a further evolution of our political and economic institutions. The direction of this evolution will be imparted in large degree by the perspectives with which policy-makers, planners, and their constituents approach regional challenges and alternatives. There is an urgency, then, to thinking our way through the special conditions of urban efficiency and amenity to understand explicitly the policy criteria which go into this image. Superficially the choice is between urban sprawl and order; in reality it engages the whole institutional machinery for land allocation. This issue could be resolved as the inadvertent by-product of solutions to other problems; however, the leverage of this issue on the future is so great that we can afford no less than a conscious and explicit exercise of choice.

There are other requirements, also. Regional policy effectuation is not brought about by inveighing against parochialism in local government. Instead, we need to mobilize some of our institutional creativity to evolve mechanisms by which the gains and losses of regional policy-making can be more equitably shared by the communities and groups which make up the region. Equity is more likely than invocation to bring about the unreserved participation of local government in regional policy-making.

Finally, the states can be the important catalysts in this national-regional partnership. The demands for statesmanship will rest heavily upon them, for they will have to validate the new arrangements which the new multi-state metropolitan regions will require.

The past, present, and future uses of urban land can be sketched in only with revolutionary strokes. They represent only the spatial dimension of the accelerating urban revolution which in one century has carried us from a rural-agricultural society to the edge of a metropolitan civilization. Perhaps the really crucial challenge that emerges from all of this is simple—to understand at every point what is happening to us so that when we act, it will be for the better.

# NOTES

1. U.S. Bureau of the Census, *Historical Statistics of the United States, Colonial Times to 1957*, Washington, D.C., 1960, Series A 195, p. 14, and U.S. Bureau of the Census, *1960 Census of Population Advance Reports, General Social and Economic Characteristics, United States*, PC (A3)-1, Washington, D.C., 1962, Table 100, p. 4.

2. U.S. Bureau of the Census, *Historical Statistics* Series F 45, pp. 140–41.

3. See Note 1.

4. Harvey S. Perloff, Edgar S. Dunn, Eric E. Lampard, and Richard F. Muth, *Regions, Resources and Economic Growth* (Baltimore: The Johns Hopkins Press, 1960), Table 57, p. 172, and Table 120, p. 270.

5. Luther H. Gulick, *The Metropolitan Problem and American Ideas* (New York: Alfred A. Knopf, 1962), pp. 26–27.

6. Hugh H. Wooten and James R. Anderson, *Major Uses of Land in the United States, Summary for 1954*, USDA Agricultural Information Bulletin No. 168, Washington, D.C., 1957, Table 7, p. 27.

7. Donald J. Bogue, *Metropolitan Growth and the Conversion of Land to Nonagricultural Use* (Scripps Foundation for Research in Population Problems, Miami University, 1956).

8. Marion Clawson, R. Burnell Held, Charles H. Stoddard, *Land for the Future* (Baltimore: The Johns Hopkins Press, 1960), Table 16, p. 108.

9. Cf., Jean Gottman, *Megalopolis* (New York: The Twentieth Century Fund, 1961).

10. U.S. Bureau of the Census, *Current Population Reports: Population Estimates*, "Estimates of the Total Population and Components of Change, by States: 1950–1960," Series P-25, No. 247, Table 1.

11. U.S. Bureau of the Census, Series P-25, No. 247. (See Note 1.)

12. U.S. Bureau of the Census, Series P-20, No. 113. (See Note 3.) Figure 1, p. 1, and Table 1, pp. 10–11.

13. U.S. Bureau of the Census, *Current Population Reports: Population Characteristics*, "Mobility of the Population of the United States, March 1959–60," Series P-20, No. 113, January 22, 1962, Table 3, p. 13.

14. U.S. Bureau of the Census, *1960 Census of Population: Supplementary Reports*, PC(S1)-1, Tables 1 and 2, p. 7.

15. U.S. Bureau of the Census, *1956 National Housing Inventory*, Vol. 1., "Components of Change 1950 to 1956," Part 1, U.S. and Regions, Washington, D.C., 1958.

16. U.S. Bureau of the Census, *Current Population Reports: Population Estimates*, Series P-25, No. 247, Washington, D.C., April, 1962, Table 1, p. 41.

17. Leo F. Schnore, "Municipal Annexations and the Growth of Metropolitan Suburbs, 1950–60," *The American Journal of Sociology*, LXVII, No. 4 (January, 1962), pp. 406–17, esp. Table 3, p. 411.

18. Donald J. Bogue, *Population of the United States* (Glencoe, Ill.: Free Press, 1959), Table 15-15, p. 408.

19. Bogue, *ibid.*

20. Schnore, *op. cit.*, Tables 5 and 7. Schnore found that 203 of 211 Standard Metropolitan Statistical Areas were decentralizing between 1950 and 1960.

21. A. J. Bone and Martin Wohl, "Massachusetts Route 128 Impact Study" in Highway Research Board, National Academy of Science-National Research Council, *Highways and Economic Development*, Bulletin 227, Washington, D.C., 1959, pp. 21–49.

22. Harland Bartholomew, *Land Use in American Cities* (Cambridge: Harvard University Press, 1955).

23. John R. Hamburg, "Land Use Projections for Predicting Future Traffic" in *Trip Characteristics and Traffic Assignment*, Highway Research Board Bulletin 224 (Washington: National Academy of Sciences-National Research Council, 1959), p. 74, Fig. 1.

24. For an illuminating contrast with U.S. urbanization see Jack C. Fisher, "The City of Socialist Man" in *Cornell Alumni News*, June, 1962, pp. 5–11.

25. Stanley J. Tankel, "Open Space: Its Use and Non-use." A paper presented at the Symposium on the Future Use of Urban Space, the 1962 Resources for the Future Forum, Washington, March 26–27, 1962.

26. Charles M. Haar, "Zoning for Minimum Standards: The Wayne Township Case," 66 *Harvard Law Rev.*, 1051 (1953). Also Haar, "Zoning for Whom?—In Brief Reply," 67 *ibid.*, 986 (1954).

27. Charles M. Haar, "The Social Control of Urban Space," a paper presented at the Symposium on the Future Use of Urban Space, the 1962 Resources for the Future Forum, Washington, March 26–27, 1962.

28. Lowdon Wingo, Jr., *Transportation and Urban Land* (Washington, D.C.: Resources for the Future, Inc., 1961), Fig. 5, p. 25.

29. Donald J. Bogue, *The Population of the United States*, Table 15-11, p. 388.

30. Jerome P. Pickard, *Metropolitanization of the United States*, Research Monograph 2 (Washington, D.C.: The Urban Land Institute, 1959), Table 3, p. 15, and Table 10, p. 33.

RALEIGH BARLOWE

# Land for Recreation

SIXTY-NINE YEARS HAVE NOW PASSED since Frederick Jackson
Turner presented his famous paper on "The Significance of the
Frontier in American History." In this paper, Turner outlined
the thesis that: "Up to our own day American history has been
to a large degree the history of the colonization of the Great
West. The existence of an area of free land, its continuous reces-
sion, and the advance of American settlement westward, explain
American development."[1]

Turner's hypothesis has had a significant influence on historical thought and is directly related to the subject matter of
this symposium. The Homestead Act of 1862 may be viewed as
the culmination of a series of settler-oriented changes in the
nation's public land disposal policies. And like many other
policies and events, it had an important impact on the settlement of the West and the development of our national economy.

One might well ask, however, what relationship exists between
Turner's hypothesis, the Homestead Act, and the subject matter
of this paper. The Homestead Act was designed to facilitate the
movement of land into farms, not into recreation. Turner recognized that the nation's land frontier was already disappearing as
a contiguous area in 1893; and there certainly was little public
appreciation of need for land for recreation at the time. How
then does the demand for land for recreation fit into the picture?
For an answer to this question, let us look at the place of recreation in the American Dream.

## RECREATION AND THE AMERICAN DREAM

Land ownership was a major goal for many of the thousands
of European colonists and settlers who migrated to the American continent during the 1700's and 1800's. But it was not their
only objective. To a large measure, they sought opportunities
for economic and social advancement. Religious freedom, political and social equality, and the promise of economic opportuni-

ties that could lead to higher levels of life were all part of the American Dream.

With a continent to be settled and developed and with millions of landless people from Europe seeking opportunities for farm and home ownership, it was not unnatural that heavy emphasis was given to land disposal and settlement policies during the 1800's. Indeed, it would have been surprising if the activities on the western frontier had not had major impacts on national policies and if policies comparable to the Homestead Act had not evolved.

Frontier settlement represented an important aspect of the fulfillment of the American Dream; but it did not stand alone. The rise of popular sovereignty, progress in industrialization, and increasing individual productivity also contributed to realization of the nation's goals. With the disappearance of the land frontier, other aspects of the American Dream emerged as significant new frontiers requiring action; and these frontiers, like the land frontier of the last century, have often generated ideas and pressures that have exerted significant effects upon national policy.

The quest for opportunities for outdoor recreation, for the constructive use of leisure time, may properly be regarded as one of these emerging frontiers. Now that we have progressed nationally to the point at which we are willing to substitute leisure time for the production that could be obtained from more hours of labor, the use we make of leisure time has become a matter of significance. Our hope that the benefits of our rising levels of life may be extended to all people makes the problem of providing land for recreation as significant in the twentieth century as the provision of free homesteads was a century ago. Like land ownership, opportunities for recreation have become a significant part of the American Dream; and private and public efforts are being directed toward the realization of this goal.

## RECREATION IN THE PAST

Our present demand for land for recreation has its roots in the past. It is appropriate, therefore, that consideration be given to a review of past experience. Before turning to this subject though, a word should be said about the concept of recreation.

Recreation may be defined in a dictionary sense as "refreshment of strength and spirits after toil, diversion or a mode of diversion."[2] Ordinarily we think of recreation as a process that refreshes or revitalizes the mind or body. This concept is embodied in Hutchinson's definition of recreation as "a worthwhile, socially accepted leisure experience that provides immediate and inherent satisfaction to the individual who voluntarily participates in an activity."[3]

Recreation is normally enjoyable; but a distinction is needed between the concept of enjoyed activities and recreation. Many people enjoy their work and also the talking, eating, sleeping, shopping, and other routine activities necessary for day-to-day existence. These activities are properly considered as parts of the income-earning and individual and family housekeeping processes. For our purposes, recreation may be viewed as leisure-time activities that people engage in from choice.[4]

RECREATION IN PRE-INDUSTRIAL SOCIETIES

With this concept of recreation in hand, let us consider the relative demand for recreation in the past. Anthropological studies show that the demand for leisure and recreation among primitive peoples has usually been higher than in more advanced societies. Evidence of this may be found in a comparison of the attitudes of the American Indians with those of the white settlers who replaced them along the frontier. The Indian braves disdained most types of work and preferred to spend their time in hunting, fighting, games, festivities, and relaxation. Among them, work was usually the province of the squaws and old men. The white settlers, on the other hand, made a virtue of work and often had time for little else.

Burch and Taves have traced the changing functions of recreation in human society by comparing the leisure patterns reported in a series of ethnographic studies which provide a continuum from preindustrial to modern industrial societies.[5] Their study shows that leisure is regarded as a prime goal in preindustrial communities. Work necessary for survival is accepted but is intermixed with play and is viewed negatively. Celebrations often accompany the completion of work.

As society moves into a transitional phase, distinctions develop between periods spent at work and play; labor is viewed more positively, and emphasis shifts to the acceptance of a work ethic. In a still more advanced society such as our own, consumption activities take their place alongside production as a major function of the economy; a new synthesis develops with work acquiring aspects of play and play aspects of work; recreation emerges as a big business; and people again think of work, in many cases, as a means to the recreational use of leisure.

### AMERICAN ATTITUDES CONCERNING RECREATION BEFORE 1900

The general attitude toward recreation in the American colonies and the early United States was that of a transitional society. Puritanic concepts regarding the virtue of hard work and the ever-present danger of idle minds becoming the devil's workshop colored much of our early thinking. People experienced many of the joys of hunting, fishing, camping, and hiking but largely as part of the normal process of making a living. Occasional softenings of the prevailing attitude could be noted as more and more time was spent, at least by some people, for social gatherings, horse racing, relaxation, or visits to taverns and grog shops. On the whole, however, society frowned on the pursuit of happiness through play; and there was little appreciation of need for reserving or developing land for public recreation.

Outdoor recreation, as we now think of it, started to emerge as a matter of public policy during the 1800's. Village commons and town squares gradually became parks. A park of twenty-four acres was developed in Philadelphia in 1828. William Cullen Bryant campaigned as a New York City newspaper editor at the middle of the century for the acquisition of park lands on the upper end of Manhattan Island; and the purchase of Central Park was started in 1853. Yosemite Valley became a California state park in 1864; Yellowstone National Park was established in 1872; and our first national forest reserves were proclaimed in 1891.

Much of the emerging interest during the late 1800's in the

acquisition of parks stemmed from a growing realization that our cities were sprawling outward and destroying the open spaces that once had been only a few moments walk from downtown centers. Parks were acquired in some areas as part of the "city beautiful" movement that started with the Chicago World Fair of 1893. Desire to preserve natural wonderlands prompted the creation of some national and state parks. But the big reason for the growing emphasis on parks in the late 1800's and early 1900's was the changing attitude of the American people.

New sentiments regarding the importance of recreation and play began to emerge during the late 1800's with the rise of a moneyed class and with increasing urbanization, rising real incomes, and an increase in leisure time. Between 1850 and 1900 the population of the nation more than tripled and the proportion of this population found in cities increased from 15.3 to 39.7 per cent. The length of the average work week dropped from seventy to sixty hours; and the average productivity per man-hour more than doubled. (Cf. Table 1.)

These changes were coupled with the rise of sports. Baseball was started in 1839 and the National League was organized for professional ball in 1876. Roller skating started in 1863. Bicycling was introduced during the 1870's and became a national craze during the 1880's. Tennis was first played in the United States in 1873 and its popularity led to the organization of the United States Lawn Tennis Association in 1881. Polo was introduced in 1876. A revival of interest in canoeing brought the organization of an American Canoe Association in 1880. Yachting became a sport for the wealthy during the latter half of the century; horse racing attracted new interest; and boxing acquired respectability as a sport. America's first golf tournament was held in 1894. Meanwhile, football and other college sports came in vogue; and the automobile made its debut at the turn of the century.

Sports have exerted a tremendous role in modifying our heritage of Puritanism and in making America recreation-conscious. Frederic L. Paxson in his discussion of the rise of sports says:

> It was the open frontier that kept America young during its first century of national existence. . . . When the frontier closed in the eighties the habit of an open life was too strong

## TABLE 1

### TRENDS IN POPULATION, AVERAGE HOURS OF WORK PER WEEK, AND LABOR PRODUCTIVITY, UNITED STATES, 1850–1960

| Year | Total Population (in Millions) | Proportion of Population Classified as Urban (Percentage) | Average Length of Work Week (Hours) | Average Productivity per Man-Hour (Measured in Constant 1950 Dollars) |
|------|------|------|------|------|
| 1850 | 23.2 | 15.3 | 69.8 | 33.7 cents |
| 1860 | 31.4 | 19.8 | 68.0 | 40.6 |
| 1870 | 39.8 | 25.7 | 65.4 | 42.6 |
| 1880 | 50.2 | 28.2 | 64.0 | 44.4 |
| 1890 | 62.9 | 35.1 | 61.9 | 61.1 |
| 1900 | 76.0 | 39.7 | 60.2 | 75.5 |
| 1910 | 92.0 | 45.8 | 55.1 | 89.6 |
| 1920 | 105.7 | 51.2 | 49.7 | 93.2 |
| 1930 | 122.8 | 56.2 | 42.4 | 106.9 |
| 1940 | 131.7 | 56.5 | 43.3 | 131.5 |
| 1950 | 150.7 | 64.0 | 40.0 | 193.5 |
| 1960 | 178.5 | 69.3 | 39.7 | 241.8 (approx.) |

Source: Data for 1850–1950 from J. Frederic Dewhurst and Associates, *America's Needs and Resources*, (New York: Twentieth Century Fund, 1955), p. 40. Data for 1960 computed from information reported in *Statistical Abstract of the United States, 1961*.

to be changed offhand. The search for sport revealed a partial substitute for pioneer life. . . .

But the causes of the rise of sport, whether in the needs of city life, or in the automatic adaptation of a society whose old safety-valve, free land, was closing down, or in the aptitudes of a community inured to frontier conditions and now deprived of them, are of slighter consequence than their effect on America. No one can probe national character, personal conduct, public opinion today without bringing out their difference from that which formerly prevailed.[6]

The change in our attitudes regarding recreation did not come about rapidly and was not even felt by many people. Outdoor recreation was a far-off dream for much of our population during the 1800's and remained so for many until recent times. True, most boys were able to find time for fishing and an occasional ball game; there was a growing class of people who had the money and free time for travel or relaxation at various vacation spots; and writers such as Bryant, Emerson, and Thoreau did write in glowing terms of the beauties of nature.

Most of our population, however, was too busily involved in the process of making a living and trying to get ahead in the world to give much emphasis to recreation. Hamlin Garland's picture of the hard life endured on the middle frontier during the 1870's and 1880's is not atypical of the situation experienced by large groups of farm and nonfarm workers throughout the nation generally. From late childhood to old age, most average workers faced the prospect of a life of toil and labor punctuated with only occasional visits to town, to a circus or fair, or perhaps to a neighborhood social or a revival meeting. Except for the necessary care of livestock and for emergency work in the shops or fields, Sunday was regarded and usually treated as a day of rest. But aside from this partial respite from work, life for many people was a long routine of toil with few infrequent days off for rest, relaxation, or recreation.

DEVELOPMENTS SINCE 1900

Our present attitudes regarding the desirability of recreation and our local, state, and national policies concerning the acquisition and development of land for recreation have their roots in the last century. The nurturing of these roots and the resulting growth of demand and facilities for outdoor recreation are largely a product of the last six decades.

New York, Boston, Minneapolis, Philadelphia, and other cities started ambitious park development programs before 1900.[7] But the impetus for most city and other local park programs came during the 1920's and 1930's. California and New York had state park reserves before the turn of the century; but most of our state park agencies came into being during the 1920's and the bulk of their park acreages were acquired during the 1930's. The National Park Service was organized in 1916; and seventeen national parks plus several national monuments were established between 1900 and 1932. Additional areas have been acquired since then for national parks, monuments, memorials, and recreation areas; and programs such as Mission 66 have been used to advantage to provide improved facilities.[8]

Other national policies affecting outdoor recreation have also taken form in recent decades. Important among these are the designation of wilderness areas and the development of recreation facilities in the national forests; the development of wildlife refuges; the creation of the Fish and Wildlife Service in 1940 and its partial successor, the Bureau of Sport Fisheries and Wildlife, in 1956; the development of recreation areas on Bureau of Reclamation, Tennessee Valley Authority, and Corps of Engineer projects; and the recent (March, 1962) establishment of a Bureau of Outdoor Recreation in the Department of Interior.

The mounting concern in public policy over the provision of land for recreation has been prompted by continuation of the trends noted between 1850 and 1900. Between 1900 and 1960, the nation's population more than doubled; the proportion classed as urban increased from 39.7 to 69.3 per cent; the average work week dropped from sixty to forty hours; and average productivity per man-hour more than tripled. (Table 1.) The combination of a larger population with considerably more leisure time and higher real incomes has brought greatly increased demand for recreation opportunities.

Other factors such as mounting mobility, changing attitudes, and the advertising activities of the growing recreation business also had their effect in generating new demand. Widespread ownership of automobiles, the development of a nationwide network of highways, and the growing popularity of air travel made the average American far more mobile in 1960 than at the turn of the century. Recreation programs sponsored by schools, communities, the military services, and other organizations broke down old resistances and made most people recreation-conscious. Meanwhile, recreation emerged as a multi-billion dollar business which profited both from its voluminous advertising activities and from the favorable treatment it has received from the nation's press.

## RECREATION IN 1962

When one turns to consideration of the role recreation plays in our lives and in land use and public policy decisions in 1962, it is easy to bog down in detail. A few aspects of the overall picture, however, can be identified and used as general measures of the present situation. Among these, our expenditures of time and money for recreation, current patterns of demand, and the nature of the areas available for recreation deserve attention.

### TIME SPENT ON RECREATION

People who work with statistics on recreation are usually impressed with the dearth of data on many matters and the generally confusing manner in which most of the available figures are reported. This situation applies very definitely to the data concerning expenditures of time on recreation. Most of the data we have involve estimates and approximations.

In considering the question of how much time we spend on recreation, let us start by asking: How much time could we reasonably expect to spend on recreation? Our average work week in 1960 called for forty hours and the average worker received two weeks of paid vacation. If one assumes a five-day work week in which the average worker spends eight hours a day (including coffee breaks) at work, an hour a day in travel to and from work, eight hours in sleeping, and five hours in eating, dressing, shopping, and other individual and family housekeeping activities, it appears that two hours a day may be available on the average for recreational pursuits. In addition to this leisure time, the worker has the free time represented by holidays, his two days off from work each weekend, and his two weeks of paid vacation that he can use for recreation. Housewives may have more or less free time depending upon their household routines. Youngsters in school normally have more than this amount of free time available; and small children have considerable free time for play.

How people spend their free time poses another problem. Much free time is spent attending classes and meetings and in household and other work. Some is spent in sleeping and relaxation. Considerable amounts are used for indoor recreation activities that range from reading, listening to music, or watching television, to participation in or being a spectator of indoor sports, going to theaters, playing cards, working on hobbies, and other similar activities. Except for walking and riding in automobiles, outdoor recreation tends to be more the exception than the rule for adults. Only a small proportion of our adult workers spend much of the free time they have at the end of the day in outdoor recreation. There is a greater tendency to spend time over the weekend in outdoor activities; and some outdoor recreation activity has become an accepted part of the annual vacation.

Reports have been issued for many years by individual park and recreation area agencies on total annual visitations. The National Park Service reported 79.2 million visits in 1960, an increase of 239 per cent above 1950. The National Forests had 102 million visits in 1961, a 340 per cent increase over 1951. The Corps of Engineers projects had 120 million visits in 1961, almost five times the number of 1952. The Tennessee Valley Authority areas had 42 million visitations and the Bureau of Reclamation projects 24 million in 1960 while the Wildlife Refuges had 7.6 million visitations in 1956, all substantially more than the numbers they had a decade earlier. Some 255 million visitations were reported for state parks in 1960 and 724 million for municipal and county parks in 1955. Still another measure of the time spent on outdoor recreation is suggested by the fact that 14.5 million hunting licenses and 43.2 million fishing licenses were sold in 1956.

Reports on park and other area visitations provide a general measure of the increasing popularity of outdoor recreation. These figures can be misleading, however, as they emphasize number of visits rather than time actually spent in outdoor recreation. Each of the many trips that frequent visitors and service workers make into an area count as much as the single visits made by many recreationists. Moreover, equal weight is given to the visits of people who are merely traveling through on highways that cross areas, people who stop a few hours for picnics or other activities, and people who stop for a week or more of camping and general vacationing.

The studies of the Outdoor Recreation Resources Review Commission provide several statistics that go beyond straight visitation counts. One of these studies estimates that the 133.3 million persons, twelve years and over, in the United States in 1960 participated 4,377 million times, measured in terms of separate days of activity, in seventeen leading outdoor recreation activities during the months of June, July, and August (September through November in the case of hunting) in 1960.[9] This calculation indicates that the average individual, twelve years of age or over, participated, during the study, 32.8 different times in driving for pleasure, swimming, walking for pleasure, playing outdoor games or sports, sightseeing, picnicking, fishing, bicycling, attending outdoor sport events, boating other than sailing or canoeing, nature walks, hunting, camping, horseback riding, water skiing, hiking, or attending outdoor concerts and shows.

Another tabulation from the same report covers the whole range of outdoor recreation activities and indicates that on the average persons twelve years and over had 92.2 days of activity-participation in various activities during the year from June, 1960 through May, 1961.[10] This study reported an average of 33.6 activity-participation days per person during the summer months, 19.4 during the fall, 18.4 during the winter, and 20.9 during the spring.

Driving for pleasure, the single most popular activity, accounted for an average of 20.7 activity days per person and more than 22 per cent of the total number of activity occasions. Driving for pleasure and walking for pleasure accounted for 41 per cent of the total. These two activities, plus playing outdoor games and sports, swimming, sightseeing, and bicycling accounted for 75 per cent of the total outdoor activity occasions.

Mueller and Gurin found in a study of the recreation activities of a nationwide sample of 2,759 adults that 71 per cent had participated in automobile riding for sightseeing and relaxation purposes during the preceeding year.[11] Sixty-six per cent had gone on picnics, 45 per cent had participated in outdoor swimming or going to the beach, 38 per cent in fishing, 28 per cent in boating or canoeing, 19 per cent in hiking, 17 per cent in hunting, 15 per cent in camping, 14 per cent in nature or bird walks, 7 per cent in horseback riding, and 6 per cent in skiing or other winter sports.

The Outdoor Recreation Resources Review Commission estimated that there were 532 million day visits and 52 million overnight visits to parks and recreation areas in the 48 contiguous states of the Union in 1960.[12] Evidence concerning the nature and duration of the visits made to a nationwide sample of national, state, and regional parks and recreation areas is provided by Leslie Reid's study of *The Quality of Outdoor Recreation as Evidenced by User Satisfaction*.[13] Twenty-six per cent of the respondent user-groups in this study were on major annual vacations, 8 per cent on one of two or more shorter vacations, 11 per cent on weekend or overnight trips, 43 per cent on day outings, 2 per cent on combined business and vacation trips, 7 per cent on trips that combined vacations with visits to friends or relatives, while 3 per cent had other explanations. Vacations accounted for 72 per cent of the visits to the areas classified as major sightseeing attraction areas and for 72 per cent of those to camping areas while day outings and weekend or overnight trips accounted for 70 per cent of the visits to areas where swimming was the major attraction, 84 per cent to the skiing areas, 82 per cent to the fishing and boating areas, and 83 per cent to the picnicking areas.

Information collected from the respondents in Reid's study show that more than half of the user-groups in the swimming, skiing, and boating and fishing areas, and three-fourths of those in the picnicking areas spent less than half a day at these sites.

In contrast, more than 30 per cent of the user-groups in the boating and fishing areas and 40 per cent of those at the skiing sites spent between one and three days at these areas. Over half of the user-groups in the camping areas stayed for four days or more and three-fourths stayed for more than one day.

## EXPENDITURES OF MONEY

Expenditures of money as well as time can be used as an indication of the effective demand for recreation. The use of this measure is complicated by the fact that many of the best things in outdoor recreation, as well as life, are still free and by the problems that arise in determining whether expenditures should be credited to recreation or to other types of demands.

Personal consumption expenditures for recreation in 1959 have been reported as totaling $18.3 billion.[14] This represents 4.6 per cent of the national income and 6.3 per cent of the nation's consumption expenditures for 1959. Around 70 per cent or more of the expenditures included in this total involve payments for theater admissions, books, magazines, club dues, radio and television sets, and other similar expenses for indoor recreation. Expenditures for outdoor activities account for around $4.8 billions of the total. Questions can be raised about the acceptability of this total, however, as it makes no allowance for the cost of automobiles, travel expenses, luggage, clothing outlays, food and beverages, lodging, or the souvenirs so often associated with vacations and outdoor recreation.

There is considerable evidence that individual and national expenditures for outdoor recreation and recreation generally are rising. No attempt will be made here to determine the amounts actually expended for recreation. It is sufficient for our purpose to note that significant sums are spent for this purpose and that the demand for recreation in this country is backed up with both willingness and ability to pay.

## PATTERNS OF DEMAND FOR RECREATION

Individual and group interests in recreation vary over a wide range. Some people place low priorities on recreation or on particular recreation activities. Many use most of their free time for reading, listening to the radio, or watching television. Others are particularly interested in hobbies, sports, or outdoor activities.

The report of the Outdoor Recreation Resources Review Commission shows that age, income, education, occupation, and place of residence have significant effects on the amounts and types of outdoor recreation in which people participate.[15] Swimming and bicycling are popular activities but these activities, along with horseback riding and participation in sports, are engaged in primarily by the young. People in the 25–64 year age groups retain some interest in swimming but their interest is less than that of teenagers. Interest in camping, fishing, sightseeing, boating, and nature walks continues at a high level until late in life; and interest in walking for pleasure is high among youngsters, declines during the middle years, and tends to increase again for people past the age of forty-five.

Tabulations on the relationship of income to participation in outdoor recreation show that participation increases as family income increases. Persons from families with incomes of less than $3,000 a year had activity-participation rates of only 18.5 days per person as compared with 33.4 days for persons from families with incomes of between $3,000 and $5,999, and averages of 40 to 50 days for persons from family income groups of $6,000 or more. Problems of aging, unemployment, and inability to afford travel to recreation areas explains much of the low participation rate among persons from low-income families.

Activities such as boating, camping, and horseback riding are participated in most often by persons from the higher income families. Walking, on the other hand, is a source of enjoyment to both the rich and poor; and fishing has its highest participation rate among persons from families with incomes in the $3,000 to $9,999 range.[16]

Years of educational attainment, perhaps because of its positive correlation with incomes, has a comparable influence on participation in outdoor recreation. Among persons twenty-five years of age and over, activity-participation rates are higher for playing games, swimming, sightseeing, and driving for pleasure among college graduates than among high school graduates and higher among high school graduates than among those who did not finish or did not enter high school. Activity-participation for walking for pleasure was highest among people with college training, second highest among those who did not enter high school, and lowest among those with high school training only.[17]

Occupations also have a direct bearing on participation in outdoor recreation activities. The data assembled by the Outdoor Recreation Resources Review Commission show that persons not in the labor force reported the highest number of days of activity-participation. Their average of 37.9 days was followed by averages of 36.7 for professional, technical, and kindred workers; 32.8 for clerical and sales (white collar) workers; 30.0 for craftsmen, foremen, and kindred workers; 27.0 for operatives and kindred workers and laborers; 26.0 for service workers; 24.4 for managers, officials, and proprietors (except farmers); and 16.8 for farm workers. Students and yet-to-be-employed young people explain the high rate among the nonlabor force. Among the others, professional workers and workers with paid vacations have definitely higher rates than farm workers and others who are less likely to enjoy paid vacation privileges.

The data on place of residence show that persons who live in suburban and adjacent areas participate to a greater extent in driving for pleasure, picnicking, outdoor swimming, hunting, fishing, and camping than residents of cities. Suburbanites also participate in driving for pleasure, picnicking, and outdoor swimming more than the residents of outlying (predominantly rural) areas. People in more rural areas, however, do more fishing and hunting and about the same amount of camping as the suburbanites.

Differences in user-groups also has an effect on activity choices and preferences. Reid classified the types of activities rated as most enjoyable by six different types of user groups.[18] His findings show that sightseeing with stops, swimming, and camping were rated as the three most enjoyed activities by user-groups traveling as family units. Swimming, picnicking, and sightseeing with stops were rated as most enjoyable by groups composed of two-or-more family groups and also by the groups made up of families plus friends or relatives. Snow skiing and swimming were rated as most enjoyed by persons traveling alone and by groups of friends while picnicking, swimming, and camping were given top billing by organized groups (clubs, troops, teams) of travelers.

## LAND FOR RECREATION

Closely related to the question of demand for recreation is the matter of how much land we have available for recreation. It would seem that a simple tabulation could be presented to show the amount of land used for recreation; but the data on this point are confusing to say the least. Recreation is frequently considered as a multiple use of land and water; and whether an area is counted as available for recreation often depends on the emphasis one gives to other uses. In an overall sense, the whole surface of the earth is or could be said to be available for recreational use. Far more limited areas are involved when one thinks of areas used primarily for recreation or those that are subject to intensive or even moderate recreational use.

Studies of the Outdoor Recreation Resources Review Commission show that 234 million acres in the forty-eight contiguous states of the Union and 283 million acres in these states plus Alaska, Hawaii, Puerto Rico, and the Virgin Islands have been designated as public recreation areas.[19] These designated areas represent 12.1 and 12.2 per cent, respectively, of the land area of the forty-eight contiguous states and of the United States as a whole.

The figures from ORRRC for the forty-eight contiguous states show that we have 3.5 million acres of county and local park and recreation lands, 32 million acres of state areas, and 198 million acres of federal lands designated as recreation areas. Approximately two-thirds of the county and local areas are county and municipal forest areas, areas which in most cases have limited value for intensive recreational use. More than half of the state lands are administered by forest agencies and more than a fourth by fish and wildlife agencies. Of the federal lands, 165.2 million acres or almost 84 per cent of the total area is administered by the U.S. Forest Service, 17.2 million acres by the National Park Service, 9.6 million acres by the Bureau of Sport Fisheries and Wildlife, 3.9 million acres by the Corps of Engineers, 766,000 by the Bureau of Reclamation, 648,000 acres by the Tennessee Valley Authority, and 113,000 acres by miscellaneous agencies.

Most of the public lands designated as recreation areas involve expanses of forests, mountains, deserts, and wilderness areas which have value as scenery but are not really available for intensive or even moderate recreational use. The total area available for these uses probably does not exceed 10 per cent of the total public designated area. Evidence to this effect is suggested by the data on size of recreation area units. Of the 24,048 units included in the ORRRC tabulation, 75 per cent involved less than 100 acres and 90 per cent less than 1,000 acres. The smallest 90 per cent of the units accounted for only one-half of the percent of the total land area. Units of less than 1,000 acres accounted for 93 per cent of the state and the county and local units but for only 30 per cent of the federal units.

Only scattered data are available to indicate the areas of privately owned land which are used for recreation. Small areas occupied by businesses representing large investments are used in most urban areas for theaters, sports palaces, bowling alleys, night clubs, dining rooms, and other places that specialize in indoor recreation. Larger urban areas must be added in when one considers the use of homes and yards for recreation. Large, privately owned areas in rural settings also are used for indoor recreation but particularly for such outdoor uses as camp grounds, beaches, country clubs, golf courses, tourist resorts, dude ranches, boating and fishing, and hunting areas.

No census has been made of the area of private lands used for recreation. It appears, however, that when we include the play areas in family backyards that we may have as much privately owned land as public land used on an intensive and moderate scale for recreation. The area of privately owned farm and forest land used for hunting, hiking, and other less intensive recreational uses is large and probably exceeds the total area of publicly owned land that has been designated as available for recreational use. From a practical standpoint, we must recognize that we have more recreational land in private ownership than in public ownership in the United States.

## FUTURE DEMANDS FOR LAND FOR RECREATION

Let us turn our attention now to the future demand for land for recreation and to the problems that will arise in the fulfillment of this demand. How much land we will need in the future will depend on the total demand for recreation and the manner in which we develop and use our land resources. Probable levels of demand and expected issues in recreation land management thus become key aspects of the problem of the future.

### PROJECTIONS OF DEMAND

Demand for recreation is a function of population numbers, individual choices, and the willingness and economic ability of people to spend time and money on recreational pursuits. In order to arrive at estimates of future demand, several assumptions are needed concerning the nature of things to come. A basic assumption is needed concerning the continuation of conditions of world peace and prosperity. With peace and prosperity, it is reasonable to expect increasing demand. War, however, could disrupt and even destroy the basis for our future hopes and aspirations, while a prolonged economic depression could have a stagnating effect on the economy that could lead to lower income levels and low rates of population growth.

Other important assumptions must be made concerning trends in population numbers, concentration of the future population, amounts of leisure time, levels of income, and individual mobility. The Outdoor Recreation Resources Review Commission assumes that our total population will rise to around 230 million in 1976 and to 350 million by the year 2000. It is assumed that almost three-fourths of our people will live in metropolitan areas by the end of the century. Leisure time will increase as the average work week drops to 36 hours in 1976 and 32 hours by 2000. With an assumed annual growth rate in gross national product of 3.5 per cent a year, disposable incomes will rise from $354 billion in 1960 to $706 billion in 1976 and $1,437 billion in 2000; and the average real income per family is expected to almost double by the end of the century. Great advances in individual mobility and travel also are expected.[20]

The joint effect of these indicators spells a tremendous increase in the demand for outdoor recreation. Clawson suggested in his much-quoted article on "The Crisis in Outdoor Recreation" that the "increase in recreational demand might be as small as five times or as great as fifteen times" by the end of the century.[21] The U.S. Forest Service has thought in terms of a four-fold increase in its Operation Out-of-Doors program. The ORRRC projects a three-fold increase in outdoor recreational activity-participation by 2000, part of it stemming from more population and part from an increase of 184 per cent in the average rate of individual participation in outdoor activities.[22]

There is no need here for another projection of future demand. Most signs point to an increase in the demand for recreation and we know that this increase will be substantial. But at the same time that we predict marked increases in demand, a certain amount of caution should be urged. We know that we cannot base our predictions on straight-line projections of recently reported park and recreation area visitation rates. This approach could soon get us to the point at which every man, woman, and child would have to spend his life in a frantic rush from one area to another to get in his annual quota of visitations.

Estimates of future demand must give some attention to the uncertainties associated with changing tastes and preferences. Our parks and recreation areas will be much more crowded in the future than at present and it remains to be seen whether people will want to visit them as much as now. Reports from states such as Michigan show that the number of hunting and fishing licenses sold has declined at a steady rate in recent years. Similar trends could affect other types of activities. The increasing use of outdoor patios, barbecues, and family swimming pools for home-oriented recreation could portend some reduction in the expected demand for public facilities. Rising incomes could lead to more participation in country club programs and less in the use of public parks. Rising incomes and greater mobility could channel significant amounts of potential demand into foreign travel and recreation. It must also be recognized that the hobbies and interests of a new generation of people, most of whom will be reared in metropolitan areas, may differ as much from those of their fathers as ours differ from those of the last century.

## Land for Future Recreation

Higher demands for recreation, and particularly for outdoor recreation, suggest a need for acquiring and developing more land for this purpose. Before we start multiplying present land areas by indices of expected population increase or of expected activity-participation rates to determine future area needs, however, consideration should be given to the types of lands that will be needed for future recreation.

Of the many criteria that can be used in classifying recreation lands, "type of attraction" and "location with respect to user-groups" have particular significance. With the joint use of these criteria, one can speak of three major classes of lands—the resource-based, user-oriented, and intermediate-use areas.[23] Emphasis with the resource-based areas is normally placed on the nature of the attraction, not on location with respect to users. These areas include our national parks and forests and many state park and forest holdings that contain natural resource attractions such as water, mountains, geologic rarities, wildlife, forests, and grass- or desert-cover that give the areas special value for recreation and scenery purposes. Traditionally, much of the emphasis in these areas has been placed on preserving and maintaining the natural attractions. Sites of historical significance also may be regarded as resource-based attractions.

User-oriented areas, in contrast, must be located within a few blocks or within a few minutes of travel-time of most of their visitors. These areas range from local tot-lots and playgrounds to city and local parks and from downtown amusement centers and backyard play areas to the privately owned dance halls, golf courses, and country clubs found near our cities. State and national parks located near large population centers often take on the characteristics of user-oriented areas even when they have the qualities of resource-based attractions.

Intermediate-use areas represent a middle classification. These areas must be located within a few hours drive of most of their users. They can involve resource-based attractions and are usually more attractive if they do. But the emphasis in these areas is more on the provision of facilities for camping and other types of outdoor recreation than on the preservation of wonders of nature. As a result, intermediate-use areas can involve the moving of terrain, the planting of trees, the creation of artificial lakes, and other man-made developments.

The types of lands acquired and developed for future use should reflect expected patterns of leisure. A shorter work day can mean more demand for local user-oriented park and recreation facilities. More holidays or longer weekends can create need for more regional and intermediate-use areas. Longer paid vacations, on the other hand, can contribute to greater use of the resource-based attractions found in national and many state parks.

Present indications suggest that most of the expected increase in demand for recreation will probably be associated with use of the user-oriented and intermediate-use areas. This means that most of the emphasis in providing additional lands for recreation should be directed towards the acquisition and development of these types of areas. Fortunately, the land needs associated with these uses are moderate; and most of our emerging needs can be provided quite easily through purchase of relatively small tracts of farm and forest land.

The fact that most of our need is for local parks and intermediate-use recreation areas does not mean that the federal government should discontinue its land acquisition programs. Important reasons can be advanced for acquiring tracts of seashore and other natural wonders and converting them into public recreational attractions. States also should be encouraged to expand their park and recreation programs through the acquisition of additional sites that have natural or historical significance. It must be recognized, however, that the supply of high-calibre resource-based sites that have not already been incorporated into public recreation areas is running low. The end of our national acquisition program of resource-based areas is or should be in sight.[24] Future emphasis can be expected to center on the provision of user-oriented and intermediate-use areas.

Closely related to the types of land in demand, is the question of levels of area development. As was observed earlier, many of our recreation lands, both those in public and private ownership, are subject to intensive use; but a far larger percentage is used primarily as scenery and for extensive recreational uses such as hunting, occasional hiking, or camping. With increasing demand, it appears that a larger acreage must be made available for intensive use. The large tracts reserved as wilderness areas can and properly should remain relatively unused until population pressure forces a change. Many of the wild and underdeveloped areas close to population centers, however, should be shifted to more intensive use.

The process of designing and developing areas for more intensive and larger-scale use calls for ingenuity and administrative know-how. At this point, we must recognize that park administration is a calling that demands professional ability and training. The satisfactions to be garnered through the use of recreation areas and the future popularity of these areas can be affected favorably or adversely by managerial decisions concerning levels and patterns of area development.

Another important aspect of the problem of meeting the demand for more land for recreation concerns the use of private lands. Much of the opportunity provided for recreation in the future can and logically should be expected to come from the private sphere. Recreation is a big business in the United States; and the people engaged in this business are already making plans to provide for many of our emerging demands.

Many private operators in the recreation field have had considerable experience in their undertakings. There are numerous instances, however, of operators who could provide desired types of outdoor recreation but who first need some type of public guidance or assistance. Farmers may need organizational assistance if they are to supplement their incomes through the leasing of hunting rights. Newcomers in the motel and resort businesses often could benefit from technical advice on how best to operate. Credit is needed in many instances to finance desired improvements. Cooperation of public administrative agencies also is needed at times to permit the private operation of concessions, motels, restaurants, and other similar facilities adjacent to or in conjunction with public recreation areas.

## FINANCING NEW FACILITIES

Still another major problem we must face in the provision of new public facilities is the matter of finance. The acquisition, development, operation, and maintenance of recreation areas costs money. In the past, and even now, many of our facilities have been provided to the public without charge or with the payment of nominal fees.

New demands and the high cost of meeting these demands are forcing a change in this situation. The day is passing when the beauties of nature and the joys of outdoor activity can be enjoyed as a free commodity. Funds, both public and private, are needed to protect nature from the depredations of man and to develop outdoor recreation facilities so that they can be used to best advantage.

Several programs involving solicitation of donations, state and local bond issues, and the collection of fees have been initiated to provide funds for the acquisition and development of recreation facilities. More programs of this nature are both needed and to be expected. As we look ahead, it appears that additional public support will be needed. Some people argue that taxes should continue to provide most of the cost of supplying new and improved facilities. Consideration should be given to this argument. At the same time, however, recognition must be given to the fact that our legislatures have many competing uses for every tax dollar at their disposal. It can be argued that recreation is important, that its place in the American Dream gives it a high priority. But valid questions can be raised concerning how far the public should go in providing free or relatively free opportunities for recreation.

Questions also may be raised as to whether we can justify area developments that will be used to capacity only on an occasional holiday or Sunday afternoon during the summer months. It is logical to assume that the people who use public facilities at peak hours in the future must expect to find facilities crowded; sometimes they will be required to make advance reservations, perhaps pay admission fees, and at times be turned away. Whether we like it or not, charges and fees in all likelihood will become an increasingly prominent part of our means of financing recreational developments.

## THE SHADOW OF THE FUTURE

By way of summary, let us look briefly into the shadow of the future. As we consider the emerging need for land for recreation, it is obvious that our expectations will be affected by factors we do not and cannot recognize. War, pestilence, or a major depression could have impacts on our population, national productivity, and way of life; we find these unpleasant to contemplate. Should the dreary predictions of the neo-Malthusians come true, all of our land could be needed to feed the human race. Wilderness areas and city parks could disappear as we find it necessary to plow them up and shift to the production of carrots and potatoes. On the other hand, if the emerging vision of an era of abundance becomes a reality, millions of acres of farmland could shift to scenery, parks, and playing fields.

Fortunately, the trend in the United States today is towards abundance, not scarcity. The U.S. Department of Agriculture speaks knowingly of rising productivity and of a need to shift some 51 million acres out of agricultural cropland by 1980.[25] It is confidently hoped that much of this land will shift to privately or publicly owned recreation areas. Meanwhile, our expectations on population growth, leisure time, real incomes, and individual mobility all point to mounting demands that can and probably will call for the use of more land for recreation.

What we see in the shadow of the future is challenging and, for the most part, pleasing to contemplate. The dreams we have of things to come, however, will not be fulfilled by themselves. Action programs are needed to acquire and develop recreation areas at the places where they are most needed. Programs of federal assistance to the states and local communities may well be needed. Programs also are needed to help private operators in the recreation field provide the services that can reasonably be expected of them.

Parks and recreation areas in the future will probably feature the same natural attractions of grass, water, trees, and scenery they do today. With more people, however, they will generally be more crowded. Most areas will be developed and used more intensively than at present. And in all likelihood, a higher proportion of the cost of developing, operating, and maintaining these facilities will be financed from user fees.

## A PHILOSOPHIC VIEW OF THE EMERGING SITUATION

As I approach the conclusion of this paper, I am impressed with the fact that we have traveled almost a full circle. Preindustrial man placed high value on leisure and loved the out-of-doors for its scenery and the hunting and playgrounds it provided. The men and women who settled this part of the American continent held to a work ethic that caused them to shift the forests, prairies, and plains into farms which represented their concept of the highest and best use of the land. Modern technology and our growing concern over consumption and leisure time have made us again recreation conscious and now have us shifting land out of farms and back into recreation areas.

Perhaps it is not unfitting that I conclude with a few words spoken in the manner of a sachem from one of our American Indian tribes:

> We have walked in the way where the world is narrow. Our journey has brought us past the thicket of theory and through a bog of statistics. Now we are leaving the forest, the sky overhead is blue again. Let us gather for a moment by a fire at the edge of the forest while we puff a pipe, and you contemplate my message. I have not spoken with a forked tongue, nor thrown ashes in your eyes. My words have been those of one who talks of a dream.
>
> Many winters ago, the redman roamed across this land. He loved the forests, the prairies, and the open spaces. When the paleface came, he shared his heritage. But the paleface wanted land. He said it was destiny that the forests and meadows change to a domain of fields and work. Today we Indians are few and you have the land. But you also have learned the secret of our fathers. You have found the joy that comes when one lives and plays with nature. More and more, your fields look like the hunting grounds of my people.

May the time you spend outdoors bring you new life and contentment. May your affections for the beauties of nature blossom and grow with the coming of each new day.

## NOTES

1. Frederick Jackson Turner, *The Frontier in American History* (New York: Henry Holt and Co., 1920), p. 1.

2. *Webster's New Collegiate Dictionary.*

3. John L. Hutchinson, *Principles of Recreation* (New York: A. S. Barnes and Co., 1949), p. 2.

4. Marion Clawson, in the manuscript of a forthcoming book on Outdoor Recreation for the Future, describes recreation as "activity (or inactivity) undertaken because one wants to do it. As such, it contrasts with work, done primarily to earn money or otherwise to provide the 'necessities' of life, or ... with the mechanics of life, such as eating, sleeping, operations to keep house, dishes, clothing, and person clean, whether these are for one's self or for his or her family."

5. Cf. William Burch and Marvin J. Taves, "Changing Functions of Recreation in Human Society," *Outdoor Recreation in the Upper Great Lakes Area*, Lake States Forest Experiment Station Paper No. 89, pp. 8–15, 1961.

6. Frederic L. Paxson, "The Rise of Sport," *Mississippi Valley Historical Review*, Vol. 4, p. 167, September, 1917.

7. Cf. Charles E. Doell and Gerald B. Fitzgerald, *A Brief History of Parks and Recreation in the United States* (Chicago: The Athletic Institute, 1954), pp. 23–36.

8. For a detailed discussion of national park policy, cf. John Ise, *Our National Park Policy* (Baltimore: The Johns Hopkins Press, 1961).

9. Cf. Outdoor Recreation Resources Review Commission, *Outdoor Recreation for America* (Government Printing Office, 1962), p. 220, Table 22. The background information for this tabulation is reported in *National Recreational Survey*, ORRRC Study Report 19, pp. 120–21.

10. Cf. *ibid.*, pp. 34 and 212, Table 1. The concept of days of activity-participation does not indicate separate days of activity. Active recreationists could secure credit for several days of activity-participation in a single day by participating in several activities.

11. Cf. Eva Mueller and Gerald Gurin, *Participation in Outdoor Recreation*, ORRRC Study Report 20, p. 5.

12. Cf. *Outdoor Recreation for America*, p. 62.

13. Cf. Leslie M. Reid *et al.*, *The Quality of Outdoor Recreation as Evidenced by User Satisfaction*, ORRRC Study Report 5, pp. 18–25.

14. Cf. *Statistical Abstract of the United States*, 1961, p. 197.

15. Cf. *Outdoor Recreation for America*, pp. 27–29 and 36–41.

16. Cf. *Outdoor Recreation for America*, p. 215, Table 8.

17. Cf. *ibid.*, p. 215, Table 9.

18. Cf. Reid, *op. cit.*, p. 26.

19. Cf. *Outdoor Recreation for America*, pp. 223–24, Tables 27 and 28; and *List of Public Outdoor Recreation Areas*, 1960, ORRRC Study Report 2, pp. 3–4.

20. Cf. *Outdoor Recreation for America*, pp. 30–32 and 219–20.

21. Marion Clawson, "The Crisis in Outdoor Recreation," *American Forests,* March and April, 1959.

22. Cf. *Outdoor Recreation for America*, pp. 32 and 221.

23. This classification follows that suggested by Clawson *op. cit.,* and Marion Clawson, R. Burnell Held, and Charles H. Stoddard, *Land for the Future* (Baltimore: The Johns Hopkins Press, 1960), pp. 153–83. A more complicated classification scheme is used by ORRRC (*Outdoor Recreation for America,* pp. 97–120).

24. Even though future acquisitions may add only slightly to the areas of resource-based lands in public ownership, changes can be expected in the administrative arrangements associated with their management and use. Many areas now administered by particular federal or state agencies will probably be shifted for various reasons to the administrative jurisidiction of other agencies.

25. Cf. *Land and Water Resources: A Policy Guide,* U.S. Department of Agriculture, May, 1962, p. 1.

M. M. KELSO

# Resolving Land Use Conflicts

WHEN THE FIRST NOMADIC HUNTER drove another from the water hole about which he found his quarry, a land use conflict took place. When the early American frontiersman pushed into the wilderness with his gun, powder horn, shot pouch, and hand axe to protect himself from the prior claims of the aborigines, a land use conflict took place. So did one occur, too, when the later settler in the same community intimidated the federal government's land agents who were attempting to expel the earlier settlers from lands they had never legally acquired from the sovereign power that owned them. And again one occurred when the western cattleman "shot up" the sheepherder's flock and, in solemn assembly with his peers, voted favorably for "law and order" by approving a resolution to his state's legislature asking that it declare the killing of a sheepherder to be a misdemeanor. Again did land use conflict arise when the increasing demands of California placer miners for water for their sluice boxes led earlier users to declare the doctrines that ripened into the American common law of "first in time, first in right" embodied in water law.

And so we could go on—Germany's "Lebensraum" of World War II, the Japanese in Manchuria in the 1930's, the distaste felt in any urban neighborhood for a saloon close to a school or for the abattoir on the next street, the concern felt by the citizenry for the unnecessary loss of the top six inches of soil on which life depends or over the ejection by some of effluvium, flotsam, and jetsam into the water we use and play in, or into the air we breathe. So could we point to the exploding city, the "encroachment" of suburban dwellers onto the rural countryside and the resultant conflicts over schools and sewage disposal and taxes, and over trespass on the farmer's fields and harassment of his livestock and himself.

This seemingly unnecessarily long repetition of homely and familiar conflicts serves a purpose. Land use conflicts run like a

282

thread—or like a number of threads—through the fabric of all cultural history and are weaving forward in the fabric of contemporary life no less, perhaps more vigorously and pervasively than ever before. To discuss land use conflicts and their resolution, then, is, in a sense, to discuss a prevalent divisive force in social living and a main element in the conflict pattern that constitutes social organization and process.

## WHY DO LAND USE CONFLICTS ARISE?

Land resources are limited, wants are limitless. In this basic premise of economic and political theory lies the basic cause of land use conflicts.

Wants not only are limitless but are diverse. Different persons have different wants and different value-structures for the ranking of those wants.

Persons are the bearers and expressers of wants. Different persons are transient in different degrees; the want-structures each has likewise differ in their fluidity. Hence, the structure of wants in a community changes as time passes and as people move about.

Land, in contrast, is far more rigid in its fundamental attributes of spaciousness, location, and elemental content. Spaciousness and location, as fundamental physical attributes of land, are absolutely inflexible; land's elemental content is relatively inflexible, though some of its elements may be depreciable under appropriate circumstances.*

It is a reasonable generalization, then, that land use conflicts arise because people and their want-structures are transient and transitory whereas land is fixed in space and content.

Land use conflicts arise as different people having different and changing want-structures contend for the control and use of inflexible units of land resource. The "persons" among whom such conflicts occur may be individuals, groups, or institutions.

* In a fundamental aggregative sense, even the elemental content of land is absolutely inflexible for what is an *increase* in one site necessitates an equal and offsetting *decrease* somewhere else. Only "capital" and the elemental content of land viewed as partial units are increasable or depreciable. In the strict fundamental aggregative sense, land is absolutely inflexible in all its attributes.

But whatever they are, their want-structures differ among them in space and time.

Superficially, this conflict appears no different than the identical conflict that appears between people over any scarce property object. What gives peculiar dimensions to land use conflicts are: (1) land is completely passive in the conflict. A land unit is what it is; its fundamental supply of location, space, and elemental content cannot be increased through entrepreneurial choice and the dynamic process of creation, use, depreciation, and replacement.* (2) The land unit cannot move to or away from situations of scarcity or surplus. (3) The only way by which one use of land can expand is by displacing another use, not by "creating" an enlarged "supply." (4) Because land and its attendant uses are peculiarly tied to locations, it frequently happens that the use made of one land unit affects the uses made of other land units, and no one of the units can move into a more favorable or away from a less favorable situation. The user of the land can move but only by disinvesting one use on one tract and reinvesting it on another tract elsewhere. "Sunk" investments in land take on the immovable characteristic of land but not of fixity of content—sunk investments are depreciable in a sense and to a degree that land is not. (5) Man may, to a degree, affect the elemental content of land, particularly in a way which may cause diminution of the elements it contains. Some of this diminution may be reversed only with great difficulty. In consequence, intertemporal conflict between different land users at different times is ever-present. (6) Land is, in a peculiar sense,

---

* *Increasing* the elemental supply content of a site by the decision maker is an act of *investing;* the increase is *capital ex ante.* Thus, *ex ante,* all *increases* in land content are capital. However, when, *ex post,* such "capital" turns out to be "sunk" and irremovable, it transforms conceptually into "land" and the then enhanced elemental content of the site may be depreciated through use. Consequently, from this point of view, the elemental content of land can never be *appreciable* but only *depreciable.*

Technology has a similar character vis-à-vis land. The discovery of "new" elemental content in a site, such as an increase in productivity, is a "knowledge" input or a form of capital when first applied but, once "known," the knowledge remains and subsequent decisions are made in the context of such existing and unchanging knowledge.

the "reality" on which societies stand and live. The use of all land units will always be endowed with values to the society as an aggregate of members that transcend and may conflict with those of the transient human occupants of each unit. The user of land today will always be in conflict with the shadowy user of the future and with his present self-appointed spokesman.[1]

Conflicts over land use arise for all these reasons between and in all combinations of single individuals, private groups, institutions, uses, and time periods. To say that land use conflicts involve all single individuals, private groups and institutions, and all land uses in all time periods is but to re-emphasize that land use conflicts are diffused throughout the fabric of all cultural history and are a main element in the conflict pattern of social organization and process.

## SOURCES OF LAND USE CONFLICTS

Among what persons and in what situations do land use conflicts arise, and over what issues? It will be most useful to consider such sources of land use conflicts in the context of the pairings of persons and their institutions between which the conflicts occur. These "pairings" for the study of conflict are (1) between and among private users; (2) between private and public users; (3) between and among different public users; (4) between current and future users; and (5) among uses.

### CONFLICT BETWEEN AND AMONG PRIVATE USERS

Control over a land unit is sought by a private person or group in order to practice a use or combination of uses on it. Conflict between private individuals or groups, then, really turns out to be conflict between *uses* or between *ways* in which a given use can be practiced on the unit. Uses, or ways of use, are outcomes of management and decision making; therefore, conflicts between individuals further turn out to be conflicts over management decision making relative to uses or ways of carrying out a use on a land unit. One individual says a certain unit of land should be used for cotton farming; another says it should be used for urban subdivision. This is conflict over use between private individuals. Or, one individual says that the best he can get out of a tract of land is $75 an acre farming it to cotton whereas another individual says that he can get $150 an acre out of that same tract of land farming it to cotton, and "takes" it away from the first, or tries to do so, through the conflict process of "bargaining." This is a conflict over management decisions relative to the use of a given unit of land.

The individuals among whom these conflicts take place will be flesh-and-blood persons acting in their own interests or as representatives of institutions such as corporations, cooperatives, clubs, etc.

One source of conflict over land uses then, is a conflict between private parties over how "best" to use a given land site. Such conflict may involve "on site" conflicts, "off site" or "between site" conflicts, and even conflicts between years of use. *On*-site conflicts are those such as the cotton farming versus urban development illustration used above. *Off*-site conflicts are those in which the use of one site has repercussions on another site, such as exploitive use of a watershed creating flood and silt damage to other sites downstream. Interyear conflicts are those between users of a land site today and those who will or expect to be users of the site tomorrow. This conflict is more fully discussed below (see p. 11).

## Conflicts Between Private and Public Users

A line is hard to define between private groups and institutions and that sovereign group we call "the public." For our purpose, the crucial line of distinction turns on the source of power over land. The public, relative to land use, is that group to which power over land attaches solely because the land unit lies within the area of political sovereignty of that group; private groups and institutions are those to which power over a land unit attaches by virtue of a relinquishment of power to the private group or institution by the public sovereign.

The structure of wants of the public group embraces many high utility wants the satisfaction of which is not attainable by private individuals or groups, hence, they do not enter into the determination of "market value." Market values will not, therefore, reflect all values included by the public within its calculus.

Conflict arises because private individuals and groups approach the use of a particular land unit with a different structure of wants and ordering of values than do public groups possibly composed of the same individuals. These differing structures of wants and ordering of values relative to land use arise from differences in (1) the wider array of utilities included in the public's (in contrast to the private person's) want-structure at a single point in time, and (2) in the time structure of utilities of private individuals and groups in contrast to that of public groups.

*Breadth of Utility Inclusion and Land Use Conflict.*—The public stands for the widest possible grouping of parties of interest in the use of a particular land unit. The structure of wants and ordering of values of this most inclusive of all possible social entities will necessarily and always be different from the structure of wants and ordering of values of private groups and private individuals. Because the structure of wants and ordering of values as between the private and public users of a land site inevitably will be different, judgment by each as to what constitutes "best" use of that site will necessarily also differ and be in conflict.

Any decision-making unit experiences economies and diseconomies that are external to its sphere of control. External economies and diseconomies have the peculiar economic significance that their impingement on the user of a given land site causes his management decisions about the use of that site to be different than they would be were he to bear or enjoy a proportionate share of the offsetting costs or benefits that apply; in other words, his management decisions are different than they would be if the benefits and costs were *internal* economies and diseconomies. As between the public and private interests in the use of a particular tract, economies and diseconomies that are external to the private user are virtually certain to be internal to the public user. Being external to the one and internal to the other causes such economies and diseconomies to have differing significance in decision making as to what is "best" use for that site. Even in those not uncommon cases wherein a public group also experiences external economies and diseconomies in the use of a given site due to the fact that some of the consequences of its use lie outside the political boundaries of the public concerned, even in such cases the structure of economies and diseconomies as seen by the public group will be different from those experienced by the private users of interest. Being different, they will be in conflict.

*Time Structure of Utilities and Land Use Conflict.*—In addition to land use conflicts growing out of differences in the breadth of utility inclusion by the public in contrast to private persons over land use are those land use conflicts growing out of differences in the time structure of utilities as between the private and public users. The public interest usually expresses more concern about "generations yet unborn" than do private individuals and groups. Why this difference should exist is not our purpose to go into here. It may be simply that the elected representatives of private individuals, once in the legislature, are no longer closely associated with private interest in land use and hence can be more "social" minded and "impersonal" about it; or it may be that the institutional pressures for perpetuation of the political institutions and culture of the group cause public policy makers to be more concerned about the welfare of the future than is true of individual decision makers acting as individuals. But whatever the reason, difference in concern between private and public decision makers over the welfare of those vague and shadowy individuals who will compose the future results in a further difference in the structure of wants and ordering of values as between public and private groups and a consequent difference in judgments as to what constitutes best land use for a particular site.

CONFLICT BETWEEN DIFFERENT PUBLICS

In the United States, a hierarchy of publics exists with sharpest cleavage between state and federal sectors. Also in the United States, different bureaus within a single governmental sector have responsibility or concern over land use. Consequently, conflict over land use in the United States may arise between these different public units as well as between different individual users and between public sectors and the private sectors generally. Each of the "political publics" that constitute the United States from municipality to federal and each of the governmental bureaus of all these "publics" that has some responsibility or concern over land use will have a different hierarchy of wants and ordering of values and hence will express conflicting judgments as to which uses of particular land sites will maximize attainment of its goal. In this respect, conflict between public sectors concerning land use arises from the same basic cause and expresses itself in an essentially similar manner to conflicts among private individuals and groups. The differing "publics" have different value structures because they represent different combinations of individuals and serve different legislatively established ends. Not only will their value-structures differ, but the qualities and magnitudes of the external economies and diseconomies peculiar to each also will differ. Consequently, it is no more strange for the federal government and a state government to be in conflict over the "best use" of the waters of the Missouri River or over the ownership of the public grazing lands, or for the Forest Service of the Department of Agriculture to be in conflict with the Bureau of Land Management of the Department of Interior over best use of their intermingled holdings than it is for private individuals to come into conflict over similar questions.

CONFLICT BETWEEN CURRENT AND FUTURE WANTS

Whether a conflict over land use is interprivate, private versus public, or interpublic, differing values attaching to time will influence the structure of wants and the ordering of values of each contender in the conflict and hence will color the judgment of each party as to "best use" of the land site in question. Present satisfactions from the use of a land site, in contrast to alternative identical future satisfactions, will have different values due to differences in time preference and in the marginal productivity of capital to the different individuals and groups. Time preference reflects the psychology of decision makers relative to waiting for satisfactions in place of enjoying them now and is a composite of the psychology of self-denial and an appraisal of the risks and uncertainties entailed. The marginal productivity of capital is a measure of the net addition to want-satisfying production generated by additional units of capital investment. The propensity for saving versus spending, together with the marginal value product of additional capital investment, determines the marginal discount for time in the value-structure of each individual group or public. The marginal rate of time discount sets the limit of profitable deferral of consumption and of investment and hence determines the time cost of investment for that decision maker. When this time cost is low, land uses that exhibit long continuing output streams, albeit at lower current levels of output, will be favored over uses whose output stream is larger at present but of shorter duration. When this time cost is high, the reverse will be the preferred choice. As a result, differing valuations by different people, different private groups, and different publics concerning time preference, together with different managerial decisions concerning the marginal value product of capital in different uses will affect decisions by these different parties as to what is "best" use for any land site at any given time. Conflicts arise because of differences in the way individuals and groups, both private and public, appraise and evaluate the future.

## Conflicts Among Uses

It turns out that whether the land use conflict is between private parties, between the private and public sectors of the economy, between public groups, or between current and future wants, it is really a conflict between land uses. Land uses are a product of decision making; decision making is an outcome of value structures and the niggardliness of nature as it is expressed in diminishing returns. It is because the structure of wants and value orderings differ as between individuals, private groups, and public bodies, and because for each the structure of wants and values varies as between the present and the future that conflict over land use occurs. Land *use* conflict is broader even than conflict among different individuals, for conflict between *uses* can impinge on even a single individual. An individual may be "in conflict" with himself. Decisions must be made by him as to "best" use of the site on which his interest is centered; if a decision problem for him exists, alternative uses exist; if alternative uses exist, they are in conflict "for" the site. When such different alternative uses represent different "individuals," the conflict is interindividual as well as interuse; when they impinge on but a single individual, they are intraindividual but interuse.

It turns out that land use conflicts arise because of differences in the structure of wants and orderings of values among different individuals and groups and differences in the judgments of individuals over the productivity of given sites in different uses in different time periods.

## DISSOCIATION OF THE INCIDENCE OF BENEFITS AND COSTS

The incidence of external economies and diseconomies has been given prominence in the foregoing discussion as a source of land use conflicts. External economies and diseconomies are synonymous with dissociation of the incidence of benefits and costs. External economies and diseconomies are simply benefits and costs that impinge upon the decision maker but over which his power of decision contains no power. He bears costs dissociated from attendant benefits or he enjoys benefits dissociated from attendant costs. If all parties of interest in the use of any land site shared in costs incident to use of the site and proportional to their expected benefits, and if all shared in benefits proportional to their incurred costs, then the market process of "bargaining," and the purchase and sale of privileges and burdens associated with land uses could be relied upon to resolve all land use conflicts.

But it is just because this Elysian perfection seldom, if ever, obtains and because individuals, private groups, and publics are trying continuously to gain benefits and repel costs incident to land use that something more than pure market process must be relied upon for the resolution of land use conflicts. Conflicts growing out of the dissociation of benefits and costs are always interpersonal conflicts, but they have their intertemporal and interspatial dimensions as well.

It frequently occurs that use of one space unit endows another space unit with costs (but no benefits) or with benefits (and no off-setting costs). The recipient of such windfall *benefits* usually resists attempts to assess charges against him for the benefits, whereas the recipients of windfall *costs* usually push upon their source for remedy. Sometimes, when the recipient of the windfall *costs* is the intangible, faceless, formless "general public," push on the source of the costs for remedy is slow and halting. Under other circumstances, when the recipient of the windfall costs is one, or one of a few, private persons and such costs stem from public action for general public benefit, the burdened private persons are ineffectual in their push for remedy because of disparity in political and economic strength.

Such conflicts growing, as they do, out of dissociation of benefits and costs cannot be resolved within the framework of the market economy so long as there exists no way in the institutional structure to assess costs proportional to benefits or to claim benefits proportional to costs.

Dissociation of benefits and costs has its intertemporal dimension also. When a land site is committed to a present use at the expense of an alternative future use, or vice versa, it frequently occurs that the future benefits or burdens will accrue to individuals not yet on the scene, hence truly voiceless at the moment when the crucial decisions must be taken. Conflict then arises between those who admittedly favor the present (or short-run) uses against those individuals existent at the same point in time who have a more highly valued future benefit or who have an emotional attachment to those shadowy future persons whose spokesmen these present individuals elect themselves to be. Upon occasion, the conflict may run the other way. It sometimes happens that those who hold a long-run beneficial interest are in the position to control, over against those who see a more valuable (to themselves or to society) short-run value from larger current outputs at the expense of future outputs. In either event, the conflict grows out of differing dissociation of benefits and costs as between present and future users.

Both of these types of conflict, whether interspatial or intertemporal, are apt to reduce the level of want satisfaction of which a land site is capable. If benefits and costs are dissociated, the production of benefits unconnected with costs will be pushed to marginal products of zero value, whereas unavoidable costs incurred without off-setting benefits cannot be curtailed to equilibrate with resultant marginal value product. Hence, "too many" inputs will be committed to the production of "uncosted" benefits or to the imposition of "unbenefited costs." Dissociation conflicts result in distorted land use and development.

## ARE LAND USE CONFLICTS GROWING IN NUMBER AND INTENSITY?

Though there is no ready way to measure their intensity, it would seem quite obvious that land use conflicts are growing in number. It would seem quite logical, too, that they are growing in intensity. Primarily this rise in number and intensity of land use conflicts would seem to result from increasing population, an increasingly complex society, and rising levels of want satisfaction in the society.

### An Increasing Population and Land Use Conflicts

An increasing population means simply that an increasing weight of people puts more pressure on the resource base, more pressure on space, more crowding, more jostling, more stepping on toes. Interpersonal, private versus public, present versus future conflicts relative to land use will increase. Public versus private conflicts will grow as the public groups become more aware of their collective needs and more vigorous in curbing individual land uses that run counter to the public's welfare; the greater pressure of population on resources will increase the concern that many have for the future resource base, space for future men to live in, and will lead to more vigorous action to curb present uses in favor of the future.

### An Increasingly Complex Society and Land Use Conflict

Our contemporary society is marked by a growing population, a more intricately structured economy, and a more richly developed governmental system. The social machine is more complex, more efficient, and more productive but more sensitive and more temperamental. All this brings increasing possibility of conflict between individuals, groups, and publics in all areas of life. Conflicts over land use are no exception.

## Rising Standards of Living and Land Use Conflicts

One outstanding characteristic of our contemporary society is its ability to satisfy rising levels of want satisfaction because of rising technological ability for resource exploitation. Because we can satisfy our wants increasingly far down the utility scale, increasingly far removed from the basic animal wants of pure survival, an increasing number of individuals in our society reach, in their utility systems, articulate levels of concern for the yet inarticulate future generations. Simultaneously and in a contrary direction, other individuals are able to reach farther down their personal utility scale for present want satisfaction in preference to future satisfaction because technology has lifted (for them) the specter of future resource shortage. Conflict over land use decisions increases between the group that asserts we can afford now more than ever to protect the future against land shortage and the other group that says we can afford now more than ever "to live high on the hog" because technology will take care of the future.

## LAND USE CONFLICTS AND RESOURCE DEVELOPMENT

Superficially viewed, conflict over land use may appear to be a deterrent to efficient land use and resource development. But a more thoughtful analysis reveals that maximum efficiency of use and maximum development can occur *only* in the context of conflict over land use. An absence of conflict implies a static society; a static society is a nondeveloping society.

Development is dynamic; it implies the existence of a dynamic society. Dynamics *are* change; change *is* alteration in land uses within and over time. Hence, necessarily and implicitly, dynamics are conflicts between proponents of divergent and alternative land uses. Development can only occur within a context of change and change only occurs within a context of conflict.

It is not conflict that is the deterrent to efficient resource use and development. The deterrent is failure to resolve the conflicts that necessarily must arise so that the changes that imply development can proceed in an effective and orderly manner. An enhanced efficiency of resource use and development does not rest on the elimination of conflict but upon its timely and orderly resolution. The few remaining pages of this paper will be devoted to an examination of where attention must center for the attainment of timely and orderly resolution of land use conflicts.*

## RESOLVING LAND USE CONFLICTS

Resolving land use conflicts involves much more than prescribing goals such as maximum land use efficiency, or maximum area income or aggregate benefit; nor is it a problem of technology or of cost minimization; nor is it a matter of engineering, nor of production economics. Resolving land use conflicts consists in the attainment of workable relations between people—people as individuals, as private groups, and as publics—through the volitional and institutional devices that have been called *bargaining* and *rationing* transactions.

### Collective Action and the Control of Individual Action

Resolving interpersonal conflicts outside the pale of organized society is a matter of pure physical power, of the law of tooth and claw. Exactly similar conflicts are resolved within the *framework* of organized society because there is also a recognized and realized mutuality of dependent interests—interdependence as well as conflict. Within organized society, collective power prescribes working rules under which interpersonal conflicts, in the interest of attaining mutuality, may be or must be resolved. The establishment and enforcement of such working rules by the collective superior against the citizen inferiors are *rationing* transactions. Conflicts resolved between citizens as equals within prescriptions laid down by these "superior" working rules are *bargaining* transactions. In either case, conflicts are resolved through

* I am not defining "land use development" as progression "ever onward and upward." The resolution of conflict over land use simply permits "change" to occur. The ultimate determinate of whether the conflict resolution that permits change has been development or retrogression in some value sense must be left to the judgment of history and of moral philosophers. All that can be said here is that the resolution of land use conflicts will facilitate land use changes. We can only hope that history proves them to be developments in the ever upward and onward sense.

collective action in control, liberation, and expansion of individual action.[2]

Wherein lies the collective power that is the source of collective action in an organized democratic society? It lies in group or public sovereignty which is "collective action in control of violence"[3] or in the democratic monopoly of physical power. Public sovereignty is epitomized by physical power as distinguished from private sovereignty which rests in economic and moral power. It is public sovereignty that makes things lawfully useful for it bestows ownership without which use is illegal and with which specific uses are prohibited or required or classed as permissive. Public sovereignty, which is collective action, is inseparable from property and vice versa. The public sovereign in an organized democracy is composed, collectively, of the politicians, the legislators, the executive, and the judiciary. It is the policy-making power of the sovereign, i.e., of the electorate or the legislature, that lays down the rights, duties, liberties, and exposures of its constituent "citizens" relative to their interpersonal relations over land sites and the uses thereof. A republican democracy, such as that of the United States, is a complex, interrelated structure of such prescriptions laid down by the whole body politic, by the elected representatives of the whole, by the executive enforcing the legislative rules as he interprets them, and by the judiciary interpreting the meanings of words and the limits to the sovereign power. Such land policy prescriptions by the democratic sovereign define the limits to, and the content of, property which turn out to be working-rules that define the interpersonal rights, duties, liberties, and exposures of citizens relative to some common land site and its use. Those working-rules govern individual actions toward one another as they are jointly involved in the same land site. The processes by which these working-rules are specified and enforced are rationing transactions; their consequence is the rationing of freedoms and restraints among persons toward one another and toward land.

## RATIONING TRANSACTIONS AND LAND USE CONFLICTS

Rationing transactions "apportion access to the benefits and burdens"[4] of land use among persons, and they specify the limits within which land use decision making will be left to bargaining between legal equals. Rationing transactions apportion the rights, duties, liberties, and exposures of affected persons toward one another to the extent that each has or may have common interest in a unit of land and its use. Rationing transactions define the limits to and the content of rights over land use held by each person who falls into some defined relation to that land; it defines simultaneously the correlative duties of all other persons to respect those rights; further, it defines the limits to and the content of the liberty, which is the freedom, of the right-holder to act as he pleases relative to the use of that land subject to his correlative exposure to the liberties, that is the freedoms, of all other persons to act as they please toward the use of that same land.

Thus, rationing transactions serve as resolvers of land use conflicts. Such conflicts are resolved in a democracy by that "bargaining" process called "rationing" which lays down the working rules which specify who can or who may do what with what land. Some of these rules will define limits of use and of benefit available to specified persons relative to any land whatever; others of the rules will define such limits of use and benefit available to any person whatever relative to some specified class of land. Zoning, for example, directs that no person whatever can apply a specified use to a specified site; on the other hand, restrictions on transfer of title to land, for example, may direct that no person of the class "owner," relative to any land whatever, can specify in his bequest of that land to his heir that it must henceforth and forever be transferred only to the eldest son. Another example: restrictions on transfer of title may specify that no person of the class "oriental," may hold fee simple title to any land whatever. The working-rules laid down as a result of rationing transactions turn out to be outright statements of what any person or specified classes of persons "must" and "cannot," "may" and "need not," do with land in general or with some defined class of land.

The working-rules laid down by rationing transactions are best represented in the United States by the following familiar property and property regulating institutions: urban, metropolitan, and rural zoning; real estate taxation; trespass and right-of-way regulation; rights to access and use of surface and ground waters; laws and regulations pertaining to the disposal of the public lands, and to mining, grazing, and logging thereon; crop acreage allotments; land use regulations for erosion control; weed-control laws; legal provisions for the organization and operation of land and water districts of many sorts; provisions of law requiring the "unitizing" and otherwise regulating extraction of oil from the ground, and many more.

What is it that all of these rationing rules have in common? Each is an expression of sovereign power, rationing among specified persons or persons in general rights to use of and control over specified classes of land or over land in general together with specification of the correlative duties imposed upon all other persons not to interfere; further, each specifies the limits to the liberty of the right-holder to bargain with and propagandize others over the use and control of that land together with his correlative exposure to the bargaining and propaganda powers of others.

When land use conflicts arise, they may be resolved by alteration of the existing rationing rules; for example, when scattered settlement in the cut-over areas of Wisconsin led to conflicts between such settlers and the residents of the more thickly settled portions of the counties, "rural zoning" as a new "working-rule" was developed. Resolving land use conflicts under rationing rules results, in other cases, *not* in alteration of the existing rules, but in the application and enforcement of the existing rules to a particular conflict situation. When the rationing rule specifies that no farmer shall produce more than a specified acreage of cotton, it simultaneously specifies the limits to his duty to obey the orders of the federal enforcing officer, and the limits to his rights to appeal the order to higher authority and to the courts. The rationing rule, by specifying the content and the limits of the farmer's and the officer's rights and duties, may resolve the conflict, but, if not, it will be resolved by the judiciary determining the facts of the case and the meanings of the words that compose the rule. The process is the same, only its content changes, when the conflict is over the establishment of a disagreeable business within a community, or over the size of lots on which a builder may build homes, or over the time and volume of diversion of water from a common supply. In all such cases, the working-rules have been laid down by rationing transactions embedded in the political and legislative process. They are then applied in practice by agents of the sovereign who, in the eyes of the court, are equal but not superior to the citizens, or, if the conflict is between two citizens, each as an equal before the court.*

Rationing transactions resolve land use conflicts, then, by specifying the rights, duties, liberties, and exposures of parties in conflict concerning access to and control over the use of land. Resolving the conflict may be the result of new rules laid down by the rule-making (i.e., the legislative) arm of the sovereign, or through the interpretation and enforcement of existing rules through the executive and judicial arms of the sovereign.

## BARGAINING TRANSACTIONS AND LAND USE CONFLICTS

The working-rules that result from rationing transactions specify what must and what need not, but may be done, by and between persons relative to land. By their very nature, i.e., setting up the "must" and "need not" limits of one party and the correlative "must not" and "may" limits of all other parties, these rules specify the uses and benefits of land that are left open to free and equal bargaining between persons. This is the area of permissiveness—where persons may do or may refrain from doing whatever they can get away with through negotiation with and persuasion on their rivals. This is the area of the bargaining transaction. Within this area, the limits to and content of which are defined by the rationing transaction, each party is subject to the negotiational power of each other party, and land use conflicts are resolvable through bargaining; that is, by buying and selling among legal equals, rather than by order from legal superiors,

---

* I am not unmindful that in not infrequent situations in the United States, it appears and, in fact may be true, that parties in conflict over land use appear before the court not as equals but as unequals due to economic, social, or racial differences. In such cases it is not that the individuals appear before the court as unequals but that the working-rules laid down by the legislative process of the sovereign, and as interpreted and enforced by the executive and judicial arms of the sovereign, have classified persons into groups to which different rights, duties, liberties, and exposures pertain.

the benefits and burdens that go with land control and use. This is the area of negotiation between equals under law, of freedom of choice from among alternatives by contenders in conflict. Within the limits of the bargaining transaction, the conflicting parties are free to discuss, dicker, cajole, persuade, propagandize others relative to any land site and its use in which they have mutual interest. It is the area within which one has the liberty to use any tactic designated by the working rules as persuasive (but not coercive) and in which, at the same time, one is exposed to actions growing out of an equal degree of liberty on the part of others. Herein, one is restrained from using—that is, has the duty not to use—any tactic defined as coercive, subject to the right of the sovereign's agent to restrain him with force, if necessary.

This area of conflict resolution has been deeply tilled by economists, for this is the area of "utility maximization" through market exchange of land use privileges and through maximization of efficiency through management. There is no need for me to repeat here the elaborate structure of economic principles that has been erected to explain, rationalize, and prescribe the behavior of people in resolving conflicts within the limits of their liberty to bargain and to manage.

Working-rules pertaining to land use may prescribe that title to, control over, or use of specified tracts or classes of land for specified use may be taken by the sovereign for public use with compensation to the private claimant. But working-rules may, on the other hand, prescribe that in the case of certain public conflicts with private owners over land use and control, the public cannot, through the superior-inferior relation of rationing, take the land use privilege from the private individual. The rules may specify, in such cases, that the public can act only through its agent behaving as an equal to the citizen-owner and can acquire access to control over or use of the land in question only through the mechanism of the bargaining transaction. In other words, the working-rules relative to land and its use may specify that the public and the citizen are equals and must resolve their conflicts toward specified uses of specified lands through the process of negotiation, persuasion, and voluntary sale. Thus, bargaining transactions not only resolve land use and control conflicts between private citizens, but also between private citizens and the publics within spheres specified by the working rules of the society as worked out through rationing transactions.

## ARE LAND USE CONFLICTS RESOLVED—AND HOW?

If, in the context of these questions, one means by "resolved" that inner and outer tensions have been relaxed, one must admit that conflicts are not resolved in this sense. Conflicts are not "resolved" in the sense that the sources of irritation—like a stone in the shoe—have been removed, but only in the sense that a workable degree of social order and interpersonal mutuality have been maintained by (1) collective rationing of rights of access to land use privileges among private individuals and groups and the collective itself, together with (2) the rationing of liberties to bargain among legal equals in the resolution of those of their interpersonal conflicts not covered by their assigned rights. In this manner, practical order and working mutuality have been maintained in the course of the history of land policy in the United States. Conflicts have not always been resolved easily or quickly, or even rightly, but social order has been generally maintained. Neither have land use conflicts always been resolved equitably—that is, with an abstract, ideal degree of mutuality. The big step forward taken by the United States during the last one hundred and fifty years in the age-long struggle of man towards the ideals of mutuality and equity has been the working out of a system wherein the sovereign superior who prescribes the working-rules for land use and decision making has become, himself, a collective of the citizenry. The outcome, of importance that transcends all else, has been that the working-rules laid down in the United States governing relations among people regarding land use and control are a consequence of rationing transactions wherein the policy-making representatives of the citizenry "bargain" among themselves to apportion the benefits and burdens, the privileges and penalties, the liberties and exposures attendant upon land use. The advent and slow perfection of the rationing transaction in western democracy over the past several hundred years has resulted, finally, in the elimination of the previously dominant master-servant relation from the area of policy making and has made policy making, in land use and control as in all else, the prerogative of the citizen-collective prescribing working-rules arrived at through rationing transactions. In this way, the citizen-collective governs itself by maintaining workable order and practicable mutuality *among* its citizen-members and *between* its citizen-members and itself. By perfecting the rationing transaction, the resolution of land use conflicts in the United States has been made democratic and capitalistic rather than monarchic, feudal, and dictatorial. It is the rationing transaction, as it evolves and develops, that will in the future resolve the problems of the public interest in private land, of the private interest in public land, and of interpersonal conflicts with respect to land use in space and time. As we pursue our research and planning for political and economic growth in the area of land use and control, our attention must center, increasingly, on the content and process of the rationing transaction in our politico-economic system for it is here that more orderly and more equitable resolutions of many current and prospective land use conflicts will be found.

## NOTES

1. "There are therefore special attitudes toward land, sometimes mystic, recognizing its permanence and man's dependence on it. The result seems to be a more frequent, conscious, often economically purposeful elaboration of rights and regulations of land use and disposal. 'Land ... has hardly ever or anywhere ceased to invest even its most private users with at least a touch of public character.'" Frank E. Horack, Jr.; Val Nolan, Jr., *Land Use Controls: Supplementary Materials on Real Property* (St. Paul, Minn.: Webb Publishing Co., 1955). The quotation is from Brinkmann, "Land Tenure," *Encyclopedia of the Social Sciences,* IX and X, (1933), pp. 73 ff.

2. "If we endeavor to find a universal principle, common to all behavior known as institutional, we may define an institution as Collective Action in Control of Individual Action...

"Collective Action is more than *control* of individual action—it is, by the very act of control, as indicated by the auxiliary verbs, a *liberation* of individual action from coercion, duress, discrimination, or unfair competition, by means of restraints placed on other individuals...

"And Collective Action is more than restraint and liberation of individual action—it is *expansion* of the will of the individual far beyond what he can do by his own puny acts. The head of a great corporation gives orders which execute his will at the ends of the earth. . . .

"Since liberation and expansion for some persons consist in restraint, for their benefit, of other persons, and while the short definition of an institution is collective action in control of individual action, the derived definition is: collective action in restraint, liberation, and expansion of individual action."

John R. Commons, *Institutional Economics* (New York: Macmillan Co., 1934), pp. 69 and 73.

3. John R. Commons, *The Economics of Collective Action* (New York: Macmillan Co., 1950), p. 74.

4. John R. Commons, *Institutional Economics, op. cit.,* pp. 67 ff.

CONTROL OF LAND RESOURCES

# MARSHALL HARRIS

## Private Interest in Private Lands:
## Intra- and Inter-Private

"THERE IS NOTHING," according to Blackstone in his *Commentaries on the Laws of England*, "which so generally strikes the imagination, and engages the affections of mankind, as the right of property; or that sole and despotic dominion which one man claims and exercises over the external things of the world, in total exclusion of the right of any other individual in the universe. And yet there are very few that will give themselves the trouble to consider the original and foundation of this right." (Book II, 2.)

This essay is focused on the origin and foundation of private rights in privately held land, including the nature of the right of property. Little has been said in earlier essays and probably little will be said in later essays, and properly so, about the nature of the rights that the Daniel Freeman family and other homesteaders were given in their homestead land. The conditions of tenure under which the land would be held were as important as major factors of public land policy in the homestead movement, whether sale, or squatting, or preemption, or homesteading; whether one hundred and sixty, or three hundred and twenty, or six hundred and forty acres; whether compact or scattered settlement; and so on. Attention is focused, therefore, on rights that homesteaders received in their land, without detracting from the land-policy conditions under which homestead grants were made.

We will present the nature of private interests in private land, mention the long struggle over three-quarters of a millenium to establish and secure these rights, and indicate how they may affect land use and development today. Borrowing the idea, an effort will be made to make the past contemporaneous, to give perspective to the present, and to illuminate the future.

The central thesis of this essay is that the rights the homesteader acquired in his land are of crucial importance in determining the success of homesteading our western land. A collateral thesis is that our present land tenure system gives the individual a maximum, yet not absolute, freedom of action in the control, use, and development of land resources. A corollary thesis is that commensurate responsibility has not accompanied the high degree of freedom. The low level of responsibility and the high degree of freedom are results of the economic, social, and political milieu out of which our land system evolved.

Interests in privately held land, whether intra- or inter-private, are concerned with property relations among and between private parties as to the object—land resources—of those interests. Property or tenure relations are exclusively man-man; they are never man-land relations. The man-land relation is a use relation solely, that is, man's dependence upon land (interpreted broadly) for food, clothing, and shelter.

This essay is concerned, therefore, with man-man relations regarding the ownership and control of land resources. Of strategic importance is the effect of these tenure relations on the use of our land. These man-man relations will be considered from two viewpoints: (1) The way established relations affect the individual personally, that is, the intra-private interests, those that influence his motivation and consequent action, and (2) the way established relations affect individuals in their use and development of land resources, that is, the inter-private interests, those involved when the action is between or among individuals. The former is a consideration of the impact of tenure relations on individual action solely within the individual; the latter is a consideration of the impact of tenure relations on individual action as two or more parties act jointly.

## ORIGINS OF PRIVATE PROPERTY IN LAND

Most antiquarians agree that property rights were first recognized in movables, in common parlance, personal property or chattels. Few movables were suitable for use, except immediate consumption, until reshaped by man, the commonest user.

The personal labor thus incorporated in the object, it was reasoned, gave an exclusive property right in the thing.

The argument ran somewhat as follows: Every man has a "property right" in his own person. This is an exclusive right. No one has a right to a man's labor except himself. If a man's labor is properly his own, whatever that labor produces is his own. This he may possess and hold against the claims of all comers. Although the earth and the fullness thereof were originally common to all men, every man acquired a right in any movable object in which his labor was incorporated.

When man began to plant and cultivate, the land itself was appropriated by the cultivator, because his labor was incorporated in it—he had mixed himself with the land. It remained his so long as he occupied and cultivated it. But if he vacated it, the land reverted to common ownership. Finally, continued occupancy, it was agreed, gave the original right to permanent property in land itself. This is the philosophic basis for moving from the idea of common property of primitive man to private property of civilized man.

Several theories have been developed to explain and justify private property in land. One of the earliest was the *natural rights* theory. According to this theory, individuals existed prior to society, and as a consequence they have rights that are not created by society. Such rights, which include the rights of property, are not and cannot be destroyed by society any more than can individuals themselves. On the other hand, some rights are created by society; for example, the right to incorporate. Societal created rights can be destroyed by society.

Another theory—the *prescription* theory—accepts the socio-economic-political situation and argues that the right of enjoyment of a thing, or title to it, may be asserted on the ground of having hitherto had the uninterrupted and immemorial enjoyment of it. As Blackstone would say "... so long that the memory of man runneth not to the contrary." By long-continued enjoyment through occupancy and use, private property in land may be acquired. Thus, a mere possessor and user acquires ownership of that which is possessed by the continuance of his possession and use. A form of this basic idea is recognized in modern property law as adverse possession.

The prescription theory is closely related to the *historical* theory, which holds that the just rights of property are those that have been dedicated and consecrated by history. The prescription theory is also closely related to the *conventional* theory, which holds that modern property rights are conventional rights, created by tacit agreement in the social contract in accord with the established custom.

With the emergence of the classical school of economics a new theory of property—the *utility* theory—came into being, if indeed one can say that the political economists of the classical school bothered to have a theory. They did not deny the natural rights theory of property, but they began to speak of *utility* rather than *right*. They twisted the natural rights theory into the labor theory of value, which was the nub of their economic thinking. But the economists were not interested ostensibly in the property rights of the individual. They accepted the economic system which existed and tried to analyze its workings. Any concern with the rights of private property was purely incidental.

The utility theory holds that private ownership, and the legal system that supports it, has its origin in utility. Private property is justified on the basis of its intrinsic worth. In this context utility is equated with the rules of justice that experience has shown are necessary to promote industry. The basic principle is that in order to encourage men to work, society ought to secure to each man the results of his labors.

American thought regarding private property in land is a unique admixture of the various theories. American states proclaimed the natural rights theory whenever they put in their basic social compacts the idea that acquiring, possessing, and protecting property is an essential, natural, and inalienable right, as many of them did. Thus, the rights to life, liberty, and property are natural rights with which man is endowed at birth. The theory is that these he cannot contract away. Also, no form of government can take away these rights. They are, therefore, guaranteed to him by our constitutions and laws. The prescription theory may be found in modern law in the principle of adverse possession, as we have seen. The historical theory may be found in the historical sequence of affirming land titles—the rights in land honored by history. The conventional theory finds its support in arguments for social control over property rights. The utility theory emerges when economics is the controlling element in the interpretation and understanding of property rights. The kind of mix that guides each of us in our study of property rights is influenced by the ideas that our respective disciplines hold to be important.

Almost a century before our Revolutionary Period, Locke had included life, liberty, and property as the trinity of natural rights. But Jefferson substituted "pursuit of happiness" for "property" in the Declaration of Independence. Why did not Jefferson include property as one of the natural rights? He must have given the matter considerable thought, for according to Chinard, Jefferson had bracketed "Propriété" in the copy of a Declaration of the Rights of Man drafted by Lafayette. The shift is significant, for both versions were held to be self-evident—the trinity in each case being exactly what men should hold as inalienable.

As society became more complex and land became more scarce, it became equally self-evident that the natural rights theory, as adjusted and supported by other current theories of property, was an insufficient basis to justify or explain private property in land. Thus, the bold assertion of "life, liberty, and property" was adjusted so that property rights acquired by an individual could be taken away from him, in the earlier day because of transgressions of the civil law and later for public use. In addition, more was demanded than mere acquisition, possession, and protection. For example, the rights involved in the inheritance process were deemed wise and effectual. But they had no basis in natural law. The rights were clearly political, that is, mere civil rights. If private property in land was first based upon the laws of nature, it was later sustained and made workable under the idea of the social contract of civil societies that were created to secure these and other rights. If this is true, the state can expand or contract, extend or abridge, many of the so-called natural rights.

Regardless of the theory of the origin of property in land, an adequate understanding of the concepts of private property is possible only if we comprehend our English feudal heritage. When William the Conqueror crossed the English Channel in 1066 and established himself as lord and chief of all the land of England, he foisted upon an unsuspecting population the most abominable land system ever devised until modern Communism. The system was known as feudalism and involved both a land system and a system of government. For feudalism has been described as a system of government based upon the organization of people upon the land.

Control over land and people was maintained by a series of "incidents" placed upon the land and personal services required of the people. At the height of feudalism the incidents numbered nine: fealty, homage, wardship, marriage, relief, primer seisin, aids, fines for alienation, and escheat. They were uncertain in amount and some of them as to frequency of collection. Their burden on the land depended in large part on the exigencies of the situation. For example, aids consisted generally, but only after they were brought under control, of payments to the lord: (1) to ransom him when captured, (2) to pay the expenses involved in knighting his son, and (3) to provide a dowry for his eldest daughter when she married. There was no way of knowing when or how frequently the lord might be captured. The other occasions for aids, likewise, were uncertain as to time.

The nine incidents gave the feudal lord considerable control over the land held by his under-tenant. They may have been quite reasonable when first imposed, but they soon became burdensome and prevented free transfer of rights in land. For example, under wardship the land was not transferred to a minor heir—the lord kept the profits from the feud until the minor became of age; under marriage the lord had to give his consent first to the marriage of a daughter and later of a son—a money payment was used to encourage the lord to give his consent; under relief the heir encouraged the lord to accept him as tenant by making a payment, usually the profits for a year; under primer seisin the lord held the property until relief was paid; and a fine for alienation was a payment made for the privilege of transferring the land to another.

By 1660, when the Statute of Tenures was enacted, the feudal system ceased to exist in its pristine purity. Many parliamentary enactments, proclamations, and ordinances had already toppled the noble structure. The statute converted knight-service tenures (land held directly of the king but subject to the feudal incidents) into free and common socage (under which only nominal annual charges were paid to the lord). This abolished homage, wardship, marriage, relief, primer seisin, aids, and fines for alienation. Escheat for felony continued. Quitrent, that is, a cash payment, was substituted for personal services. The last vestiges of feudal tenure, however, remained to harass the farmers of England until 1922 when copyholders, the lowest class of English tenants, converted their tenure into free and common socage.

Constant effort was made throughout feudal times in England to adapt tenure relations to meet contemporary requirements. But social evolution appeared to lag far behind technical requirements of the existing situation. Slow-to-change tenure arrangements seemed to hold up economic progress. Once a tenure adjustment was made it outlived its usefulness. For example, the practices of primogeniture and entails remained long after their need and justification had disappeared. This inheritance process was even brought to America. So were some of the burdensome feudal incidents, although they were outlawed in England in 1660, before much of America was settled.

## ORIGINS OF OUR LAND SYSTEM

Our land tenure system is a direct descendant of the feudal tenures of England. The legal system and governmental organization that supported it were based upon the common law of England and English civil government. The feudal land system, however, did not survive the Colonial-Revolutionary period. The form of government also has changed with the emergence of our national system. The common law, however, remains the fundamental legal system that controls land tenure relations. But it too had been adjusted in many particulars through enactments of the Colonial assemblies by the time we became a nation.

Changes in the land system, although infrequently the subject of discussion, are among the most dramatic and far-reaching of any that took place during the Colonial period. We will first consider tenure adjustments prior to the Revolution and then present changes that were worked out during the Revolutionary Period.

## TENURE ADJUSTMENTS PRIOR TO THE REVOLUTION

The *right to tax* land was not reserved in the land grants from the English crown. The various Colonial governments held this right, as do our state governments today. The federal government does not tax real estate; and the state governments do not tax federally owned land. The right to tax was unquestioned then as it is now. Land taxes were common throughout the Colonies and were levied at an early date, as early as 1645 in Virginia, for example. The Colonial governments established the principle of equal taxation, although varying rates were applied occasionally, as for example, a double rate was levied on certain absentee owners. The ideas of the right of appeal if a landowner thought the rate was too high and of forfeiture in case of failure to pay the levy were also well accepted during the Colonial period. The tax rate could be changed from time to time, special levies could be assessed for special purposes, and certain land could be exempt from taxation.

The right of *eminent domain* also was recognized in Colonial America. General enactments to govern the taking of private property were infrequent. Usually, the local governing body passed a special act each time land was to be taken. The commonest takings were for public buildings, towns and forts, and water mills, wharves, and ferry sites to be operated by private parties. The procedures for justifying the taking of the land and for determining the price to be paid were usually outlined in the special act.

The *police power* was not used extensively in the Colonial period, although the right was clearly established and adapted to existing conditions. The chief police-power concern of the Colonial governments in regard to land was about fences, livestock, hunting, and fishing. Generally the law specified what would be considered a good and sufficient fence and the responsibility for partition or division line fences. This regulation was made effective by holding the owner of livestock responsible for damages done by them, if he did not maintain good and sufficient fences.

Hunting and fishing rights were given to the landowner by the colonizing agent who had received them in the original grant from the crown. Hunting on another's land without permission was forbidden and severe penalties were imposed on violators, but anyone could hunt on vacant land. Hunting on the Sabbath was generally prohibited.

In Colonial America land *escheated* for failure to plant and occupy it or to meet other conditions in the grant. If the landowner could not be located or if he were an alien the land would revert to the grantor. Failure to pay quitrent and taxes also caused the land to revert. The land was forfeited by suicide. In general, Colonial laws regulating escheat were vague and difficult of administration.

The right to *alienate land* by sale was fully recognized throughout Colonial America, although numerous minor restrictions were found. In some Colonies the landowner might not sell his land if he had not paid the purchase price and received a patent, or if he had not been resident in the Colony for two years. These restrictions were evidently designed to curb speculation. Numerous regulations restricted the sale of land by minors, married women, executors, administrators, corporate bodies, and persons holding less than fee simple estates. Special legislation dealt with the sale of property by church bodies; usually a separate enactment dealt with each transaction.

One of the more fascinating land tenure experiences of Colonial America was concerned with the system of *inheritance*. Testate and intestate succession were recognized. In intestate descent, the major rules that the Colonists brought with them to America may be summarized as follows: Inheritances lineally descended but never ascended, males were preferred to females, the eldest was preferred to younger sons, females inherited equally, full blood was preferred to half blood, grandchildren could inherit by representation and primogeniture was practiced. Let us look at these ideas about inheritance and observe changes that were made during the Colonial era.

Although most American states have now discarded the old feudal rule that inheritances descend but never ascend, the Colonies apparently did not make this adjustment. Also, the old rules on dower were generally followed and it appears that no significant adjustment was made in them.

The preference of males over females was well established in English law. The Colonists, however, began early to dethrone male heirs. Some provided that male heirs were to receive only two portions to one portion for females, according to Hebraic law. Some of them provided that the eldest son should have only a double portion, not the entire estate. The idea of primogeniture began to decay at the very beginning of settlement. It fell into disuse in many Colonies, particularly in New England, long before the Revolution. The barring of entails was first possible by action of the legislative bodies dealing with each case individually. This soon became too burdensome and small estates in fee tail could be alienated in fee simple under general acts of the legislature. Little progress was made, until the Revolutionary period, against the rule of the full blood, under which half-blood heirs were generally disinherited. It remained until after the Revolution to complete the drive toward equal devolution among children.

*Quitrents* were common in all of the Colonies, except in New England. The amount of the rent varied from Colony to Colony and from time to time. In some places the quitrent attached immediately, while in others it was not due for a period of years, up to five. The diversity of conditions of levying and the ineffective collection procedures were among the reasons for eventual failure of the quitrent system. Quitrents had fallen into disrepute prior to independence. Following independence they were outlawed specifically in some of the Colonies, while in others they were allowed to die.

Each Colony had its own system of *recording* deeds, mortgages, and wills, and of *surveying* the land. Some Colonies began keeping land records early, while in others many years elapsed before an attempt was made to keep a record of conveyances in land. Most Colonies, however, experienced great difficulty in getting the deeds recorded within the time specified, but gradual improvement was observed as the country became settled. Two general systems were used in surveying: metes and bounds and the rectangular survey system. Colonial experience with rectangular surveying, although somewhat unhappy, was the basis for the system later to be adopted in regard to much of the land west of the original Colonies.

Contrary to what might be expected, *leasing* of land was quite common in Colonial America, and sharecropping existed from the very beginning.

By the end of the Colonial period we find that the rights of private parties in land were less than absolute. They were diminished by the rights held by society: the right to tax, the right of eminent domain, the right to promulgate police power regulations, and the right of escheat. We also find that the right to alienate land by sale was rather firmly established. Progress was observed in adapting inheritance practices to the new situation. Quitrents were disappearing rapidly. Progress was being made in recording rights in land and in surveying procedures. Leasing appeared throughout the Colonies, and was subject to few regulations, as it is today. The general contours of the emerging land system were being formed and a sound foundation was laid for adjustments during the Revolutionary period.

### ADJUSTMENTS DURING THE REVOLUTIONARY PERIOD

An interesting aspect of the ideas that were developing in regard to the control of land was the distinction in the Declaration of Independence between human and property rights. Jefferson made the distinction clear in the Declaration by including, among the inalienable rights of man, the "pursuit of happiness" in the place of "property." It seems that Jefferson was consciously separating human rights, which are inherent and inalienable, from property rights, which are not necessarily inherent, natural, nor inalienable. Jefferson understood the need for abridging certain existing property rights. For within a short time he began his effective legislative endeavor to take from the individual property holder the right to entail a landed estate and later to outlaw primogeniture in intestate succession.

Between the Declaration of Independence and the acceptance of the Constitution several plans were put forth for the handling of the new public domain. Among them was the Land Report of 1784 which laid out in detail a complete system for handling the vast public domain. But the Congress voted not to consider the report. One of the eminent authorities on Jefferson places the 1784 report on the level of the Declaration of Independence and second only to the Constitution among the state papers of that day. The report was superseded by the Ordinances of 1785 and 1787.

The Ordinances of 1785 provided, among other things, for appointment of surveyors by the Congress, and for rectangular surveying, military bounties, a minimum price of one dollar per acre, reservation of one section of each township for educational purposes, transfer by deeds, recording in the state land office, and fee simple tenure. The 1785 Ordinance was never put into effect; it was supplemented and amplified by the 1787 Ordinance. The latter Ordinance was the foundation upon which was built the disposition of the public domain. Its basic principles continue to affect the land system.

Major land tenure provisions of the Ordinance may be summarized briefly as follows: The estates of persons dying intestate would descend equally to all heirs of equal consanguinity, the principle of representation would be followed, with no distinction between the full and half blood, and the widow would receive one-third of the real and personal property; estates could be devised by will; deeds and wills would be recorded within a year; real property would be transferred by lease and release or by bargain and sale, while personal property would be transferred by delivery; taxes would be equal on residents and nonresidents; no tax would be levied on land belonging to the federal government; and no person would be deprived of his property except in public exigencies and upon just compensation. Amendments to the Ordinance were made as experience pointed the way.

The Southwest Ordinance of 1790 added nothing of significance to the land tenure arrangements and the land policy provisions of the earlier Ordinances. It extended the same land system and plan of government to the southwest area.

The impact of the three Ordinances upon the land tenure system and the pattern of land occupancy remains to this day. The liberal provisions influenced legislative enactments and judicial interpretations for many years. The Land Report and the Land Ordinances were the forerunners of the Preemption (1841) and the Homestead (1862) Acts.

In order to understand the evolving land system, we need to comprehend the ideas prevailing at the time of its emergence. Numerous attitudes and values could be selected to present the situation, but only four will be used. They are chosen on the basis of their importance at that time, but also for their current relevancy. They are equality, freedom, security, and the family farm, and they will be discussed in that order.

The concept of *equality* was probably the most powerful philosophical yet practical idea that came into full bloom as our land system emerged at the time of the Revolution. The concept had occupied the minds of thoughtful men for generations. Plato and Aristotle both held that equality was a fundamental principle that should govern the distribution of land. They suggested, in general terms, that the state should regulate inheritance and gift as well as the sale of land to prevent inequality in landholding, that the laws of inheritance should be used to decrease existing inequality, that the most stable states are those with a large middle class of landowners, and that in an agricultural democracy laws should provide that every farmer has some land of his own. Obviously they were referring to free men for they were writing in a slave-holding state where slaves owned no property. It remained for Cicero to assert that all men, not just free men, are equal by the laws of nature. Thus ancient and modern thought on the subject were joined, though it took generations to effectuate the idea.

Discussion of the pros and cons of the concept of equal distribution of the land waxed and waned throughout the Colonial period, but it did not attain full fruition until the Revolutionary era. At the time of the formation of our national government, between 1776 and 1789, many political philosophers believed that the democratic form of government was no respecter of property. Democracy, it was feared, might destroy the property idea in the name of equality—the tides of equality were running so strongly at the time. Some held that the establishment of equality was a chimera—a frightful and foolish creature of the imagination. The only progress that could be made, they proposed, was in diminishing inequality. To resolve the dilemma, it was suggested that large fortunes could be dispersed by a judicious regulation of inheritance, without either depriving present landowners of their property or violating seriously the expectations of their heirs. Equality should not be attained at the expense of confiscation, when the same could be accomplished by a more gradual process.

It was argued by some that justice requires an unequal division of property, for human personalities are unequal and need unequal amounts of things to realize their fullest development. It was suggested also that justice requires that all men are equal before the law and need equal protection through equal participation in governmental processes. At the time of the emergence of our land system the two notions were intermixed and confused. Also, on the scene was the emerging economic thought of the era, which held that the desired measure of equality would result automatically from the spontaneous action of economic law, particularly if the most glaring deficiencies of feudalism and mercantilist policy were eliminated.

The reasoning regarding equality from the political viewpoint ran about as follows: Man as an individual antedated man as a citizen; as individuals, men were free and equal; men formed government for purely prudential reasons; and the originally free and equal men must remain free and equal. But the idea of political equality was rather flexible; its meaning varied and changed with time and place. The basic thought, however, was that all men are created free and equal, but to accommodate both human slavery and human equality, as was necessary in some states, the idea was twisted around until it came out "all free men, when they form a social compact, are equal."

In any event, the idea of equality was so strong that Jefferson used it as a guiding principle in formulating his notions about land reform. His fight against entails was successful, for he was convinced that the maintenance of large estates in the same family from generation to generation did not meet his standards of equality in the distribution of land resources. His fight against primogeniture likewise was successful for equal devolution alone could meet this concept of equality—Jefferson could not even tolerate the Hebraic idea of a double portion for the eldest son.

The change from the eldest son take all, the preference of males over females, and the preference of the full to half blood, past the idea of a double portion for the eldest son, to equal devolution was truly monumental. But the battle is not completely won; much progress yet remains to be achieved. For example, we have long subscribed to the scriptural and common law idea that husband and wife become one, but we have found it difficult to get away from the property idea that *he* is the *one* to the idea that husband and wife are equal in property relations.

Perhaps the second most influential idea that engrossed the Revolutionary mind was the concept of *freedom*. The freedom complex like the idea of equality, had an effect upon the land system that emerged at the time of the Revolution.

A major influence behind the idea of freedom was the unfree feudal system of land and government from which the colonists fled. Many of the hardy souls who ventured to these shores were fleeing from severe limitations on their freedom. The ideas of freedom were indeed only embryonic in contemporary Western Europe. But some inroads had been made on old systems of sociopolitical control and conformance. The unfree land system was of much concern. Under primogeniture and entail equal heirs were not free to acquire ownership of the family's land: it all went to the eldest son. The landowner was not free to transfer land to whomever he pleased, when under the iron thumb of primogeniture and entail. Competition for available land resources was anything but free. The trend, however, toward a free land system was distinct and sharp.

Perhaps the strongest idea of freedom was in the area of religion. The thesis that the free land system could not have arisen except for the religious reformation in Colonial America would be difficult to prove. But the idea of religious freedom,

it must be conceded, contributed to the free land tenure system
and to the plans for a liberal policy in distribution of the
public domain.

The general ideas of freedom in vogue during the Revolutionary period were worked into the land system in numerous
ways. Examples are the unbridled freedom to buy and sell, the
unrestricted freedom of the owner to waste his land, the almost
complete freedom accorded the landowner who would take the
trouble to control the disposition of his estate through testa-
mentary devise, and the absolute freedom of concentration and
fragmentation.

Another philosophic feature that had become embedded in
our land system was the idea of *security*. At the time of its emergence the idea was quite different than it is today. Originally,
if a person owned a farm he had a high degree of economic and
social security. He was assured of a place to work; he did not
have to look to anyone for employment. He was assured a living
through good times and bad, for his farm would always supply
him with food and clothing. He was assured a living during old
age. His farm, in fact, was a kind of savings bank out of which
he could draw for his needs during the evening of life.

The land ordinances, under which the Northwest Territory
would be settled, indicated the nature of the rights that fee
simple ownership would give a landowner. This added to the
security with which he held rights in his land. They also provided
for a fairly cohesive system that would be basic in all of the new
territory. The states were free, of course, to enact land laws to
meet their individual needs, but new legislation had to be within
the framework of the tenure system laid down in the land ordinances. The provisions for surveying and recording made the
landholder's ownership of land more secure. The revised eminent
domain procedure also added to his feeling of security.

A fourth philosophic idea built into our land system was
the *family farm* concept. Although the term probably was not
used in those days, the basic ideal was the same as it is today.
The land of the New England Colonies was farmed largely by
individual families on units suited to their condition. Some large
farms were found in the Middle Colonies, as exemplified by the

Dutch patroonships in New York and the manor-like holdings in Pennsylvania and Maryland. Large farms were also found in the Southern Colonies as plantations. Even in the Colonies where larger-than-family farms were most common, many farms were operated by individual families, and could properly be thought of as family farms. All of the units, whether large or small, were, for the most part, subsistence units in those days. They all produced, as nearly as they could, the things necessary to sustain human life.

The small farmer of that time was in apposition to the plantation or other large unit. The ideal of the independent family upon the land was worked out in light of the existing situation. The actions of our founding fathers in regard to land ownership and control must be interpreted in the setting in which the drama was unfolding. For example, Jefferson's visualization of a countryside of small farmers was in contrast to a countryside of large plantations. He was not selecting the subsistence farm of today in preference to the highly productive commercial farm operated largely with the labor of one family. There is no indication whatsoever that Jefferson and those who followed his leadership, if they were on the scene today, would select as a policy objective the low-income subsistence farm in preference to the typical family farm. There is no doubt but that they would select the family farm over large-scale units of today.

The actions taken by our nation's leaders in those days laid the foundation upon which was built the present system of family farming. The elimination of primogeniture and entails, the introduction of equal devolution, and the distribution of land in family-sized units tipped the scales in favor of family farming.

To summarize, adjustments in our land tenure system during the Revolutionary period were incorporated largely in the land ordinances. Four attitudes and values that had significant impacts upon our land system were equality, freedom, security, and the family farm. The concepts of equality and freedom are hallmarks of the Revolutionary era and colored most of the actions taken regarding our land system. The ideas of security and family farming, although less easy to trace, were first-order philosophic attributes of the emerging system of land tenure.

## THE HOMESTEAD AS A CONCEPT

Following the Revolutionary era, experience with disposal of the public domain contributed little to basic elements of our land tenure system. The experience with squatters and the Pre-emption Act, however, paved the way for the Homestead Act. But at about the time of the Preemption Act other homestead ideas were emerging. To understand the Homestead Act, there-fore, we must look at the homestead as a concept, and we will consider it from two viewpoints. The commoner concept is that a homestead is a piece of land granted a settler under conditions that he live on it, cultivate and improve it, or otherwise use it in making a living for his family. Another equally important view-point is that a homestead is a piece of land, including the dwell-ing thereon, that is given special treatment by certain laws to preserve the integrity of the family as the basic element of social organization. The Homestead Act of 1862, at least in part, was based on the philosophy that underlies the latter viewpoint. The connection between the two viewpoints has not been a matter of deep concern to social scientists, judging by the dearth of writing on the association. We will try to explore the relation-ship in sufficient depth, however, for the purposes of this book and possibly to encourage a more thorough study of the subject.

The idea in the federal Homestead Act is largely an American invention. It is deeply rooted in our Colonial experience and in our progressive settling of the public domain from its origin to 1862. The ideas expressed in the special state homestead laws are likewise largely American. They are deeply rooted in the need to protect the family against loss of its residence—from forced sales in satisfaction of debt and in other ways. The obvious purposes of the federal Homestead Act and the special state homestead laws are entirely different, except in one particular, although their origin is in the same socio-economic-political com-plex. The one similarity is that the federal statute protects the home from execution as do the state statutes. The federal act declares that homesteaded land shall be exempt from liability to forced sale for debts incurred previous to the issuance of the patent therefor.

The basic policy of the state homestead laws is to protect the home, the family residence, and not the individuals, as are the personal exemption laws. The protection of the homestead was not complete, for many exceptions are spelled out in the laws and are permitted by positive action of those who hold the homestead right.

In pursuance of the policy of protecting the family residence, the wife of the owner of homestead property has the right to control its disposition during their lives. She must sign instruments that transfer ownership rights in the homestead property, and she is protected in many ways against coercion to sign the transfer instrument. Also, the husband cannot defeat his wife's right to a homestead by devise of the property to another person. In some states the widow is entitled to both dower and homestead; in other states she is entitled to only one, but she may select which one. Almost invariably the wife has some kind of homestead interest in the land, if she survives her husband.

In addition to the homestead claims of the wife, in some states the statutes provide that the minors of the marriage have a right of homestead until they arrive at majority.

Several states provide an additional protection for the homestead through exemption from a limited amount of property taxes. The tax exemption applies only if the property is owned and occupied as a homestead. Although the tax exemption usually is not great, it is another indication of the public's attitude and value judgment in favor of the owner-occupier.

Parenthetically and from another viewpoint, the idea has developed that a man's homestead, his place of residence, is his castle. The privacy of the home cannot be invaded except under due process of law. The establishment of this idea was a slow and sometimes painful process. It is safeguarded with all diligence. If it gives way one of the great bulwarks of the common law is lost. We are so accustomed to the protection afforded that we assume it is a natural right that cannot be altered by man. Yet, its abridgment is possible, particularly if the right of privacy is taken too lightly.

The homestead idea is important to the family in protection of its privacy, in the advantages afforded by its exemption from execution for debt, in the restrictions placed upon the freedom with which it can be alienated, and in its exemption from taxation in certain jurisdictions. The homestead idea adds to the stability of the family and as a consequence has social values worthy of note. The concepts embodied in the homestead exemption idea were important in the establishment of the Homestead Act, although they were alike in only one particular. It was easy to find a name for the Homestead Act, for the settlers and the Congress were interested in the advantages afforded by the homestead idea.

It would appear that the ideas embodied in the Homestead Act and in the state homestead exemption laws had their origins in the frontier conditions involved in the settlement of our western lands. The state homestead exemption laws, and the various ideas that surrounded the family's homestead, antedated the Homestead Act. The characteristic features of the homestead as already developed found ready acceptance in the Homestead Act. The exemption from execution for debt features were quite similar. The two homestead ideas working in harmony were complementary in effect. In discussing the federal Homestead Act we should not lose sight of the special attention given the family's homestead in the state homestead laws. For the homesteader and his family were afforded some additional protection by the general land laws that encompassed the sanctity of the homestead as a concept.

## CHARACTERISTIC FEATURES OF OUR
## LAND TENURE SYSTEM

The essential features of our present system of land tenure have been foreshadowed in the preceding paragraphs. It remains only necessary to summarize them briefly and to focus attention on specific private interests in privately held land.

We have divided the control of land resources into two simple dichotomies: (1) private and public interests in *privately* held land, and (2) private and public interests in *publicly* held land.

The public holds all of the basic rights in all publicly held land. Certain use rights in such land may be leased or otherwise transferred to private parties, usually for a specified period of time. All members of society hold equal interest in some public land, the Homestead Monument at Beatrice, Nebraska for example.

The public also holds certain rights in all privately held land. These rights are retained by the government, or they are given to society by the landowner, whichever theory you may prefer. They traditionally include the right to tax, the police power, the power of eminent domain, and the right of escheat. In recent years a fifth right has emerged in the form of the spending power, as for example in various conservation and adjustment programs.

Private interests or rights in privately held land include all of those not held by the public. The interests of the private landowner in his land can be looked at from many viewpoints. When considered from a legal viewpoint and *in toto* these interests make up a large part of the whole field of real property. From an economic viewpoint, they may be considered at the level of the firm or an aggregation of firms. They may also be considered as to how they affect the actions of the private owner individually and personally and how they affect his actions in connection with others. In general these rights are regulated by state law, with each state making its own law within the framework of applicable constitutional provisions.

The task would be endless to isolate and describe every one of the possible separate interests or rights that private parties hold in their privately owned land. Suffice it to pick out a few for illustrative purposes. They will be considered under the dichotomy of intra-private and inter-private.

Four pairs of the most common intra-private interests are as follows: (1) possession and occupancy (2) devise and give (3) waste and conserve, and (4) use or leave idle.

Although *possession* and *occupancy* when applied to land are nearly synonymous terms, they are slightly different, especially in a legal sense. Possession is the control of the land for one's use and enjoyment, either as owner or proprietor and either personally or by a person who exercises the right in one's place or name. Occupancy is used in the sense of occupation or physically holding possession. It is always actual, as distinguished from possession, which may be actual or constructive.

Our land tenure system gives the private owner highly secure, yet not quite absolute, rights of possession and occupancy. The owner-occupier has the greatest security, that is, the greatest assurance that his possession and occupancy will not be disturbed. The occupier who holds a lesser estate, a tenant, for example, has less freedom from disturbance of his possession and occupancy. The security with which the land user, whether he be farmer or urban dweller, holds his rights has a tremendous influence upon his use and enjoyment of the land.

The second pair of intra-private rights in land are *devise* and *gift*. A devise is a conveyance of property by the last will and testament of the owner. An *inter vivos* gift is usually a transfer of property without pecuniary reward and not necessarily in consideration of blood or family relations. Before the middle of the thirteenth century, land could not be transferred during life. In some countries today, land cannot be sold. The long struggle of the English landowner for the right to dispose of his land is one of the most fascinating developments in the history of land tenures. It was not until 1540, for example, that the oft-married Henry VIII sponsored an act, called the Statute of Wills, that gave landholders limited right to dispose of their land by will. So today we enjoy the fruits of the hard-earned rights of past generations.

The private landowner is also free to *waste* or *conserve* his land as he sees fit. He need not maintain it in its present physical condition. He may permit it to erode, gully, or become denuded. Or he may improve it by drainage, irrigation, clearing, leveling, or building structures upon it. If he is the owner, the sky is about the limit as to either waste and deterioration or conservation and development. If he is not the owner and merely holds a lesser estate, as a life tenant or ordinary tenant, his actions are regulated, albeit rather ineffectively, by the laws of waste. It has long been a principle of the common law (since the thirteenth century) that the interests of a person in reversion or remainder shall be protected against waste. But the laws against waste have been ineffectual in cases of gradual deterioration. The whole conservation movement might have been unnecessary if the laws of waste had been effective and had applied to owners as well as holders of lesser estates. In society's effort to establish the freest of tenures the pendulum probably swung too far toward complete freedom. For freedom without responsibility may result in unwanted ends.

Another pair of intra-private rights of the landowner is that he may *use* his land or he may leave it *idle*. He has almost complete freedom in the uses he may make of his land. But he cannot use it for unlawful purposes or so as to injure adjoining landowners. Although land is an economic good, the owner need not use it for productive purposes; he may leave it idle. Or he may use it for purposes for which it is not suited. As we have seen recently, society may use the spending power to encourage the owner to take his land out of production. Conservation and land retirement are two current exercises of the spending power that influence the land system.

There are also four pairs of inter-private interests that may be considered. They are: (1) buy and sell, (2) mortgage and lease, (3) give easement and prevent trespass, and (4) subdivide and consolidate.

One of the most economically important attributes of our land tenure system is the freedom with which land is *bought* and *sold,* an inter-private transaction. In general, no controls are exerted over who can buy land. The buyer may be a citizen or alien, male or female, young or old, resident or absentee, wealthy or poor, and capable or unqualified. The only essential characteristic is that he has the money, or can get it. The freedom with which land is bought and sold, according to economic theory, would tend to put land in the most economically capable hands. This is the usual but not the universal result. Freedom to buy and sell, however, is an essential characteristic of a free enterprise economic system.

Another set of inter-private interests in land are the rights to *mortgage* and to *lease*. The private landowner may share his rights with another by either or both of these means. There is practically no limitation on the right to mortgage. The mortgage may represent only a small portion of the value of the land or it may be for more than the land would sell for on the market. The formality of writing and recording is not a limitation of the right; they are procedures to make effective the sharing of the right with another—of adding security to the holding of rights in land. The landowner likewise has an unrestricted right to lease his land; he may lease all or a part of it to whomever he pleases for whatever rent he can obtain.

The freedom to mortgage facilitates buying and selling whenever the purchaser does not have the money to pay cash. The right to lease makes it possible to separate ownership from management. These two inter-private interests in land are regulated more or less by the laws of the several states. The regulations generally are nonrestrictive, that is, they do not reduce significantly the freedom with which the individual may act; they are designed basically to safeguard and protect the respective interests of the two parties—to add security to the relationship.

A third pair of inter-private interests in land are the rights to grant an *easement* and to prevent *trespass*. The former makes it possible for the owner to share specified use rights with another; under the latter the owner may prevent others from forcing upon him the sharing of his use rights. An easement may arise in many ways; it may be by prescription, that is, long-continued enjoyment, by existing conditions that would be obvious upon inspection, or by an outright grant, whether oral or written and recorded. The owner may prevent the other party from trespassing upon his property, that is, from unlawfully coming upon it or causing injury to it. The laws against trespass are designed to assure the owner quiet and peaceful possession and occupancy of his property. These two inter-private interests increase the number of people who may use the land and add to the security with which the owner holds his rights. Both increase the efficiency with which the land may be used.

The freedom with which the landowner may *subdivide* his holdings or *consolidate* it with other land are other major inter-private features of our land system. The facility with which adjustments can be made in the size of ownership units is of crucial importance in a rapidly changing economy. We observe numerous acts of subdivision at the growing edge of many metropolitan areas and even smaller cities. Less dramatic, but of comparable importance, is the frequent consolidation of farms in the agricultural sector of the economy. No limit is placed upon the smallness or the largeness of the parcel of land that a person may own, and one person may hold as many parcels in as many states as he can acquire. Segmentation of holdings and concentration of land have never been viewed with alarm. The freedom to subdivide and to consolidate land, wherever it is situated, has contributed much to the economic and social effectiveness of our land system.

## THE LAND SYSTEM AND ECONOMIC PERFORMANCE

We have seen that rights in land may be divided into intra-private and inter-private interests—those that affect the individual personally in his enjoyment of the land, and those that affect two or more individuals in their joint control and use of it. We have shown the general nature of such rights or interests and have amplified what is involved by illustrations of different kinds of rights or interests. Some reference has been made of the effect of land tenure upon land use. We need now to examine how various rights in land, as specified in our tenure system, affects the economic performance of those who control and use the resource.

The protection thrown around the owner-occupier gives him maximum, but not absolute, assurance (security) that he may reap the fruits of all long-term investments of labor and capital that he applies to the land in such a way that it becomes a part of the real estate. The advantages of quiet possession and occupancy also permit the owner-occupier to use the land in any way that he sees fit, whether on a long-term or short-term basis. He may decide that it is to his economic advantage to build up the productivity of the land through various means. Or he may calculate that he can make more money by letting the soil erode and the buildings become dilapidated. He may use the land at its highest use or he may leave it entirely idle. The land system gives him almost complete freedom of choice, yet it fails to impose upon him commensurate responsibilities.

The land system not only grants this maximum freedom of action, it also assures the owner-occupier that his privately held rights in land will be taken from him only under the due process of law and then at just compensation. His neighbors cannot infringe upon this quiet and peaceful occupancy and use. So he is protected against interference from either private or public sources. This does not mean that he has absolute security, but there is a minimum of laws that in any way reduces the security with which he holds his land.

The land system provides that parcels of land can be put together freely to enlarge operating units in meeting the technological requirements of modern society. Likewise, the owner can subdivide his land into any size units that may yield to him the highest economic return. We have developed neither a set of laws nor a group of attitudes and values to deter consolidation or subdivision of land.

Our land tenure system also accords the landowner a maximum degree of freedom in granting to others the rights that he holds—sharing inter-private rights. Thus, he is relatively free in working out a lease with his tenant or a mortgage in case he wants to use the land as security for a loan. The land tenure system affords some protection of the property against waste by a nonowner who holds the use rights. But we have developed, over the years, the attitude that the owner should be permitted to waste the land if he so decides. This attitude has made it difficult for a strict interpretation and effective administration of the laws against waste.

Thus it can be said in summary that the rights of private landowners permit the maximum economic use of the land. Since the owner receives, except for taxation, the full benefit of any increments to the physical quality of the land and whatever is attached to it, it can be said that the tenure rights of the owner actually encourage its fullest economic development. Also, since the owner must stand the loss for any decrements in the physical quality of the real estate, he is encouraged to maintain and to develop the land to its optimum productiveness.

Others who hold lesser interest in land than the owner are more restricted in the use of the land. The holder of a life estate, an administrator or executor, or a trustee, for example, must use the land under well-developed principles formulated in our law. But generally these controls neither prevent nor make difficult the highest economic use of the land.

From another viewpoint, the security with which the owner holds rights in the land encourages him to develop and use it to the place of maximum economic returns. He is assured, insofar as the conditions of tenure under which the land is held can offer such assurance, that he will be able to capture the benefits of his investment of capital and labor. This is not only true for variable annual or short-term inputs, but also for fixed, long-term inputs. This assurance acts as an encouragement rather than a deterrent to the maximum economic use of the land.

The owner's planning horizon can be as long as his life expectancy, or limited only by his own unique economic planning. In fact, it can be said that the right to decide who may use the land after his death may encourage the owner to extend his planning horizon beyond his death. But this condition may cease the minute he transfers to another any substantial right in the real estate. For example, if the owner gives a mortgage on the land or if he holds only an equitable ownership interest, as under a land contract, the security with which he holds the land has been reduced by the provisions of the mortgage or contract. This possibility of forfeiture or foreclosure, as the case may be, may act as a deterrent in making improvements and may actually cause the owner to use the land so as to cause disinvestments in it.

Leased land may be used at less than the optimum. Its use may be circumscribed in the lease, inputs may be poorly related to income shares, or the possibility of not collecting all of the rent due may be deterrents to optimum land use. The planning horizon of the tenant under customary leasing arrangement is not sufficiently long to permit a well-informed tenant to use the land at the optimum. It can be said, in summary, that whereas the owner is encouraged by the security with which he holds his rights in the land to use it at the optimum, the insecure tenure with which the tenant holds his rights offers less encouragement.

It should be pointed out that no system of land ownership and control can be devised to overcome deficiencies in other aspects of the economic milieu in which the holders of use-rights in land perform their function. Land tenure arrangements cannot overcome any deficiency in knowledge, or any lack of initiative, or any inclination toward thriftlessness. Likewise, land tenure arrangements cannot overcome any deficiency that might exist because of the malallocation of capital and labor.

In summary, our land tenure system gives the owner a high degree of freedom and substantial encouragement in the optimum use of his land. There is practically no intra-private barrier to cause the owner to use his land at less than the optimum. Thus he is assured quiet possession and peaceful occupancy; he can devise or give the land to anyone that he may choose, subject only to his wife's interest; he can waste it or improve it; and he can use it as he sees fit or let it lie idle. The rules and regulations that govern inter-private relations in regard to land likewise permit a high degree of freedom in transactions among and between private holders of rights in land. The land tenure system expedites the purchase and sale of rights in land; it permits consolidation and fragmentation without questioning the efficacy of the action; it facilitates mortgaging and leasing under almost any arrangement that the parties may desire; and the owner may grant lesser rights to other parties as through an easement or he may prevent other parties from trespassing upon his land.

In general, those were the conditions of private rights in private land under which the homesteader received his land. Equal claimants were given equal rights to the available homesteads. Yet with the passing of homesteading little has been done to maintain and encourage equal access to landed property. The molders of our tenure system gave much thought to according the holders of various rights in land maximum freedom in the control and use of those resources. Freedom of action had been curbed slightly by the idea that the rights of those who hold lesser interests should be secure. Land laws in general added to the security with which the various rights are held. Undergirding the whole land system was a fundamental idea that private property in the land resources of the nation should be distributed widely—in family farms. Maintenance of a nice balance among various objectives was the tight rope upon which performed the framers of our land system.

KRIS KRISTJANSON

and RAYMOND J. PENN

# Public Interest in Private Land:
# Private and Public Conflicts

THE PUBLIC INTEREST, broadly defined, is best served by working toward a situation in which all people in the world community can look forward to having adequate food, clothing, and shelter. Private land can be an effective instrument in enhancing the public interest thus defined.

The Honorable Chester Bowles, the President's special representative and adviser on African, Asian, and Latin American Affairs has said,[1]

> ... this year marks the hundredth anniversary of two of the most decisive documents of American history, documents which assured that American land would be used for the common good—the Homestead Act of May 20, 1862, and the Morrill Land Grant College Act of July 2, 1862.
>
> Although the importance of this legislation to our national development is dramatic in terms of physical progress, its greatest importance may lie in the way it shaped our national character and gave depth to our belief in the dignity of the individual.
>
> Since the passage of the Homestead Act, more than 270 million acres of free land have been distributed to American farmers. The Morrill Land Grant College Act led to the creation of sixty-eight great public educational institutions, still committed largely to promote the development of rural America.

The basic concept underlying the Land Grant College Act was relatively simple; namely, that an opportunity should be provided to the young men and women of America to study the science of agriculture and the industrial arts. This opportunity was to be available, not only to the members of the wealthier classes, but also to the sons and daughters of the working classes actively engaged in building a better America.

When one reflects upon the tremendous progress made during the short period of one hundred years in raising the living standards of the American people, it is exciting to think about the possibilities for the next fifty to one hundred years. If the basic concepts underlying the Homestead Act and the Morrill Act could be directed toward creating a world community in which adequate food, clothing, and shelter were available for every man, woman, and child on this earth, there does not seem to be any reason why this objective could not be attained. This goal can be achieved only of we are firmly committed to it. The Land Grant colleges continue to have a major role to play toward this end.

This chapter focuses attention on two major areas of study where the people in the Land Grant colleges can make a significant contribution. There is a need to gain a better understanding of the relevance of the basic principles of the Homestead Act to the people of Asia, Africa, and Latin America. There is a need also to learn how to modify our ideas about distribution in order to keep pace with the tremendous improvements in technology. This is necessary to help raise the level of living in the rapidly developing countries, but it is also necessary to maintain a maximum degree of freedom for the farmers and other producers of America. In order to take full advantage of the improved technology, research workers and public administrators need to direct more attention to the effectiveness of the institutional arrangements which apply to distribution.

The first part of this paper is based on the writings of Professor Penn in order to provide readers with an opportunity to share some of Professor Penn's experiences and thoughts about land reform in Latin America.

The second part deals with some of the institutional factors which govern the distribution of the rewards of our improved technology. It is based, in part, on the Canadian experience with the sale of wheat to China, with some speculation about the importance of being able and willing to modify the institutional arrangements which apply to distribution, thus making possible more effective use of our productive capacity to satisfy the needs of a greater number of people. Attention is drawn to the importance of finding new markets to maintain a wide measure of freedom of action for the individual farm owners and operators in rural America.

The two issues of ownership and distribution were fundamental to the success of the Homestead Act. The understanding of their relevance to the problems of accelerating development in the less developed areas of the world is fundamental to attaining the objective of an adequate level of living for all.

The people associated with the Land Grant colleges have made phenomenal progress in attaining their initial objectives during the short period of one hundred years. This progress can be expected to continue at an accelerating rate. The Land Grant colleges of the United States have provided training for the men and women who operate the farms and factories of the nation. This training process, along with such programs as the extension service and farm credit, has been so successful that it is possible to produce far more than is required to meet existing demands, despite the fact that the agricultural and industrial plant of North America has been operating at less than full capacity for a long period of time. If those who drafted the Morrill Act could observe the consequences of their work, they would say that the results far exceeded their fondest expectations.

The benefits have not been confined to the United States. In Canada, for example, most of the engineering and agricultural colleges are staffed by people who have had the privilege of studying at one or more of the United States Land Grant colleges. This has had its effect on the rate of development of Canada's industry and agriculture. Students from almost every country in the world have attended many of the United States' colleges with similar beneficial effects. By now there are a great many professors and students from United States Land Grant colleges working in other countries, and it would be interesting to trace their influence on the improvement of productivity throughout the world.

The fact that the United States has had such phenomenal success with increasing its own productivity has in turn created problems of distribution. The technological progress has not been matched by the same degree of progress in understanding and modifying the institutional arrangements which affect the ownership and distribution of the fruits of this improved technology. As a matter of fact, we find ourselves in the somewhat ridiculous position of speaking of the agricultural problem in the United States by which we usually mean the oversupply of agricultural commodities. Despite this, the major effort in the United States Department of Agriculture and the Land Grant colleges continues to be directed towards improving efficiency in the techniques of production. This increased knowledge thus accumulated is very efficiently transmitted to the farmers through a well-organized extension service. When the government tries to institute production controls of one kind or another, it finds that the farmers, through the application of the improved technology, produce more on fewer acres. This basic inconsistency tends to make a mockery of the various production control programs. The overall production control designed to reduce total output does not make sense in terms of the world situation.

In the United States, progress has been made possible by a willingness to adapt institutional arrangements to meet the needs of the changing times. For example, the basic concepts about land ownership have been subject to modification. If progress is to be made in the underdeveloped countries of the world, there is a need for a clearer understanding of the rights, privileges, and responsibilities which ought to be associated with land ownership in each particular situation.

Some research work is being done in this field by workers in the Land Grant colleges. Much more needs to be done if the objective of eliminating hunger and poverty is to be attained.

The following discussion is based on Professor Penn's analysis of the significance of land reform as a factor in the economic development of Latin America and is intended to draw attention to the need for more study in this field.

Every serious plan for economic development in Latin America today includes some kind of land reform. No magic formula for Latin America's economic ills is so widely accepted— and so little understood.

On the surface, the landless of South America look to land

reform to assure them of food and shelter. Actually, they seek something much broader and quite different. They want relief from a feudalism which we North Americans find hard to comprehend.

What we must understand is that in much of the world today the ownership of land carries with it ownership of government—the right to tax, the right to judge, the power to enact and enforce police regulations. It dominates every crucial decision about investments in social capital—education, transportation, hospitals, power projects.

To the *campesino*, ownership of land is more than a source of wealth. It is the source of prestige, political power, and social justice. It gives him the right to build his own house in which to raise his family. It gives him, too, the right to tax himself to build a school. It lets him share in the bundle of rights which have so long been a prerogative of the large landholder and denied to the landless.

The pressure for land reform, then, must be seen for what it is—pressure for a major reform in the government, the society, and the economy. Peaceful or violent, it is nothing more or less than a revolutionary movement.

We might well ask ourselves what specific expectations the landless of Latin America have from land reform.

*Economic Security.*—Of course, the families see in the ownership of a piece of land a kind of job protection and assurance that whatever happens they will at least have food and shelter.

*Political and Social Justice.*—Through land ownership the landless hope for status in their communities, freedom to act and speak freely, the opportunity to see their children given an education, and the right to share in control over their government.

*Use of Resources in the Broad Public Interest.*—Latin Americans are increasingly aware that the way they live depends not simply on their own efforts, but also on the total national production. Too much of Latin America's wealth—land as well as other resources—is not fully used. Large estates often do not produce the harvests they could with more intensive management. Virgin land has not yet been cleared for agricultural use. Without roads and markets, it can add nothing to national production and wealth. Thus, national land policies can directly affect the health and well-being of the individual and his family.

These, then, are the expectations from land reform.

It should be obvious that breaking up large estates will not, by itself, fulfill such hopes. Much more is involved. But it is quite natural that we in the United States tend to see land reform as a rather simple matter. Our Constitution was established on the liberal ideas of those who knew what European feudalism had been and why it must be abandoned.

This is why land ownership in the United States is not an absolute right, and why it does not carry other political and social rights with it. It is also one of the reasons that we in the United States have devised ways to give the landless some very substantial protections.

In the courts, landed or landless can in general expect fair and equal treatment.

People without property can vote and can put pressure on their legislatures for social security, minimum wages, job safety standards, and unemployment protection.

Credit sources make land purchase feasible, and the landless can also obtain property rights in the industry or, through their unions, acquire legal security in their jobs.

These facts are perhaps the major reason capitalism has not blown apart as Marx and Engels said it would. The power accompanying ownership of productive resources has not become as concentrated as they predicted. Even where concentrations of ownership have occurred, a far-sighted governmental structure has provided ways to give the man without property some other resources to use to protect his own and the larger public interest.

In this country, one major step in land reform was the opening up of western lands. For many years homesteads were available to anyone with the courage to move and the minimum resources to get established on new free land.

More than courage is needed for the settlement projects in the *llanos* of Colombia and Venezuela and along the Pacific fringe of Guatemala. New settlers need roads, schools, and markets. They need equipment in this modern day, and they may also need credit and technical help.

Supervised credit programs are an element of land reform in a number of Latin American countries. Farming cannot survive the 25–35 per cent interest rates which are common in many countries.

Property taxation is not common in Latin America, and it is another most urgent measure of land reform. Property taxes can discourage an owner from leaving his land idle or unproductive. They can raise money to build and maintain schools and roads and other public services. They can also reclaim some of the special benefits that are added to land values as a result of these social investments.

Legal procedures may be another vital element of land reform. In the Philippine Islands, special courts have been developed to give tenants more protection and both owner and tenant more responsibility in conflicts about land ownership and use.

Land reform is not, then, a simple matter. Why does it come to its bitterest focus in the issue of breaking up large estates? Because these holdings dramatize the economic, political, and social inequalities which stir the spirit of human justice.

Often large estates are on the best agricultural land—the irrigated valleys in Peru, the *pampas* in Argentina, the *savannahs* around Bogota and Cali in Colombia. Here the landless live in hunger, poverty, and squalor, with the large landowner an obvious explanation for their plight and target for their discontent.

This is a situation on which the politically cynical will capitalize. It is a situation the politically naive will misinterpret in their eager hope for speedy results from land distribution. Only the political realist will accept all the complexity of a true land reform program.

The political realist will demand a kind of land reform that guarantees regular and continuing machinery for expressing the public interest through rules about land ownership and use. And the political realist will find that these are not legal questions of land title, but questions of practical democracy.

Public interest cannot be determined by government edict—as we too often think, even in this country. It can only be determined by people who have the right to get together in groups and arrive at decisions and who have the bargaining power to put those group decisions into effect.

Procedures are important. True land reform must set up procedures to help in arriving at group decisions (planning or policy formation). It must provide procedures to put these decisions into operation. And, of course, it must include procedures to protect minority views and rights.

The force of public interest thus defined can be brought to bear not only on the recalcitrant individual but, also, on a governmental agency that is failing to do a job that is needed. At its best, it may even be brought to bear on the government itself.

Thus, the most important ingredient in economic development becomes the ability of the public to express its interest. This interest is far too seldom given voice in Latin America today, and our United States programs do not always help in its expression.

To return to our initial argument, most current talk about land reform assumes that widespread ownership of land is an adequate channel for expressing the public interest. It can be, of course, but the United States' experience suggests that additional channels must also be devised.

Let me very briefly review some of the other procedures we employ in the United States to make private property serve the public interest.

*Police Power.*—Through their governments, people can limit the individual's property rights to protect health, safety, security, and national welfare. This is the power under which laws are made that require us to stop at stop signs, prevent us from opening a store in a residential area, or keep us from plowing up the prairie sod to create wheatland in some soil conservation districts in the Great Plains. This is strong authority, so it is limited. It cannot be arbitrary. It cannot confiscate property. In addition, when it affects the use of property the owner must be notified, have an opportunity to be heard, and have access to the court if he feels he had been damaged.

*Taxation.*—People can levy taxes on land and income to support their government. These taxes must be uniform; similar pieces of land must pay the same tax. They must be used for public purposes. Technically, they must not be used for regulation, though in fact they sometimes are. History gives ample evidence that taxation can do much to make private ownership more sensitive and responsive. Particularly, it can force a reluctant owner to put land to its highest economic use if the plan of taxation is devised with that purpose in mind.

*Eminent Domain.*—When the public needs a piece of private land, it can take it. This, too, is a power so strong that rigid limits have been placed on it. Land taken by the government must be used for a public purpose—highways, railroads and public utilities, and schools. In general, we could not use this authority to take land from one private person and give it to another for private use, as would be done in a land distribution program. Urban redevelopment (slum clearance), however, has used this authority to take private land, change its use, and return it to private use. The owner is compensated for the land taken, but his only basis for contesting the action is the adequacy of the compensation and the validity of the public interest.

*Spending Power.*—Governments can have major effects on land use by their decisions about spending. Roads, schools, power projects, airports, defense, and other government purchases all can influence the value and use of land. Subsidies, as well as taxes, can guide the nature of private land use.

The United States has gone through, but not stopped with, its own land reform program. This continent was settled with large landed estates, but these were soon broken up. There was even more significance in the Homestead Acts, which created numerous family-farm units from the large reserves of unused land.

Those were strong democratizing measures, and to them we added an arsenal of other basic tools by which the people could express their public interest in private property. Changes in ownership have not been as important when we have so many other good ways of influencing the use of private property in the public interest.

The United States has, of course, developed its own particular peculiar combination of land tenure rules, growing out of its own history and culture. Other cultures may find quite different ways in which people can give form and force to their interest.

There is no question that large landholdings must and will be broken up as Latin America's economic and social revolution progresses. Mechanisms to make such changes without violence are the great strength and the vital need of democracy.

But none of the three goals of land reform which were stated earlier will be achieved by a land distribution program conceived in haste and directed by slogans.

Latin America needs to be thinking, and we with her, of two other vital steps. First, she must make sure that the new land-owners have the help they will need to farm well and market their produce. Second, she must develop continuing and durable ways to enforce the public concern about private land no matter who holds title to it.

For the urban landless and jobless, land reform is not the solution the idealist will hope or the demagogue pretend. Making agricultural pioneers out of urban unemployed is not a realistic way of handling these major population groups.

For the *campesino* a piece of land is only part of the answer without the sources of credit, technical advice, transportation, and market facilities to make ownership meaningful.

For both groups, and for every other citizen, land reform does not relieve us of the need to seek other lasting ways to make private property serve the public interest. This is the issue in Latin America today. It may well be the supreme test for both the political and the economic systems we cherish and defend.

Perhaps the worst thing any of us can do is to hope for too much from the first stages of land reform. They are a necessary, but by no means a sufficient, condition for the liberal democracy we hope to encourage throughout this troubled world.

Professor Penn's discussion of land reform in Latin America emphasizes the vital importance of a sound land ownership pattern in achieving a higher level of living for the people of Latin America. If we are serious about participating in a vigorous way in the process of eliminating hunger, we must gain a better understanding of the role of private property in helping to attain this objective in different parts of the world.

Another way in which the Land Grant colleges can make a

significant contribution is by gaining a better understanding of the modifications in trading patterns and basic concepts about distribution which are necessary to resolve the companion problems of hunger and overburdening surpluses.

In the United States and Canada there has been a concerted effort to control production on individual farms through all types of public programs such as acreage allotments, marketing quotas, soil banks and so forth. Despite these efforts, the farmers have persistently increased overall production.

Canada's recent experience with the sale of wheat to China demonstrates very forcefully the impact of a slight modification in the philosophy and techniques of distribution on the overall agricultural situation in the exporting country. The modification has made a profound difference to the freedom of action of the individual Canadian farmer in the use of his property.

This experience demonstrates the importance of defining in broad terms the consumption objective before deciding on the nature of the production controls. It is well known that about two-thirds of the world's people have inadequate diets. Therefore, something is basically wrong with spending huge sums of money to control production without first exploring all possible avenues for moving food into those areas where it is most needed. The United States has had considerable success with some aspects of its Public Law 480 designed to dispose of surplus agricultural commodities in the underdeveloped areas. In the administration of this program some of the producing countries, and particularly the wheat-producing countries, were critical of the United States program for wheat disposal. I think it would be fair to say that Canada was particularly sensitive about some aspects of the United States disposal programs. This was mainly because Canada, like the United States, had a serious surplus problem.

About two years ago almost everyone associated with the wheat industry in Canada was concerned with what they considered an unmanageable surplus of wheat production. The Canadian Wheat Board had a very carefully formulated program of marketing quotas designed to limit the amount of wheat to be marketed by any one farmer. Grain elevators were filled to capacity. Existing storage facilities on farms were taxed to capacity.

About a year ago the Canadian Wheat Board agreed to sell 186 million bushels of wheat to China. This was made possible by some flexibility in credit arrangements. The Chinese have proved to be very meticulous in living up to their contractual obligations, and it is expected that they will continue to do so. The wheat sale, which coincided with a short crop, made it possible for the Canadian Wheat Board to remove marketing quotas, thus enabling farmers to exercise a greater degree of freedom of choice in the use of their land. It also stimulated employment in the transportation industry which has always operated far below capacity in Canada. The act of making this sale transformed the entire wheat economy of Western Canada. It seems to me that this demonstrates the need for new ideas about how the surplus agricultural products of North America can be effectively used to meet the requirements of the rapidly developing nations. It is likely that these sales will continue and that they can be expanded. The extent of the expansion will depend on our ability to devise new trade patterns which will make it possible for the rapidly developing nations to earn dollars to pay for wheat and other agricultural commodities produced in North America.

There is evidence that the Chinese would like to buy more soft wheats. Canada has a shortage of low-quality soft wheats. On the other hand, it is likely that the production of high-protein hard wheat can be increased. France produces an abundance of the kind of soft wheat desired by the Chinese. The French and British consumers prefer hard wheat for rolls and white bread. There might be a possibility of an arrangement whereby the Chinese buy wheat from France and Canada, and the United States increase its exports of hard wheats to Europe. This is just one illustration of the type of modifications in trade patterns which could be of mutual benefit to all concerned. If the United States does not wish to sell wheat to China because of some political philosophy, it might also make sense for the United States to ship wheat to Canada at reasonable prices for resale to China. This is the kind of issue which requires systematic analysis. Certainly the Canadian experience with the wheat sale to China demonstrates the profound effect of such a transaction on the degree of freedom of choice which can be exercised by the Canadian farmer. The public interest in private land is very much a function of the role to be played by North American agriculture in world development.

While we consider these two areas of study important in terms of making the greatest possible contribution toward the attainment of a higher level of living within the world community, we want to emphasize that this kind of work should complement work now underway, rather than be considered a substitute for it. As is well known, many of the scholars from United States Land Grant colleges are actively engaged in assisting people in other countries to learn the techniques for improving productivity. Relatively few are concerned with the institutional arrangements which govern the ownership and control of the natural resources. Even fewer people are concerned with improving the methods of distribution.

In thinking about the nature of the different forms of participation in the development of the underdeveloped nations, we should bear in mind that the overall effort by North Americans is very small.

The contribution of some nations is more insignificant than others. For example, during the period from 1951 to 1960, Canada contributed some 0.7 per cent of the Gross National Product[2] to underdeveloped areas (foreign aid) compared to 1.24 per cent by the United States. Nonmilitary assistance was 0.10 per cent and 0.61 per cent, respectively. In 1960, Canada shows up somewhat better at 0.17 per cent contributed, compared to 0.53 per cent in the United States.[3]

It is noteworthy that contributions, as a per cent of the Gross National Product, have declined in both countries since the 1951–55 period. This drop is due entirely to reductions in military aid. The nonmilitary aid as a proportion of the Gross National Product has remained relatively level in the United States, while in Canada it has increased slightly since 1958. However, when measured as a percentage of the Gross National Product, the Canadian contribution is only about one-third as large as that of the United States.

Neither country has really begun to play a significant role in relation to the problems and possibilities which lie ahead.

In summary, we have tried to focus attention on the progress made by the Land Grant colleges in providing training in agriculture and the industrial arts and to consider the nature of the contribution to be made in the future. We have suggested that it is entirely realistic to assume that within the next fifty to one hundred years it will be possible to create a world situation in which every man, woman, and child has adequate food, clothing, and shelter. To attain this objective we must be committed to it. Having accepted this as an objective of public policy, the Land Grant colleges have a significant contribution to make in helping attain it. Two areas of study have been discussed which require more attention than they have received heretofore. First, there is a need to gain a clearer understanding of the role of property rights in economic development. Second, we need a clearer understanding of how to modify the institutional arrangements which inhibit distribution of the rewards of our improved technology.

In conclusion, I would again like to quote from Chester Bowles who asks,[3]

> Can we, now the richest people on earth, become creative participants in the unprecedented revolutionary changes of our era, changes that most privileged people will oppose tooth and nail, but which for the bulk of mankind offer the hopeful prospect of a little more food, a little more opportunity, a doctor for their sick child, and a sense of personal dignity?

Chester Bowles answers his own question in the affirmative, and I believe he speaks for all of us, when he says,

> I believe we can draw lessons from our own experience that may play a decisive role in the building of prosperous, peaceful and dignified rural societies in Asia, Africa and Latin America.

## NOTES

1. *Department of State for the Press*, No. 332, May 24, 1962.

2. *Canada Year Book*, 1952–53 to 1961. Commercial Letter; Canadian Imperial Bank of Commerce, September, 1961.

3. *Statistical Abstract of the United States*, 1956, 1958 and 1961. United States Department of Commerce; Bureau of the Census.

MARION CLAWSON

# Public and Private Interest
# in Public Land

AN EXTENSIVE PUBLIC OWNERSHIP of land has characterized the American culture since the earliest Colonial days. More than three-fourths the total national area has been in public ownership at one time or another; more than one-third still is publicly owned. The largest part of the federal lands are in the eleven western states and in Alaska. Half of the eleven western states is federally owned; nearly all of Alaska is publicly owned, with the overwhelming part still in federal ownership. But there are some federal, state, and local government public lands in every state, and in nearly every major part of each state. Although the largest part of the publicly owned land is forest or grazing land, highways, streets, parks, and land around public buildings are a form of public land ownership which reaches directly into our larger cities.

Perhaps private enterprise plays a larger role in the United States than in any other country; certainly large segments of our population continuously emphasize the role of private enterprise. The possible conflict between heavy endorsement of private activity and a large public land ownership has, in general, not materialized. There have been, and are, critics of public land ownership; but political support for public land ownership has prevailed to the extent that large areas have continued in or been added to public ownership. The explanation lies largely in the fact that the publicly owned lands have been used by individuals and corporations for private activity. Timber, forage, minerals, and other resources on public lands are typically exploited by private enterprise. Individuals use public lands for private purposes. The opportunity to use public lands, usually under rather carefully defined conditions and restrictions, has greatly mollified the possible criticisms that would have arisen had the economic development of these resources been undertaken by government corporations or bureaus.

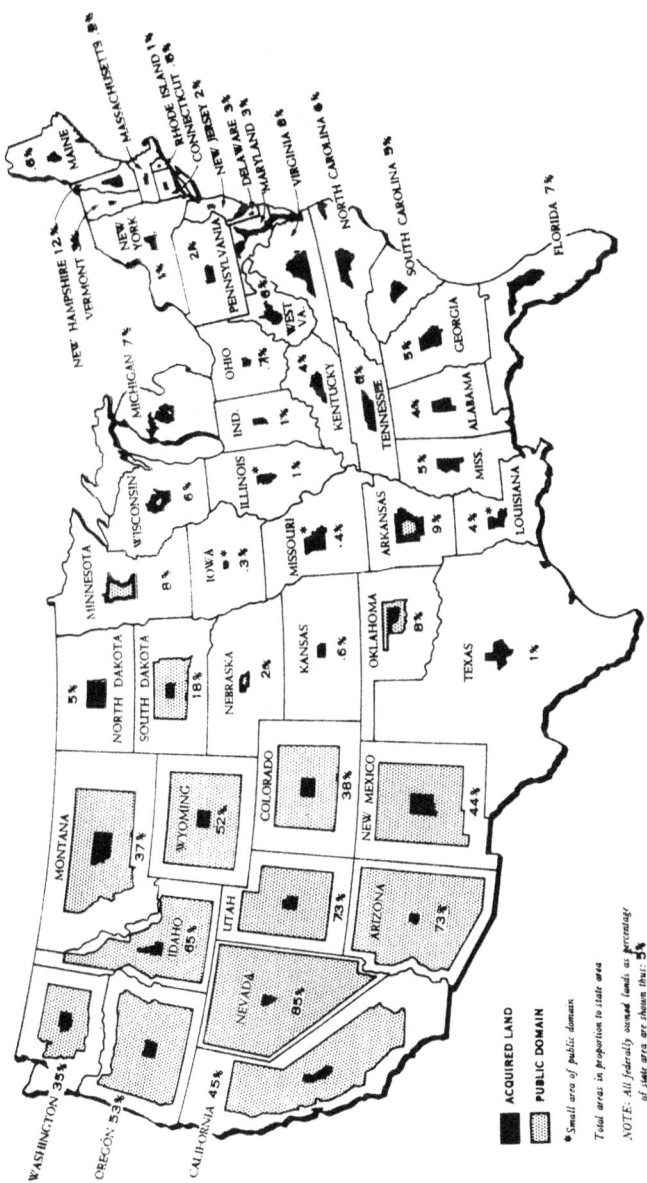

# PRESENT FEDERALLY OWNED LANDS

FIG. 14.1

Source: The Federal Lands

WASHINGTON 35%
OREGON 53%
CALIFORNIA 45%
MONTANA 37%
IDAHO 65%
NEVADA 85%
UTAH 73%
ARIZONA 73%
WYOMING 52%
COLORADO 38%
NEW MEXICO 44%
NORTH DAKOTA 5%
SOUTH DAKOTA 18%
NEBRASKA 2%
KANSAS .6%
OKLAHOMA 8%
TEXAS 1%
MINNESOTA 8%
IOWA .3%
MISSOURI .4%
ARKANSAS 9%
LOUISIANA 4%
WISCONSIN 6%
ILLINOIS 1%
MICHIGAN 7%
INDIANA 1%
OHIO 7%
KENTUCKY 6%
TENNESSEE 5%
MISS. 5%
ALABAMA 4%
GEORGIA 5%
FLORIDA 7%
SOUTH CAROLINA 5%
NORTH CAROLINA 6%
VIRGINIA 6%
WEST VA. 6%
PENNSYLVANIA 2%
NEW YORK 1%
VERMONT 2%
NEW HAMPSHIRE 12%
MAINE 6%
MASSACHUSETTS 9%
RHODE ISLAND 1%
CONNECTICUT 6%
NEW JERSEY 2%
DELAWARE 3%
MARYLAND 3%

ACQUIRED LAND

PUBLIC DOMAIN

*Small area of public domain.

Total area: in proportion to state area

NOTE: All federally owned lands as percentage of state area are shown thus: 5%

351

Most other countries of the world have public lands—some, very extensive areas. This is true of highly developed European countries, where forests, marshes, moors, and parks are often publicly owned, as well as streets and other heavily used public areas. It is also true of most Latin American countries, where extensive areas of high mountains, deserts, and jungle are publicly owned. In this discussion, we cannot get into the problems of public land ownership and management in countries other than the United States. Some of those problems are peculiar to each country, but many are similar to those found in the United States.

## A BRIEF LOOK AT FEDERAL LAND HISTORY

Federal land history in the United States falls into five major eras: acquisition, disposal, reservation, custodial management, and intensive management.

The new nation actually began to acquire lands before the Constitution was adopted. The new states—formerly Colonies— ceded much of their land to the new national government. This is the land east of the Mississippi but west of the Atlantic coastal states, for the most part. The first great further acquisition was the Louisiana Purchase, which included the whole present state of Nebraska as well as many millions of acres in this general region. As a result of our war with Mexico, we acquired the Southwest; and by treaty with Great Britain our claims to the Pacific Northwest were confirmed. Other smaller acquisitions rounded out the area of the contiguous forty-eight states. In 1867, we bought Alaska from Russia, completing the major acquisitions of public land.

Disposal of federal land began immediately, but for many years was at a relatively slow rate, partly because the new states themselves still had substantial areas of land for disposal on relatively favorable terms. Although disposal continued, the areas acquired overshadowed those disposed of, so that the total area within the forty-eight contiguous states rose until about 1850. The area of federal land in these states declined continuously from that high point until about 1930, since which date the area has about leveled off. With the addition of Alaska, the net area in federal ownership rose again in 1867, to a new peak; after that date, the line of net area including Alaska continued to fall. Disposition was by several means: cash sales, grants to states, grants to railroads and other transportation companies, homesteads for settlers, and others.

Concern over the headlong, heedless disposal of land, over the unproductive condition in which natural forestlands were left after cutting, and concern over the extensive tenancy that developed on farmlands, all led to a demand that some of the federal land remain in public ownership. Yellowstone National Park in 1872 was the first major land reservation, although there had been several smaller ones previously. The idea of major, permanent federal reservations dates from 1891 when the first forest reserves were established. Reservation as a major process in the forty-eight contiguous states came to an end with the passage of the Taylor Grazing Act in 1934, which withdrew the remaining public domain from disposal except as it was classified and made available for disposition. Outside Alaska, all federal lands today may be considered as reserved for continued public use, although some further disposals will take place. The legal situation in Alaska is not so clear-cut, yet it seems probably that most federal lands there will remain in federal ownership, except for those extensive areas required to be turned over to the new state as it requests them.

Custodial management of the reserved federal lands began at once, though on a very low level for many years. Forest fires were put out, if possible, and trespass prevented. Gradually, more intensive methods of management developed. Timber was sold, on open public bid and under carefully specified conditions of cutting. Grazing was permitted under license or permit which specified numbers of livestock, length of season, and other management practices. Recreation was allowed from the beginning, and picnic areas and campgrounds were developed as the need arose. Timber, grazing, and other surveys provided the administrator with information about the land he was responsible for. Gradually, management became more intensive in numerous ways. It is impossible to give a date which marks clearly the transition from custodial to intensive management. We chose 1950 as marking the change; in that year, for the first time, cash

354 CONTROL OF LAND RESOURCES

receipts from all federal lands equalled total appropriations for their management and improvement. This is at least one measure of intensity of management.

A few general comments should be made at this point about federal land management during this long period:

*First,* the early federal land ownership was involuntary, in the sense that the national government did not want to own land but did so only until it could be disposed of.

*Second,* throughout most of the nineteenth century, the disposal ideology was dominant, and it continued powerful into the first two or three decades of the twentieth century. Many disposal measures were supported or tolerated which now seem to us obviously unwise, but they did not seem so when it was believed that all public land would eventually be in privately owned farms.

*Third,* the idea of permanent federal ownership of certain types of land was accepted only slowly and reluctantly.

*Fourth,* today however, there is a strong public conviction in favor of continued federal ownership of parts, forests, and grazing districts. Disposal on a large scale is no longer a real political alternative, in the opinion of this writer.

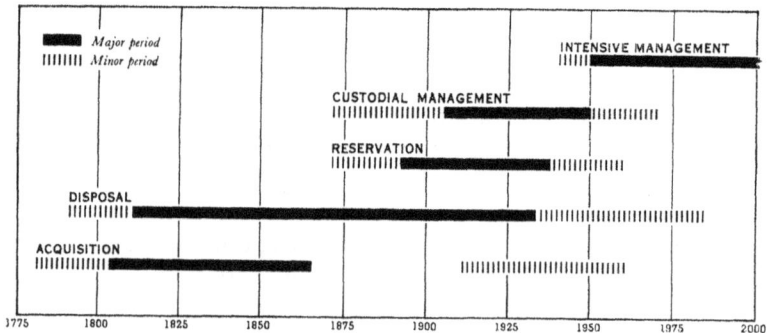

MAJOR ERAS IN FEDERAL LANDOWNERSHIP AND LAND MANAGEMENT IN THE UNITED STATES, 1800-2000

Source: *The Federal Lands*

FIG. 14.2

## BRIEF REVIEW OF OTHER PUBLIC LAND HISTORY

Although most public land in the United States is owned by the federal government, significant amounts of land are owned by other units of government.

The original states along the Atlantic coast acquired land during their early history, some of which has been retained throughout. More commonly, however, these states today own land that they have bought in more recent times for parks and forests. All of the states created out of the public domain received substantial grants from the federal government. These grants took different forms: some were place grants, such as the grants for common schools, of one, two, or four sections out of the thirty-six sections in each township; some were quantity grants, for so many thousands of acres for, say, an agricultural college, school of mines, or for an insane hospital; some were type-of-land

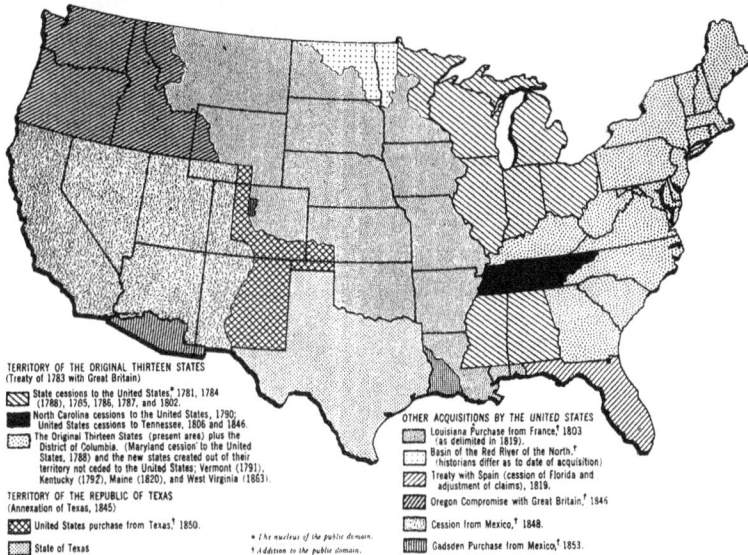

TERRITORY OF THE ORIGINAL THIRTEEN STATES
(Treaty of 1783 with Great Britain)

State cessions to the United States,* 1781, 1784 (1788), 1785, 1786, 1787, and 1802.

North Carolina cessions to the United States, 1790; United States cessions to Tennessee, 1806 and 1846.

The Original Thirteen States (present area) plus the District of Columbia. (Maryland cession to the United States, 1788) and the new states created out of their territory not ceded to the United States; Vermont (1791), Kentucky (1792), Maine (1820), and West Virginia (1863).

TERRITORY OF THE REPUBLIC OF TEXAS
(Annexation of Texas, 1845)

United States purchase from Texas,† 1850.

State of Texas

* The nucleus of the public domain.
† Addition to the public domain.

OTHER ACQUISITIONS BY THE UNITED STATES

Louisiana Purchase from France,† 1803 (as delimited in 1819).

Basin of the Red River of the North.† (historians differ as to date of acquisition)

Treaty with Spain (cession of Florida and adjustment of claims), 1819.

Oregon Compromise with Great Britain,† 1846

Cession from Mexico,† 1848.

Gadsden Purchase from Mexico,† 1853.

**ACQUISITION OF THE TERRITORY OF THE UNITED STATES AND ORIGIN OF THE PUBLIC DOMAIN, 48 CONTIGUOUS STATES**

Source: U.S. Department of the Interior, Bureau of Land Management.

FIG. 14.3

grants, such as swamps and overflow land. The total area granted to states within the forty-eight contiguous states has been 225 million acres, or 12 per cent of their area. Alaska has been a special case; it has been given a grant nearly one-third its total area, most of which has not yet been selected. Texas is another special case; as an independent republic before it joined the Union, it owned all its lands, and never surrendered them to the United States.

The states, like the federal government, at first looked upon grant lands as a source of revenue. Most states have disposed of most or all their original grant lands. State land ownership, in states receiving grants, is only about a third of the area which they were granted. Most states, for a long time, gave their lands only the most casual management. In recent years, state land administration has improved. Many states now manage forest, grazing, and mineral lands with reasonable efficiency and regard for future productivity. However, most persons familiar with both state and federal land administration will agree that state land management has lagged badly.

States have also acquired land for many purposes. One particular purpose of state land acquisition has been for parks. Although the area of state parks is small relative to the total land area of the nation, yet such lands are often highly important in the lives of its citizens. States have also acquired land for forestry and other extensive purposes. States have also acquired limited areas of highly strategic lands—the major highways of the nation. In many instances, individual landowners donated land for road rights of way, feeling that a public road so enhanced the value of their land as to far more than offset the value of the donated land. While these roads were usually narrow and unimproved at first, over the decades they have often developed into major highways. Title to the right of way has often been transferred to the states, as state and federal money (funneled through state organizations) has been used to improve the roads. Where new major highways have followed different routes than the old roads, the states have had to buy the necessary land from private landowners.

Counties also own land in the United States. Most of this

today consists of land the counties purchased for special uses, such as parks, roads, schools, and the like. Counties acquire a kind of title to land when they seize private land on which taxes have not been paid. Although such land can be sold to other individuals, the titles so acquired are imperfect in many states. It had always been assumed that this type of county land ownership was temporary, a mere stage between one private individual who would not or could not pay his taxes and another private individual who would and could pay them. During the great Depression, tax delinquency assumed very large proportions, and the counties of the nation at one time owned 10 million acres or more land. However, most of this has now gone back to private ownership. A few counties own forestland for continued management.

Cities also own land. While the acreages are small compared with state-owned areas, and even more so as compared with federal land areas, the values are relatively high. City-owned land has almost without exception been purchased from individual owners and is held for special-purpose uses. City parks include less than a million acres of land, but are highly important in the total recreation picture. School areas, other public building sites, and various special uses are also typically publicly owned. Most important are the streets and alleys, which, in a typical American city, occupy about 30 per cent of the urban used area. These are publicly owned. The city spends large sums of money on them and has control over their use.

In large part because of the history of selective land disposal in the United States, most types of public land are not large solid blocks, but are interspersed to varying degree with private land. The smaller the public land area and the more intensively it is used, the more likely all of the land within the exterior boundaries will be publicly owned. Conversely, the larger the area and the later it was reserved for permanent public ownership, the more likely the publicly owned lands are to be intermingled with private lands. Few city parks have enclaves of private land; state parks sometimes have a little yet are typically wholly public. About 4 per cent of the area within national park boundaries is privately owned; about 25 per cent within national forest

boundaries; and about 40 per cent within grazing district boundaries. Moreover, the privately owned land in these types of federal holdings does not typically lie in large solid blocks, but tends
to consist of many relatively smaller tracts scattered widely. Many
observers of this situation have concluded that what is needed is
a system of land exchanges to block up public and private holdings. They overlook the fact that most private owners get substantial advantages in use of public lands by reason of their scattered location.

Partly because of this land ownership history, the various
governmental agencies and levels of government do not own
physically distinct types of land. That is, forested land is owned
by several federal agencies, by states, and even in local parks
and forests. Within a given natural region or district, there is
often little or no correlation between type of land and managing
agency. With very few exceptions, government in the United
States does not own cropland. That is about the only physical
type of land not publicly owned, and about the only major type
of land use not carried out on public land.

## WHY PERMANENT PUBLIC LAND OWNERSHIP?

We have noted the widespread public support for continued
public ownership of certain types of land in the United States.
Within the confines of this paper, it is not feasible to provide
evidence supporting this statement; the reader is asked to accept
the author's judgment that such evidence does exist and that this
is in fact the situation. It is worthwhile, however, to explore
briefly how this attitude came about and why it is strongly
held today.

Almost no one would argue against public ownership of
streets, alleys, roads, and highways—we long ago abandoned the
idea of toll roads. So has every other advanced nation in the
world. Likewise, no one would argue against public ownership
of the land occupied by public schools, other public buildings,
and various public functions. Divergences of opinion might arise
over parks, although most people would agree that some of these
at least should be public; but differences are particularly likely
to exist about forest and grazing lands. Some of the latter are

indeed privately owned, yet, in fact, a significant proportion of each is publicly owned and seems certain to remain so. Why?

The dominant reason for strong public support for large-scale public ownership of forest, grazing, and other relatively "wild" lands is the widespread conviction that these lands will be more efficiently managed, more conservatively managed, if publicly than if privately owned. This conviction grows out of the early history of land use in the United States. The private forest owner, and even more the timber harvester trespassing on the public land, cut the virgin timber he found without regard for its reproduction and replacement. Fires were allowed to burn uncontrolled; no provisions were made for seed trees, nor was young unmerchantable growth protected from logging damage. If the land were shortly to be cleared for farming, as many believed, then there was no point whatever in forest protection. The rancher using public grazing land typically over-used it, often knowing that if he did not, some one else would, for he lacked power to control its use.

Concern over abuses of land use was at first expressed by a few leaders, beginning mostly in the third quarter of the nineteenth century. But they persuaded others of the dangers of exploitation of natural resources with little apparent concern for the future. The various federal land reservations were the concrete outgrowth of this concern. The success of the federal agencies in managing lands and their resources have materially strengthened this belief in the wisdom of public land ownership. The Forest Service, for example, has built an international reputation for integrity, competence, and dedication to the public interest.

Many people may argue that this common public attitude is not wholly in accord with the facts or that it rests upon a false interpretation of history. Defenders of private forestry and of private grazing land use will argue that well-managed private lands today are as conservatively used as are public lands. The impartial student of land use will note that many, if not all, types of land use have undergone material changes over the past decades. For instance, the larger private forest land holdings are now managed about as well, on the average, as are the federal forest-lands. Although no comprehensive studies have been made recently, it is altogether possible that the same is true for grazing lands.

Regardless of the facts of land use today, few would deny that there is strong public support for public ownership of certain types of land. In my judgment, there is little to be gained from considering the relative merits of public and private ownership of land of these types, for it is most unlikely that there will be a major change in the relative proportions of each.

Perhaps a stronger, if less widely expressed, current reason for continued public land ownership lies in the multiple-use possibilities of public land. Much public land has forestry, grazing, recreation, and other on-site use potential, and nearly all has watershed values that may be rather large. It is possible that all these values will be given reasonable consideration in private

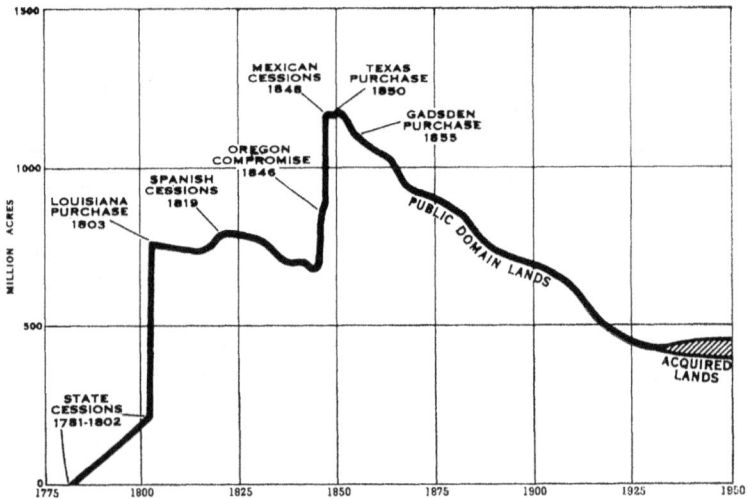

APPROXIMATE AREA OF FEDERAL LANDS IN THE UNITED STATES, 1781-1950, WITH DATES OF IMPORTANT ACQUISITIONS

Source: U.S. Department of the Interior, Bureau of Land Management

FIG. 14.4

ownership, yet it is unlikely that they will. The man who owns land for grazing is less likely to consider its recreational values than the public land manager; and similarly for each other combination of land uses. Moreover, the private landowner can find no way to capture the benefits of improved watershed conditions, which benefit people far lower down. Granted that multiple-use management has been the subject of much sentimental nonsense, yet there remains a lot of substance in this point.

## USE CATEGORIES ON PUBLIC LANDS

The number of persons who use the public lands is large, and their uses are varied. At the risk of some over-simplification, these uses can be grouped into three broad classes: commercial, noncommercial on-site, and noncommercial off-site.

The chief commercial uses of public lands are forest harvest, grazing, mineral exploitation, and occupancy under lease or permit. About one-fourth the sawtimber harvested in the United States comes from federal lands. This volume is especially large in the West. Many sawmills there are heavily dependent upon federal timber. The federal forests contain a disproportionately large part of the old mature timber of the nation, and increasingly occupy a larger place as a supplier of certain grades of timber. Their role in supply of pulpwood is smaller, but still important. The federal lands provide some forage to approximately a seventh of the nation's roughage-consuming livestock. Their role is much larger in the West, where they supply some forage to over half of the total. While the federal lands often provide only a small part of the total forage for these animals, yet that part may be critical seasonally. Drastic changes in the western range livestock industry would be required if the federal grazing were no longer available. About 5 per cent of the oil and gas of the nation comes from federal lands. Modest amounts of other minerals are taken from them also. Many thousands of businesses or homes are located on federal land, under lease.

The motivation for these uses of federal land is the prospect of private profit. Those obtaining such resources pay for them; in the case of timber and the leasable minerals, the rate of pay is about the same as for private lands. Grazing is obtained at a rate below that on private land, yet significant fees are paid. The number of persons directly involved in this type of federal land use is relatively small, even in the regions where federal lands predominate. The total revenue raised from these activities on federal lands is not small, however—something of the magnitude of $300 million annually in recent years.

The chief noncommercial on-site use is outdoor recreation. For this use, the motivation is personal enjoyment, not financial gain. "Noncommercial" does not in the least imply "less highly regarded"—as any public land manager who has had conflicts between sportsmen groups and livestock interests, or any other pair of conflicting interests, can testify. In the threefold grouping of recreation areas into user-oriented, intermediate, and resource-based, which I have used extensively elsewhere, the federal lands provide the chief publicly owned resource-based areas. As such, they include some of the most outstanding areas of the United States. One can easily think of Yellowstone, Grand Canyon, Yosemite, and other noted national parks, as well as extensive areas of national forest almost equally attractive to the connoisseur of outdoor areas. These areas have been in high demand as vacation areas, and their use for this purpose will almost certainly rise steadily in the future.

Recreation is a major activity of lands owned by government at all levels. It is often the chief or sole use of many areas, especially parks. The total number of visits, or admissions, to all kinds of publicly owned recreation areas exceeds the total number of people in the nation by several times. The average citizen obtains at least six days (or part thereof, where the typical visit is less than a day in length) recreation on public land annually. Although precise data are lacking, the best indications are that about half of the entire populace actually uses such areas. The other half does not wish to partake of outdoor recreation, or is physically or financially unable to do so, or has no ready opportunity for such enjoyment. Recreation is now the use of public lands which touches the largest proportion of the population (except for public transportation routes and perhaps for schools), and it is likely further to extend its leadership in this regard in the future.

The chief noncommercial off-site use of public lands is as watershed. All land is watershed, in some degree. The mountainous federal lands are especially important sources of water in the West, and to a lesser extent in the East as well. Some of the grazing lands are heavy contributors of sediment although their water yield is often low. It is extremely difficult to measure the contribution of good resource management to stream flow, either of quantity or of quality. Many extravagant statements about the role of forests have been made in the past, for instance. Foresters, range managers, and other land administrators have usually sought to keep the water running off their lands clear and free of sediment. Only in recent years has it seemed possible to influence water yield significantly by manipulation of vegetation. The value of the water arising from federal lands has almost surely risen, but it is impossible to say to what extent the management of these lands has contributed to or subtracted from the value changes that a developing economy brought.

Watershed is a use of land which affects significant numbers of people, perhaps vitally—although, as we have noted, we cannot be sure to what degree. But, even if one concedes that a western city dweller is deeply dependent upon federal land management for his water supply, yet in many cases the person involved would have little realization of the physical, economic, and governmental relations involved.

Possibly one other important noncommercial off-site benefit from public lands should be mentioned, although it defies precise measurement or perhaps even precise definition. Many of us have a sense of well-being from knowing that certain things exist, although we personally may enjoy them little or not at all. To this author, big-league baseball, art galleries, and opera fall in this category; if others were no more active in their support than he, they would fail. Yet he regards them as desirable attributes of the city in which he lives. The same may be true of some public land. There seems to be widespread public support for wilderness areas, for instance; yet many supporters could not define such areas and never have used them or expect to use them. The same may well be true of many wildlife refuges—note the national interest in the whooping cranes, mostly by people who never have or never will see one. Many of us will defend a national park against some threat, real or imagined, although we may never see the area itself. It could well be argued that the nation is richer for some of its public landownership, merely because of this rather general public attitude.

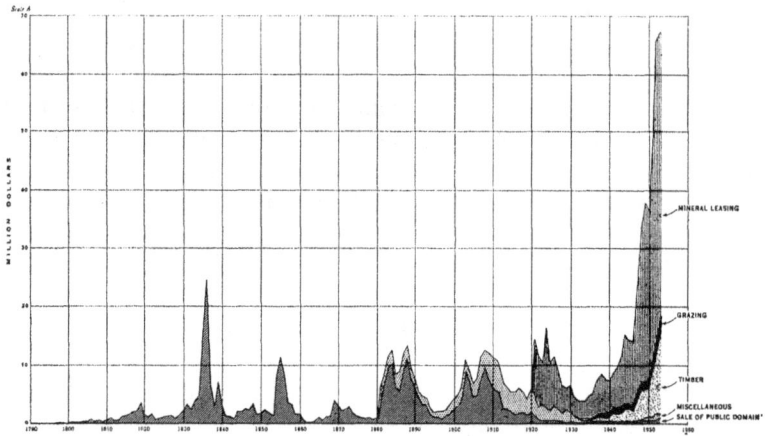

RECEIPTS FROM SALE AND LEASE OF PUBLIC DOMAIN, REVESTED AND ACQUIRED LANDS AND THEIR PRODUCTS, 1796-1952. Excludes some receipts prior to 1881, notably fees, commissions, and the sale of Indian lands—items that make up the miscellaneous category from 1881.

Source: *The Federal Lands*

FIG. 14.5

## PRIVATE DEMANDS AFFECT PUBLIC LAND ADMINISTRATION

The most important single determinant of public land administration is the nature and volume of the demands by private individuals for the land, its separable resources and its uses. The actions of the public speak far louder than do any words its members may utter.

If the demand for resources and services of public lands is low, then management of such lands will almost surely be extensive. The emphasis will be largely upon protection from fire and from trespass. Such uses as are requested can often or usually be granted, with only infrequent interference with other proposed uses of the same land. The administrator is not forced to choose among potential uses and between would-be users. Under these circumstances, multiple use is likely to be more a slogan than an operating program, because all the desired uses can be granted without modification of others. Because the level of demand is low, the administrator is likely not to be exposed to much political pressure. But, on the other hand, when political pressure does arise, there is likely not to be any countervailing pressure from other segments of the public. The administrator is forced to oppose such political pressures largely unaided.

There are many variants of the above, but it represents in general the situation on federal lands some decades ago; it has been more or less typical of some other public lands at earlier times.

At present, when the demand for uses and resources of public lands is often relatively high, the resulting management is quite different. The public land manager is forced to employ intensive management practices, so far as available funds will permit; and the situation enables him to make a good case for larger appropriations each year. While protection continues important, now he must give more attention to serving the needs of the land users. Roads must be built, campgrounds and other recreation areas provided, detailed management surveys made, timber sold, and scores of other important actions taken. Because demand is relatively heavy, the land manager can no longer grant almost everything the public requests; what one person or group wants would preclude what another person or group wants. The land manager is forced to pick and choose among uses and among users; some of this, such as timber sales, can be accomplished through competitive bidding, where the rival claimants battle it out. But often the land manager must make choices on other grounds, among dissimilar uses, where law or custom has foreclosed the use of competitive bidding as a means of choice.

Under conditions of heavy demand for public land uses and resources, the land manager is likely to be exposed to many political pressures. Groups denied some use, or threatened with loss of use they consider reasonable, are likely to take their case to their elected political representative, or to the land manager directly, with intervention by political representatives in the background. On the other hand, under these circumstances of heavy demand for public land, it is highly probable that there will be countervailing political pressures from other user groups. The recreation group asking or demanding retention or reservation of an area as wilderness is likely to be faced with lumber, mining, and other interests arguing the opposite side of the issue. And so on, for almost any use conflicts one can imagine. Multiple-use management now becomes vastly more difficult; it may also become much more important.

## THE NATURE OF POLITICAL PRESSURES ON PUBLIC LAND MANAGEMENT

The nature of political pressures exerted by user groups on public land managers and on the governmental structure generally is closely related to the nature of the use itself. Let us look briefly at the kinds of pressures exerted by the three major user groups described above.

The various commercial user groups exert their political pressures in their own ways. Such groups are generally small in numbers. On the other hand, they have a direct financial interest in the public land management. They can afford to devote time and energy to the task of trying to influence public management in their directions. They can afford to keep constant attention and pressure on critical spots in the whole legislative-appropriation-administrative process. They can often be highly effective at this, because they make it their business to be well-informed. When there is a Congressional hearing, or when an administrator is formulating a decision, they can often argue cogently for their viewpoint, sometimes bringing new facts to bear. They know what actions are possible, what factors are likely to be influential in decisions, and how to influence action. They make up in skill and alertness what they lack in massive political strength. Many groups in this general class have their representatives in the national capital or in state capitals, to carry out this type of activity more skillfully and more constantly than intermittent representatives can do.

The noncommercial user groups, both on-site and off-site,

operate in their own ways also. These groups involve far larger numbers of people than do the commercial users; hence their potential political strength is great. But their individual monetary gains or advantages are often small or hard to identify; it is hard to appeal to individual members of such groups in terms of their direct economic advantage. Groups of such users often find it hard to enlist people and to obtain funds. Partly as a result, they find it hard also to observe the whole governmental process closely, and to know when and how to be most effective. When a major issue arises that can be dramatized, such groups have great political strength. They thrive on crises and slogans. Between times, they often seem to sleep. They have massive political strength which they often do not seem to know how to use effectively.

Beyond the noncommercial users is a still larger group, that general public about which we so often hear and yet which is so hard to define and locate. These people have no interest in public lands beyond that which they have in good government generally. They have little knowledge of the public lands or of political issues involving them. On the other hand, a substantial segment of the general public resents private exploitation of public resources or of public programs, when this is called to their attention. This broader general public can only rarely be aroused to political action on public land matters. The issue must be made to appear simple and must be dramatized, if this general public is to respond. If some issue is dramatized in this way—perhaps wrongly—the larger general public can often be irresistible politically. It is likely to be aroused, if at all, by groups representing the noncommercial users. However, sometimes particular commercial interest groups can enlist general public support—witness the submerged lands (mistakenly called tidelands), where private oil interests convinced a large segment of the general public of the merit of their position.

## THE ROLE OF THE PROFESSIONAL LAND MANAGER

The professional land manager is coming to play a major if not decisive role in the management of public lands of all kinds.

There are several reasons why this should be so, and some significant consequences of it.

As the intensity of public land use increases, and as the intensity of management of such lands rises in response thereto, the need for professional expertize in public land management becomes greater. Protection of forests against fire or of grazing lands against livestock trespass were important in their day, and required honest conscientious public servants. But they did not call for much training or for high degree of professional competence. Management of public land for timber harvest, for grazing, for recreation, and for all other uses today does require a great deal of knowledge and professional skill. Existing timber stands must be measured, their growth rates estimated, timber sales laid out for profitable operation of the private buyer (and hence for the best realizable prices for the public agency), and numerous intensive forest management practices followed to assure healthy forest stands and reasonable growth rates. Whereas any normal person could detect the existence of a forest fire, it takes a trained forester to ascertain the existence of a tree disease or an insect infestation, and to know what to do about it. Similar examples could be given for each of the other major uses of public land.

Another factor in the need for expert knowledge on the part of professional public land managers is the rising level of knowledge on the part of public land users. I have heard livestock men in recent years discuss grazing management of federal lands in exactly the same professional terms as used by the representatives of the federal agencies with whom they deal. Many recreationists on public land are well informed on various aspects of resource use and management. (Many are not, of course.) Moreover, especially with recreationists, users of public land in one region or state are often familiar with management of similar land in other regions or states, and are not hesitant to point out to professional land managers how certain problems have been handled elsewhere. The uninformed public land manager is increasingly at a disadvantage.

In all federal agencies and in many state and local government agencies administering public lands, the position of the professionally trained land manager is becoming increasingly entrenched and strengthened. In such instances, some minimum degree of formal professional training, usually in college, is required for employment and for advancement. Increasing attention is directed to in-service training of the men selected by each agency. Higher positions within each agency tend increasingly to be filled by promotion from within the ranks of the agency, or at least by transfer from some other agency with equally high professional standards. Top positions in various agencies are and always will be filled with an eye to the political acceptability of the man, even if he comes from within the ranks of the agency itself. But, even here, minimum professional competence and experience is becoming increasingly insisted upon. The day when just any friend of the Senator could get a good public land management job—and quite possibly do passably well at it—has passed. This increasing professionalization of public land management has, in part, taken the form of the protection of civil service personnel policies and actions, but it goes much deeper than the mere form of such actions.

Under these circumstances, the nature of the professional training of the professional land managers becomes highly important. In general, their training is likely to be in forestry or in range or wildlife management, or less commonly in some other physical science. The men so trained acquire a respect for science and for rational thought, which are major helps in doing their jobs and in adapting to new knowledge as it becomes available. The university schools in which they acquire this training usually inculcate in them a spirit of public service also. Men entering the field of public land management realize they cannot expect riches or high financial rewards, but they often realize well the opportunities they have for public service. By and large, the men trained in these ways lack much or any training in the social sciences, such as history, philosophy, economics, sociology, anthropology, and the like. Forestry schools are coming increasingly to urge or require a few basic courses in some of these fields, notably economics, from their students. In the past, however, and to a considerable extent now, such training is either not given or is minimal. It should be added that in the past its need may not have been too great; today, however, as the intensity of public land management rises and hence the need exists to make difficult choice decisions which often involve economic and social comparisons of one use with another, the need for this type of training is much greater. We can expect that it will become still more important in the future.

As a result of the growing demands for use of public lands for many purposes, professional public land managers come increasingly, either deliberately or unconsciously, to play one interest group against another. The forester who might like to make a timber sale which a private timber harvester wants, must realize that the area has important recreational values and that the recreation groups will be vocal in their criticisms if their interests are not protected. Similar examples could be cited for almost every other pair of uses of the public land. Moreover, such examples arise within what are ordinarily thought of as single uses; for instance, conflicts between speedboaters and fishermen, or between small private timber harvesters and large ones. As the volume and variety of demands on public land rise, it is inevitable that the public land manager will be exposed to a multiplicity and increased intensity of pressures from private groups. One major result of these increasing pressures from all sides, or from almost all sides, is to increase greatly the scope within which the land manager can exercise his own judgment. If he were exposed to only mild pressures but in a single direction, as often was true when use intensity was much lower in the past, he would find it difficult to resist that single pressure. But when he is exposed to a multiplicity of pressures and all the would-be users of the public land know this to be true, he must and may seek a decision which to him seems most defensible in light of the physical characteristics of the resources and of the demands for them. But this often leads the professional land manager into fields where his basic training, especially if it included no social sciences, has not equipped him to deal. He must weigh one use against another, often lacking the skill for determining the economic and social values involved in alternative resource uses.

## ECONOMIC ANALYSIS AS APPLIED TO
## PUBLIC LAND MANAGEMENT

Public land management involves substantial economic operations. Total annual revenues and total expenditures from all public lands in the United States are each well over $300 million annually. These are significant sums, even for the United States today. Many aspects of public land management produce revenue; timber sales and mineral leases are the two chief sources. Under these circumstances, one might expect economic analysis to serve as one guide to public land management. It is true that profits are not the major motive for most public land management; yet many activities—of which timber stand improvement is a good example—are undertaken because they "pay." For many such activities, comparative costs and returns are highly important criteria; even where financial returns are not large, economic tests of efficiency of operations are important.

For a number of reasons, economic analysis has not been a major factor in public land management in the past. During earlier decades, so far as federal lands are concerned, their assumed temporary status—pending their disposal to private ownership—was undoubtedly a major factor inhibiting economic planning. If land were going to be disposed of in a few years, there was little sense in any management program for it. The low level of use of federal and state lands up to perhaps thirty years ago was another major factor inhibiting economic analysis for land management. Even the minimum custodial management often cost more than any possible revenues; growth of mature forests was low or nonexistent; the lands were being protected for future date, one which was rather indefinite, for uses not clearly foreseen. Under these circumstances, it would have been hard to calculate the optimum level of management, even had there been a disposition to do so.

The fact that many of the outputs from public land are noncommercial also makes economic analysis difficult. Outdoor recreation enjoyed by millions of visitors obviously is valuable, yet the absence or low level of an entrance fee means little cash income. Water flowing from public lands also has high value, but it is very difficult to know how much to attribute to water-shed management as such. An equally important factor has been that governmental expenditures generally are not subjected to economic analysis. We have treated expenditures for resource management about as we have treated expenditures for general governmental services—necessary, perhaps inevitable, but a drain on the economy rather than a support to it. At no step in the typical budget process are marginal revenues confronted with marginal costs.

To an economist and former public land administrator (as this writer is), it appears that economic analysis could contribute significantly to two major types of managerial decisions regarding public lands. One concerns the allocation of the public land resources between competing demands or uses; the other concerns the appropriate level of intensity of public land management.

When a public land manager is confronted with competing demands for public land use, he can sometimes reduce the degree of direct competition by appropriate management devices, and thus to some extent allow each applicant to have what he wants. This is the essence of skillful multiple-use management. But a degree of conflict sometimes remains after any reconciliation of demands. When this occurs, the land manager nearly always is concerned with which use is the more "important." To an economist, there is no better measure of importance than comparative income. As we have noted, this is not easy to estimate in those cases where the services of the land are typically not priced but are rather given away. But it should be possible to devise methods of estimating the value of such resources; I have suggested methods whereby this might be done. A public land manager, or his superiors in the executive branch, or the legislature, might be unwilling to accept comparative economic returns as the sole guide to public land management. But surely comparative returns do provide one important measure; and when another course than the most profitable is followed, comparative returns show how much this costs.

We have noted that increased demands for public land make more intensive land management rational. This is true for private lands as well, of course, as the same demand factors apply there also. Technicians interested in public lands usually know a number of measures for increasing output from a given area of public land. But to what degree do the possible measures "pay"? This involves a balancing of costs against revenue, in a manner not usually undertaken for public activities. But it is particularly appropriate to some kinds of public management activities. How far does it pay to build forest access roads, in order to make timber sales, to fight fires more efficiently, to detect insect and disease infestations and either combat them or remove the damaged trees, and for other purposes? To what standards should the roads be built? How intensively should campground areas be developed, to meet the projected demand? A host of specific management questions arise, on which economic costs and returns for different levels of management would be significant.

It seems highly probable that economic analysis will play a larger role in public land management in the future than it has in the past. The increased demands for use of such lands will provide a powerful argument for more intensive management of such lands; this will require larger appropriations. The economic wisdom of specific management methods and uses is more likely to be challenged in the future than in the past. If economic analysis is to play a larger role, then it must be made more directly applicable to the problems; and it must be matched by improved appropriation and expenditure processes which can utilize the results of better economic analysis.

## WHAT OF THE FUTURE?

The future area of federal land in the United States will remain about as at present, except in the unlikely event of a program of large-scale federal acquisition of land as a means of agricultural adjustment. Some relatively minor disposals, totaling at most a few million acres, will be offset, more or less, by modest purchases of land for special purposes. Some transfers of specific tracts of land from one agency to another may occur. But neither wholesale disposal or large-scale acquisition seem probable, given the political and popular support for present federal land management activities.

The area of state, county, and city public land will almost surely rise in the future, although the actual area added may be small relative to the total national land area. A few states may continue to dispose of part of their grants from the federal government, but it seems improbable that such disposals will be large. On the other hand, a great many units of government will add land, especially for recreation. Although the latter may be rather modest in total area, yet the land values will be high and their usability for the public great.

For all types of public land, and for almost every separate tract of public land, use will grow for most of the purposes for which the land is suited. There will almost certainly be increased competition among alternative uses of land and among contending user groups. This will require increased intensity of land use. These are the kinds of changes which public land managers have faced during the past two decades; they will continue in the future probably at an accelerated rate.

The situation of relatively stable though slightly expanding land area and of greatly increased demand for public land, with consequent increased intensity of land use, is likely to mean a greater future reliance on economic analysis to guide public land management. Comparative costs and returns from different management practices, and the incidence of both costs and benefits, are likely to have a greater future influence on the land manager and upon the legislative bodies which appropriate funds. New demands are likely to be put on the economist to supply more relevant and more dependable economic analyses. Many decisions will continue to be made, entirely or partly, on other grounds, but costs and returns are likely to loom larger in the future.

All of this will almost certainly increase further the already large role of the professional land manager. The growing technical complexity of public land management will make the typical government administrator or legislator more dependent upon the technician. The growing volume of use of public lands will give rise to greater contending political pressures. However, these are likely to free, rather than to confine, the public land manager, for to a large extent they will be offsetting. The total effect will be an increased professionalization of public land management.

IMPLICATIONS FOR
FUTURE LAND POLICY

PHILIP M. RAUP

# Satisfying the Economic Demands for Natural Resources: Some Recent Developments in European Land Policy*

## INTRODUCTION

EUROPEAN AGRICULTURAL POLICY in the nineteenth century was dominated by problems incident to the dissolution of feudal tenures and the emergence of a market economy in an increasingly urban and industrial society. American agricultural policy in the nineteenth century was dominated by land problems associated with the exploration and settlement of a continent. In both areas, land tenure policies were at the center of the agricultural problem complex.

Although Europe in the nineteenth century was dismantling an old land tenure structure and the United States was creating a new one, there is a striking parallelism in the preoccupation on both continents with problems of tenure, ownership, and settlement. This preoccupation continued into the twentieth century, beyond World War I. In a number of European countries, the culmination of programs of "freeing the peasant" was not reached until the enactment of the land reform and settlement laws that followed World War I. This was true, for example, of the National Settlement Law (Reichssiedlungsgesetz) of 1919 in Germany, and the "Own Farm" settlement legislation of the same year in Sweden. For a number of European countries whose independence dated from the 1917-1919 era, there was a similar preoccupation with land policy focused on the creation of owner-

* Paper Number 1124, Miscellaneous Journal Series, Agricultural Experiment Station, University of Minnesota.

operated units of family-farm size. This was the case, for example, in Finland, Poland, Czechoslovakia, Bulgaria, Greece, and Spain.

Triggered by the collapse of agriculture prices after World War I and the continuing agricultural depression of the 1920's, the interest of agricultural economists in the United States shifted sharply from land policy to market and price policies. A major hinge point in American history occurred sometime between the Stock Raising Homestead Act of 1916 and the Rural Zoning Enabling Act passed by the Wisconsin state legislature in 1929. The policies exhibited by these two acts represent diametrically opposed concepts of agricultural and land tenure policy. On the national scene, this emerged more clearly in the Taylor Grazing Act of 1934, which placed the seal of finality on the closing of the American frontier that Fredrick Jackson Turner had proclaimed some forty years earlier in 1893.

A similar shift of focus was occurring in Europe at about the same time. The dramatic character of world agriculture price collapses in the 1930's was reflected in a shift of agricultural policy away from a focus on land and toward a focus on the market. In very rough terms, for the thirty years from 1925 to 1955, agricultural policies in both Europe and North America reflect this preoccupation with price levels and market structures. In the middle 1920's it became apparent that a focus on land policy alone was an inadequate approach to the problems of agriculture in an industrial world. It was not a sufficient solution to the agricultural problem to provide an incentive structure in which the lure of ultimate land ownership would be the major motive force for agricultural prosperity and advance. Stability and justice in a land tenure system were undoubtedly a necessary condition for agricultural development. The aftermaths of World War I underlined the fact that land ownership alone carried no guarantee that the owner would participate in the economic progress of an increasingly industrial world.

In both Europe and North America, agricultural price policies came sharply to the fore in the 1930's. For varying times and periods in the countries of Europe and the New World, land policy all but dropped from sight. Speaking again in broad terms, there has been a gradual but distinct reversal of this trend in the 1950's. Generally rising levels of income and well-being in Europe and the United States over the past fifteen years have thrown the lagging status of agriculture in sharp relief. It has become clearer that agricultural price policy is an inadequate tool with which to lift the labor rewards in agriculture to a par with rewards for similar economic contributions in nonagricultural sectors.

We are party in the 1960's to a renewed discovery of the importance of land policy to healthy agricultural growth. We have celebrated the centenary of the Homestead Act, an act that dramatized for the world a solution to the agricultural problem represented by free men on free soil with opportunity for the full and free exercise of their productive and managerial talents. This wheel of history has come full circle. We have passed through an era in which the inadequacies of land policy alone became increasingly apparent. We have passed through its antithesis in the past thirty years, in which the cure-all for the ills of agriculture was sought in the field of market and price policy. There is increasing recognition on both sides of the Atlantic that neither of these major directions of policy is adequate, taken by itself.

In America we find this change in emphasis reflected in the growing awareness of the problem of land use and rural area development. In Europe we can note similar trends reflected in the increasing concern with regional planning that extends beyond the narrow boundaries of confined states, and in a sharply renewed interest in the structural problems that inhibit agriculture's participation in a market-oriented industrial economy.

It is in this setting that we can profitably turn our attention in the United States to a study of recent developments in European agricultural policy as they affect land tenure and land use. This study of the European lesson can be particularly rewarding for it is in Europe that the confrontation between intensive agriculture and highly industrialized society has yielded the most clearly drawn policy issues. The problems of European agriculture arise from dense settlement, rigid agrarian structures, and rapidly growing industrial sectors. They occur in a setting in which major fractions of total agricultural land use and output are accounted for by part-time farms and related enterprises involving families with dual sources of income, with one foot in agriculture and one foot in the nonagricultural world. Price policy alone does not reach the roots of the agricultural problems of these regions and producers. The rigidity of agrarian institutions is so great that structural reforms are essential. The inadequacies of a narrow conception of agricultural problems, in both their economic and their geographic setting, is compelling a re-examination of the agricultural problem situation in a broad framework of interregional and intersectoral relationships.

The brief summary to follow will draw upon some recent European experience in land tenure policy development as it has sought to provide tentative answers to the following questions:

1. From the standpoint of productivity and the firm, what are the problems involved in adapting agriculture to an industrial world?

2. From the standpoint of welfare and the household, what are the problems involved in adapting rural areas to an urban world?

3. From the standpoint of resource endowments and usage, what are the problems involved in adapting agriculture dominated by the winds, the rains, and the seasons, to a world in which man is increasingly able to bend and weave the forces of nature to the pattern of his will?

This survey makes no attempt to cover the entire range of postwar land policy developments in Western Europe. It is not a status or situation report on European land tenure. It is rather an attempt to draw selectively from recent experience in two European countries those elements that promise to be of greatest interest and value to research workers in land economics in the United States. Where evaluation is involved, it will be in terms of the potential worth of European experimentation to our efforts to adapt domestic land tenure policies to the needs of the American economy in the decades immediately ahead.

## FARM SIZE EXPANSION AND RURAL
## LAND PLANNING IN SWEDEN

The nineteenth century pressure for abolition of the remnants of feudal concepts of land tenure culminated in Sweden in a law of 1896 granting virtually unlimited freedom to divide and convey land. This laissez faire land policy continued for thirty years until reversed by a law in 1926 that sharply reduced the possibility of legal division of lands. This period of freedom in land division and transfers coincided with the emergence of an active program to promote the development of owner-operated farms, first by local county agricultural societies and later with vigorous help from the national government. This "Own Farm" movement was aided by the creation of a national Own Farm Loan Fund in 1905, followed by regional Own Farm Boards in 1919 and the creation of a state Own Farm Board in 1928 supported by a network of county Own Farm Boards. "Up to 1939 the main objective of the Own Farm movement was to promote and enlarge agricultural production by encouraging the formation of small holdings, both for social and population policy reasons."[1]

A major reversal in Swedish land policy occurred between 1928 and 1939, culminating in a decree of the Riksdag virtually bringing to a stop the creation of additional new farms under the Own Farm program. This 1939 Act also marked the effective end of state programs for the subdivision of larger farms, or for the expenditure of state funds on large-scale land reclamation projects.

The sporadic efforts to combat agricultural price collapses in the 1930's, followed by disruptions generated by World War II led to the appointment in 1942 of an agricultural commission charged with a re-examination of the entire structure of Swedish agricultural policy. This commission's report, enacted into law by the Riksdag in 1947, forms the backbone of modern Swedish agricultural policy. It was this report that set a goal of parity of agricultural incomes with the rewards for labor accruing to other comparable groups of workers. The means created to achieve this goal of parity incomes in agriculture are noteworthy in that they form one of the first comprehensive statements of European agricultural policy to recognize that the control or guidance of agricultural product prices is in itself an inadequate approach to farm problems.

The means by which this goal of income parity is pursued can be grouped under three headings:

1. The improvement and rationalization of the management of individual farms.

2. The improvement of land and building layout, including drainage, reclamation within the farm, construction of farm roads and new buildings. For these activities the term *internal rationalization* is used.

3. The enlargement of farm size, combination and consolidation of farm holdings, and the replanning of the rural community. For this the term *external* or *outer rationalization* is used.

The major focus of this survey will center on the policies and measures used to guide external rationalization or the improvement of the agrarian structure.

During both the first and the second World Wars there had been repeated threats to agriculture represented by attempts on the part of nonfarmers to avoid postwar crises and inflation by purchases of farmland. To combat this threat, the Swedish Riksdag in 1945 enacted a Land Acquisition Act providing in principle that all acquisition by private persons of lands classified for taxation purposes as agricultural land required the approval of a county agricultural board before title could legally be registered. (In Sweden, privately owned forestland is also classed as agricultural land for purposes of taxation.) This act, amended in 1948 and replaced by the Land Acquisition Act of 1955, constitutes one of the major features of current Swedish land policy. The goal of this legislation has been to prevent nonfarmers from acquiring farmland or forestland which, it is believed, should remain in the hands of the farming population in the interest of a healthy agriculture. Applications for permission to acquire land need not be made in the case of land transferred by inheritance, by partition among husband and wife, or in certain cases where transfers are among close relatives or where land is acquired by the Crown or by municipalities.

These measures to prevent the use of land for speculation or as an anti-inflation hedge by the nonfarm population continued a trend in Swedish land policy that dates from 1916. In that year, an act of the Riksdag required that the acquisition of land by foreign citizens be contingent upon the approval of the King in Council. This initial restraint, directed at the intrusion of foreign capital seeking a safe haven in wartime, was later expanded in 1925 to include joint stock companies, associations, and foundations, for whom farmland acquisition was also made contingent upon approval by the King in Council. The Land Acquisition Act of 1945 extended this control to cover virtually all land sales to private, unrelated nonfarm buyers, with approval authority vested in local county agricultural boards.

The restrictions contained in the act of 1945 were given additional strength by the inclusion of a right of preemptive purchase in the subsequent 1947 legislation that established income parity as a farm policy goal. Under this preemption provision, the county agricultural board had the right to take over a property that had been sold, after the sale had been completed and at the price agreed upon between the buyer and seller. The right of preemption is not exercised if the buyer and seller are close relatives, or if the sale is to a buyer who already holds a part interest in the property.

Between 1947 and 1955, the preemption act gave the county agricultural boards the right to interfere in a sale of farmland after the title had already been registered by the buyer. This provision was changed in the Land Acquisition Act of 1955, which consolidated the preemption provisions of the 1947 act with the control of land transfer provisions of acts of 1945 and 1948. Under existing law, the approval or denial of permission to complete the transaction is the key to the exercise of subsequent rights of preemption. If a transaction has been disapproved, the seller then has the right to demand that the county agricultural board shall buy his property at the price agreed upon with the prospective purchaser. Under this act, approved applications for the acquisition of land since 1955 have ranged from a low of

5488 in 1957 to highs of 5972 in 1959 and 5902 in 1960. In the same five years the number of applications denied ranged from a low of 661 in 1958 to a high of 910 in 1960. On the average, 12 to 15 per cent of the applications have been denied in each year.

In the early years under this program some opposition from land-owners was experienced, particularly in cases in which a county agricultural board injected itself into a transaction after it had been completed and recorded. These sources of friction were largely removed by the 1955 Land Acquisition Act, with the result that in a number of counties, the agricultural boards are currently offered more land under this act than available finances will permit them to buy. The use of the act in pursuit of a policy of active acquisition has been confined as a matter of policy to agricultural areas in which the parcelization of farms created severe problems of adjustment or in which the migration of rural people out of agriculture has led to immediate need for a regroupment and expansion in size of remaining farm units.

It is important to note that existing Swedish legislation authorizes disapproval of a transaction if the buyer is a nonfarmer. It also authorizes disapproval if the buyer is a farmer, in case the land is needed to expand a nearby farm that is presently too small, or to complete a regroupment or consolidation project in the community. It was the addition of this latter provision (paragraph 5 of the 1955 Land Acquisition Act) that marked the transition from a negative policy of preventing parcelization or the sale of land to nonfarmers toward a more positive policy of improving farm configuration and increasing the size of farms.

Swedish law also authorizes the expropriation of land under certain conditions, if the land is needed to improve the agrarian structure or increase the size of farms now too small for an economic existence. Under this legislation, land can be taken from a large farm, or an entire farm can be taken from certain classes of owners not primarily included in the farming population, and forestland can be acquired. While the existence of this legislation has undoubtedly strengthened the preemption legislation and laws regulating land transfers, actual expropriation has been used in very few cases. One principal reason is that full compensation is guaranteed the owner of any expropriated land,

and the awards made in the few cases that have been attempted have been so high that resale of the land to an operating farmer has involved the expropriating authorities in a substantial loss. The combination of transfer control and preemption authority, used together with a policy of active purchase of land in the open market, has proved to be the most successful avenue open to county agricultural boards in acquiring needed land for farm consolidation and expansion.

Based on this body of legislation, the county agricultural boards in Sweden today practice what might loosely be called a form of "rural renewal," not unlike that currently practiced under the heading of "urban renewal" in the urban core sectors of American cities. The county boards have authority to acquire land, raze buildings, construct new buildings, realign field boundaries, drainage patterns, and local road systems, and combine properties to the end that a pattern of economically viable farm units shall be created in the rural community. They can acquire land through preemption, in extreme cases through expropriation, but most importantly through active purchase in the open market. The land thus acquired can be held in order to create a reserve for rural community redevelopment. In the interim, the land is rented to local farmers.

Although the rights of preemption and expropriation have been important tools in the hands of county boards, the major tool in the pursuit of rationalization policies has been the authority to buy land in the open market.

The scale of operation under this legislation has been modest over the ten years, 1951–1960. In that period county agricultural boards acquired a total of 67,846 acres of arable land, and 334,986 acres of forestland; they disposed of 53,144 acres of arable land and 237,777 acres of forestland; as of January 1, 1961, they held 19,084 acres of arable land and 160,388 acres of forestland in their revolving land funds. In 1960, the year of greatest activity during the decade, the county agricultural boards acquired 10,363 acres of agricultural land and 54, 201 acres of forestland; they sold 8,021 acres of agricultural land and 42,620 acres of forestland in 881 separate sales, involving a taxable value of 15,588,000 kronor (roughly $3,000,000).

To this body of basic land tenure legislation, the Swedish Riksdag, in 1959, made a significant addition: In revising price policies and the basis for calculation of cost and returns on "typical farms," it was laid down as policy that the support of measures designed to improve the agrarian structure should be extended to cover "two-family farms." In farm price policy negotiations between agricultural associations and the government, it was also laid down that agricultural prices for the six years 1959–1965 should be designed to yield a remuneration to labor in agriculture that would reduce the gap between farm and nonfarm wages for comparable work based on net labor earnings in typical farms in the 10–20 hectare size group (roughly 25 to 50 acres). The same agreement contained provisions that this size group should be replaced with "typical farms" in the 20 to 30 hectare size class (50 to 75 acres) in the determination of agriculture price policies for the period after 1965.

As a consequence, Sweden now possesses statutory authority to control transactions in land or to acquire land in order to expand existing farm units up to a size consistent with operation by two families. The National Board of Agriculture and the county agricultural boards also administer a system of loan guarantees and grants, to provide financial support for land purchase or for other internal and external rationalization programs. There are no separate government-operated banks or lending institutions for agricultural credit. Instead, the credit required is arranged through existing banking institutions. If the purpose and terms of the loans are approved by the county agricultural boards, the borrower is given a loan guarantee which he then takes to the bank of his choice. Amortization is typically spread over thirty years.

A system of "write-off grants" supports the guaranteed loan program for land purchase or building construction in those cases in which the borrower is an individual of limited financial means. Grants of 25 per cent of the cost of new building construction are authorized for internal rationalization, up to a total building cost of 5,000 kronor and of 15 per cent of the rest of the cost. If the measure is carried out in connection with external rationalization, grants are authorized up to a building cost of 10,000 kronor. In both cases the grants are limited to a maximum of 8,000 kronor, and are not available to farms that are larger than can be operated by two families.

This two-family-farm base for policy is in sharp contrast with existing land tenure and settlement policies in the remainder of Europe. It reflects the fact that the agricultural share of total Swedish population has declined from 30 per cent in 1930 to an estimated 12 per cent in 1960, with an average decline in the agricultural labor force of 3.5 per cent per year over the five years 1956–1960. This active demand for nonfarm labor coupled with the growing difficulty of maintaining economically viable small farms in climatically or geographically unfavorable areas has led to the appearance of actual farm abandonment in Sweden in recent years.

Much of the success of the Swedish program of rural renewal must thus be attributed to the general economic prosperity of the country. This should in no way detract from the approval that Sweden's post World War II land tenure policy merits. It reflects a sober and cautious approach to problems of structural adjustment that can be resolved only over a number of years, and that require policies that give due consideration to the interest both of the farm and the nonfarm population.

Swedish concern with the "rationalization" of agricultural production units extends to the rural communities themselves. Prior to 1952 the number of communes or minor civil divisions in Sweden was approximately 2,500, some of which had as few as 500 people. In that year a thoroughgoing reorganization of the basis of local government was undertaken, through a process of consolidation of communes, with a goal of establishing a minimum size of commune of at least 2,000 inhabitants. With this in mind the number of communes was reduced from 2,500 to some 800 in 1952.

This drastic reduction has now proved inadequate. A further reduction in the number of communes from 800 to 300 is proposed, based on a provisional goal of minimum sized communes that include at least 6,500 to 8,000 inhabitants.[2] In pusuit of this goal, the concept of "outer rationalization" has been substantially broadened. It was originally conceived with regard to the rural community surrounding an individual farm or group of farms. It has now been expanded to cover groups of rural communities. In this way Swedish land tenure policy reflects clear-cut recognition of the fact that the creation of viable farm units depends to an important degree on the creation of viable rural communities.

## GERMAN LAND TRANSFER AND SETTLEMENT LEGISLATION

On August 2, 1961, the text of a comprehensive Real Estate Transactions Law was officially published in West Germany. This law, which went into effect as of January 1, 1962, brings in closer correlation two streams in the development of German land tenure policy that trace back to 1918. In that year, a federal ordinance required that transactions in rural lands be officially approved before the title transfer could legally be recorded. Reflecting this basic policy, and with some exceptions, market transactions in German farmland have been subject to some form of official approval since the end of World War I. During the Nazi period this method of control over the sale of farm land was intensified and expanded through the "Public Notice Concerning Real Estate Transactions" (Grundstueckverkehrsbekanntmachung) of 1937. Allied Control Council Law Number 45 of 1947 contained essentially the same provisions, as they related to the commercial sale of land. Germany in this regard has probably had a longer and more continuous history of official control over the rural land market than has any other European country.

The year 1918 also dates the beginning of the modern period of German land settlement policy embodied in the "National Settlement Law" that has long been associated with the name of its principal author, Max Sering. The law of August 2, 1961 joins these land settlement and land market control threads, but it does not represent a perfect union of these twin aspects of German land tenure policy. This emerges from the full title of the 1961 law, which reads: "Law Concerning Measures for the Improvement of the Agrarian Structure and for the Protection of Agriculture and Forest Enterprises."[3] Some idea of its complexity is provided by the fact that new law sets aside fifty-two sepa-

rate state or national laws and ordinances concerning land transfers, inheritance or settlement.

With this law Germany, in 1961, has taken essentially the
same step that Sweden took with its comprehensive agricultural
legislation of 1947, 1955, and 1959. Emphasis has shifted from a
simple control over the sale of farmland, and a unilateral promotion of small settlement, toward a land tenure policy focused
more directly on the expansion of farm size and the creation of
economically viable units. Major differences remain between the
German and Swedish approaches.

Most importantly, German agriculture has lived a relatively
sheltered and protected life since the time of Bismarck. Tariff
and agriculture price policy has more or less insulated it from
the world market, an insulation made almost total during two
World Wars and intervening periods of inflation, and subsequent
Nazi rule. Official sanction of migration out of agriculture, and
an emphasis on commercial farm units that could survive in open
competition both regionally and internationally, are all relatively recent developments in German agriculture history. The
comparison with Swedish land tenure policy is also imperfect in
that public and private organizations supporting settlement and
small holding programs in Germany are substantially stronger
politically and economically than is the case in Sweden. West
Germany is also burdened with a greater concentration of very
small farm units, and the parcelization problem is much worse.

With these reservations, the basic outlines of German and
Swedish policy are strikingly similar, although the scale is different. In principle, the sale of farm land to a nonfarm buyer is
either prohibited, or subject to careful public scrutiny. The
grounds for disapproval as specified in the 1961 German law are:

1. if the sale would lead to an unsound division of the land;

2. if, as a result of the sale, a number of tracts of land that
constitute either a spatial or economic unit and that belong to
the seller are uneconomically reduced or divided;

3. if there is a gross discrepancy between the transaction price
and the value of the land.

Previous legislation requiring approval of transactions in real
estate specified that the sale should be disapproved if the buyer

was not professionally engaged in farming. In the 1961 legislation, this provision has been altered in that the approving authority (in most cases, a form of county agricultural court) *may* disapprove a sale on the ground that the buyer is a nonfarmer, but need not necessarily do so.

In order to provide a basis for the determination that a sale is leading to an unsound division of the land, the law specifies that this is presumed to be the case if the sale would leave the remaining tract of agricultural land smaller than one hectare (2.47 acres), or 3.5 hectares (8.7 acres) in the case of a forest unit. The individual *Laender* of the Federal Republic are empowered to set higher limits on the minimum size of permissible remaining holdings if they choose to do so.

The 1961 legislation is also noteworthy in that it has expanded the use that can be made of the right of preemption. In restricted form, the exercise of the preemption right dates far back in German history and was a prominent part of the National Settlement Law of 1918. Under that law, the right of preemption could be exercised in favor of an officially recognized public-law settlement association if the sale involved farmland that was within the bounds of an existing or planned settlement project. Also under the old law, this preemption right could be exercised only in case a sale of land had been given official approval by the local approval authorities. This had in the past led to seemingly inconsistent policies, in that the exercise of a right of preemption by one publicly empowered authority (a settlement organization) could take place only after another publicly empowered authority had given official permission for a voluntary sale of the land. Under the new law, this inconsistency is removed in that the preemption right can be exercised only in those cases in which official approval of a transaction in real estate has been denied. Note that a similar difficulty had arisen in Sweden, and was corrected by a comparable change in the Swedish Land Acquisition Act of 1955, see page 385 above.

One purpose of German land tenure policy is to prevent the uneconomic splitting of land holdings, whether agricultural or forest in nature. Another purpose has been to prevent inflation in land values that has repeatedly and over two generations threatened to price farm land out of reach of any operating farmer. Two World Wars followed by two major inflations with a world-wide depression in between have combined to create strong motivations in Germany for the control of land prices.

A novel variation of this control is contained in the new 1961 law. In the past, there was always some question about the accuracy of the stated price in an application for official approval of a sale of farmland. Charges have been made increasingly in recent years that it was common practice for the actual trans- action price to be three or four times the price stated in the application filed with the approval authorities. The new law states that if the transaction is disapproved and if the right of preemption is subsequently exercised, compensation for the land acquired through preemption cannot exceed the price stated in the original application for approval of the voluntary sale. This is reminiscent of ancient Chinese land tax policy, which relied on self-assessment and authorized the taxing authority to buy the land outright at the stated assessed value, in lieu of accepting the taxes based on that valuation.

In determining the value of land against which the appro- priateness of the price offered in the market sale is to be meas- ured, the common practice is to use the "yield value" (*Ertragswert*) of the land as a point of departure. This is set by law as some multiple of the annual value of the net output of the farm, after an adequate sum has been deducted for the wages and maintenance of the farm family. In the former Prussian parts of West Germany, the determination of the yield value was con- ventionally set at 25 times the annual net yield value. In Bavaria, on the contrary, the multiple has been 18. This illustrates the fact that a substantial degree of variation continues to exist among the states of the federal Republic in their administration of Federal laws.

Although labeled a "real estate transactions law," the new German legislation makes a substantial excursion into the area of inheritance law. In the case of intestate succession, the new law provides that the farm will be passed on intact to one of the heirs in case they cannot agree on a division among them- selves, or in case any one of the heirs files an official request for this form of court aid to achieve a "closed" inheritance. Although it applies only in those cases in which the deceased has left no will or testament, this law does introduce this limited form of closed inheritance throughout West Germany.

Prior to the 1961 law, this type of officially sponsored closed inheritance prevailed only in what had been the British zone of occupation. To this extent it represents an uninterrupted continuation of the main policy thread contained in the Nazi-sponsored National Hereditary Farm Law (*Erbhofgesetz*) of 1933, with the major difference that the owner can avoid this form of transfer to a single heir by exercise of his freedom to make a will. Land transferred to a single heir under this provision of the new law cannot be resold within fifteen years without obligating the single heir to compensate the remaining heirs for any difference between the sale price he receives for the land and the price it would have brought had it been sold in an open market transaction at the time he acquired it through compulsory closed inheritance.

The ancient thread of primogeniture and entail, which has never completely disappeared from German land tenure policy, reappears in this new law in that the heir benefiting from the closed inheritance has an obligation to compensate remaining heirs for the money value of their proportion of the inheritance, but at the "yield value" (*Ertragswert*) of the land and not at market price. In the booming industrial and agricultural economy of West Germany in the 1960's, this could result in a substantial degree of disinheritance, for the remaining heirs.

## CONCLUDING OBSERVATIONS

These recent modifications in land tenure policy occur in a setting that includes the clearly apparent threat of surplus agricultural productive capacity. Milk is surplus in a number of European countries today; this shows up in episodic butter surpluses and distress disposal programs. Barley production has approached surplus levels in Northwestern Europe in the past several years. The French agricultural disturbances of July, 1961 were triggered in part by potato surplus production that promises to increase in magnitude as diets shift away from heavy reliance on starchy foods.

In this setting of impending surplus the recent changes in European land tenure policy take on added relevance for the American observer. From the foregoing summary we can single out five items that merit our attention:

(1) The two-family farm base for agricultural price and land tenure policy in Sweden is clear-cut recognition of cultural phenomena of our time; early marriages and extended life expectancy. With half of all girls in the United States under age twenty-one at the time of first marriage and boys under age twenty-three, and with life expectancy approaching seventy years, at birth, it is unrealistic to expect that the average farmer is ready to retire when his son is ready to take over the family farm. Swedish farm policy emphasizes the unrealistic nature of a "one-family farm" policy goal. Given the capital accumulation problem facing beginning farmers, the increasing importance of uninterrupted continuity in farm operation at the time of transfer from generation to generation, and the extension of productive years of work through use of machinery, the two-family farm would appear to be a rational policy goal for American agriculture.

(2) Stress on policies and programs aimed at parity of agricultural income with labor returns earned outside of agriculture has thrown in sharp relief the different status of the money rewards to agricultural labor. European experience underlines the fact that actual parity between agricultural and non-agricultural incomes is unlikely to be achieved without some control over entry into agriculture. In this regard, the income gap between industrial and agricultural incomes can be interpreted in a variety of ways. It is not only a measure of the attractiveness of agriculture as a way of life but of the unattractiveness of urban life and industrial employment with their greater risks, higher levels of crowding, and more demanding social and interpersonal contact.

True parity of monetary incomes between industrial and agricultural occupations does not reflect a realistic equality in occupational choices. Where income parity has been reached or approached, the evidence is clear that more people will seek employment in agriculture than can be accommodated within the framework of income policy. With no control over the entry of nonfarm capital into the agricultural land market, a goal of parity incomes in agriculture faces almost certain defeat through the transfer of labor incomes to rental incomes through land value appreciation. At this level of analysis, the policy question is: Can parity be achieved between farm and nonfarm incomes without control of the entry of both capital and labor into agriculture?

(3) In several European countries, central governmental aid in land reclamation, drainage, irrigation, and related large-scale programs of new land development has been reduced or stopped completely. These European policy determinations, arrived at in a situation in which surpluses are more impending than real, highlight the irrationality of some American programs of public subsidy of the development of new land for agricultural purposes.

(4) European experience with wars and inflation has focused attention on the disruptive nature of capital flights into the land market. We have experienced similar pressures in the United States, but these have been on a comparatively minor scale. Instead of catastrophic fears arising from war or the fear of a currency collapse, the pressures tending to hold capital in farmland in the United States have been more subtle. Through appraisal practices at time of inheritance and through capital gains tax provisions, a substantial incentive is placed before the owner of agricultural land, or before potential investors. Where there is nonfarm income sufficient to provide a family living, and where interest can be focused on capital value appreciation at the expense of current income, our institutional setting provides strong motivation for holding capital in agricultural land beyond the limits that price and profit levels would dictate on a normal profit and loss basis. European experience with more dramatic forms of these same forces should alert us to the long-term consequences of the intrusion of nonfarm capital into the rural land market. These considerations suggest that we might well consider alternative price and nonprice methods of avoiding undesirable results, and their comparative benefits and costs.

(5) European experience offers extreme examples of the high cost of remedying the evil of unrestricted subdivision and parcel-

ization of farms. The increasing number of United States farms comprising two or more noncontiguous tracts should alert us to the fact that uneconomic parcelization can happen here.

Much more could and should be said on the basis of recent European land tenure developments. It would be pertinent to examine the experience of the Netherlands in administering their law setting price controls on agricultural land. It would be equally rewarding to analyze the operation of Danish farm policy which, in principle, specifies that no one individual can own more than two farms.

Even greater importance should attach to an analysis of the extensive agricultural legislation in France in 1960–62. The series of wide-ranging laws relating to agriculture and natural resources constitute a major reformulation of French agricultural policy. One significant feature of this recent body of French legislation concerns the creation of a new system of national parks. France in 1960 has for the first time established a system of park and nature reserve areas, reflecting the growing importance of urban and nonagricultural uses of rural lands. England in 1950 took a similar step. The national park tradition has never been prominent in Europe, and is only recently receiving the attention that the automobile era demands.

This brief summary of recent developments in Swedish and German land tenure policy gives evidence of a major change underway throughout Europe. Emphasis is shifting away from the creation of small holdings and toward a positive instead of a negative approach to the problems of farm subdivision or the prevention of nonfarm buyers from disrupting the rural land market. We can note the continuance of a determination to prevent deterioration and dismemberment of rural communities coupled with a new interest in promoting an increase in farm size. This new policy focus emerges most clearly from the Swedish legislation although even in the German legislation the impact of a highly industrial economy on an outmoded agrarian structure is clearly apparent. A number of European countries now welcome off-farm migration. Only a few years ago this topic was discussed in terms of a "flight from the land."

Repeated histories of wars and inflation have created in

Europe a highly developed awareness of the fact that nonfarm capital can completely disrupt a tenure system based on owner operation. This can occur whenever farmland is purchased for tax avoidance, or for reasons only remotely connected with farm productivity and profits. Where parity is sought between agricultural and nonagricultural incomes, most countries have found it necessary to develop some control over entry into agriculture for both men and capital. The result is a type of franchised farming, in many variations.

Mechanization and the technological revolution in agriculture have placed new emphasis on the important economies of scale to be achieved through expanding farm size. This has had a delayed but heavy impact on European agriculture in the 1950's. It is a trend we can expect to continue and to accelerate, if the goals of the European Common Market are achieved. With few exceptions, the parcelization and land consolidation problem has dominated the discussion of European land tenure policy in recent years. It has only recently become apparent that an emphasis on consolidation alone is not enough. Structural change of a major order is demanded, involving farms and rural communities alike, combined with positive policies toward agricultural education, training and off-farm migration. The Swedish and German legislation reviewed here represent major efforts to grope toward land tenure policies appropriate to an agricultural economy dominated by an urban and industrial world.

## NOTES

1. This quotation and much of the historical survey material that follows is drawn from "The Rationalization of Swedish Agriculture," National Board of Agriculture, Stockholm, 1961, and from supporting documentation presented to the Fourth Session, Working Party on Consolidation of Holdings (FAO), Stockholm, August 9–16, 1961. The author is also indebted to Hans Wetterhall, Deputy Director General, National Board of Agriculture, Stockholm, for his helpful comments on an earlier draft.

2. See "Swedish Reply to the [UN] Questionnaire Circulated in Connection With the Preparation of the 1962 Report on Land Reform," Board of Agriculture, Stockholm, 1961.

3. In the discussion that follows, principal reliance has been placed on the following sources: Friedrich Nonhoff, "Das neue Grundstueckverkehrsgesetz, insbesonders seine siedlungsrechtlichen Vorschriften," in *Bodenordnung in der modernen Gesellschaft,* "Schriftenreihe fuer Laendliche Sozialfragen" (Hannover: Verlag M. & H. Schaper, 1961), XXXIV, 77–90. J. Vorwerk, "Das Grundstueckverkehrsgesetz," *Berichte über Landwirtschaft,* XXXIX, No. 3 (1961), 400–412. A. Fritzen. "Grundstueckverkehrsgesetz und Betriebsfestigung" ("Real Estate Transactions Law and Farm Stabilization"), *Agrarwirtschaft,* XI, No. 5 (May, 1962), 152–60. "Gesetz über Massnahmen zur Verbesserung der Agrarstruktur und zur Sicherung land- und forstwirtschaftlicher Betriebe" ("Law Concerning Measures for the Improvement of the Agrarian Structure and for the Protection of Agricultural and Forest Enterprises"), text, plus comments by J. Vorwerk and J. Hastenpflug. *Innere Kolonisation,* XX, No. 11 (November, 1961), 237–56.

GENE WUNDERLICH

# Satisfying the Economic Demands for Natural Resources: Some Policy Issues for the United States

## INTRODUCTION

OUR NATURAL RESOURCES, although not unlimited, are abundant. In the short run and in isolation at least, the United States will not find serious economic restraints in its physical quantities of available natural resources. Some natural resources, however, will be used more intensively and rapidly than others. Some natural resources will expire, and others will replace them.

Our survival as a nation or a people will depend, to a great extent, on technical advances. These technical advances, with their adjustments in resource combinations, production processes, and products require counterpart adjustments in institutional systems. Moreover, as Kenneth Boulding argues,[1] institutional modifications or innovations can anticipate and encourage technical developments rather than merely respond to exigencies created by technology. But short-run expedients are not enough. Some appreciation of, if not agreement on, the need for long-run resource policy will contribute to the design of more effective institutional systems.

A book on land policy, commemorating a legislative deed one hundred years past, has some obligation to look one hundred years to the future. Some part of a resource policy should extend beyond the next decade or two to see what, if anything, can be said about the long run. A separate natural resource policy may be useful in the short run, but inadequate in the long run when account must be taken of shifts in resource use brought about by changes in knowledge, quantities of resources, and human needs. Long-run policy must include human resources, and capital as well as natural resources.

This chapter contains five related but fairly distinct parts: (1) an overview of the resource situation, concluding that the United States has enough resources *if* institutional as well as technical changes are forthcoming; (2) some concepts of organization and policy, stressing differences of short run and long run, and concluding that goals in the usual sense are more useful in the short run; (3) a look at some conservation issues illustrating the difference between long- and short-run policy, and suggesting some adaptations of resource institutions; (4) an observation on the distribution of wealth as an aspect of resource policy, illustrated by data from agriculture; and (5) an examination of the role of population policy in relation to resource policy. The chapter is directed mainly at institutions and policies, not at technical problems. Institutions and policies include, but are not limited to, government.

## PRODUCTION, RESOURCES, NEEDS

To focus attention on resource policies and institutions for the United States, a brief outline of our resources and needs will be helpful. Confinement to broad generalizations about production, and overall relationships between resources and needs will permit us to see specific problems in prespective and yet focus on organization, conservation, distribution, and population.

Abstractly, production could mean any use of means to attain expected ends, but the term is generally limited to physical resources to accomplish material needs. In this narrower sense, production is simply the process of adding location, form, or time utility to sets of resources. Although some resources, such as scenic views and space, are consumed directly, most human needs are satisfied by combining resources in production. A policy for one resource, therefore, usually will be a policy for a set of resources.

Because production processes change through advances in technology and relative availablity of resources, a wide view of policy suggests that all resources—natural, capital, and human— be included. Similarly, all human needs—basics, amenities, and social overhead—should be included, if account is taken of changing tastes. A series of matrices, such as in Figure 16.1 could be

# NEEDS AND RESOURCES*

| NEEDS | RESOURCES | | |
|---|---|---|---|
| | NATURAL | CAPITAL | HUMAN |
| BASICS | | | |
| AMENITIES | | | |
| SOCIAL OVERHEAD | | | |

*NEEDS:
　　BASICS--Food, Shelter, Clothing
　　AMENITIES--Health, Education, Leisure, Privacy, Mobility
　　SOCIAL OVERHEAD--Military, Welfare, Regulation, Knowledge

RESOURCES:
　　NATURAL--Energy, Space
　　CAPITAL--Convertible, Nonconvertible or "Sunk"
　　HUMAN--Labor, Skills, Inventiveness

FIG. 16.1

used to demonstrate changes in needs and resource combinations over time.

Different sets of needs shown in such a matrix could be filled with different combinations of resources.[2] It is easy to see that, even with a slight degree of detail, the number of possible combinations of resources and needs becomes extremely large. From the present pattern of needs and resources, what can be projected to the future? In the near future, at least, the United States might expect a rate of economic growth which exceeds the population growth by about 1 to 2 per cent a year. At this rate, the average person would be 50 to 100 per cent better off materially when he leaves the labor force than when he entered. Since the average American now has ample income to supply the minimum requirements for basics, some amenities, and contributions to social overhead,[3] a simple projection of the present could be called optimistic. If the level of material well-being were to improve as suggested, however, some shift in needs and resource use might be expected.

## THE NEEDS

No appreciable increase in the average quantity of food needed per capita is expected. Caloric intake per capita has actually decreased from 3,500 to about 3,200 in the past fifty years. Some redistribution and quality upgrading are expected, perhaps in the relatively expensive form of animal proteins. Greater energy demands, often in the form of fossil fuels, fertilizers, and other minerals,[4] will result from the need for a greater total quantity of more completely processed foods. In the short run, the requirements for space resources to produce food may decrease. In the long run, space requirements will depend on economic conditions and technological advances. Much of agriculture's capital, located on small flexible units, is convertible within a wide range of uses. As more irrigation, land-forming, and drainage are used in farming and as off-farm industries assume a larger proportion of the food production process, capital in food producing may become less flexible. Among human resources, labor and some mechanical skill will decline but scientific skill will still play an important role. Special skill in food production will be needed to carry out a continued trend in the absorption of agriculture into a larger food and fiber complex.

With present rates of population growth in the United States and in the whole of the free world, it would be imprudent to discontinue or slow up our research in food sciences.[5] Of course if population pressure were decreased, we might feel comfortable about diverting intellectual as well as other resources into other purposes.

On the average, no appreciable increase in per capita use of basic materials for clothing is anticipated. Some upgrading in durability, maintenance, and flexibility may occur. Because clothing is rather directly associated with the person, a style factor will persist and will require resources. The proportion of the household budget devoted to clothing is an increasing function of income up to the middle-income group, whereafter the relative importance of the clothing item decreases as income increases.[6] The importance of clothing, therefore, may be determined not only by the average income but by the income distribution. Materials for clothing are expected to continue to shift from natural fibers to mineral derivatives. Perhaps the main developments will be in design engineering, such as clothes molded to fit individuals, and temperature and moisture modifications for severe climates.

Assuming 1,000 square feet for work and living, shelter requirements for our present work force and population[7] would occupy about 7,200 square miles. If all this shelter were on one level under one roof, it could almost cover New Jersey. Generally, an increase in space needs per person has taken place, partly because of the movement toward single-unit dwellings.[8] Such space requirements are directly related to the amenities of privacy and convenience so an assessment of needs is difficult. However, an increase in per capita space requirements is likely, particularly for the people now in lower-income strata whose incomes may improve. Substantial upgrading in environmental modifications through heat pumps, acoustical materials, and lighting are likely. Greater amounts of energy and capital will be needed. Modular units and other developments probably will replace much labor even in construction. More skills of architects and planners will be needed.

Amenities are varied collections of comforts and conveniences the omission of which would not jeopardize human survival.[9] In Galbraith's words: "Recreation will not enter the consumer's preference system except in combination with some minimum quantity of food. Food can be present without recreation."[10] As per capita income rises, amenities may be expected to constitute a larger proportion of human needs. Between 1950 and 1959, for example, personal income increased 68 per cent and all expenditures increased 61 per cent, but amenities[11] increased 87 per cent. Optimistic economists can assume that in the United States, problems of producing the basics largely have been surmounted and, barring catastrophe, that the problems of the future lie in resources for amenities. Greater amounts of energy and space will be devoted to education and recreation. More applications of science will be concentrated on health and comfort. Advances in mobility will continue an edifying, but perhaps also a homogenizing, effect on the population.

Social overhead will probably increase. As an indicator of the increasing importance of social overhead as an element in our economic system during the last half century, we can note that the gross domestic product in constant dollars of all government has increased seven and one-half times while the GDP of the farm sector (a proxy for basics) has increased only one and one-half times, and the GDP of the rest of the private economy (a proxy for amenities) has increased five and one half times.[12]

This growth of social overhead is partly the result of an increasingly complex and interdependent social system. Communication and control requirements alone call for more resources just to keep our left hand advised of what our right hand is doing. Much of the government expenditure is, of course, military, concerned largely with external relationships.

The drain of the military establishment on our resources complicates expectations about the future, first because of its enormous size and second, because policy is affected by many circumstances beyond national control. In spite of this uncertainty, however, as a relatively wealthy country we can afford to be responsive to the welfare needs of groups and individuals encountering unusual hardship, or disadvantaged by the functioning of an ever-changing economic system. Thus, education, retraining, occupational mobility, and research probably will become increasingly important. The role of the government as a representative of future generations, specifying levels of resource conservation, will grow in importance.

The Resources

Natural resources to meet our needs appear to be adequate for the near future despite heavy use. Although shifts in use of land resources will occur, overall supplies will not seriously limit economic development, in the short run at least. Space limitations will appear locally, particularly for shelter and amenities.

Total and per capita energy consumption in the United

States probably will continue to increase. Total horsepower of all prime movers, for example, increased two and one-half times in the ten years from 1950 to 1960.[13] The United States now consumes almost twice as much petroleum as all other countries of the free world combined. It matches or exceeds all other free countries in the consumption of manganese, iron, zinc, and copper. In so doing, it is using up its reserves of nonrenewable minerals at two to three times the rate of other free countries.[14] Sam H. Schurr summarizes a monumental work on energy:

> Viewed strictly from the natural resource position and with due allowance for technological advance, the United States in 1975 or thereabouts could satisfy its demands for all energy, and for each of the energy materials of which the total is composed, from domestic sources of supply at no significant increases in costs, except for those which might be brought about by a rise in the general price level.[15]

Paul McGann reinforces Schurr and associates and indicates there will be no energy shortage for the next generation, but after that, shortages will appear in fluid fuels and other energy sources will become economic. Upon demonstrating the interdependency of capital and labor with energy supplies, he comments:

> When we look ahead several centuries, general energy supply shortages show very serious danger areas. Technological progress provides some promise that these problems will be solved. At present real income levels and constant population, energy problems would not be great for several thousand years. With rising populations and income, however, some major ecological equilibrium must be reached by mankind in his energy use at a much earlier date, perhaps only several hundred years from now.[16]

Intensive use of natural resources, coupled with growing capital,[17] has resulted in the concomitant increase in labor productivity. Real product per man-hour increased 35 per cent between 1950 and 1960. This increase in productivity often entails major adjustments in resource use. Man-hour output in agriculture, for example, increased 80 per cent from 1950 to 1960 and reduced the number of its production units from 4.7 to 3.7 million.

## TECHNOLOGY AND ORGANIZATION

Future production relationships and resource requirements will depend to a large extent on population and technology. Available knowledge from which technology flows is doubling every ten years. Ninety percent of the scientists who ever lived are alive now. Discovery of the wheel took 50,000 to 100,000 years after Homo sapiens appeared. In 4,000 more years, James Watt invented the flyball governor. In 150 more years, automatic electronic control systems were operating. Two decades later, man was orbiting earth. We have firm bases for assuming that this technological progression will continue. But, as some resources are used up and others become more productive, shifts in economic organization will be required.

A forecast of our material well-being based on optimistic projections of present trends would appear in figure 16.1 as a shift of needs downward and resources used to the left. In physical measures, our goods and services basket would contain a greater proportion of amenities and a smaller proportion of food. Our production processes would employ a greater proportion of natural resource energy and a smaller proportion of labor.

An index of material well-being could be specified as the degree to which we use our natural endowment and stock of old capital as compared to new capital (saving or sacrificed consumption) and to labor (human effort). The closer we come to living on nature without saving or working, the better off we will have become, at least by the criteria suggested in comparing Genesis 2 to Genesis 3.

Thus, resources themselves probably will not limit progress in our level of material well-being. Such estimates often assume, however, that appropriate institutions will be forthcoming. Like the eighteenth-century liberals, we could assume that if one just leaves things alone somehow everything will work out all right. However, technological and social changes are occurring at an increasing rate, and the relatively slow, hit-or-miss process of institutional change may not be adequate. Furthermore, we are faced with a new problem—organizational complexity. If we are not able to make adjustments rapidly enough, we will eventually strangle in our own complexity. Civilization would not explode, it would simply grind to a tired, congested stop.

## ORGANIZATION

### THE DESIGN OF INSTITUTIONS

In many ways, the organization of interpersonal relationships (loosely speaking, our institutions) is parallel to the organization of technical production processes. To describe either institutional or production organization we usually need to know (1) the objective or product (2) characteristics of the resources or individuals (3) controls and decisions (4) communication channels or processes available (5) sequence and duration of actions or processes, and (6) the rate at which the production or institutional system is to grow or depreciate. For many policy issues, less distinction than usual need be made between institutional and technical processes. Because most questions relating to resource policy seem to be answered in terms of some public program or action, however, organization herein generally refers to institutions.

A simple way of describing an institution is to say that it is a generally accepted way of doing things, such as selling land, borrowing money, electing representatives, paying taxes, or educating children. When we talk of developing new policies or programs to do various things we are talking about modifying our institutions.

If, as suggested here, an institution can be thought of as a way of doing something, the relationship between a policy and an institution can be expressed as: What do we want to do? and, How can we do it best? Because the world is uncertain, we could add a collateral question: How do we cover ourselves when our policies or institutions change?

Resources are important but economic development, social improvement, or political progress is impossible without some organization. The likelihood of constructing effective economic and social institutions will be increased if we understand the principle of their design. Keen judgment, an experienced eye, and persistent cutting and fitting could eventually yield a skyscraper but trained architects and engineers can see that the job is done better and faster. Economic, social, and political engineers, using the best of accumulated knowledge about their respective systems, probably can design better policies and programs to modify our institutional structure than if they rely on day-to-day expedients.

## Two Approaches to Organization and Policy

Social engineers have available to them two general approaches, one somewhat more useful in the short run, the other more useful for coping with long-run problems. Because in resource policy we have included problems with both short-run and long-run relevance, at least a brief sketch of these two approaches could be helpful later on.

Most thinking about organization engineering, its relation to policy, and the modification of our institutional structure, can be related to these two approaches which are closely related to two distinct theoretical systems.[18] One is a 1-way, means-ends, pragmatic approach; the other is a 2-way, evolutionary, biological approach. Policy engineering, in the past, has dominated the first approach. Developments in the theory of control systems during the last decade or so, however, may strengthen the second approach.

The pragmatic approach to policy simply takes certain specified objectives as given, and thereupon seeks the most effective means of reaching such objectives. Policy objectives, within the time that the means are active, are invariant. Objectives are decided, once and for all, finally (and we assume clearly) by the people or their appointed designers. Our policy, then, consists largely of filling the gap between where we think we are and where we know we want to go.

Within the pragmatic approach, there exists a large body of widely accepted economic models. Resource policy issues, such as those discussed later, may be illuminated with such models. One of the main values of these models, suggests Jan Tinbergen,[19]

> ... is in judging the consistency among objectives and between means and objectives. Where quantifiable, the rate at which two objectives substitute for each other while competing for

available resources is valuable datum for the policymaker. The level of attainment of any objective resulting from the use of each of several alternative resources also is useful for the policymaker. Even if such relationships cannot be quantified, these economic models can express the problem more precisely.

Following the pragmatic approach,[20] the policy maker (1) ascertains the present state of affairs (2) compares the present state to a desired state, and (3) judges the effects of various policy means. From this evaluation the policy maker decides whether "reforms" (changing the institutional foundations), "structural modifications" (changing specific institutions), or "minor adjustments" (changing instrument variables) are needed. He further decides which of the reforms, structural modifications, or minor adjustments should be chosen. In resource policy, reforms would apply approximately at the level of the constitution and to principles underlying whole bodies of law, such as primogeniture or equal inheritance. Structural changes would apply to institutions such as the Homestead Act, the land market, farm tenancy, and acreage allotment programs. Minor adjustments would refer to changes in "instruments" such as the rate of interest on mortgages, land rentals, and the rate of cost-sharing on soil-conserving structures.

Recognizing the limitations of such means-end pragmatic models in the long run, they are still useful as a framework for, and for partial analysis of, particular policies. In order to undertake any separate economic program, it is adequate to state a policy and then suggest specific modification of an institution in order to bring about the desired objective. Economists and many others are habituated to think in terms of such models. Schematically, this is often illustrated by bold arrows from means to ends. Only rarely will such schemes show the little arrows running in an opposite (feedback) direction. However, they are useful constructs, in the short run at least.

Unfortunately these models have serious weaknesses if we think in terms of general or long-run changes, such as those we would expect in one hundred years. For these purposes, evolutionary models may be more helpful.

The second (evolutionary) approach to policy views what would be means and ends as mutually interdependent. Means and ends are not separated; they are parts of an interdependent system, the understanding of which can be gained best through information transmitted from one part of the system to another. An evolutionary model cuts us off from the certainty of a goal or target. Ends, when specified at all, are in terms of a continuing state such as survival, mobility, or growth. An evolutionary model centers on an understanding of the process of a changing system but prescribes no date or direction for change. As policy makers, we not only act but are acted upon—often by the same environment we attempt to influence.

During the past two decades, substantial strides have been made in the theory and science of organization. The theoretical models resulting from work on communications have been applied to problems in such areas as automation of factories, medical science, and military strategy. Insights into our problems of economic, social, and governmental organization are possible through the use of these models. A common theoretical structure—cybernetics—has integrated conceptions of machines, biological organisms, and social processes. With models of social systems, cyberneticians and social scientists, hopefully, will be able to identify critical control relationhips within our economic, social, or political system.[21] They will be able to determine the limits of survival for an institution, a people's capacity to absorb change, the rate at which information flows from one sector of an economy to another, the likelihood of a revolution, and so on.

What is the significance of these two theoretical precepts to resource policy? Briefly this:

(1) That we can ignore the interdependency of means and ends in our institutional system locally and for a short time; that we can draw on available (known) means to reach a short-run goal; but that goals specific enough to be of any value in policy can be developed only for the short run.

(2) That long-run policy is more relevantly stated in terms of continuing states such as survival or growth; that modifications of our institutions is a continuous process, not a single instantaneous change; that communication between parts of an institu-

tional system is of vital importance; and that resource policy cannot be regarded as independent from other policy.

## GOALS

In the short run, we realize the value of setting goals and sorting through available means to accomplish these objectives. In 1862, however, meaningful goals for the United States in 1962 could not have been conceived. Likewise, meaningful goals for 2062 are virtually impossible, if by meaningful goal is meant some specific invariant target, usually quantifiable. "A better life" or "a stronger democracy" is not exact enough to measure against the present.[22] In the short run, it is sensible to establish goals such as a given size of farm for every family desiring one. A "goal" for the long run can be scarcely more than a design of an institutional structure capable of flexibility to accommodate future changes.

One of the fundamental purposes of an institutional system, as with any ecosystem, is to survive. Changing resources and changing goals that are a part of economic growth place an institutional system under stress. These stresses can be either resisted or absorbed. If light and short, the stress probably can be resisted. If serious and sustained, modifications probably must be made. A characteristic of a surviving institutional system, therefore, is likely to be *flexibility*.

A system presumes units or components. Coordination of these units is also likely to affect survival and growth of the system. An institutional system will depend, in large part, upon effective *communication* among its components, i.e., people or groups of people.

Resource policy needs a flexible institutional system, the parts of which communicate. What are the channels of our institutional communication system? The market, courts, legislature, newspapers, and community organizations are such channels. By information transmitted and received through these channels, individuals and groups orient their buying and selling, their legal conduct, their lobbying, their advertising, and their local politics. Through these channels they will control expenditures on reclamation and conservation, restoration of wildlife habitat, automation in industry, land use regulations, space research, public transit—to mention but a few.

## CONSERVATION

If the year 2062 is important in our thinking, then conservation of natural resources is a critical policy issue. Our level of material well-being, and that of the people living when we are dead, depends on how these resources are prorated over time. Because we hopefully assume that our society will live longer than we as individuals expect to live, conservation problems are usually identified with the public interest and the public policy.

Basic questions in conservation[23] policy relate to (1) the rate, sequence, and location of use; (2) the combination of resources; and (3) the development, discovery, and invention of new resources and techniques. One must candidly admit, however, that such questions are much easier asked than answered. In the long run, as we indicated earlier, the answers might be expressed only in terms of technical and institutional systems capable of solving emerging problems. At best, we can require a safe minimum standard in policies accounting for the uncertainty of a distant future.

In the short run, we can assume that the goals of today are the goals of tomorrow, and that presently known means to attain these goals are all the available means. In the long run, these are shaky assumptions.

### THE SHORT RUN

*USDA Land and Water Resources Report.*—In the short run, say ten to twenty years, a pragmatic approach permits an evaluation of demands for, and supplies of, resources merely by projecting present goals, present resources, and present techniques of converting resources into goals.

A report by the Department of Agriculture,[24] for example, indicates that our food, clothing, and shelter needs for 1980 can be met with fewer acres provided technological improvement is forthcoming at current rates. More intensive use of the fewer acres may be presumed. This intensification will probably be in the form of more capital, more research, more skill, but less labor.

The real "goals" of this report are inherent in its assumptions about projected requirements, i.e., a per capita real income 57 per cent higher than 1959 and some changes in wants (requirements)[25] of the 261 million people in 1980. If policies are designed to facilitate the satisfaction of these projected requirements, then such projections become targets just as surely as if they had been so labeled. Although the terms "objectives or objective functions," "targets," or "goals" were scrupulously avoided, the term "requirements" served the purpose of the report. Resources were stated largely in terms of acres devoted to major uses. Crop yields were projected in a straight line, from 1950 through 1959 to 1980. Only an 8 per cent increase in feeding efficiency could be assumed, so a net increase of 18 million acres in range was necessary. Some improvement in efficiency of forest production is assumed but a possible deficit in forest acreage needed to meet "requirements" was indicated. Thus, the assumed requirements combined with the assumed rates of conversion of resources into products yielded the shifts in resource use given in the table.[26]

| LAND USE | MILLION ACRES | |
|---|---|---|
| | 1959 | 1980 |
| Cropland | 458 | 407 |
| Grassland pasture and range | 633 | 651 |
| Forestland | 746 | 741 |
| Farmsteads and farm roads | 10 | 10 |
| Special uses | 147 | 196 |
| Miscellaneous other land | 277 | 266 |
| Total | 2,271 | 2,271 |

By maintaining the current rate of productivity increase, we can attain a per capita consumption of food, shelter, and clothing 2 per cent greater in 1980 than in 1959.[27] For all agricultural purposes—crops, livestock, and fibers—33 million fewer acres need to be used in 1980, assuming investments in land and water improvement take place at the present rate. A net withdrawal of 33 million acres in agricultural production does not imply conservation in the sense of limiting present production in favor of future production. It is a needed production adjustment. Presumably, a withdrawal of a greater acreage implies conservation by favoring the future over the present.

The importance of assumptions either about targets (e.g., population projections) or conversion coefficients (e.g., crop yields) may be illustrated by comparing crop-acre requirements used in the USDA report with the Senate Select Committee Report on National Water Resources.[28] The Land and Water Policy Report suggests a 51 million acre decrease of cropland, and the Select Committee Report, a 22 million acre increase of cropland. Thus, even for the relatively short-run projection to 1980, differences in a few assumptions can make substantial differences in the outcome. Despite the entreaties of such reports to be regarded in the light of their assumptions, "magic numbers" such as "51 million acres dismissed from crops" often are given more attention than the broad guides to policy for which the reports are intended.[29]

In recommending means to accomplish the targets of the 2 per cent increase of per capita consumption of all farm products associated with the 57 per cent increase in per capita income, the Land and Water Policy Report made several suggestions on the sequence, timing, and, to a lesser extent, the location of various public measures. Thus, this report attained a fair degree of precision, even though it was intended only as a general policy guide.

## THE LONG RUN

*Flexibility and Communication.*—In the short run, a conservation policy with a pragmatic view, such as that of the USDA Land and Water Policy Report, can attain an imperative by its statements of objectives, resources, and conversion coefficients usually not feasible in the long run.

The voice of distant generations may be too faint to tell us their objectives very specifically. Furthermore, our resources and our conversion coefficients rest in some future combinations of knowledge fragments. In the long run, therefore, we might spare our divinations of objectives and resources to develop a technological and institutional system capable of easy movement in a changing world. For our institutional system to survive the impact of technological change, *flexibility* and *communication* must be built into each of our institutions. Conservation presents problems of communication not only within the present system but between the present and future systems. In effect, we must transmit to nonexistent receivers and receive from nonexistent transmitters.

A flexible system would be one which could readily change its course when needed. A flexible resource policy might be one in which a wide range of production alternatives were developed rather than one which relied on only one process or one resource. A flexible resource policy also would avoid irreversibly depleting the productivity of a renewable resource. The siltation of reservoirs, destruction of animal species, lowering of ground water levels, and spoliation of scenic sites and wilderness areas are examples of irreversible damage to resources. In resource policy, irreversibility may depend upon the possibility of economic, not necessarily physical, reconstruction.

In policy decisions, the rate at which nonrenewable resources should be used depends upon expected substitutes and the relative value of present as against future use. Nonrenewable resources, however, can be destroyed rather than depleted. Frequently, such destruction results from a difference between processes that are publicly efficient and processes that are privately profitable. Harry Caudill[30] describes coal augering in the Appalachians, for example:

> Augering in virgin ridges is fantastically wasteful of coal. Rarely do the bits extend into the mountain more than a quarter of its width. If boring proceeds from both sides, a solid block of coal is left in the center of the ridge which contains 50 percent of the original tonnage ... the weight of the overlying rock and soil crushes the thin walls between the holes. The coal in the interior is thus sealed against the outside world.

Time is the essence of conservation and therefore represents some peculiar problems of communication in an institutional system. Today's interpreters of messages from tomorrow's generation are hampered by ignorance and sometimes by lack of motivation. Buyers and sellers of the future are not present to bid in today's marketplace. And, in contrast to the voices of the past, the voices of the future can demand no writs of inheritance, pass no laws for their own benefit, and reserve no abundance.

## On a Flexible Economic System

We may be able to develop a more flexible economic system in a number of ways, for example, by reusing final goods, organizing to prevent high peak-loads, substituting communication for transportation, and developing flexibility in governmental functions.

*Salvage and Nonterminal Production.*—Many of our resources after they are dug, washed, and cut from the earth are sent on a one-way street to a final good beyond which no economic use is possible. Thus we see the growth of scrap heaps, trash fires, and junkyards. Many goods not designed as modern one-horse shays are discarded because of failure of a miniscule component that cannot be economically replaced. Other goods are forced into premature retirement because they either were not designed for remodeling or were designed for obsolescence. Losses from corrosion have been estimated at $5.5 billion a year, thus speeding the rush of our goods into scrap.

Many goods, such as gasoline and paint, are necessarily used up in consumption. Other goods, such as automobiles and office buildings, could be designed for easy component replacement (modular building units, for example) or remodeling. Other goods, such as a water supply, could be converted into virtually continuous use. Although much could be done in product design to preserve and reuse our goods, current economic incentives have not promoted a flow concept of material. Are we, for example, devoting enough research to the use of scrap iron compared to iron recovery from taconite?

*Peak-Loads and the Flow of Use Over Time.*—Perhaps the classic example of the peak-load problem is found in the generation of electricity. Uses of electricity have created such a market that it is economical to use off-peak electricity to pump water back into a storage reservoir for generation during peak uses. For other resources, however, such pumping back is not feasible. Camp grounds, theaters, restaurants, parking lots, and highways, faced with heavy demands at certain times, are virtually idle other times. Work and play habits—an important aspect of our institutional structure—often have a herd characteristic which demands that everyone work from 9 A.M. to 5 P.M., go to a movie on Saturday night, church on Sunday morning, and the park on Sunday afternoon. Large concentrations of people compound the effect. How might the use of our offices, transport systems, and recreation facilities be spread over time? More perfectly discriminating prices, reorganization of workers into shifts, and education in use of recreational facilities can minimize the needs for excess capacity of production capital and social overhead.

*Communication and Transportation*[31].—Our transportation systems accomplish two basic, and distinct, functions: movement of material, and communication among people. Most transport systems must compromise these two functions to some degree. The competitiveness of these two functions is apparent to commuters and truckers at peak-load times. The impact also might be seen on a planner's drawing board. A railroad or highway best suited for moving commuters is not always best for moving material. But why, in an electronic age, must persons communicate through physical presence? How much might our transportation load be lightened (and how much less time wasted) by trading messages electronically? Communication wedded to transportation (*a la* pony express or commuter) can result not only in waste but in an organizational handicap.

In the short run, we must improve our transportation to avoid wasted time and material. We have an abundance of recommendations for improving transportation. In the longer run, we need to improve electronic techniques of communicating and organize our habits of doing business to move thoughts, ideas, and controls electronically rather than mechanically.

*Government by Function instead of Geography.*—A final thought, related to the previous paragraph on communication, relates to proposed change in governmental structure. One of the primary reasons for our system of local, state, and central government was communication; first, because slow (mechanical) means of transportation required accessible local government and second, because the lack of interconnection with other regions, industries, and persons created a more easily identifiable local interest. The physical necessity for small, multifunction government units has greatly declined, but the institution of local and state government hangs on (often against economic, social, and even political pressures to the contrary). We are aware of frequent inadequacies of some of our geographic units to deal with such resource problems as location of new industry, migration, water development, and local services such as schools. As our governmental needs change more rapidly in response to improvements in technology and shifts in wants, government must be more responsive. In many instances, this will require local responsiveness coupled with centralized association of problems, access to resources, and authority. A layering of government is not necessary for communication and direct channels along functional lines can aid in the responsiveness to problems. Excessive bureaucracy is deadening because so much of the original message is lost in the transmission system. The organization of government along functional lines (that is, problem-oriented by industry, resource, or enterprise) could facilitate communication. Of course, the actual form of government will be determined by other considerations also.

COMMUNICATING WITH OUTER TIME

Conservation, in the long run, will involve the organization of institutions flexible enough to meet future needs. In the absence of clearly defined goals, resources might be used so that salvage and re-use are possible, so that renewable resources are not irreversibly depleted, and so that substitutes for nonrenewable resources can be developed to offset depletion. A government in a society of growing complexity must continue to adapt and improve communication between the components of its resource policy. Especially critical will be the problems of "communicating" with future generations whose faint voices may be drowned out by current cries. "The problems of immediacy always have the advantage of attracting notice—those that lie in the future fare poorly in the competition for attention and money."[32]

## DISTRIBUTION

Thomas Jefferson, visiting a village near Paris in 1785, wrote to Bishop Madison about the conditions of the working poor and unemployed. He contrasted their position with that of the very wealthy in whose hands the property of France was "absolutely concentrated."

> I am conscious that an equal division of property is impracticable, but the consequences of this enormous inequality producing so much misery to the bulk of mankind, legislators cannot invent too many devices for subdividing property . . .[33]
>
> . . . it is not too soon to provide by every possible means that as few as possible shall be without a little portion of land. The small landholders are the most precious part of a state . . .[34]

The sentiment expressed by Jefferson characterizes our basic precepts favoring the wide distribution of property. The Constitution, the Homestead Act, and the Sherman Anti-Trust Act are but a few of the overt efforts of the United States to encourage widespread holding of property and to discourage the restraint of economic opportunity. Although this sentiment persists, economic conditions within which it is expressed have changed. Owner-proprietorship of farms, for example, may be favored under the illusion that they are still adequate expressions of the egalitarian sentiments. But owner-proprietorship of farms does not necessarily provide either widespread ownership of property or equal economic opportunity.

With the intention of opening the distribution issue, we might examine the concentration of resource ownership and control, first in the economy generally, and second in agriculture specifically.

### THE ECONOMIC SYSTEM AND THE DISTRIBUTION OF OWNERSHIP

Notwithstanding numerous modifications, our economic system still relies on the assumption that an owner's preference of more to less of anything will induce him to move resources into uses where they create the most valuable product. This allocative function of the market system also performs the distributive function, because the same rate of return which is the incentive for the resource owner to allocate his resources to their "highest" (most lucrative) use is the owner's reward for making a correct decision. In a competitive situation the resource market sets the value of the resource regardless of its owner. Thus the market has an important, though only partial, bearing on whether a resource owner will be rich or poor. More completely, a property holder's income is a function of (1) the amount of property he owns (2) the unit return of the property, and (3) his personal taxes or bounties.

Of these, (2) and (3) are easier to adjust in the short run through bargaining, negotiation, and legislation, with interest or rental rate adjustments, tax changes, incentive bounties, price supports, cost-sharing, and other manipulations of the owner's rate of return on his resources or his personal income directly.[35] Changes in property rights are relatively more difficult and time consuming to bring about, hence are less well suited for short-run policy. Thus, the ownership of property and the modification of the structure of property might best be treated as a long-run issue.

In Jefferson's world, just emerging from feudalism, the assumption that property ownership meant economic power was reasonable. Since the classic treatment of the corporation by Berle and Means, we have been on notice that such an assumption is naive. The ingenious institution of the corporation, which Adam Smith said would never be of economic importance, has vested great power in the hands of a few decision makers by owners of resources whose power is diluted by their large numbers. So effective has been this device that we have imposed legal restrictions on corporations in order to protect not only consumers but the owners of property.

With the exception of agriculture and miscellaneous services, the corporation dominates all United States industry. Large concentrations of resources are controlled by relatively few organizations. In 1959, for example, 75 per cent of our firms controlled only about 4 per cent of our productive assets. On the other end of the size scale, about 75 per cent of our productive assets were controlled by 1 per cent of the firms. The decision makers of giant corporations own a very small proportion of the resources they control. Thus, tremendous economic power can be attained without property. However, the location of this power and its consequences on resource owners, consumers, and the public at large will depend not only on an organizational form, such as a corporation, but on the entire institutional milieu within which it functions.

Bigness is not necessarily strength, as witness consumers—the largest and apparently weakest sector in the economy. The basic ingredient of power (economic or other) is coordination of the components of a system for specific objectives. Consumers lack economic power because they communicate *through* the market, rather than *ahead* of (in order to influence) the market.

A basic issue then is how economic and political coordination is to be encouraged or discouraged in relation to our national interest.

## DISTRIBUTION OF RESOURCE OWNERSHIP AND CONTROL IN AGRICULTURE

Among the roots of most supports for the family farm is the sentiment against concentration of wealth in the hands of a few. Whether they are motivated by concern for political freedom, as was Jefferson, or by belief in the economic superiority of the family farm, as are more modern advocates, concentration of ownership or control of agricultural resources has been generally disfavored by Americans.

Sometimes our sentiments curve in on us like dilemmas on crumpled horns. Agricultural land policy seems to be faced with such a dilemma; namely, that (1) land should be widely held (2) land should be held by the tiller, but (3) tillers are now a small proportion of the population and their number is decreasing. As an aid in clarifying some of the issues surrounding the family farm and the structure of agriculture, a few observations can be made about the meaning, trends, and implications of concentration of ownership and control.

Some assistance on the problems of concentration can be had merely from definitions. What do we mean by "concentrated" or "held by a few"? First, a distinction between ownership and control is sometimes useful. A working simplification is that ownership or title determines where the returns to the factor of production go; and control is the authority for decisions about use of the resource.[36] Second, a group among whom resource ownership or control is concentrated should be circumscribed. When "a few" own or control the land, of whom are they a few? Are they a few of all men, women, and children in the world; a few of the adults in a nation who could be owners or operators; or a few of the persons who do own or control some land? Much increase in the concentration of land ownership and control of agricultural land in the United States could be attributed to the rapidly diminishing proportion of farm people in the American population. A measurable interpretation of concentration is best limited to the distribution of ownership or control among those who own or control the resources at the time of measurement.

Third, a persistent inclination for static definitions exists even for problems that are essentially dynamic. Fixed-size classes (for example, Census of Agriculture's Economic Class or Size of Farm) contain no inherent comparability over time, and force their users to adjust them with exogenous factors such as price indexes. These fixed classes can create some strange illusions for the nonperceptive. For example, as farm size and output increase generally, more and more farms climb into the upper brackets, leading to cries of dangerous concentration by the alarmists and assurances of healthy, prosperous agriculture by the mollifiers. Concentration and distribution are relative terms and their definitions need to reflect this relativity.

What then, can be said of concentration of resources in agriculture? With some exceptions, such as in production of poultry and some truck-farm crops, the distribution of ownership of nonland resources is roughly in proportion to the land on which the nonland resources are used. Therefore, an examination of the concentration of land ownership and operation will roughly proxy for a view of the structure of agriculture.

The familiar Lorenz curves and concentration ratios can be used as demonstrations. These devices permit comparisons between time periods, forms of wealth, and different populations without adjustment. The curve shows the accumulated portion

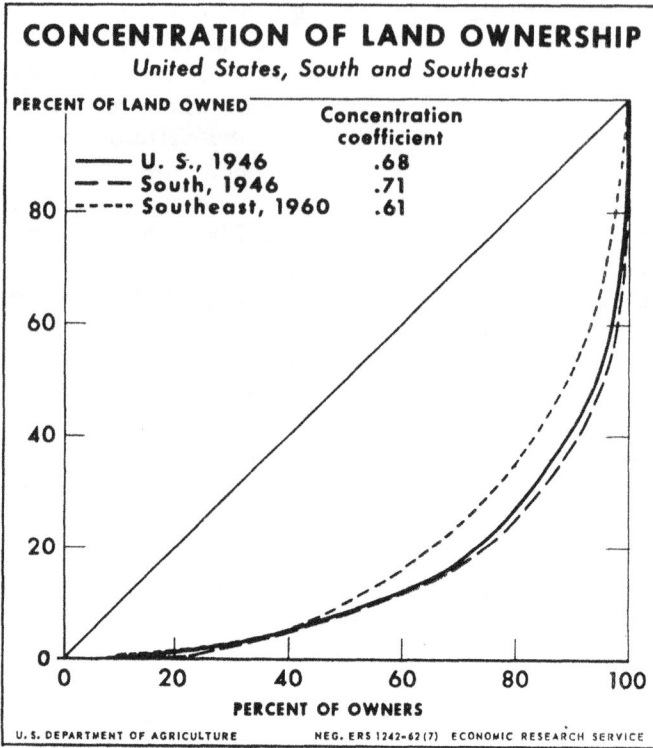

## CONCENTRATION OF LAND OWNERSHIP
### United States, South and Southeast

PERCENT OF LAND OWNED

|  | Concentration coefficient |
|---|---|
| ——— U. S., 1946 | .68 |
| — — South, 1946 | .71 |
| =----- Southeast, 1960 | .61 |

PERCENT OF OWNERS

U. S. DEPARTMENT OF AGRICULTURE          NEG. ERS 1242-62(7)   ECONOMIC RESEARCH SERVICE

Fig. 16.2

of land owned or operated by the accumulated portion of owners or operators. Figure 2, for example, shows that 50 per cent of the owners in the Southeast in 1960 owned less than 10 per cent of the land, and 95 per cent owned less than 50 per cent (conversely, 5 per cent owned over 50 per cent of the land). The concentration ratio (0 to 1) is the area between the Lorenz curve and the diagonal, divided by the area of the triangle described by the diagonal and two axes. Thus, the more the curve bows downward, the larger is the concentration ratio.

*Concentration of Ownership.*—Only one complete survey of farmland ownership in the United States has been made in recent times. This survey, reported by Inman and Fippin,[37] was made in 1946. In 1958 and in 1960, respectively, surveys of land ownership were completed in the Great Plains and in the South-eastern States.[38] Figure 2 illustrates the degree of concentration in the United States in 1946, in the South in 1946, and in the Southeast in 1960. Figure 3 shows the changes in concentration in the Great Plains between 1946 and 1958.

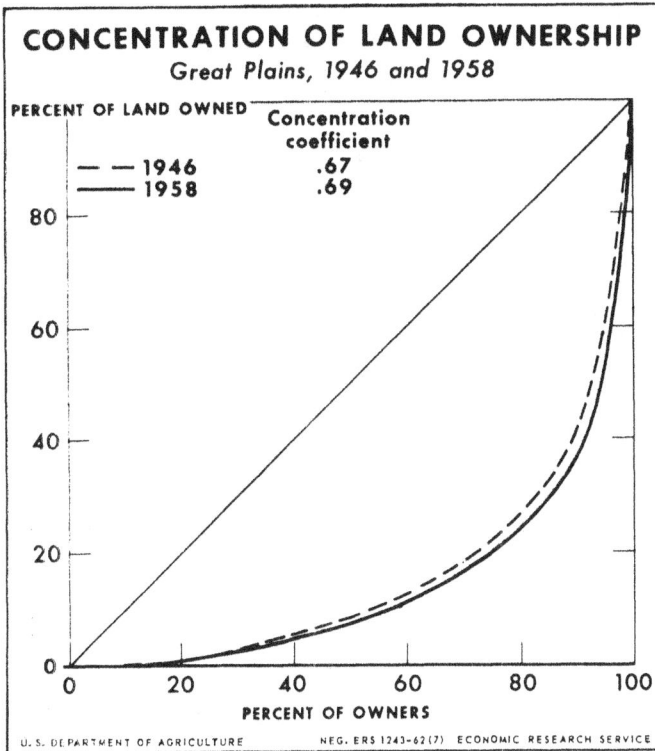

FIG. 16.3

Concentration of land ownership appears approximately the same as the concentration of all wealth of the United States.[39] The limited information on ownership does not permit a definitive statement on changes in concentration for the United States. However, the small increases in two major agricultural areas can be accounted for either in errors of estimate or in differences in the areas covered. On the basis of some information on transfers, there does appear to be little recent change in concentration of ownership.

*Concentration of Operation.*—Historical data on concentration of farm operating units are more abundant than data on ownership. The curve in Figure 4 shows concentration in the United

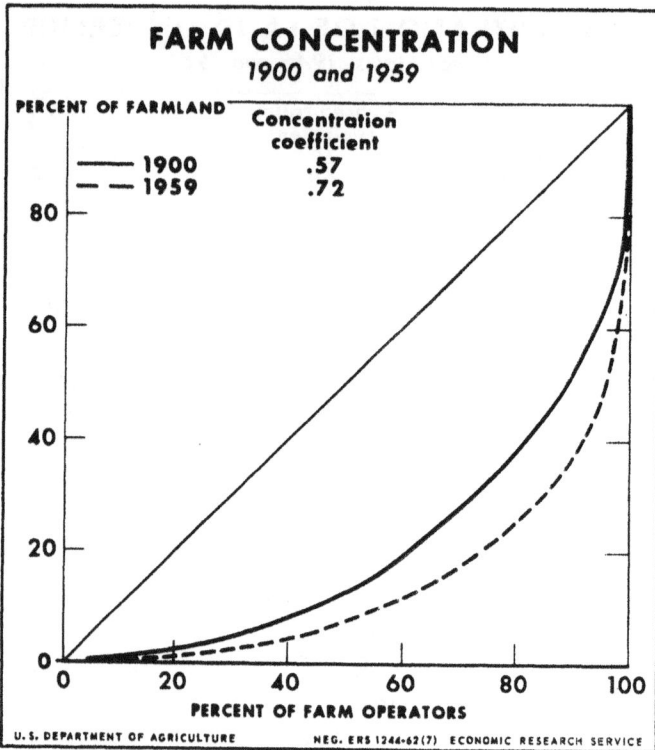

FIG. 16.4

States for 1900 and 1959. The concentration coefficients represented by these curves have increased from 0.57 in 1900 to 0.72 in 1959. Because data on the concentration of farm operations are taken from complete censuses, errors of estimate are minimized. Changes in census definition of farm between 1900 and

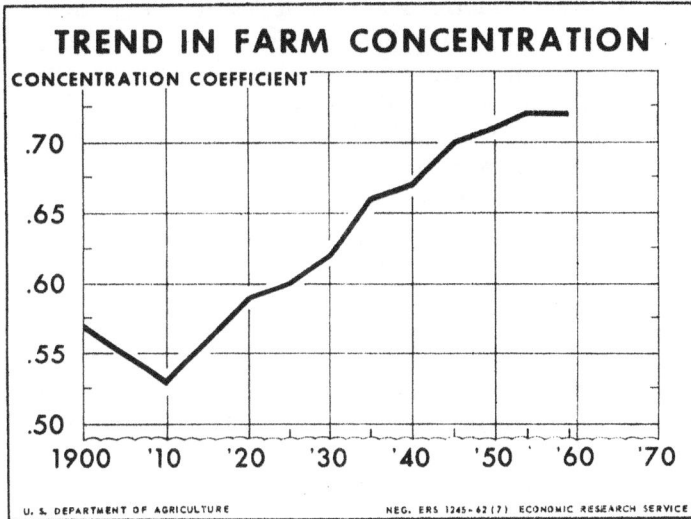

## TREND IN FARM CONCENTRATION

CONCENTRATION COEFFICIENT

| | | | | | | | |
|---|---|---|---|---|---|---|---|

.70

.65

.60

.55

.50

1900  '10  '20  '30  '40  '50  '60  '70

U. S. DEPARTMENT OF AGRICULTURE        NEG. ERS 1245-62(7) ECONOMIC RESEARCH SERVICE

Fɪɢ. 16.5

1954 are probably unimportant. The effect, if any, of the 1959 change in definition, is to lower the concentration ratio slightly.

There is little doubt that concentration of farm operations has increased since 1900, and that this increase was not limited to the last few years. Furthermore, this concept of concentration tends to be conservative because it refers only to the distribution of land among operators at any particular time. The effect of fewer operators in absolute numbers, or a smaller proportion of farmers in the entire population, is excluded.[40]

The distribution of control is only partly explained by the concentration of operations. The loci of decisions, even in the relatively simple organization of a farm, are extremely difficult to identify. As the farm becomes more closely integrated with a prefarm and a postfarm stage of production, the so-called agribusiness gains complexity comparable to that of manufacturing firms. Changes in the structure will be measured in part, however, by the gains or losses in decision making about the resources entering and the products leaving the farm. Some attempts are now being made to measure these gains and losses in decision making between producers and contractors in written integration contracts. Eventually it may be possible to trace the exchange of decisions as we now trace a flow of funds.

Precise measurement of the factors affecting concentration or dispersion of control remains for future research, but some of these factors can perhaps be identified. Concentration will result, in part, simply from the growth in economic size of farm. Part of the concentration we have experienced in the United States may be due to decline in farm numbers to the lowest number since the homestead era. In some areas, for some types of farming, intensification and specialization may be accompanied by concentration of control.

Family assistance and intergenerational accumulation accompanied by migration of farm youth may cause a buildup of substantial estates by those who remain in agriculture. Inheritance, however, can have a dispersing effect by breaking up estates. The long-run effects of family assistance and inheritance on the number of farms and the rationing of opportunities have not been adequately determined.

Factors tending to disperse ownership are vertical integration contracts, farm management services, purchased and contracted inputs, leases, partnerships, and farm corporations. While it is quite clear that most of these arrangements will disperse ownership, the effect on control is not clear.[41] The growth in part ownership (owners who rent additional land),[42] partnerships, and corporations[43] would appear to indicate that larger farms favor dispersion of ownership and concentration of control.

As the number of farms continues to shrink, a point may be reached where reconsideration of our policy on ownership and control of agricultural resources may be in order. Perhaps resources cannot be both widely owned and operator owned. Do we want to encourage owner-operatorship? Contrariwise, if resources are widely owned but controlled by a few operators, will we have an organizational form typical of other industries but regarded unfavorably for agriculture?

As a concluding note to this section, the following thesis is suggested. Agriculture in the United States is advancing into an organizational form nowhere duplicated in the world now or in the past. We moved through the Domestic Stage characterized by largely self-sufficient units and motivated mainly by self-preservation; and through the Commercial Stage characterized by off-farm contact with the product markets and motivated by family income. We have now entered the Industrial Stage characterized by close interdependence with both resource and product markets and motivated by firm profits.

The implications of this new stage in the organization of agriculture will be particularly noticeable in the relatively underdeveloped markets for resources in agriculture that have been historically small, local, and individualistic. Changes are taking place, however, and already some enterprises have become part of a food and fiber producing industry, no longer just a type of farming.

## POPULATION

Our human resources, although of increasing interest to a large number of scientists and educators, have not been exhaustively considered in terms of a public population policy. In a sense, of course, compulsory school attendance, subsidies to education, tax concessions for children, and views on dissemination of contraceptive information, indirectly reflect some attitudes about the desired quality or quantity of population in the United States. More realistically, these measures, which indirectly bear upon the dimensions of the population, are aimed toward other objectives. A public population policy, as such, apparently does not exist.

Yet the relation between the quantity and quality of our human resources and our level of material well-being seems to be close enough to warrant our serious attention and that of others concerned with resource policy.

Surely the number and talents of our people will have an effect on the composition and amount of goods and services making up our material well-being in the future. The quality and quantity of our human resources will affect the use of our natural and capital resources. How can a land policy avoid being, sooner or later, a people policy?

A more complete population policy will have to face the issue of people as ends as well as means (resources). With respect to ends and means, the human resources particularly are distinguished from natural or capital resources. Although people are basic inputs in the production of goods and services, people are also the decision makers who specify the objectives of production.

The orientation of this chapter toward material well-being suggests that consideration of population policy herein be confined to people as resources. The subject of population as an end or objective extends considerably beyond the scope of this chapter.[44]

Of the many possible aspects of a population policy, such as numbers, age, health, migration, and composition, perhaps two will suffice to focus attention on population considerations that relate to resource policy. These two aspects will be called, for the sake of brevity, quantity and quality. Quantity will refer simply to the number of people, largely in terms of human resources. Quality will refer primarily to the level of skills and knowledge of a population, with perhaps a word on biological capacity.

A short-term policy on population quality would include (1) education (2) training and adult education (3) retirement, and (4) health and welfare assistance. Quantity policy in short run would include (1) health measures (2) migration (3) public subsidies such as income tax concessions, and (4) birth control. Longer-run policies would be much the same but would depend mostly upon appraisal and modifications of basic institutions including public finance, attitudes on family planning, employment, retirement, and education. The irreversibility of population growth in a country with a high value on the sanctity of life means that population considerations almost automatically are long-run considerations.

How many human resources will be needed? This question can be answered somewhat better by separating human resources into labor, skill, and inventiveness. As a power source, man is extremely limited and, to a large extent, machines have either replaced man or so augmented his energy that they have made him a director or decision maker. Mechanical sources of energy, when linked with computers, are replacing many hand skills also.

In 1961, testimony before the Joint Economic Committee

investigating the expected impact of automation on the economy included the prediction that

> ... we must realistically look forward to the day, perhaps not more than a generation away, when there will be no human labor, other than supervisory or maintenance engaged in the manufacture of many of the mass-produced necessities of American life ... the drudgery of routine jobs will be handled by inexpensive robots rather than sensitive human beings.[45]

Computers are performing routine management tasks. Even many technical and scientific activities are being "cybernated" away from people. In a report to the Center for the Study of Democratic Institutions, Don Michael announced that: "There is every reason to believe that within the next two decades machines will be available outside the laboratory that will do a credible job of original thinking, certainly as good thinking as that expected of most middle-level people who are supposed to 'use their minds.' "[46]

Human genius in the arts or sciences is for the time being irreplaceable, but brainpower has acquired tremendous leverage through electronics and mechanics.

A recent report stated that machines would "eliminate at least 200,000 jobs a year in the next decade."[47] Another report indicated that in just six years, 1,500,000 jobs had been eliminated in manufacturing alone.[48] The Bureau of Labor Statistics has estimated, optimistically, that between 1960 and 1970—an era in which all employment will rise 20 per cent—professional and technical personnel will increase 40 per cent. Proprietors and managers would increase at about the overall average. No increase is anticipated among unskilled workers and a decline in farmers and farm workers is anticipated.[49]

In a paper on the effects of population growth on capital formation, 300,000 to 500,000 workers annually were estimated to be excess labor[50]—that is, technologically obsolescent. Unskilled labor will probably feel the greatest impact of the current trend toward cybernated industry. Based on the current experience of those who do not complete high school, unemployment rates of 30 to 60 per cent among the relatively unskilled may be expected. However, many skilled blue collar and white collar workers also will find they are no match for lightning fast, perfectly accurate control systems. Such diverse activities as retailing, accounting, livestock feeding, trucking, translating, manufacturing, medicine, law, and economics all will feel the effect of computer advances.

The outcome of an ever-increasing rate of automated production and electronic thinking in as distant an era as 2062 is impossible to guess. New combinations of knowledge are rapidly falling into place and are creating whole new possibilities for production. For example, the new science of control systems—cybernetics—has been developed in less than two decades.

Out of this science, machines have been designed to learn by cognition, generalization, and correction of errors, in the same way man learns. Such machines in control of production lines could produce a large part of the consumer goods. Perhaps it is not wholly irresponsible to say that *potentially* most of our material needs[51] could be satisfied by machines. What our institutions—property, customs, unions, tax concessions and subsidies, lobbyists, and others—will permit is another question.

If the needed quantity of human resources seems to be limited, what of the quality of these resources? The answer, in part at least, seems to follow from the considerations of quantity. The men who can understand, manipulate, and develop the complex controls required for production of greater material well-being, must be talented, skilled, and educated; i.e., those in whom enormous investments have been made. These people probably will be older than present-day workers before they begin to produce. Their production will be intermittent because of retraining and education. Their productive life can be extended into later years.[52] Demands on physical strength or dexterity will be met with steel and electricity instead of muscle and nerve. Our human resources will need to be much wiser and perhaps, as a consequence, somewhat older.

We can claim at least a partial success; our human resources are becoming older.

The newborn of 1862 could look forward to little more than forty-one years of life. Today's newborn can expect almost seventy years of life. Those who made it to age fifteen in the Homestead era could expect to live forty-five years and die with their boots on. Today's fifteen-year-olds can expect to live fifty-six more years—six years beyond the institutionally determined limit of their productive life.

And from where will the resources for the added education and training come? One possible source is the savings resulting from a reduced rate of birth. Strohbehn estimates, for example, that the capitalized value of savings from a reduction in births equivalent merely to the hard-core technologically unemployed would be "more than \$2.3 billion" or about "one-fourth of our 1959 [public] expenditures for elementary and secondary education."[53]

A long-run policy on population limitation, of course, will need to be judged for consistency with other policies. Furthermore, in order to be implemented, such a public policy must be attuned to individual objectives which also may be inconsistent. In his theoretical treatment of economic policy, Jan Tinbergen[54] commented:

> Among the important and widespread inconsistencies in individual economic behavior, and hence short-term aims, are those referring to the choice of education and to the creation of a family. Generally speaking, too many young people choose too little education and care too little about family planning; very evidently because of the shortsightedness of others as well as of themselves. The test of inconsistency is that, if they could have chosen again, they would have chosen differently, and that this continues to be true for successive generations.

For the largest gains in per capita well-being, in the long run, the need for continued increases in population—as resources —appears doubtful. If a larger population is desired, it will have to be argued on other grounds. The need for improved skills and education of human resources appears obvious.[55] Surely if we expect to continue to make the material gains which we ascribe largely to knowledge, we must continue to invest in education and training.

The implications of continued population growth on our

economic and social organization are perhaps even more important than the implications of population on the technical capacity to produce. As the number of people increases, and their contacts with each other increase, so also does the complexity of their relationships tend to increase.[56] In a society of large numbers, rules and codes supplant personal contacts. Other things remaining the same, organizational overhead—the resources used just to keep a system in control of itself—changes geometrically with a change in the population.[57] As Arthur S. Miller stated as his central thesis of the political economy of population growth:[58]

> ... population growth will create the need for more organization which, in turn, will result in the further enhancement of group (including societal), rather than individual, values. If continued, the tendency could result in such a diminution of personal freedoms as to approximate the conditions of totalitarianism.

A population policy will involve problems perhaps much greater than the role of human resources in production. The legal, political, and social problems appear to dwarf what we might view as substantial economic problems. Immensity of the problem, however, is hardly an excuse for avoiding an attempt at its solution.

The neo-cornucopian argument that we appear to be ahead in the food-people race has not been discussed. Whether the increase in the food/people ratio is because of, or in spite of, population increases would be appropriate for a more exhaustive treatment. Such a treatment might explore the thesis suggested by Colin Clark and most Marxians that a letup in the upward spiral of consumption would bring about the collapse of our economic structure.

Predictions of food-producing capacity vis-à-vis population probably avoid more important issues. Some goods, such as the space and privacy Harrison Brown[59] refers to, are not produced without limit. And bread alone, at its best, is a dull diet.

## MORE THAN A NATION

Although this chapter was confined to the resources and needs of the United States, the relationship of our resource policy to other countries cannot go unmentioned. Few responsible persons today deny America's commitment, first, to the nations now comprising the free world, and eventually to all nations willing to cooperate in raising the level of material well-being as one means for human ennoblement. It was in such a context that the Paley Commission report was written. The Commission believed that

> ... if we fail to work for a rise in the standard of living of the rest of the free world, we thereby hamper and impede the further rise of our own, and equally lessen the chances of democracy to prosper and peace to reign the world over.[60]

Although not sufficient, intelligent use of our resources will do much for the enrichment and development of an American civilization. This thought can be expressed no better than with the words of Will Durant in the opening of his *Story of Civilization:*

> Civilization is social order promoting cultural creation. Four elements constitute it: economic provision, political organization, moral traditions, and the pursuit of knowledge and the arts. It begins where chaos and insecurity end. For when fear is overcome, curiosity and constructiveness are free, and man passes by natural impulse towards the understanding and embellishment of life.[61]

## NOTES

1. Kenneth Boulding, *The Organizational Revolution* (New York: Harper and Brothers, 1953).

2. Presumably, the rows, columns, and cells of this matrix could be filled with quantities such as energy or energy displacement equivalents. The sum of all the needs then could be expressed in energy transfers. Meier, using an energy transfer criterion, arrives at current needs of $4 \times (10)^7$ calories per year in North America. Meier's estimates were composed of caloric requirements of water, food, fiber, fuel, power, materials, metals, and paper. The overall estimate includes about 80 per cent waste (not directed to human purposes) in interchanges of energy sources. He expresses these needs as a range of "adequate" levels for the world at present standards, 1 to $4 \times (10)^7$. See R. L. Meier, *Science and Economic Development: New Patterns of Living* (New

York: Massachusetts Institute of Technology and John Wiley and Sons, 1956), p. 10.

3. Based on personal consumption expenditures and personal income data in U.S. Bureau of the Census, *Statistical Abstract of the United States, 1961* (Washington, D.C.: GPO, 1961), Table 413.

4. Glen T. Barton and Ralph A. Loomis, *Productivity of Agriculture, United States, 1870–1958,* USDA Technical Bulletin 1238, Washington, D. C., April, 1961.

5. If the Schmookler-Brownlee thesis that inventiveness follows rather than leads investment is correct, the decapitalization of agriculture relative to other segments of the economy could induce a climate of stagnation in food science. Such stagnation could be a disaster in the long run. Jacob Schmookler and Oswald Brownlee, however, did not refer specifically to agriculture in their general model in "Determinants of Inventive Activity," *American Economic Review,* LII, No. 2 (May, 1962), 165-85.

6. Based on Series G 244-330 of the *Historical Statistics of the United States, Colonial Times to 1957—A Statistical Abstract Supplement,* prepared by the U.S. Bureau of the Census (Consumption Expenditures by Income Class, 1874–1950).

7. Based on average square footage of new construction and population increases, 1950–60, of 850 square feet per person upgraded to 1,000 square feet per person; with shelter requirements of about 60 per cent, 20 per cent, and 20 per cent for residential, commercial-industrial, and other, respectively.

8. Dwelling-unit starts were 65 per cent 1-family in 1900 and 80 per cent 1-family in 1959.

9. Omission of many of the amenities, however, might drastically alter the character of our civilization. In no way, therefore, can we assume that amenities are "luxuries" or "unnecessary."

10. John K. Galbraith, *The Affluent Society* (Boston: Houghton Mifflin Co., 1958), p. 150.

11. Calculated in current dollars on the basis of selected, not all, amenity expenditures. Jewelry and pleasure trips, for example, were confounded in categories that were primarily basic and thereby excluded.

12. Based on Series F 44–48 of the *Historical Statistics* (Gross Domestic Product, 1904–1955).

13. U. S. Bureau of the Census, *Statistical Abstract of the United States, 1961* (Washington: GPO, 1961), p. 522. Total horsepower, prime movers: 4.7 bil. hp. 1950 to 11.4 bil. hp. 1960.

14. A report to the President by The President's Materials Policy Commission, *Resources for Freedom,* I, "Foundations for Growth and Security," Wm. S. Paley, Chairman (Washington, D.C., GPO, June, 1952, 82nd Congress, 2nd Session).

15. Sam H. Schurr, Bruce Netschert, *et al., Energy in the American Economy, 1850–1975* (Baltimore: Johns Hopkins Press, 1960).

16. As an indicator, the real value of nonresidential structures and pro-

ducer durables increased from $186.2 billion to $251.6 billion (35 per cent) from 1950 to 1958, or about 4.5 per cent a year: *Statistical Abstract of the United States, 1961*, Table 444, p. 325.

17. Paul W. McGann, "Technological Progress and Minerals," (p. 80) in J. J. Spengler, ed., *Natural Resources and Economic Growth* (Baltimore: Johns Hopkins Press, 1961).

18. Herbert A. Simon, in developing F-theory and O-theory models, illustrates many of the differences of these two approaches. See especially pp. 170–82 of his *Models of Man: Social and Rational* (New York: John Wiley and Sons, 1957).

19. Jan Tinbergen, *Economic Policy: Principles and Design* (Amsterdam: North Holland Publishing Co., 1956).

20. Approximately according to Tinbergen's scheme.

21. Arnold Tustin, for example, constructed a cybernetic model for Keynes' "General Theory" in the *Mechanism of Economic Systems* (Cambridge: Harvard University Press, 1953).

22. Karen Dovring acidly comments on some "goal" literature in "Scientoid Manifesto," *American Behavioral Scientist*, IV, No. 9 (May, 1961), 36, 37.

23. With some relaxations in the rigor of his definitions, the concept of conservation used here is that of S. V. Ciriacy-Wantrup in *Resource Conservation, Economics and Policies* (Berkeley: University of California Press, 1952), p. 51. He defines conservation in terms of "changes in the intertemporal distribution of use. In conservation, the redistribution of use is in the direction of the future; in depletion, in the direction of the present."

24. Land and Water Policy Committee, USDA, *Land and Water Resources, a Policy Guide*, May, 1962.

25. Domestic use of farm products was expected to rise 50 per cent based on 48 per cent population increase and 4 per cent increase in food consumption, assuming some upgrading in diet. Nonfood requirements were expected to decrease 19 per cent between 1959 and 1980, that is, at less than the 25 per cent decrease of the previous decade. Timber requirements were expected to rise one-third.

26. Adapted from *Land and Water Resources, a Policy Guide*, USDA, Land and Water Policy Committee, May, 1962, p. 43.

27. This 2 per cent increase in per capita demand in all farm products was all that was anticipated at the prices expected in 1980. *Land and Water Resources, op. cit.*, p. 37.

28. Based on projected 480.5 million acres in 1980. U.S. Senate Select Committee on National Water Resources, *Land and Water Potentials and Future Requirements for Water*, December, 1959, p. 64.

29. Generalized models which readily reveal the effect of a change in an assumption are a helpful antidote for the mesmerizing effect of magic numbers. For a good example, see George Tolley's "Interrelated Land Development Possibilities" in *Modern Land Policy* (Urbana: University of Illinois Press, 1960), p. 121–40.

30. Harry Caudill, "The Rape of the Appalachians," *Atlantic*, April, 1962, p. 40.

31. Transportation of people and materials consumes 20 per cent of our energy and is expected to require one-fourth of our energy by 1975. Sam H. Schurr and Bruce Netschert, *Energy in the American Economy, 1850–1975* (Baltimore: Johns Hopkins Press, 1960), p. 264. According to R. L. Meier, *Science and Economic Development, op. cit.,* almost 40 per cent of our energy is used for transportation if we include the manufacture of vehicles and facilities.

32. U.S. Department of Interior Annual Report, "Resources for Tomorrow," 1961, p. 27. Quotation from President John F. Kennedy.

33. Koch and Peden, *The Life and Selected Writings of Jefferson* (New York: Random House, 1944) (A letter to the Rev. James Madison, President of William and Mary College, October 28, 1785) p. 389.

34. *Ibid.,* p. 390.

35. Walter E. Chryst and John F. Timmons, "The Economic Role of Land Resource Institutions in Agricultural Adjustment," *Dynamics of Land Use: Needed Adjustment* (Ames: Iowa State University Press, 1961). See especially pp. 254–57.

36. This is a functional definition—owners sometimes partake of decision making and decision makers sometimes partake of resource returns, at least in the short run.

37. Buis T. Inman and William Fippin, *Farm Land Ownership in the United States,* U. S. Department of Agriculture Miscellaneous Publication 699, 1949.

38. Roger W. Strohbehn and Gene Wunderlich, *Land Ownership in the Great Plains States, 1958,* U.S. Department of Agriculture Statistical Bulletin 261, 1960. The Southeast study (unpublished) includes all rural land in the States of Virginia, North Carolina, South Carolina, Georgia, Florida, Alabama, and Tennessee. The concentration curve in Figure 2 is for farmland only, however.

39. Concentration coefficient for the value of gross estates in the United States is 0.61 and in England and Wales is 0.85, as calculated from data in Tables 99 and 100 in Robert J. Lampman, *The Share of Top Wealth Holders in National Wealth,* National Bureau of Economic Research 74 (Princeton: Princeton University Press), pp. 213–16. Concentration coefficients of land ownership are about 0.10 lower when based on value rather than on acreage.

40. The effect of a relatively diminishing agricultural population on concentration can be calculated by giving a zero value to nonfarm households. If the nonfarm households are included at zero value, the concentration coefficients are 0.85 in 1910 and 0.97 in 1959 rather than 0.53 and 0.72 in the same years.

41. Walter G. Miller, "Farm Tenure Perspective of Vertical Integration," *Journal of Farm Economics,* XLII, No. 2 (May, 1960) 307–16.

42. R. S. Crickenberger and W. L. Gibson, Jr., *Farming as a Part Owner*, Virginia Polytechnic Institute Bulletin 504, April, 1959.

43. Tentative estimates based on 1959 data show 130,000 farm partnerships and 10,000 farm corporations in the United States. These farms account for acreage and production much out of proportion to their small number.

44. As a point of departure, the author offers the following summary of possible objectives of a population quantity policy from an economic point of view: I. Maximum number of people: Suggests a subsistence level of living. II. Maximum production: Suggests a population such that additions thereto would not increase total product. III. Maximum average product: Suggests a population at which production per capita is at a maximum.

45. Joint Economic Committee, 86th Congress, 2nd Session, "New Views on Automation," p. 337. Statement of John I. Snyder, Chairman, U. S. Industries, Inc.

46. Donald N. Michael, *Cybernation: The Silent Conquest*, California: Center for the Study of Democratic Institutions, 1962, p. 9.

47. Ewan Clague and Leon Greenberg, Report before American Assembly, Harriman, New York, May 4, 1962 (from Washington *Post*, May 5, 1962).

48. Donald N. Michael, *op cit.*, p. 14.

49. "New Views on Automation," *op. cit.*, p. 211.

50. Roger W. Strohbehn, "Impact of Population Growth on Capital Formation," Association of Southern Agricultural Workers, Jackson, Mississippi, 1961.

51. In discussions of automation, the case for greater opportunities for displaced workers in personal service in industries can be overstated. Cheap replacements can substitute for repairs, machines instead of sales personnel can dispense merchandise (and perhaps provide more information about a product), and shorter work weeks will permit many consumers to perform their own services.

52. Although expected life has been increased, a very small proportion are reaching what appears to be a physical limit of slightly over one hundred years. For information on possible limits of life, see Louis I. Dublin, Alfred Lotka, and Mortimer Spiegelman, *Length of Life* (New York: Ronald Press, 1949).

53. Roger W. Strohbehn, *op. cit.*, p. 5.

54. Jan Tinbergen, *Economic Policy: Principles and Design* (Amsterdam: North Holland Publishing Co., 1956), p. 20.

55. Skills and education can be considered independently of capacity or talent. The biological selection for improvement of humans is quite beyond the scope of this chapter but the relation of capacity to the absorption of skills and knowledge has not been overlooked. Jean Rostand, "Can Man be Modified?" "Adventures of the Mind," No. 26, *Saturday Evening Post*, May 2, 1959, p. 25, 97–100.

56. "The task of studying a system in a scientific way is therefore rather a special one. A system consists of $n$ elements. Before we started talking about

systems, this would have meant $n$ investigations to find out what this set of things was like. Once we declare the set of things to be a system, however, there are not only the $n$ elements themselves to examine, but $n$ $(n-1)$ relations between the elements to be examined. (This is the right number by the way; the relation between A and B is not necessarily the same as the relation of B to A.) Think of a system with only seven elements. This has forty-two relations within itself. If we define a state of this system as the pattern produced in the network when each of these relations is either in being or not in being (which is not a very detailed account of the relationships), then there will be $(2)^{42}$ different states of the system. This is a fantastically large number; more than four millions of millions." Stafford Beer, *Cybernetics and Management* (New York: John Wiley and Sons, 1959), p. 10–11.

57. Organizational complexity is a function not only of the number of people but also of the number of transactions (to use the J. R. Commons term) among or between people. At one extreme, a large population in anarchy may require no organizational overhead. At the other extreme, a small population can attain monolithic uniformity with tight organization.

58. Arthur S. Miller, "Some Observations on the Political Economy of Population Growth," *Law and Contemporary Problems*, XXV (Summer, 1960), 614–29.

59. Harrison Brown, "The Human Spirit Needs Space," *Saturday Review*, XLV, (February 17, 1962), 16–17.

60. The President's Materials Policy Commission, *Resources for Freedom*, "Foundations for Growth and Security," I (June, 1952), 3.

61. Will Durant, *The Story of Civilization* (New York: Simon and Schuster, 1954), p. 1.

WALTER C. NEALE

# Developing Countries: Role of Land Policy in Providing Incentives for Development and Sharing More Widely the Benefits of Development

THE BELIEF THAT LAND POLICY should be directed to assuring that cultivators be owner-operators has received almost universal assent from the disinterested since Arthur Young first commented on how the peasants of the Pas-de-Calais had "turned sand into gold" and John Stuart Mill asserted that peasant proprietorship was the best system for agriculture. Since cultivating proprietorship has been the exception over much of the earth's surface, the approved policy has generally been land reform. Until the Russian Revolution, land reform was understood to mean owner-operation, although occasionally the cooperative farm was suggested. Since the Russian Revolution, the term has come to encompass large-scale collective and cooperative farms, although both forms are still based on the idea that the cultivators shall be directly or indirectly the owners of the land they farm. Over much of the world it remains true that land reform means the transfer of title to land from landlord to cultivating farmer.

I shall argue that reform of tenurial systems is at best a secondary means of stimulating development and improving the level of living of the cultivating farmer; and that such associated innovations as credit cooperatives cannot be as effective as is often hoped. Progress in rural areas depends upon opportunities and initiative. Opportunities are limited by natural endowment, by the rural social structure, and by the absence of sources of off-farm supply. Initiative is restrained by the attitudes of the cultivating peasantry toward innovation and toward government.

441

These attitudes are themselves an integral part of the institutional structure.

Little need be said about why we want to see growth in the output of agriculture in the developing lands. It is, of course, that we wish to see the larger part of the world's population escape from poverty, and the road to this end is more food for more people and increased off-farm disposal of this increased production. More food must move to feed the growing population of the towns; and other agricultural produce is needed in larger quantities to meet the new demands of developing industries. To achieve these larger outputs, systems of water-basin control are necessary as are the adoption of new farming techniques, different equipment, new rotations, and new crops. No difficult technical or engineering questions arise about the sort of thing needed; rather the big problems are how to organize the changes, how to get people to accept them and to work them—in short, how to build a progressive element into the rural economic and social structure. And it is here—where adaptability, innovation, and thrift are required—that reformers from John Stuart Mill to the United Nations have agreed that the best incentive is peasant ownership of the land.

In discussing land policy for developing countries generally, and in evaluating the idea of peasant proprietorship, I shall deal first with the contrasts between the underlying characteristics of American experience and of Asian experience; second, with the primary needs of Asian agriculture; third, with the obstacles to fulfilling the needs; and lastly, with the changes in institutions serving agriculture which are thought to be important in building into the rural society of developing lands the incentives and the means for sustained progress.

## THE CONTRASTS BETWEEN AMERICA AND ASIA

American success with family farming has been based in part on a generous helping of arable land. What population there was in this country when the settlers arrived was disposed of. The ratio of population to arable area, and even more the ratio of population to potential arable area, during the nineteenth century was unusually low by any standards. Whereas the assumption upon which the Homestead Act was based was that all the land needed was a man to farm it, in South Asia the opposite assumption is common: all that the man needs is land to farm. It is not true that Asians have not had opportunities to move into virgin lands in the past century, for they have—notably into southern Burma and into the Outer Isles of the Indonesian archipelago; and there is evidence of vacant land throughout South Asia over a century ago. But the pattern of settlement has been different. When the Burmese moved south they filled up the delta area, spawning daughter villages until all the lowlands were covered. Within half a century they faced the same situation of limited arable land that had been faced in India and in Java from an earlier date, and which is now quite commonly faced throughout South Asia. Squatter settlements in Sumatra today appear to follow the same pattern. The rapid decline of new opportunities was partly a result of the larger population at the time settlement of the new areas began and partly a result of the smaller area available for settlement. Partly, however, it resulted from the absence of alternative opportunities for making a livelihood and from the poverty of the settlers.

The pattern of land settlement in South Asia has been one of extension to the limits of cultivation, limits defined by technical knowledge, by the tools in use and by the capital available to bring the less productive or less accessible areas under the plow. In any case, today the Asian peasant has little land, and that which he has has been much more thoroughly "mined" than the American farmer's acreage; while it is probably fair to say that in the United States we have never pressed to the limits of accessible land.

There are reasons why the patterns of settlement in Asia and in the United States have been very different. In the United States we have had the means to use extensive agriculture. Even in the earliest days, our draft animals were horses, and the amount of land which can be plowed by a man and a horse is a good deal greater than the amount of land that can be plowed by a man and a pair of oxen. More recently, the contrast has become even greater since we have been able to employ inanimate energy to extend vastly the area which one man can handle.

If the contrast between the sources of power is the most striking difference, there are, nevertheless, lesser ones which have contributed appreciably to the difference in the pattern of settlement. Whether one thinks of a steel moldboard plow on the one hand and a roughly shapened root upon the other, or whether one considers the difference between a scythe and a sickle, it is clear that the equipment available to the American farmer permitted him to use a much larger area of land for his farming operations than the equipment of the Indian, the Burmese, and the Javanese peasant allowed. The typical pattern of Middle-Western farming of a hundred and sixty acres or more is by Indian standards immense. In India the average holding in some regions is three to four acres, and even in the Punjab where, for India, agriculture is extensive, a man is considered well-to-do if he farms fifteen to twenty acres. Elsewhere one finds larger holdings, but never on the European let alone the American scale, and in Java and the delta areas of southeast Asia the Indian pattern is repeated.

When the development of modern industrial society began in the United States the lands were new. Whether farming practices were bad or good the lands were, at least for a time, highly productive. And when they became less productive, they could always be put back to fallow or the farmer could pass on to another area. In much of India the land has been farmed for centuries, and there are those who say that Indian land cannot deteriorate further because farming practices have already reduced fertility to a permanent biochemical minimum.

Another major contrast is in the concepts of ownership and of control of the decision-making process in the United States and in traditional village society. Our idea of ownership goes back to the Romans' *usus, abusus, et usufructus.* That a man in the United States could farm his land as he pleased has meant, of course, that he could be pigheaded, but it has meant also that he could be original if he so chose. It was, in any case, his land to do with as he saw fit. The owner of freehold land has the right and the responsibility to decide. In a village community, the locus of the right to decide and the responsibility for decisions is never clear. As in the case of government by committee, nobody knows who is responsible and nobody knows who to blame, so that the power of veto is always greater than the power of originality. But more important perhaps than any inherent indecisiveness of groups, initiative is restrained when many different sorts of people have different kinds of rights in the land. There may be a hierarchy of power or prestige, and there is usually a hierarchy of wealth, but, nevertheless, even the lowliest man in these hierarchies has his rights, some claim upon the harvest, some claim for an opportunity to work in order to justify his rights in the harvest. In addition, there may be ritual requirements, there may be traditional ways of doing things: the common knowledge or the common sense of the community which restricts a man to a narrow band of choices even if, in principle, he has the right to deviate from the norm. Lastly, there is the intermeshing of operations by the many different cultivators in a village community, an intermeshing with which we are familiar from our own past in Europe under the manorial system—the three-field system, the common harvesting, the common grazing.

The way in which a man visualizes opportunities and risks is in part a function of the situation in which he finds himself, but it is also a function of the way he has been brought up to think about situations—what is important, what is desirable, what is permissable. Different societies provide different myths to rationalize and justify activities, and these myths structure the "same" situation differently in different cultures. The result is, of course, varying evaluations of the advisability of possible courses of action, and even varying interpretations of the nature of the real world—that is, of cause and effect.

"Objectively" the peasants' situation may differ because he is cut off topographically from his market; because his market consists of varying numbers of buyers and consequently is subject to large fluctuations in price; because he may need money in a hurry and have no credit facilities; because he may be tied in his marketing arrangements to a money-lender; or because he may face—and this is very common in India—a buyers' market for land so strongly entrenched that sale is not an alternative but a disaster.[1] In India, in particular, the peasant faces extreme variations in the character of the seasons from year to year. If other farmers face similar risks—the farmers of the American plains, for instance—it is still true that the variations are seldom so great nor distributed with such unpredictable randomness; and furthermore, in the developed countries of the world, farmers have resources or publicly provided facilities to tide them over. So, even on the level of the measurable or observable characteristics of a situation the rational and informed Indian peasant will reach conclusions different from those of the American farmer because different solutions are appropriate to his riskier situation.

The institutional structuring of the situation in which a peasant finds himself also affects his decisions. The risk of losing land is given far greater weight not only because the return to land is proportionately much higher than in the United States, but also because a larger loss of prestige and political power is consequent upon the loss of land. Futhermore, it is much harder to start anew as a landholding peasant. On the other hand, some of the most satisfying prestigious rewards come from noneconomic activities. These noneconomic activities are often not so much spiritual as ritual or political. There is the satisfaction of abiding by the moral law or of doing the "done thing." The joy of looking upon a large following is never to be underrated, and, perhaps less agreeable to our prejudices, bossing servants and clients has its pleasures, as does doing nothing while others work.

Institutions themselves provide different rules for choice, different limitations upon the permissible and impermissible. There are situations of long-standing mutual obligation in which it is impermissible to dispense with hired labor although there is nothing for the labor to do; and situations in which it is permissible to demand extra work without paying additional compensation. The network of kin to which one is obligated is far more extensive than in European society—this is true not only of the Indian extended family, but of lineage societies in West Africa, for instance. The Bantu of Central Africa must support his in-laws, while the Chinese in Malaya have an as yet unstudied system of extensive mutual obligations.[2]

When someone speaks of the ignorance or superstition of the illiterate peasant, and then quite reasonably recommends education as a solution to his problems, he ignores the fact that everybody is educated—some more effectively, others less—in the basic elements of his culture. What in fact the uneducated lack is the ability to read and write—the smaller part of our own system of education—and the particular set of beliefs which we have absorbed from our system. The Asian peasant learns, as all of us do, from the experiences of participating in the workings of his own society—including the formal schools—and from the precepts of those he loves, respects, or fears. In some school systems in the world the children learn that educated thought is memorizing facts or methods; in others they learn it is putting up a good argument to prove the teacher is wrong. In similar vein, the child in an Asian village—"tradition-oriented" is the descriptive phrase we use—learns that wisdom is respect for the older people, for the powerful, for the advice of holy men. He learns from experience that defiance of the authorities—that is, innovation—results in unpleasantness, often painful. He learns he cannot divorce himself from the activities and rules of his society —a lesson we all learn but which we are apt to be less aware of in America because our rules provide for  areas where innovation is not defiance—for the man at odds with his society is helpless. Thus he is not foolish or ignorant but rational and educated when he behaves in the fashion native to his society—he would be in real trouble if he did not. So, when what we call opportunities are presented to him to change or improve, he often does not see them as "incentives for progress" or a chance to share "more widely the benefits of development." What he sees is the probability of conflict with the respectable or the powerful or the divine and, like a wise man, he avoids such false opportunities.

The political and social structure of a country affects both attitudes toward change and the possibilities of making improvements. The American political structure has been democratic and our social structure has been egalitarian. On the one hand this has given the American farmer the power to adopt and to adapt; on the other, it has given him the feeling that he has a right to make changes and to act independently of the norm. In Asia, instead of being democratic and egalitarian, peasant com-

munities are typically authoritarian and hierarchical. The hierarchies of ritual status, of economic power, and of political power are not always identical, but they are closely intertwined. Local
councils of elders, headmen, landowners, and money-lending
merchants both can and will make it very difficult for the in-
novator of whom they disapprove. The wise peasant will not
pick a fight which he cannot win. The Homestead Act is a concrete manifestation of the American attitudes of equality and
opportunity; the Indian ladder of rights in land is a reflection
of the Indian view of society as consisting of distinct layers.

The Asian's attitude toward government in general and
officials of the government in particular is usually one of distrust
colored by fear. Typically his relationships with the bureaucracy
have concerned taxation, land law, and the criminal law, and,
in all three cases, officials appear to the peasant either grasping
or callous. The appearance may be false—is false in frequent
cases, for many civil servants have sincerely had the interests of
their charges at heart—but it is how it looks to the peasant that
counts. Taxation may be fair by the usual canons, but when
assessments tend to rise, as they do when the responsibilities of
government increase or productivity rises, the tax assessor looks
greedy if one does not understand his objectives and reasoning.
When there is a question of title to land or other rights in land,
the practices of the judicial officers are so strange as to appear
arbitrary if not random. The British typically introduced Anglo-
Saxon concepts of relevancy of evidence. These concepts are
closely related to our ideas of scientific objectivity and observation,* and they work fairly well in societies where the same
kind of idea structure permeates many institutions (although we
should be aware that they do not by any means work perfectly).
But in other societies they are not so obviously the way to achieve
justice. Equality before the law is closely related to the idea of
an egalitarian society; but where the society accepts hierarchy as
normal, status will be as important as observation in establish-

* It is an interesting question whether our ideas of science have affected
our ideas of how to administer justice, or whether the scientific revolution in
England owes a great deal to the customary way of ascertaining the truth in
court.

ing justice, since justice itself is a reflection of the values of a particular society and not a universal, equally applicable in one form anywhere. Where the experience that goes with age means wisdom and knowledge of how the people around one behave, the source of truth is the elder as much, if not more, than the observer. Yet Western law assumes all are equal as participants in a dispute or as witnesses to the truth. It was—and is—strange to the Asian peasant to see his standards ignored in courts designed to enforce standards, and no one should be surprised if perjury occurs and court procedures are corrupted.

The criminal law has brought the peasant in contact with the police, who have not been noted for gentleness or honesty. Be it said for the police, they are greatly tempted (it is always easier to resist the temptation to increase one's income by 10 per cent than it is to resist the temptation to increase it by 100 per cent) and are under pressure from those above to solve crimes: that is, to get convictions. But the police themselves represent the taxing government and the national courts, and so are "strangers" to the village populations and do not represent the local society in the way that the followers of the former rulers did (which should not be interpreted to mean that the former enforcers of a ruler's will were gentle—only that they fitted into the ideas and expectations of the villagers better than the modern policeman does).

The American farmer has not, throughout his history, had a high regard for the government, but his distrust has been tempered by the facts that national (or state) governments grow out of the same value-system as his own and that the officials of government are necessarily responsive to his feelings. Furthermore, the American farmers' distrust of government has not been tinged, to say nothing of dominated, by fear of bureaucracy.

If I may be permitted a mechanical analogy, the history of the legislative framework of American agriculture is a poor model for Asian countries in the same sense that a Rolls Royce piston is a poor part to use in repairing a Ford pickup truck. The inherent merits of piston or of truck are irrelevant—it is simply impossible to use one with the other.

## THE NEEDS OF ASIAN AGRICULTURE

To be more productive many changes are necessary in both the circumstances and the practices of the Asian peasant. Some are within this control, at least in the sense that the effective unit for making the operational changes could be the farming family. Others, however, are beyond the capacities of a family or even a village, and among the necessary changes these are as important and probably more important than those which the family can make.

When one looks at the operation of the typical Asian cultivated holding with the eye of an agricultural expert it is apparent that the peasant needs better tools, different crop strains, changes in his cropping pattern, fertilizers and natural manures, and often water.* A farm management consultant notes the need for easier contact with markets, more stable marketing arrangements, and both long- and short-term credit to finance the commercial operations of the peasant. But few indeed of these improvements are within the power of the individual peasant to make alone.

Different crop rotations are possible wherever the peasant farms his own plot, as is now common, and cooperative credit institutions can be established by small groups of peasants. Here, the trouble is not that the actions are beyond the capacities of small numbers, but rather that the social pressures, reinforced by more overt restraints, prevent all but the most courageous from engaging in the new forms of activity. A redistribution of land ownership will not change these attitudes; and, where attitudes are changing, present tenure arrangements do not prevent innovations. Where a village suffers from water-logging the cultivators can jointly ditch the land; but with the very small holdings in Asia a single peasant can accomplish nothing this way. However, even the matter of drainage is not a straight-forward local problem, for when many villages feel the need for better drainage the water must go somewhere. Countries or districts fronting on the sea with large or many rivers can let gravity solve the problem once the water is led into the rivers; but other areas face topo-

* Where there is not a shortage of water the problem is frequently the reverse—water-logging and floods.

graphic and political problems. For instance, since the building of large canals in Punjab flooding and water-logging has become widespread. Either the water must be run off through Pakistan or routed into the Junna River. The latter solution would only worsen the flood problems of Uttar Pradesh and Bihar. And, on a smaller scale, similar difficulties arise in many places.

Supplies from off the farm are essential to economic growth in rural areas. The improvements in farming technique which depend upon off-farm supplies—while immediately operated by the cultivator—require the cooperation of resources and activities from distant points and industries. Steel plows and fertilizers come from heavy industrial plants which require large amounts of capital and skilled workers and managers. To be useful the inputs must be transported over long distances. In India today, a bottleneck to increased outturn in numerous areas is insufficient transportation. Although the fertilizers are produced, there are places distant from the plants where the fertilizers do not arrive at the right time or in large enough quantity. But more transport means more railway capacity, and this in turn requires more steel, more fabricating plants, and immediately more coal, which means more mines, which means more machinery and power. Seed farms require little capital but to be useful there must be a well-organized distributive network on a larger-than-village scale. The cultivator cannot affect his own productivity until a large part of the rest of the economy has provided facilities on a national scale.* Management of the Ganges watershed will include the states of Uttar Pradesh, Bihar, and Bengal, and parts of Punjab, Madhya Pradesh, and Orissa. All of Burma and much of Thailand should be treated as integrated valley-plains, as should the states of former French Indo-China and northwestern Thailand. For the states of southeast Asia the relevant area for

---

* All this is true of any economy, but in the developed world we are not usually aware of the importance of interdependence once the first chapter of the elementary economics text is read. Crises do arise occasionally, but non-delivery of goods to the farmer is not a chronic cause of failure to progress. National scale can here be taken to include such regions as north India with a population of 200 million.

supplies of equipment and working capital is even larger than the nation.

The system of tenure under which the peasant operates is not therefore *the* primary problem in assuring a larger supply of farm produce to the developing nations. At two points the system of tenure does become important: first, in its relationship to the peasant's willingness to adopt new tools and techniques when they become effectively available; and second, in its effect upon the distribution of the produce, what we are here calling "sharing more widely in the benefits of development."

## SOCIAL AND POLITICAL PROBLEMS
## IN REFORMING TENURES

The social obstacles to reform arise because the peasant places reliance upon a different kind of experience from that which American farmers have had, and upon different myths. Specifically, the Asian peasant has a different view of the aims and trustworthiness of bureaucracy, of the risk and rewards inherent in his alternatives, and of the character of the natural world. Even his knowledge or ignorance, which many emphasize as a major barrier to development, should itself be treated as an outgrowth of his experience within a specific institutional structure.

The lesson of community projects in India, and of the precursor efforts at village uplift, is that information and all varieties of exhortation, while necessary, are totally insufficient as causes of change or foundations for reform. Law as a vehicle of reform may be treated as a bureaucratic-informational exhortation to behave differently, and is likely to prove ineffective. The analyses of Indian land reform laws[3] agree that the intentions of the laws have been ignored or subverted; that enactment of titular rights is not enough, and the structure of rules and attitudes governing behavior in the villages is one reason why.[4]

What is needed is a change in the relevant experiences. Some such changes will inevitably grow out of development—experiences with schools, cities, and enlarged markets, and the existence of modern industrial techniques. Other changes needed for agrarian progress will be frustrated by the experiences of development and independence—administrative failures and "unfair" shifts in relative income, for instance. Still a third group of changes will depend upon conscious structural alterations in institutions other than tenurial ones—changes in the level of loyalties from family, tribe, caste, or locality to nation, and changes in the forms of dependency and responsibility from village councils and headmen to broader political action in parties and pressure groups, to national bureaucracies, and to the courts. So long as the headman administers justice; so long as the decent person abides by the precepts of the elders; so long as men regard themselves as rightfully in the place to which the nature of the universe has assigned them; so long as these remain, the legislative granting of land titles to tenants will be subverted or, if somehow carried through in law, will be ineffective as instruments of progress.* The political obstacles to reform originate in the hierarchical, ritualistic power structure of underdeveloped lands. Both land reform and economic development threaten the position of the present possessors of high status. Even when they do not threaten the dominance of these groups, they introduce strains by forcing the ruling groups to change their techniques of control. Daniel Thorner has complained[5] that the legislatures of the Indian states have undermined reform by legislatively defining self-cultivation as to permit landlords to retain their lands. But this is not surprising, for political power and social prestige are as enjoyable as wealth, and quite naturally those who enjoy these nonmaterial utilities do their best to preserve them. It is not a simple problem of a few aristocrats versus a "mass" of the people, but rather it exists at every level and involves people all the way down the hierarchy. If one restricts one's gaze to the relationship of tenant to landlord in an Indian village, it appears that the tenant has nothing to lose but his inferiority. But the view is too narrow, for he has superiority as well—economically over the landless laborer, ritually over the outcaste. Even among outcastes there are levels of prestige and acceptability, so that political unions for the purpose of subvert-

---

* An anology can be made here with the position of the American Negro. His effective freedom dates not from the Emancipation Proclamation, but from his recent refusal to submit and from his own belief in the possibility of equality.

ing reform legislation can be made between much larger groups than might at first appear likely.

Each country's new agrarian system must be a unique adaptation to industrial society—uniqueness made necessary by the differing sets of social myths which must be adapted, as well as by the differing social structures upon which modernization acts. The dangers of uncritical importation of systems which have proved successful elsewhere have been analyzed by Furnivall in his economic history of Burma and the Netherlands Indies.[6] When new social goals and new rules governing the achievement of these goals are introduced into a society, the result may in the end be successful adaptation, but there is likely to be a long period during which the conflict between the new and the old causes a breakdown in the old restraints (what Furnivall calls the disappearance of a "social will") while the new rules do not take on the morally imperative character needed to make them function as limits to unbridled self interest. The phenomenon is analogous on the scale of an entire region to the state of anomie or normlessness in individuals.[7]

India has probably made the best adaptation of the countries of Asia, yet even here the conflict between new goal and old rule and between old goal and new rule continues to create disruptive tensions, tensions which take the form of "casteism," "corruption," and disapproval of political processes. To adapt a cliché of the London *Economist,* progress must not only be attempted, it must be seen that what is attempted is progress.

## CHANGES IN INSTITUTIONS AND LAWS
## TO BENEFIT THE FARMER

The institutional changes needed in marketing, credit, and extension will vary both with the existing social structure and with the specific resources and the specific developmental objectives of the society. The American pattern will be relevant only in a country not suffering from a shortage of land, which already has an egalitarian society, and which does not need to exert great pressure upon its farmers to mobilize the real resources of the rural areas to build the urban industries and national social overheads.

In large parts of sub-Saharan Africa a quasi-American pattern is possible where the problem is interracial distribution of land, as in British East and Central Africa, where the man/land ratio is generous to man and the internal tribal structures are not markedly hierarchical. In such places, capital for intensive industries producing for the domestic market is not likely to develop, while foreign capital is likely to be plentiful relative to the population.

On the other hand, India and Indonesia both need to draw heavily upon the rural population in both real and financial terms in order to establish an industrial base for a populous national society; yet there the man/land ratio limits the marketable surplus and the capacity of the peasantry to save. Unmodified freehold tenure will dampen industrial growth, so that ways are needed to channel produce into the modern sectors. Burma probably presents an intermediate case where the establishment of a small-holding yeomanry would have immediate advantages in increasing family welfare, but where in the longer run the typically peasant orientation of the villagers would lead to such multiplication of small-holding villages that an intensive population problem would be created by the very security so beneficial in the short run.

Policy can aim at one extreme at creating credit and marketing institutions which maximize the disposable income of the farmer, to institutions at the other extreme which attempt to divert to the state or the cities—in any case, to industry—as much as possible of the produce of the countryside. Thus we now find the Congress government in India favoring—so far ineffectively—the creation of village-wide cooperative farming societies. Whatever the philosophic rationale of the Congress, certainly realization that such cooperatives would be easier to deal with and more amenable to government pressure than are individual peasants has been an important contributing element.

Similarly, the type of information or of technological help given by extension services will vary depending upon whether the objective is to maximize the range of free choice consciously and effectively enjoyed by cultivators, or whether the objective is to direct the cultivators' activities in directions desired by the indus-

trializing authorities. Again, India provides an example of the
conflict: the community projects are designed, in part after the
United States extension service, to teach the farmer how to make
the best of his resources and to show him what his alternatives
are; whereas the programs of the Ministry of Agriculture are
designed to increase the outturn of grain and fibers whether or
not the cultivator is convinced of the suitability of the program
to his own welfare. State trading in foodgrains is perhaps a more
striking example of the urge to mobilize and manipulate rather
than to persuade for the farmers' own benefit.

Other conflicts will arise with the introduction of modern,
western institutions into the societies of developing lands. Credit
and marketing cooperatives, which have increased the return to
the farmer in egalitarian societies, work differently in hierarchical cultures. Local leaders often take control of these organizations and use them to reinforce the existing power structure.[8]
To charge that these institutions are corrupt is to make the
further mistake of exporting our classifications of behavior as
well as our institutions: what happens is that the existing social
structure adapts the imported form to its habitual procedures.
It is only "right"—that is, to be expected within the traditional
structure of attitudes—that the leaders of all the other village
activities should become the leaders of the village cooperatives.
The mistake made is to assume that, because Scandinavians and
Scottish cooperatives are democratic, Indian ones will also be
democratic. Once in control, it is only "natural" that the leaders
should take advantage of their position, for that has always been
their reward.

What is needed to create effective new institutions and adaptations of old institutions is knowledge about how the societies
in each developing land react to and alter the new structures,
and of this knowledge we do not have nearly enough. More
credit, more stable markets, more help from extension services, all
these are needed in all the underdeveloped lands. But in each
country, the modern means must be fitted into different agricultural patterns—cocoa for export in West Africa, rubber for export
in Malaya and Sumatra, rice for export in Burma and Thailand,
food grain and fiber production for on-farm as well as off-farm

consumption in India, rice for domestic consumption in Ceylon, tea for export in India and Ceylon—agricultural patterns in each case uniquely affected by sociological patterns which in turn will transform the new institutions.

## SOCIETY, CHANGE, AND DEVELOPMENT

The picture presented here may seem to be so pessimistic as to lead to a policy of inaction. If readers feel depressed because I argue that the peoples of developing lands will not become "like us," then they are right to feel depressed, for the peoples of Asia will not become Hindu, Moslem, and Buddhist devotees of the American way. But if I have given the impression that tenure reform, credit cooperatives, regulated markets, and extension officers cannot lift the peasantry from its poverty, then I have fulfilled my intentions.

This is not pessimism. It is an argument that the main impetus must come from outside the legal and economic structure of the rural areas. Two sources of change, mutually interdependent, can change the rural areas and not only permit but encourage progress. One is the growth of industrial society which will provide the farmer with the instruments and capital for more productive farming. The other is a slow alteration in the structure of rules and myths so that initiative and attention to productivity is encouraged. Rules and myths will change because industrial societies create a "world of fact" and demand the same characteristic attitudes as do modern farming practices. The rules and myths will change also because the doctrines of nationalism and the requirements of a modern national government are incompatible with tribal or hierarchial social structures.

Land reform will be a useful ancillary policy in the development of a modern national economic society but it cannot be the prime mover in its creation, even in the countryside. Traditionally the argument has been that ownership creates the incentives to save and invest, and to learn, and doubtless it does contribute to these desirable activities. But the question is whether incentive is enough, and in the absence of available means, it is not; in the face of local powers opposed to change, it is not. As effective in neutralizing innovation as the feeling that others

will get all the benefit is the fear that one cannot or dares not
innovate.

It should be remembered that the peasantry is not incapable
of saving under present tenure arrangements, nor was it incapable
of saving in days when the law provided even less protection to
the cultivators. Then and now, "savings" eventually go into "cere-
monial consumption," jewelry, and land.[9] Sooner or later "savings" turn into consumption because the saver does not invest in
real capital but in existing values or in activities preserving or
earning prestige. Where the saver lends it is not to enterprise
but to the needy. Thus again we find that developmentally inappropriate idea- or value-systems hinder development and the
long-term enjoyment of growing wealth.

It is also argued that land reform will destroy the old hierarchies and so establish the external conditions necessary for initiative in farming. To some degree it will, and this is why we
can regard it as a useful but secondary policy. Land reform is,
in fact, carried out almost in proportion as the lower orders of
society feel they have the right and the courage to demand equality and freedom from the higher orders. It is not irrelevant that
the most thoroughgoing reforms in India were carried out in
Uttar Pradesh, where the Congress national movement made an
alliance with the tenants forty-three years ago, and in Kashmir,
where the War of Partition disrupted the old society. Elsewhere,
reforms have been evaded as fast as they have been enacted. Limitations on rents are ignored where the traditional rental share is
considered fair, or where the immediately powerful are more
real to the tenant than are distant officials. In Uttar Pradesh itself
there is evidence that many failed to get the rights the reform
law promised and illegal sharecropping continues.[10] "Land
reforms," Baljit Singh writes about Uttar Pradesh, "have
obviously not brought about any institutional change in the
structure of cultivation."[11] The landless—those without rights in
land before reform—have no rights in land today. Where there
is a will tenure reform eases the way, but it does not create
the will.

In sharing the larger product of a developing society what
has already been said about the ineffectiveness of legislative land

reforms applies with equal force. The profits of farming in modern style, the savings from cooperative credit and supply institutions, and the increased realizations from better organized markets accrue to the cultivator only to the degree society, as an integrated system, allows him to exercise power. In other words, the institutions serving the farmers, like the laws granting rights, formally recognize a power and initiative already achieved. In addition, however, to the social restraints upon the farmer, his enjoyment of the fruits of development also depends upon his place in the economic system. If he is engaged in one of the more highly productive activities he will become richer, but if he is employed in a low-productivity field his earnings will tend to approximate the low average productivity of such labor, if not the even lower marginal productivity. In a heavily populated country the laborer in the field will earn a low income because labor makes but a small marginal contribution to ouput. In such countries the farmers' returns will rise only when much labor has been drawn into industrial and commercial pursuits and the supply of capital in agriculture has increased appreciably. In other countries where land is more plentiful the farmer will benefit more quickly.

In India an assault upon the whole system of ideas and the whole social structure of the village has been initiated by the community projects. The community project program has spread to many other nations, but with the possible exception of Pakistan, where the "basic democracy" program is a modified, "guided democracy" version of the Indian program, it is no more than incipient. The Indian idea of community projects is not to legislate or command but to persuade. As a land policy it is as hopeful as tenure reform. It has met the obstacles which all developmental efforts have met—to which much of this paper has been devoted—and so far has not been clearly successful. But the idea behind community projects—that human action springs from belief modified by experience and from experience understood in terms of one's world view, and that both experience and belief must be altered to achieve change in the countryside—this idea is at least as plausible a basis for policy as the belief that the springs of human action are property and gain.

In India the system of local government has been revised recently so that local councils are elected by secret ballot and have funds and, one hopes, power. If the analysis presented here is correct, this reform is as likely to release initiative as are economic reforms because it provides a means of bypassing the traditional hierarchy of control; but whether it will succeed depends, again, on the willingness of the lower orders to seize the opportunity.

What, then, can be said about a policy of rural reform to stimulate growth? First, that the contrasts between American and Asian circumstances make our system an inappropriate model for the developing lands of Asia. Second, that the social structures and systems of ideas in the developing lands will change or frustrate efforts to adopt the institutions which have served American and European farmers. Third, that progress and wealth in the villages will depend primarily upon the unification and growth of the other parts of the national economy. Fourth, that legislative changes in titles to land cannot initiate growth, but can only recognize changes in social and political power in the countryside. And lastly, that we can approve of all efforts to alter the social, political, and idea systems of the rural areas—by legislative reform of tenures, by providing new routes to political power, and by acting upon the minds of men through extension services —that we can approve these programs so long as we recognize that they are secondary reinforcements and not prime movers.

Major land reforms are important dates in history. They are symptoms of great changes which require reform and which make them possible; but they are not measures which can be carried through in isolation as the means of initiating progress.

## NOTES

1. Cf. F. G. Bailey, *Caste and the Economic Frontier* (Manchester: Manchester Universty Press, 1958), pp. 58–62.

2. On the non-Indian societies see Paul J. Bohannan, "Tiv Trade and Markets," unpublished private paper; Phillip Mason, *The Birth of a Dilemma* (London: R.I.I.A., 1959); Godfrey Wilson, *An Essay on the Economics of Detribalization* (Lusaka: Rhodes-Livingstone Institute, 1940); Margaret Read,

"Migrant Labour in Africa and Its Effects on Tribal Life," *International Labour Review*, XLV (1942), 605–31; T. H. Silcock, *The Commonwealth Economy in Southeast Asia* (Durham: Duke University Press, 1959).

3. Cf. Daniel Thorner, *The Agrarian Prospect in India* (Delhi: Delhi University Press, 1956); V. M. Dandekar and G. J. Khudanpur, *Working of Bombay Tenancy Act, 1948: Report of Investigation* (Poona: Gokhale Institute Publication No. 35, 1957); Baljit Singh, *Next Step in Village India* (Bombay: Asia Publishing House, 1960).

4. The argument is spelled out in greater detail, with illustrative material, in my *Economic Change in Rural India* (New Haven: Yale University Press, 1962), pp. 192–208.

5. Thorner, *Agrarian Prospect . . .*, *op. cit.*

6. J. S. Furnivall, *Colonial Policy and Practice* (New York: New York University Press, 1956); *Netherlands India: A Study of Plural Economy* (Cambridge: Cambridge University Press, 1944).

7. Cf. Robert K. Merton, *Social Theory and Social Structure* (Glencoe, Illinois: The Free Press, 1949), pp. 131–61.

8. Cf. Daniel Thorner, "Context for Cooperatives in Rural India," *The Economic Weekly* (Bombay), XIV (Annual Number, 1962), pp. 251–66.

9. Bailey, *op. cit.*, pp. 47–173, for a clear description of how potential real savings become "consumption" via the mechanism of changing "asset portfolios."

10. Singh, *Next Step in Village India*, *op. cit.*, pp. 25–36.

11. *Ibid.*, p. 33.

WAYNE N. ASPINALL

# Making Policy for Land Use

ONE HUNDRED YEARS after the signing of the Homestead Act, it is natural for Americans to take stock of our land programs— past, present, and future. We cannot examine the Homestead Act or any other individual public land law in a vacuum. We cannot isolate problems of public land from private land any more than we can isolate problems affecting agricultural lands from today's pressing need of land for rights-of-way for superhighways and for the support of urban and suburban growth. There is need for review and analysis of every aspect of land use.

Reading the history of the Homestead Act—particularly the legislative history—leaves one wondering whether those persons who were involved actually recognized the full historical significance of what they were doing. In my opinion they did not. Consider the circumstances at the time of passage of the Homestead Act: a country at war within itself with the future of the Union uncertain.

When the Homestead Act became effective on January 1, 1863, an event of greater significance to the national administration, and certainly to President Lincoln himself, also took effect—the Emancipation Proclamation. I shall not attempt to compare the significance of these two measures.

Nor will I comment on problems concerned with the developing countries and the implications of our land policy experience in other parts of the world. Rather, I shall confine my remarks to the land use policy which is made by the federal Congress for the United States.

No single event or circumstance more clearly highlights the changes that the nation has undergone than does the Homestead Act which, although not based on a scientifically planned use program, has been highly successful. However, those who today would point to such national progress without planning as justification for not planning for the future are attempting to deny the changes that have taken place in one hundred years. They

462

refuse to face the facts of national life in the mid-twentieth century. These conclusions will, I think, become clear as I develop my subject.

In the early history of our republic, the great expanse of almost endless fertile fields invited the settlers and the government alike to put the land to use. History shows that while there were some who talked of land classification, by and large there was no land use program within the present-day meaning of that term. Even the Homestead Act itself, which was an agricultural measure, relied upon classification by nature rather than classification by man. In other words, the lands that would be open for entry were not specifically identified or set aside by the government. The only qualification was that the individual comply with the law by entering upon not more than a quarter section of unappropriated public land and develop it into his farm home. Nor does the question of classification or diversified use seem to have entered significantly in the debate preceding passage of the act.

In this connection, I would like to make a point I have made recently and repeatedly. When President Buchanan vetoed the first Homestead bill in 1860, one of his main arguments was one he had used in vetoing the first Land-Grant College Act, namely, that the Congress had no power to "give away" the public lands either to states or to individuals. For the record, let us stop referring to these lands as free lands; let us nail down the fact that this was no "give away." Over 1,600,000 persons have gained title to over 270 million acres of public lands by paying in hard work and by donating to the United States a farm production capability greater than that existing elsewhere.

The principle had been the same throughout our land policy prior to the Homestead Act. First, Congress adopted policies of selling lands for revenue to fill the national treasury and of giving land as the reward or payment for services rendered. We rewarded our soldiers, such as Daniel Boone, with land; and to the explorers of an earlier age we presented grants of land instead of medals. I refer to Lewis and Clark as the outstanding example of those so honored. We also encouraged the construction of railroads and the expansion of education through land grants.

In this connection, I also note that Congress did not adopt recommendations of the General Land Office to amend the Homestead Act in order to limit it to arable agricultural lands with lands chiefly valuable for timber to be excluded from settlement. This was an affirmative rejection of classification.

Land was then plentiful. Settlement was the important national policy. I therefore conclude that a scientific discussion at or about the time of the adoption of the Homestead Act would have had little influence in establishing land use policy. Once the most desirable lands were settled; once the development pattern of the West had taken shape, we could and did benefit from intensive scientific studies of land use in formulating our policy. Lest I be misunderstood, let me hasten to add that this does not mean that Congress has always adopted the blanket recommendations of the land planners and land economists or that Congress will do so in the future. Neither does this diminish the fact that we need scientific advice and guidance.

At the 1962 White House Conference on Conservation, in referring to the broader aspects of the subject, I pointed out that Congress had followed a moderate course providing for the use of our natural resources. That use was and is, of course, based on good management with the maximum good for the maximum number. This policy decision concerning our land resource is exemplified in the Homestead Act and all of its amendments or extensions. It was in the extensions of this act that land classification started.

I refer to the Desert Land Act, the Kinkaid Act, which, in 1904, allowed entry on up to 640 acres in the semi-arid areas of Nebraska, the Enlarged Homestead Act, the Reclamation Act with its specialized homestead, and the National Forest Homestead Act. The fact that the Kinkaid Act set up special rules in the state of Nebraska and the enlarged Homestead Act permitted 320-acre homesteads in seven western states, including my own state of Colorado, and that subsequently the Alaska Homestead Act recognized the peculiar problems of that area emphasize the groping for special use conditions that today are called "classification." As happened so many times in our history, out of the cauldron of congressional debate came a wise practical policy for America.

In bridging the gap between the past and the present, I think we will all accept as fact that not all land laws have fulfilled the hopes of their sponsors. The Desert Land Act, for example, seems today to be attracting more applicants for entry on land that cannot qualify under the act than for entry on land suitable for development. Other laws have outlived their usefulness; for example, the Department of Agriculture has recommended the repeal of the National Forest Homestead Act. Still other laws have only limited potential today and their revision has been recommended by the Secretary of the Interior. We have pending, in the Interior and Insular Affairs Committee, bills that cumulatively would revise the entire system of use or disposition of the public lands.

The extent to which the Secretaries of the Interior and Agriculture have consulted with or have had the benefit of advice from land economists and professors, such as the authors of these papers, is not known to me. But if the Executive Branch does not avail itself of advice from skilled technicians and academicians, then economists' and professors' influence in the molding of national policy may be minimal, if not lost entirely, unless they seriously consider what I am about to say.

They are specialists in their fields. I fear though that, with few exceptions, their knowledge of the practical side of law-making may be rather limited. This much I am sure they all know: the work of Congress is done in its committees. This means that the committees, or the subcommittees, hold hearings, take testimony, hear all sides of the question and, prior to recommending legislation, build a record on which a report can be made. I wonder how many professors who are now with universities have, in their academic capacities, appeared before a congressional committee in an effort to outline a basic land use concept upon which the committee could attempt to build a particular land law?

We hear from the Executive agencies and we hear from groups who seek to benefit from, or hold off possible harmful effects of, legislation. With all due respect to the dedication to service that our government employees have in connection with the average bill coming before a congressional committee, the government representative who testifies has a narrow field of responsibility and speaks from his particular vantage point. On the committee staffs we have professionals who read economists' reports and attend their meetings; but they can only advise the committees in connection with the analysis of testimony: they do not themselves appear and testify.

Let me give an example. Our Subcommittee on Public Lands in the House of Representatives has held hearings both in the West and in Washington, D.C., on legislation designed to establish a Wilderness Preservation System. In the western states, 231 witnesses were heard. Basically, these witnesses were users and would-be users or their representatives. Those college professors who appeared gave testimony as users of wilderness. In Washington, D.C., an additional fifty nongovernment witnesses were heard and of these, two from geology professors who spoke of the mineral potential in wilderness areas. Not one land economist, speaking academically, was heard. The same is true in connection with hearings on a sweeping revision that has been proposed for disposition of our nonmineral public lands.

Conceptually, it is up to all land economists to think in terms of overall programs. It is gratifying, therefore, to see that attention is being given to the necessary ingredients of a modern land policy. I do not jump to the conclusion that this symposium will delineate a set of rules that will resolve all of our land problems. I do, however, look forward to a broad outline of principles that can act as a blueprint to assist all of us charged with responsibilities in land management. The need for such blueprint becomes more readily apparent if we study for a moment the manner in which Congress makes policy for land use.

The Committee on Agriculture has before it a proposal to divert to recreational use, 50 million acres of privately owned agricultural land no longer needed for farming. The Agriculture committee also has jurisdiction over the proposal I mentioned before to repeal the National Forest Homestead Act, and in addition, has general jurisdiction over agriculture and over forest reserves other than those created from the public domain. The Banking and Currency Committee considers legislation designed to permit the acquisition or retention of green-belts, or open spaces, in and around urban areas because it is the committee that has jurisdiction over housing programs and urban renewal in connection with which it is logical to provide federal assistance for urban breathing space. The Government Operations Committee has before it a bill that would permit the disposition of certain surplus federal property for public park, forest, wildlife refuge, public recreational area, or historic monument purposes. The Committee on Public Works, which has general jurisdiction over flood control and public roads, is concerned with land use at Corps of Engineers reservoirs and the rights-of-way of our fast-growing interstate highway system. The Committee on Merchant Marine and Fisheries has jurisdiction over wildlife refuges and has recommended a bill that the House of Representatives passed on April 2, 1962, relating to public recreational use of wildlife refuges. In this context I would also like to relate back to my earlier reference to the Wilderness Bill and remind you that, as passed by the Senate, there is authorization provided, in certain circumstances, for the inclusion of portions of wildlife refuges in the Wilderness Preservation System.

This, then, is how Congress is developing policy for land use. What is the practical lesson of this recitation? One lesson to be gained is that in becoming a highly specialized and complex government, we have carved out neat cubicles for each category. Everything must fit in a precast mold. The second observation is the one I mentioned before, namely, that unless people from the study and classrooms bring the general picture before the committee, the congressional group doing the work on the legislation may obtain only a limited viewpoint.

In this complex system and procedure, how then should Congress make up its mind? How is policy finally going to be formed? To a great extent the theory of our founding fathers still holds true and Congressman represents the people in his district while the United States Senator represents the state. So we have local and sectional interests represented in the Congress. As a Congressman I must eventually re-examine each proposal in the

light of the overall national interests before casting my vote;
but initially I am expected to represent my people who sent me
to Congress.

Conversely, our society today no longer has all of its needs
and aspirations bound up in small geographic areas. Many large
groups, spread throughout the nation, have a common interest.
These people are joined together in literally thousands of organizations, many of which have Washington representatives whose
duty and obligation, among other things, are to keep an eye on
legislation that might be of interest to or affect the people they
represent and, if warranted, appear before the committees
handling the legislation.

The bicameral legislature and the system under which it
operates is in large measure responsible for the moderate policy
for wise use of our land resources pursued by Congress. That it
is a moderate course, and not extremist, is demonstrated by the
fact that the several different committees, each having limited
jurisdiction, have reported favorably bills with a general relationship to the central theme of wise use, conservation, and good
public management.

It is this fragmentation of legislative responsibility for development of land use policy that underlines the need for intensive
general study. The contribution of land economists to the next
one hundred years of land development will be of great significance if they develop "a perspective of national land policy
from the vantage point" of the past hundred years and attain
their objectives of identifying the major land problems with
which we are confronted and suggesting alternative lines of action
concerning the future land policy of the United States. The published proceedings may then offer benchmarks for those who
follow.

In a specialized age, where semantics are very important, and
phrases quickly become words of art with special meaning, land
economists can make another contribution if they provide precise definitions of terminology utilized by those concerned with
the subject of land use. Here is an example of what I have
in mind.

Several years ago the term "land reserve" was applied to privately owned acreage taken out of agricultural use; and recommendations for land retirement programs envisioned such areas as becoming a great land reserve. More recently we have been told in connection with our work in public lands that the public domain not now in actual use for some specific purpose represents a "land reserve" which, on occasion, has even been referred to as "THE national land reserve."

This raises some very interesting questions.

First, can we—and I see no reason why we should not—co-mingle private and public lands in our planning? To me, the next question then is: Does the term "land reserve" connote nonuse except in emergencies? Our whole history of public land management has been to encourage use, even though the use may not be very active, as in the case of a national forest reserve or wilderness preservation area.

In an era when labels seem to mean so much, we should guard against changing our land policy by the adoption of a designation which, to many, indicates the opposite of use. So, it may be that it would be better, if we were to look to the *use* of our public lands, to restrict the designation of "land reserve" to areas that will be "retired" and set aside for possible, but not certain, use at a later date.

As individuals, land economists should take some action to make certain that the principles outlined for a proposed land policy are brought to the attention of the various committees of Congress and related to specific pieces of legislation being considered by them. If they do this, we can have a good mixture of the theoretical with the practical needs of the users, possibly tempering the sometimes exaggerated hopes and fears, and continue to have what I consider to be a well-balanced, moderate land use policy.

# The Contributors

THOMAS LE DUC, Professor, Department of History, Oberlin University.

PAUL W. GATES, Professor, Department of History, Cornell University.

MARI SANDOZ, writer, New York City.

CARL O. SAUER, Professor Emeritus, Department of Geography, University of California.

JOHN M. BREWSTER, Agricultural Economist, Economic Research Service, U.S. Department of Agriculture.

ROSS B. TALBOT, Professor, Department of History, Government, and Philosophy, Iowa State University.

W. B. BACK, Professor, Agricultural Economics Department, Oklahoma State University.

HARRY A. STEELE, Chief, Land and Water Economics Branch, Economic Research Service, U.S. Department of Agriculture.

NORMAN E. LANDGREN, Land and Water Economics Branch, Economic Research Service, U.S. Department of Agriculture.

LOWDON WINGO, JR., Economist, Resources for the Future, Inc., Washington, D.C.

RALEIGH BARLOWE, Head, Department of Resource Development, Michigan State University.

M. M. KELSO, Professor, Department of Agricultural Economics, University of Arizona.

MARSHALL HARRIS, Agricultural Economist, Farm Economics Division, Economics Research Service, U.S. Department of Agriculture, and Research Professor, Agricultural Law Center, State University of Iowa.

KRIS KRISTJANSON, Director, Economics Division, Manitoba Hydro, Winnipeg, Manitoba.

RAYMOND J. PENN, Professor, Department of Agricultural Economics, University of Wisconsin.

MARION CLAWSON, Director, Land and Management Program, Resources for the Future, Inc., Washington, D.C.

PHILIP M. RAUP, Professor, Department of Agricultural Economics, University of Minnesota.

GENE WUNDERLICH, Farm Economics Division, Economic Research Service, U.S. Department of Agriculture.

WALTER C. NEALE, Professor, Department of Economics, University of Texas.

WAYNE N. ASPINALL, Representative in Congress from Colorado, and Chairman of the House Committee on Interior and Insular Affairs.

HOWARD OTTOSON, Chairman of Department of Agricultural Economics, University of Nebraska.

470

www.ingramcontent.com/pod-product-compliance
Lightning Source LLC
Chambersburg PA
CBHW021544210326
41599CB00010B/306